'I knew from the first time I heard THE THE that it was important. The music resonated with my punk/new-wave leanings, but Matt's lyrics are otherworldly. By the time Mind Bomb was released, it felt like he was a modern-day philosopher and possible seer. His original music is still relevant in more ways than he could have imagined – and the new stuff is powerfully evolved.'
Tony Hawk – Professional Skateboarder

'I heard Infected when I was a postgrad student at the LSE. It was probably "Heartland" that really struck me first – just an extraordinary song and words. "Heartland", I would say, is the greatest political lyric in British music.'
Mark Curtis – Historian & Analyst – Declassified UK

'I've had the pleasure of filming Mr Johnson in the brothels of Harlem, beneath a steam train, in a studio lit by electric fires, in the alligator-infested swamplands of Louisiana, on stage at the Royal Albert Hall... and can honestly say he's the loveliest man in show business.'
Tim Pope – Music Video & Film Director

'Matt Johnson's ability to evoke longing, lust or wonder with a chord change or a phrase is preternatural. The production and engineering of his albums is staggeringly gorgeous. I can't say enough about his music's beauty and vitality; it has provided a soundtrack to my life.'
Rob Delaney – Actor & Writer

'For many years, through his music, Matt Johnson has traversed a dark landscape of injustice and broken systems, of brittle bones and raw emotional transparency. It's fascinating and compelling to read the minutiae and myth behind the man. All hail Chairman Matt!'
JG Thirlwell – Composer & Musician

'Matt was an early inspiration as I found my way into my creative endeavours. I grew up watching what he did, and it pushed me to carve out my own path. Years later, his music has become the sound of my films, infused into the atmosphere and emotion of everything I make.'
Gerard Johnson – Brother & Film Director

'Matt Johnson was instrumental for me finding my voice as a writer. While recording Pretty Hate Machine alone in London, I'd walk the streets daily listening to Soul Mining to stay sane.'
Trent Reznor – Musician & Film Composer

'Matt Johnson is not only one of the greatest songwriters this septic isle has ever produced, but he's also an astute commentator and storyteller. I so enjoyed devouring this journey through Matt's intriguing past.'
Marc Riley – Broadcaster

'Matt is an extraordinary musician, composer and artist. He is rooted in the history of London, its artists and its musicians. He is unique and universal. Like the city he comes from, he has the ability to enchant, surprise, shock and charm with sharp humour. He is a great man and dear friend.'
Jools Holland

'Matt Johnson's approach to making music has always been thrilling and intriguing. This book offers a beautiful insight into the ideas, artistry and attitude of one of pop music's greatest mavericks.'
Samira Ahmed – Writer & Broadcaster

'Matt Johnson will always be the intrepid London boy with a music soul – and the man of many worlds with a writer's heart. Funny fucker too!'
Johnny Marr – Musician & Songwriter

'Matt Johnson is a fidgety auto-didact who learnt early on that you should never be afraid to be unique. Cognitive Dissident is an inspiring extended conversation with fellow traveller Jason Wood that delves into politics, class, architecture, and the changing face of London. And, always, there's music – from stealing out of his parents' till to feed his 7-inch single habit, to working at the De Wolfe Music library, to the first THE THE records, released in the fertile post-punk world, this is an evocative, often sad, but properly fascinating story.'
Bob Stanley – Writer & Musician

'From the first page, Cognitive Dissident drew me in with its warm, engaging and intimate view into the life of the thoughtful, self-taught visionary who has captured the hearts and minds of multiple generations through his deep passion for music, film and politics. I was completely captivated and enchanted by the rich and detailed stories from Matt's life which provided so much insight into the creativity and influences which shaped the incredibly talented artist who I have long admired.'
Cheryl Waters – KEXP DJ & Host

'THE THE's songs aren't just ear worms, they're spirit worms; emotional, fascinating and often contradictory amalgams, full of curiosity and rage, irony and social commentary, hope and desperation.'
JJ Abrams – Film Director

'Before THE THE, my collection of 'fuzzy warbles' focused mostly on love, loss, and heartbreak. After THE THE, it focused on love, sex, war, life, death, politics, God, anxiety, self-loathing, and spiritual yearning. Cognitive Dissident is the inside story of how Matt Johnson burned a hole through the plastic pop of the corporate monoculture to give the world an experience of full human dissent. Here is the truth about what it means to be a thinking, feeling human being in a society prostituted to the dirty dollar and Perpetual War. Simply unmissable.'
David Edwards – Media Lens co-editor

COGNITIVE DISSIDENT

CONVERSATIONS WITH THE THE'S MATT JOHNSON

MATT JOHNSON

WITH JASON WOOD

Copyright © 2026 Cinéola Limited under exclusive license to
Omnibus Press (A Division of Wise Music Limited)
14-15 Berners Street
London W1T 3LJ
England

Cover photograph by John Claridge
Cover design by Martin Lewis
Image editing by Gillian Glover and Angela Roberts
Picture research by Matt Johnson

ISBN: 978-1-9158-4165-0
Special Edition ISBN: 978-1-9172-7424-1

Matt Johnson hereby asserts his right to be identified as the author of this work in accordance with Sections 77 to 78 of the Copyright, Designs and Patents Act 1988.

All rights reserved. No part of this book may be reproduced in any form or by any electronic or mechanical means, including information storage or retrieval systems, without permission in writing from the publisher, except by a reviewer who may quote brief passages.

Every effort has been made to trace the copyright holders of the photographs in this book but one or two were unreachable. We would be grateful if the photographers concerned would contact us.

A catalogue record for this book is available from the British Library.

Designed and typeset in Palatino
by Palimpsest Book Production Ltd, Falkirk, Stirlingshire

Printed in the Czech Republic
www.omnibuspress.com

CONTENTS

Introductions:

Nothing Is What It Seems by Jason Wood   1

Fragments Of Thought by Matt Johnson   5

Chapter One:	Roots Lie Deeper Than Bones	7
Chapter Two:	The Desire Of The Moth For The Star	47
Chapter Three:	This Is The Day Your Life Will Surely Change	105
Chapter Four:	I Was Trying So Hard To Be Myself I Was Turning Into Somebody Else	144
Chapter Five:	Through The Ether And The Mists Of The Mind	200
Chapter Six:	The More I See The Less I Know	227
Chapter Seven:	Like A Stranger In The Night	255
Chapter Eight:	The Only Thing That Stays The Same Is That Everything Must Change	277
Chapter Nine:	The Lust For Unsung Dreams	315
Chapter Ten:	You Would Think, By Now, That People Would Know Better Than To Ask Me What I've Been Doing With My Time	337

Chapter Eleven:	The Bonfire Is Burning, The Birds Returning	370
Chapter Twelve:	Brain Fevered, Body Limp, In Altered States The Truth Is Glimpsed	394
Chapter Thirteen:	The Future Is Closer Than We Think	415
Chapter Fourteen:	Every Step Of The Climb Led You To This Place And Time	464

Acknowledgements	483
Filmography and Discography	485
Bibliography	488
Permissions and Image Credits	490

NOTHING IS WHAT IT SEEMS
Introduction By Jason Wood

I FIRST ENCOUNTERED MATT JOHNSON IN PERSON AFTER A period in which he had remained relatively silent as a singer–songwriter. However, to quote filmmaker Nicolas Roeg, 'Nothing is what it seems'.

Having last performed in public in 2002, Johnson had placed THE THE – formed when he was just 17 years old – on what felt like an indefinite hiatus as he entered a period of quiet contemplation.

An intensely personal and political writer whose search for truth evolved from the position of lived experience, through his songwriting Johnson mined issues not rigorously covered by mainstream media – amongst them: Britain as a colonised 51st state of America; the corporate takeover of our cities; and the connection between war and profit. But when we first met he found himself in a period of relative inertia and in his slumber turned to focus his efforts on conservation issues as the London he had grown up with was ruthlessly exploited by property developers with a bloodlust for profit. Observing from the sidelines, he witnessed corporate state propaganda swamp the cultural airwaves, the insidious rise of the right and what Johnson detects as the neoliberal capture of the left in politics and in public life.

Burning Blue Soul (1981), initially released under the name

Matt Johnson instead of THE THE, had intrigued me with its experimental sonic textures, introducing my fertile ears to new sounds formed against the backdrop of an emerging DIY aesthetic that included bands such as Scritti Politti, Cabaret Voltaire and This Heat. But in all honesty, *Burning Blue Soul* was more a record for my brother and his music-obsessed friends. I was just fortunate enough to experience it through osmosis. *Soul Mining* (1983) and *Infected* (1986), however, felt wholly mine.

These records, with their distinctive artwork, signalled a musical journey that was unafraid to embrace diverse influences and to resist formula and easy categorisation. Made by an autodidact from a working-class background, they also highlighted that creativity was not the sole province of the privileged and the elite and made me, perhaps for the first time, want to question the status quo, hold ideologies to account and be unafraid to err towards introspection.

The band, with revolving members and collaborators but always with Johnson at its centre, continued an upward commercial and artistic trajectory through *Mind Bomb* (1989), *Dusk* (1993) and *Hanky Panky* – 1995's fascinating detour into the tortured soul and artistry of Hank Williams.

Matt Johnson's discography, as this book will reveal, is not black and white. There are shelved and aborted projects, as well as a number of more recent musical resurrections through his own Cinéola label. Established after one bruising encounter too many with major label corporations, his independent label has become a crucial creative outlet, seeping out across film, music and publishing.

Repetition is not something that Matt Johnson seems much interested in as a writer and musician, and so after the release of *NakedSelf* (2000), a release that was not without pressure and pain and which holds a slightly spectral presence, there began a retreat. In reality, Johnson was working on other projects, perhaps most significantly developing his work as a soundtrack artist in collaboration with documentarian Johanna St Michaels and his writer–director brother, Gerard, whose films I had programmed.

It was actually cinema that pulled me personally into Johnson's orbit and eventually to the book you now hold in your hands. Johnson had been introduced to British-born, Los Angeles-based poet John Tottenham's *The Inertia Variations* by friend and collaborator JG Thirlwell. An ennui-tinged collection that documented the act of idling, the compendium inspired a decision to give up what Johnson described as his existence as a flâneur to embark on a characteristically ambitious, collaborative and expansive mixed media project, which took its name from Tottenham's collection of poems.

The resulting documentary directed by Johanna St Michaels, *The Inertia Variations* (2017), had its international premiere at Copenhagen International Documentary Film Festival and its UK premiere at Edinburgh International Film Festival before enjoying a run of sell-out screenings at cinemas worldwide. As the Creative Director at the independent arts centre HOME in Manchester at the time, I arranged for it to be screened. The reaction to the film, which details in a candid and moving manner the value of friends and family, the need for political engagement and the value of conceptual art as both a creative endeavour and as a therapeutic release valve, was stunning – and proved that the appetite for Johnson's work had not been sated.

Few works deal so eloquently with the rebirth that bereavement can allow – Matt's older brother Andrew having passed away during the making of the documentary – and precipitated a frenetic period of new THE THE-related activity, beginning with the 2018 The Comeback Special Tour, a new album, *The Comeback Special: Live at the Royal Albert Hall*, another Gerard Johnson soundtrack, *Muscle* (2019) and a concert movie, directed by Tim Pope.

More recently we have had the release of *Ensoulment* (2024), an album of entirely original music involving longstanding THE THE members James Eller (bass) DC Collard (keyboards) and Earl Harvin (drums), along with Barrie Cadogan (lead guitar), Gillian Glover (backing vocals), Terry Edwards (horns), Sonya Cullingford (fiddle) and Danny Cummings (percussion). Additionally, the album marked the return of co-producer Warne Livesey, who previously worked on *Infected* and *Mind Bomb*. The Ensouled World Tour followed soon after the release of *Ensoulment*. Both album and tour were critically and commercially successful and re-ignited a creative flurry of new activity that shows no signs of slowing.

It was whilst preparing for and subsequently interviewing Johnson for *The Inertia Variations* that I detected a sense of kinship and a connection that went beyond promotional duties. We kept circling back to each other, talking about a five-decade-long career but also other areas relating to culture, geo-politics and the pleasures and pain of contemporary existence. This book is a result of those conversations.

Evolving over multiple years, our dialogues were almost all conducted in person until COVID-19 intervened. Rather than go on hiatus we continued our talks over Zoom until we were able to meet again in person including a pleasant sojourn to Mallorca. From memory, only three of the interviews occurred remotely.

Some of the discussion around Matt's soundtrack work was conducted by Nick McKay for the 'Kino' edition of *The Modernist* magazine, which I guest edited. Nick offers an intelligent deep dive into soundtrack composition and Johnson's abiding love of cinema. Matt, Gillian (who also works as Cinéola's production manager) and I took a road trip through the places of his childhood and early adulthood. With a 7 a.m. start we travelled to the Two Puddings pub in Stratford, East London, then onto Essex and Suffolk, tracing the trajectory of family moves and the pubs that his parents ran as landlords. These pubs, with their atmospheric cellars, provided the space for the Johnson brothers to establish their first music and artist studios.

This book is obviously intended as succour for admirers of THE THE and it functions as a reliable memoir. But I think it's also more than that. I advise that you think of it as a map or a series of polaroid snapshots. It charts a creative and personal journey, but is unlikely to be the final destination.

Jason Wood, 2026

FRAGMENTS OF THOUGHT
Introduction From Matt Johnson

I FIRST MET JASON WOOD WHEN HE WAS RUNNING THE ARTS centre HOME in Manchester. We were introduced by Nico Marzano from London's ICA (Institute of Contemporary Arts), who had recently screened the documentary I was involved with, *The Inertia Variations*. Nico had spoken very warmly of him and suggested we'd get along. Subsequently, Jason arranged a screening of the film and I headed up to Manchester with director Johanna St Michaels. The event itself was a big success, but the evening was notable for me as the start of our friendship.

There are some people you meet in life where you know instantly that a friendship will develop. The conversation is easy, but it also goes very deep, very quickly. It was like that with Jason, and we both acknowledged that evening that we would become friends. He's my favourite kind of person: street-smart, working-class, good-humoured, hard-working, overachieving and thirsty for culture and life.

We kept in touch, met up a few times and he then put forward the idea of us doing a book together. I instantly agreed. He suggested the conversational format, which made sense to me. This is not a conventional autobiography, memoir, diary or journal and many of the people I know, places I've been and events of my life aren't covered here. I say this because I do know a lot of people and I don't want anyone – friends, family, colleagues or acquaintances – to feel offended if they don't see their names mentioned!

Jason and I shared about sixteen recorded conversations over several years during the creation of this book. I think we have come up with something different, yet complementary, to the biography *Long Shadows, High Hopes* by Neil Fraser (2018), which was, by definition, written from the outside looking in, whereas this book is told from the inside looking out. There is inevitably some crossover between the two books though – and in fact even with interviews I've done in the past – as certain events happened a certain way and naturally cropped up during the course of our conversations.

Life does not always unfold in a linear fashion that lends itself to straightforward chronological recounting but rather as a spiralling series of criss-crossing, concurrent events. Therefore, *Cognitive Dissident* is more a scrapbook – fragments of thought, influence and observation from a life spent drifting between worlds: music, film and politics.

It isn't about nostalgia, though there's plenty of that. It's about trying to understand where my generation has come from, how we got here and where we might be headed next. It touches on music, bereavement, memory, class, politics, culture, family, friendship and philosophy – and the strange, winding path that has carried me from the bomb sites of East London in the sixties, through the smoky little clubs of the post-punk underground in the late seventies, across to live in Spain, America and Sweden for periods of time in the intervening decades, back to England – and now into the emerging landscape of AI and humanoid robotics.

Matt Johnson, 2026

CHAPTER ONE

Roots Lie Deeper Than Bones

Matt Johnson grew up in a loving, working-class family in East London with his publican parents and brothers, Andrew, Eugene and Gerard. Later moves to Suffolk and then Essex didn't dampen Matt's love of London and in fact provided the creative spark for early music-related activity, writing and his first public performance.

Jason Wood: Where were you born?

Matt Johnson: My older brother Andrew and I were both born at the maternity hospital in Walthamstow. I'm quite a mongrel I suppose in that my parents and grandparents were all Cockneys but with familial roots that are a combination of Portuguese, German and Irish as well as English. Growing up in East London in the sixties it felt like a post-war city as everyone seemed to be talking about the war. You would still see lots of old bomb sites in the east of the city, albeit some now containing pre-fabs.* Andrew and I would even sometimes get to play on some of those sites – possibly the same ones our dad played on when he was a boy.

---

* Cheap, pre-fabricated, temporary housing.

JW: And as it was the sixties, London was about to start 'swinging'.

MJ: Yes, it was changing fast although my early childhood coincided with the fag-end of a notable period in the East End's history, one marked by the relationship between Cockneys – the native working-class Londoners, often of English-Irish descent – and Jewish immigrants, mainly from eastern Europe. Despite linguistic and religious differences, there was a lot of everyday mixing. Jewish culture – Kosher food shops, Yiddish theatre, tailoring shops – had become an essential part of East End life and something I vividly remember. The combination of these two communities was quite interesting as there were tensions at times but also a shared remembrance of the infamous Battle of Cable Street when they came together along with the Irish Dockers and the Socialists to fight the Fascists.*

By the 1950s and '60s, many in the Jewish community were leaving the East End for places like Gants Hill, Golders Green and Redbridge – as social mobility and housing opportunities improved. Many Cockneys – including parts of my own family – also left. The East End has since become home to newer waves of immigrants – notably, since the 1970s, Bangladeshis and other Muslim groups but also young, hipster middle-class White British who romanticise the idea of living somewhere 'edgy'.

My memories of the Cockney-Jewish coexistence of early childhood have now faded into folklore. There will soon be little left of the London I knew and few people left who care that much either. Cities are always evolving, of course, and London now seems home to a more transient community. Consequently, there are many who don't feel so much affinity to the areas they live in because they don't have roots there and seem to pass through more quickly than previous generations.

---

* The Battle of Cable Street on 4 March 1936 saw anti-fascist demonstrators clash with the Metropolitan Police who were protecting a march by the British Union of Fascists led by Oswald Mosely.

JW: It is a very different city to the one we both grew up in. What are your memories of Stratford? Is there much remaining from when you were growing up there?

MJ: I have strong memories from when I was a child. The streets, buildings, people. Around the corner from the Two Puddings on West Ham Lane used to be the old Queen Mary Hospital. My brother Eugene was born there. I spent a couple of nights in there myself after Andrew pushed me down a flight of stairs! My Aunt Joey worked there for a few years too. It was closed down in the mid-seventies and was demolished in the eighties. There's still the old Town Hall next to the Puddings plus a remaining mixture of Victorian and Edwardian buildings along the Broadway – although most have been demolished, sadly.

It was a proper high street back then on both sides of the Broadway with a wide variety of shops. I remember seeing the old tram lines along there too. I have vivid memories of walking in the rain along West Ham Lane with my dad to the local newsagent. Those types of shops had a certain fragrance – a combination of fresh tobacco, newsprint and sweets – and always felt warmly underlit. The old Routemaster buses had the little tungsten bulbs that also gave them a very inviting cosy glow as they glided past in the rain with their windows steamed up. I was a kid of course but it all seemed human-scale as there were none of the modern, overbearing, soulless building monstrosities in the area then.

Across the road from the pub was my primary school, The Grove, on Salway Place. It was Victorian and quite foreboding with high ceilings, polished wooden floors and the smell of carbolic soap in the toilets. It was demolished in 1971. Very close to the site it stood on is the famous old Theatre Royal – still hanging in there. In the seventies the Stratford Shopping Centre was built after they'd demolished many much-loved old buildings to make way for it. It was hated then and is hated now. Yet even that – in its turn – has been superseded by the even more loathsome Westfields.

There was a beautiful old department store on Stratford

Broadway called Boardmans that I'd sometimes go to with my mum when she was shopping. It always felt very grand with huge winding staircases, thick carpets and a hushed sense of peace. That was demolished in the seventies. And opposite that – sitting astride two sections of the Broadway is the imposing St John's Church. My dad, Eddie, would sometimes sneak off to sit in the grounds under the trees to read a book when he was feeling stressed. The whole area was much nicer then.

JW: So, you remember quite a lot about your time walking around those streets as a boy?

MJ: Yes, and I still vividly remember walking with my dad through the bustling Angel Lane Market when coming back from school. He seemed to know everyone. He couldn't walk ten yards without stopping for a chat or a joke. Angel Lane was famous in the East End. The Beatles filmed their promo video for 'Penny Lane' there. But it was demolished in the seventies too – a crime against the local population.

So many old shops I remember. The building next to the Two Puddings was occupied by the gentlemen's outfitters Dunn & Co. When that closed my dad and Uncle Kenny took out a lease there and opened a restaurant called Keneddy's – a pun on their names. It didn't work out too well though as they had problems with a manager, who turned out to be a crook, and ran off to the north with some of their money. They had someone track him down to deal with him. Then they asked my Uncle Freddie to run the place for a while, renaming it Frederick's.

Behind the building that housed the Two Puddings are the remnants of the former fire brigade station – parts of it demolished now. I remember as a toddler lying in bed with my mum for afternoon naps and often hearing firemen practising on the drill tower. There was some sort of tall radio aerial on top of the main building and I remember hearing messages broadcast over their Tannoy system.

JW: And where do you think your love of design and architecture comes from? You have an attentive eye for detail.

MJ: My love of old buildings comes from my mum, Shirley, as she loved old things and had a keen eye for furniture, buildings, antiques. She was a very perceptive person and a hard worker all her life. Before becoming a landlady – and mother to four boys – she'd worked as an orderly at Forest Gate Maternity Hospital – sometimes working through from 1 p.m. until 6 a.m. My dad remembered her telling him once how – in the dark basement there – she'd seen babies and various monstrosities squeezed into glass jars!

JW: Did your mum have any other jobs before becoming a famous landlady at one of East London's busiest pubs?

MJ: She'd also worked at some nearby factories: Clarnico's chocolate factory, Bryant & May match factory, Tate & Lyle's sugar factory. Quite a few members of our family also worked at those and other nearby factories such as Lesney – which made Matchbox Toys – and Yardley London, purveyors of soaps and fragrances. The job my mum really loved though was working in a little record shop on Stratford Broadway just along from the Two Puddings – next to the King Edward VII pub – until the man who owned it went bankrupt.

Although my mum was a pretty, striking girl, growing up she was actually a streetwise tomboy who hung around in the boys' gang rather than sat at home playing with dolls. Her dad taught her how to box so as a young girl growing up in the streets of the East End she knew how to fight and look after herself.

I think she would have loved to have been in fashion when she grew up. She used to design her own clothes, creating drawings of coats and dresses and taking them to a dressmaker to have made – she even had her own suits made at a men's tailor in Hackney. When we were living above the Puddings she bought a Singer sewing machine and designed and made extremely detailed fancy dress costumes for Andrew and me for our end-of-year school competitions – dressing us up as a snowman, a pirate, a Roman emperor and a Viking. We won every year.

She'd often take us to Petticoat Lane in the east or to Carnaby Street in the west to buy us the latest fashionable clothes – even dress us up in the same outfits sometimes so we looked like twins (which was quite irritating for us)! She meant well and we looked nice, I suppose – but it could be awkward for Andrew and me as we were attending a rough, tough inner London school with thuggish kids!

Maybe in contrast to her glamorous persona as landlady of a successful 'swingin' sixties' London pub and her love of the latest fashions, she was actually a highly moral person. As kids watching TV we'd be aware of her discomfort when anything too sexual or lewd came on the screen. Neither of my parents were churchgoers but my mum might say, 'God will punish you!' on the odd occasion we did something beyond the pale.

She had a very strong sense of family and instilled in us from an early age the adage 'blood is thicker than water' – that you can never fully trust anyone outside the clan. In later years Andrew and I used to find humour in the fact that 'Johnson Family' was a term that regularly appeared in the later works of William S. Burroughs – particularly *The Place of Dead Roads* (1983). In his books, the 'Johnsons' were a metaphor for people who lived by a code of mutual respect, honesty and personal freedom – though it was actually a late-19th century American expression referring to 'honourable' members of the underclass who might defy the conventions of society but adhered to an implicit code of conduct.

JW: So, what other qualities do you feel your mother imbued you with?

MJ: The quality I remember most about my mum was her innate sense of fairness. Whenever we had cousins or friends to stay it always stuck in my mind that she'd ensure everyone was treated fairly. Each got the same as everyone else. No favouritism was shown to any of us brothers either. She was a modest person who disliked boastful people and played things down. Even when my parents were earning very good money as the Puddings became one of East London's busiest pubs she would never brag or belittle – always mindful of other people's feelings. She also drilled it into us to be polite and exhibit nice manners.

But she was also a very direct person and if someone did anything to hurt or upset her or her family she'd look them in the eyes and say exactly how she felt. She had quite a temper at times and was the one who disciplined my brothers and I more than our dad. But she was always emotionally available and sympathetic when we were going through a hard time. She was highly intuitive and could read my brothers and me like open books.

JW: So, in the Two Puddings where your mum and dad worked, what kind of clientele did they serve? Did it attract a lot of West Ham United supporters?

MJ: Yes. And a lot of West Ham players too. Whereas footballers are very cossetted these days, living more isolated lives in mansions and hiding behind management entourages and security teams, it was a different world back then. West Ham and England captain Bobby Moore would have a drink in the Puddings – and his father-in-law, Eddie, was quite a character. He reminded us of TV personality Monty Modlyn* – and would sometimes stay with us. He'd arrange West Ham-related treats for Andrew (who was the Hammers fan of the house), such as a personal tour of Upton Park where he met a naked Geoff Hurst! The hattrick hero was in the treatment room on a massage table when a shy, blushing Andrew was led into the room. Geoff was very courteous and friendly and duly signed the autograph book my brother proffered. In later years Bobby Moore took over the next pub along the Broadway – The Black Bull – and renamed it Mooro's. You'd also have Billy Bonds or Frank Lampard Sr in the Puddings at various times – Harry Redknapp met his wife there. Lots of footballers went there. Jackie Charlton came in to celebrate the night England won the World Cup!

---

* Montague (Monty) Modlyn (1921–1994) was a Cockney market trader-turned-broadcaster, remembered for his chirpy and down-to-earth style.

JW: Billy Bonds is my all-time favourite footballer.

MJ: Yes, he was old-school. Andrew really liked Billy Bonds.

JW: And why was it called the Two Puddings?

MJ: Well, in Edwardian times the establishment was called the Refreshment Rooms – there was a public house on the ground floor and a dining room on the first floor. Every Christmas the governor at that time would have two gigantic puddings made in the kitchen and serve up free helpings for the local poor. So, it received a local nickname which then stuck.

JW: When my dad used to take me in the pubs as a kid they'd give you roast potatoes on a Sunday.

MJ: In East London pubs on Sunday mornings it was also about seafood, cockles, shrimps – and jellied eels of course!

JW: Were Sundays entirely joyful family moments?

MJ: Not for me. Sundays were ruined thinking about Mondays – I used to cry on Monday mornings as I just didn't want to go to school. There were certain routines and rituals on Sundays for us. We'd usually go to Petticoat Lane Market early in the morning with our parents – they'd pick up biegels, smoked salmon, potato latkes etc. from Mark's Deli for supper. Or we might go to Blooms, the kosher restaurant on Whitechapel High Street. We might spend the rest of the morning wandering the market or walking round the deserted streets of the City. (Now there are bars, shops and restaurants everywhere but back then the City was completely shut down over weekends and quite eerie.) Later in the afternoon we'd usually have a Sunday roast – our mum was a wonderful cook – and in the evening she'd give us a bath and we'd all have supper. There would be Victoria sponge cake too.

On the TV in the corner of the room on Sunday evenings would be Jake Thackray – who I developed a Pavlovian response to. Best described as a Yorkshire chansonnier, I suppose, he'd be on TV plucking his nylon-strung guitar with his hangdog expression and instantly make me feel mournful. Just the sound of his voice made me think of Monday mornings. In later years he actually performed occasionally for my parents at their folk events at another pub we lived above – the Kings Head in Ongar. I'd then hear Jake Thackray's voice on Sunday evenings drifting up the dumb waiter to the flat above. There was no escape! Actually, once I'd grown up I came to really enjoy and respect his brilliant lyricism and songwriting but back then he triggered a terrible sense of dread.

JW: And you lived in the flat above the Two Puddings?

MJ: Yes. You can just about see the small, front balcony from the pavement outside – the flat was set back from that. I was a one-year-old when we moved there. Lots of happy memories. For Andrew and me, Christmas was the highlight of our year. Our mum always made the flat look beautiful with decorations and lights and there was always so much lovely food, fruits, nuts, biscuits and sweets laid out. We used to get so excited on Christmas Eve that we couldn't sleep for hours after hanging up our pillow-cases. We used to get a lot of toys and were quite spoilt looking back. We had Beatles wallpaper in our bedroom – we even had Beatles wigs – Dalek outfits and Thunderbirds costumes – and God knows how many other toys over the years. Many ended up broken by Boxing Day as we were quite rough – with each other and our toys. Our dad was always keen to remind us to be thankful by telling us how little he got for Christmas as a boy – an orange, a piece of coal and a single wooden toy apparently!

JW: And your family left the pub in 2000?

MJ: Yes. My parents were the licensees of the Puddings from 1962 to 2000. Although we moved to the countryside for a few years the pub stayed in the family for nearly forty years. Our uncle Kenny was very involved with the dancehall upstairs, booking bands and singers. Different aunts and uncles managed it for my parents over the years. My mum's younger brother Uncle Peter and my Aunt Kay managed it for a while and then my dad's youngest brother Uncle Michael and my Aunt Claire took it on. My dad still came in weekly to deal with the business side of things. As a special treat when we were kids he'd take one of us with him on a Monday – 'No, it's my turn to go!' 'You went last time!' We loved it, sitting in the corner of the infamous office there, earwigging on the gossip between our dad and uncles. It was exciting as we'd overhear all sorts of stories about various crimes, shenanigans and general misbehaviour – much of it humorous.

My dad and uncles were well connected with certain characters in the London underworld. Obviously, the most famous were the Krays. They were a few months younger than my dad and he'd known them – first on nodding terms – since they were teenagers. But later on, my parents often went to the various nightclubs the Krays owned. As kids we'd often overhear them mentioning 'the twins'. There were a few members of the inner circle of the Firm who were very close to my dad and uncles as they'd grown up with them and remained lifelong friends. My family knew a lot of people from various walks of life in those days – some were friends, some were foes. It's strange to me how in the decades since, certain characters who were just a normal part of family gossip when growing up – footballers, musicians, writers, painters, gangsters – have since become legendary figures in the national consciousness.

What used to irk my brother Andrew and me though was how certain middle-class film directors attempted to appropriate working-class history. They would always get it wrong and turn East End underworld figures, for instance, into 'diamond geezers' with all that 'mockney' nonsense. The truth is, the genuinely heavy characters didn't brag, boast or talk about violence; they were softly spoken, didn't swear for the sake of it, were quite well read, well dressed and – most importantly – were extremely discreet so as not to draw attention. More in the vein of Philip Baker Hall's character in *Hard Eight* (1996) or Mikael Persbrandt's in *Odyssey* (2025) than the usual loud-mouthed thugs you find in British gangster films.

JW: What other colourful characters were regulars in the Puddings?

MJ: There were so many – the names of most have been lost to the mists of time – but the pub attracted cerebral and creative types as well as gangsters and footballers. Author and broadcaster Daniel Farson* became a friend of the family as did screenwriter Barrie Keeffe,† who based parts of Helen Mirren's character in the film *The Long Good Friday* (1980) on my mum (who he was secretly in love with, he admitted to our dad many years later!). The brilliant British photographer John Claridge was a regular and told me he had to stand on an empty beer crate to be able to see the bands playing at the pub as it was so busy and he was too short. (Incidentally, John took the portrait of me on the cover of this book). Joan Littlewood, the pioneering theatre director of the Theatre Workshop – who ran the Theatre Royal Stratford East for many years – was also a customer.

The Two Puddings was most famous as East London's best and busiest music venue. And this was down to my Uncle Kenny who'd been promoting music since the late fifties with countless concerts and dancehalls all over the UK. He used to tell me he'd promoted everyone apart from Elvis Presley and The Beatles, and it certainly seemed that way to us as kids as we'd regularly hear the names of artists he was promoting – from bluesmen such as John Lee Hooker and legendary rock'n'rollers like Gene Vincent and Jerry Lee Lewis, to up-and-coming groups like The Kinks, Small Faces and The Who and singers David Essex, Screaming Lord Sutch and Long John Baldry – plus countless others. In the sixties many of these artists would perform on the ground floor or upstairs in the dance hall at the Puddings or over at Kenny's legendary nightclub in Forest Gate, the Lotus Club. He'd also hire venues across the capital and the country. I often refer to Uncle Kenny as the George Best of our family as in the sixties and

---

* Daniel Farson was the author of *Soho in the Fifties* (1987), *Limehouse Days* (1991) and *The Gilded Gutter Life of Francis Bacon* (1994), amongst others.
† Barrie Keeffe was a British playwright and screenwriter best known for *The Long Good Friday* and his sharp, socially conscious dramas.

seventies – with his long hair, beard and penchant for big American cars – he was very charismatic and often to be found in nightclubs up the West End until the early hours gambling, drinking and fighting.

I'd grown up hearing plenty of stories about crooks in the music business and my dad mentioned more than once, 'If you ever have any nonsense from anyone let us know and we'll get it dealt with.' I never had to take him up on the offer as I liked to fight my own battles but it was always nice to know I had that behind me.

JW: And what changed? What forced your parents to give up the pub?

MJ: Under the Thatcher government the pub/brewing industry was hugely reformed*. Suddenly brewers were empowered to earn

---

* The 1989 Beer Orders were Thatcher-era regulations intended to reduce brewery control of pubs, but they led to pub-company consolidation and higher rents for many pub landlords.

far more money as property landlords than merely selling beer and so they increased the rent by ridiculous amounts – 300 per cent in some cases. My dad, uncles and many other pub landlords were involved in legal action. The Crehan v Inntrepreneur case became the test case for hundreds of publicans who believed the post-Beer Orders beer-tie agreements were anti-competitive and had forced their pubs into financial loss. Many landlords – including my dad and uncles – paid legal fees to support similar claims, but when the House of Lords ultimately ruled against Crehan in 2006, it effectively shut down those challenges and left most of the publicans without compensation. Of course, by this point, it was no longer the Watney Mann brewery based in Whitechapel that my dad had known so well and had a strong relationship with. As a consequence of a series of takeovers and mergers – and possible financial shenanigans – over the decades via front companies like Grand Metropolitan, Inntrepreneur, Enterprise Inns and Voyager Pubs, the Two Puddings ended up as part of the property portfolio of the vast Japanese investment bank, Nomura. As with so many British industries, countless old-school pub landlords were screwed over due to Thatcher's reforms. My family had been the landlords until 2000 but after those reforms the expense of running it skyrocketed and debts were incurred and they could not afford to keep the pub. That later legal ruling meant there was no compensation for the large financial losses many pub landlords suffered. The building then fell into general disrepair and became a series of low-rent, seedy bars and nightclubs. God knows who owns the building now. How many pubs do you now see boarded up all across the United Kingdom. Much of the blame for that can be laid at Thatcher's door.

JW: How many bedrooms did the flat have?

MJ: Two. There was the living room and dining room on the Broadway side and bedrooms on the other side with the kitchen and bathroom in the middle. There was a balcony at the back as well as the smaller one at the front.

JW: And were you sharing bedrooms with your brothers?

MJ: Yeah, me and Andrew. Eugene was in with our mum and dad. I have a memory of a tea stain on the wall in my parents' bedroom that has just come to my mind. It was from when my mum threw a tea pot at my dad's head!

JW: But, generally you were a happy family?

MJ: Very. A close-knit East End family with lots of lovely relatives. On my mum's side were Uncle Tommy and Aunt Joey, Uncle Peter and Aunt Kay, and Uncle Allan and Aunt Susie. On my dad's side were Uncle Kenny and Aunt Ann, Uncle Freddie and Aunt Doreen and Uncle Michael and Aunt Claire. Plus, grandparents, great aunts and great uncles and lots of lovely cousins too of course – and in recent years lots of lovely nieces and nephews. I was very lucky as there was not a member of the family I didn't like. Obviously, you get closer to some than others but I liked them all. I probably picked up my musical inclination from my mum's dad – Grandad Joe – who used to yodel, play a bit of harmonica, banjo, accordion – even spoons! My dad had quite a good voice too and used to do impressive impersonations of his favourite singer, Paul Robeson. My mum loved Edith Piaf, but couldn't sing very well.

I was sad to leave the Two Puddings as it was a magical part of my childhood and I was happy – even though we weren't allowed out to play in the streets because Stratford Broadway was such a busy road. Andrew and I actually used to think The Drifters' song 'On Broadway' was written about there! There were even neon signs on some of the shops opposite the pub – such as the jewellery chain H. Samuel – which at night gave the view from our flat quite an evocative atmosphere. A great story is when Clyde McPhatter from The Drifters visited the Puddings in the mid-sixties and got the entire pub singing 'On Broadway'! Years later I did actually live on *the* Broadway in Manhattan. Something must have drawn me to it.

JW: How many pub staff were there?

MJ: A lot. It was a very, very busy pub. The staff were lovely and always incredibly kind to us kids. You can't tell from the frontage but it was a big pub inside as it went back a long way. There were quite strict rules in those days and as a child I wasn't allowed in the pub during opening hours. When I was really little, before I started school, I used to sneakily sit at the bottom of the stairs and watch my mum working behind the bar. As a little boy I thought 'working' was actually drinking beer and eating sandwiches! The customers were all very nice too. As you do with kids, they'd sometimes ask, 'What do you want to be when you grow up?' And from the age of five I always answered, 'I'm going to be a singer or an actor.' I just knew. How? I don't know. Maybe because there was music around us all the time.

JW: And did your parents have a clear division of duties?

MJ: My mum was a harder worker than my dad. He used to acknowledge that. She'd often accuse him of being a bit lazy! But he would deal with the office side of things, the takings, going to the bank, ordering up stock etc. and she would oversee the food; but they would both serve behind the bar.

JW: Was there ever any trouble?

MJ: Lots of fights. My family didn't really trust the police as they could be quite petty and vindictive and also slow to show up when there was trouble. My dad, uncles and friends usually had to deal with it themselves.

JW: So, happy childhood, loving family... did you also have friends at this point?

MJ: We had school friends though we didn't go around to their houses to play or vice versa. Our best friend was probably Paul Terry – the son of the pub's cleaner, Rene. He'd come in with her and we'd play in the back yard of the pub. We'd also often be out and about around London with our parents going to museums and exhibitions – plus lots of visits to London Zoo to see Guy the gorilla, Goldie the eagle and Chi Chi the panda, who were the most famous animals there in those days.

JW: And were there rival pubs?

MJ: Back then there was The Swan as well as King Edward VII, the Black Bull and a few others. The Swan – which has also since shut down – was run by David Edwards, who was a close friend of my dad. In fact, not only were they neighbours in Stratford but even at the end of my dad's life – in the little Suffolk village he lived in until he died – they were still neighbours and close friends. David is a lovely man, a larger-than-life bon viveur. He and his partner John Tanner (AKA Mrs Sixpence) were regulars at the Colony Room Club as David was friends with owner Muriel Belcher. Through his connections there David's younger brother John met and became the companion of the painter Francis Bacon.* John became the subject of some of Bacon's most significant portraits and was sole heir to his fortune. Bacon liked visiting The Swan as – like many other artists in decades to come – he was intrigued by the East End, and East Enders.

JW: How was school?

MJ: I never cared for school from the start. It was quite a poor neighbourhood and the school was quite strict. I wrote a song called 'Mrs Mac' about a particularly fearsome dinner lady/ supervisor who would terrorise the children. I even vomited on my plate once, whilst she was standing over me, forcing me to eat the over-boiled greens and grey-looking kidneys. Stratford is now very multi-cultural and multi-racial, back then it wasn't.

---

* Francis Bacon (1909–1992), Irish-born British painter, was famed for his visceral, nightmarish portraits and twisted figures, and is widely regarded as one of the most powerful and influential artists of the 20th century.

There was only one black boy in my year, one Sikh boy and maybe one Indian girl. My favourite teacher was Mrs Bhattacharya, who wore wonderfully colourful, flowing saris and had a bindi on her forehead, so I assume she was Hindu. She was very kind to us kids. The area was very different then and I didn't know what racism was or meant. Throughout my entire life I never heard either of my parents make a single racist comment so as a little boy I had no sense of growing racial tensions. I do remember hearing people on the radio or TV talk about 'coloured people' though, and I recall always being on the lookout for green, blue, purple or red people when being walked to and from school!

I didn't understand what 'class' was about either. I remember something my dad said to me once about his childhood that really stuck with me. He said: 'I didn't know we were poor when I was growing up. We were such a happy family and had so many lovely neighbours who also had very little so I had nothing to compare to.' In recent decades I suppose TV and the power of advertising have created a culture of permanent want. No one feels satisfied with anything anymore. My first awareness of class was when I'd notice that my mum – who, like my dad, had a broad Cockney accent – would slightly alter the way she spoke in certain circumstances – a posh shop or restaurant. I detected a slight class discomfort within her.

JW: And how did you get on at school?

MJ: As a little boy I used to cry every Monday. I would sob and my mum would sit with me and console me and say, 'Oh, you've got the Monday morning blues.' I actually used to enjoy it when I was too unwell to go to school and I'd be lying in bed with a hot water bottle with my mum bringing me grapes, Ribena and especially Lucozade – back then it was in the glass bottle with the amber-coloured crinkly cellophane wrap.

JW: I know you weren't particularly academic at school, but were you social?

MJ: I had plenty of friends at school but because I was born in the summer I was always one of the youngest in my year. I should have been in the year below really. I always struggled because I was quite young for my age.

JW: And were you a troublemaker or were you well-behaved?

MJ: On the surface well-behaved. But I was sneaky. Later on, at secondary school, I became a truant, and was naughty and got told off. In my younger years I wasn't a troublemaker, but just one of those kids who slipped through the net. The teachers didn't notice me much.

JW: Your journey to school would have been minutes long?

MJ: Yeah, our dad and mum would take turns taking us across and picking us up.

JW: So, you really had no excuse for being late! What about local parks or green spaces? I know that as a child you'd visit Wanstead Flats, Victoria Park in Hackney or the nearby West Ham Park but were there other places?

MJ: We often visited Battersea Park. That would be a full day out. In the mid-sixties it still had remnants from 1951's Festival of Britain where it was turned into the Festival Pleasure Gardens. There was still a funfair and things like the Tree Walk and the grotto – or 'Temple of the Winds' – which was quite eerie and lit with atmospheric colours and with different scents blowing to indicate north, south, west or east winds. We'd also visit Greenwich quite often and many weekends our dad would also take us to the Embankment or walking around the quiet streets of the City.

JW: Did you go to watch football matches too? West Ham?

MJ: Yes, I sometimes went to Upton Park with Andrew and our dad. I remember seeing them play Manchester United with George Best but it was a dull game. Maybe George was hungover!

These days if I can't get up to see Manchester United with my sons I may go and watch the less-fashionable London clubs. I used to take my eldest son Jackson (I sometimes just call him Jack) to Fulham or Charlton Athletic when he was young and I take my youngest son George to Leyton Orient – or the three of us will go to watch ÖIS in Göteborg. When he was a boy my dad used to go to Arsenal but he also supported West Ham because Andrew passionately supported them.

People often ask me why I'm a Cockney Red and how can I support Manchester United when I should really support West Ham. Well, it's purely down to sibling rivalry. In the sixties West Ham were a very glamourous club who played beautiful football. Not only had they won the FA Cup in 1964 and the European Cup Winners Cup in 1965, they were largely responsible for England winning the World Cup in 1966 too. The captain was the very charismatic Bobby Moore; and Martin Peters and Geoff Hurst scored all the goals – including the latter's famous hattrick. I suppose I felt I had to be different from Andrew.

We were always bickering over something or other. Andrew chose Thunderbird One, so I went with Thunderbird Two. He chose Captain Scarlet so I was left with Captain Blue. His favourite American comic superhero was The Flash so mine was Green Lantern. On and on it went. Even in later years down to David Bowie and Marc Bolan. But in the mid-to-late sixties there was only one club that eclipsed West Ham's glamour: Manchester United had Bobby Charlton, Denis Law and the incomparable George Best. All three were Ballon d'Or Award winners and the club itself became the first English team to win the European Cup in 1968. So, that was my one-upmanship on Andrew. I was only about six or seven but as everyone in England knows, once you have a club you are stuck with them for life. And, of course, I then manipulated my sons into supporting them too, which was great for my eldest Jack in the Fergie years but not so great for my youngest son George in recent times.

JW: And how would you generally describe your relationship with Andrew? Competitive it seems!

MJ: Looking back, my relationship with Andrew fit the 'sibling ambivalence' framework, I suppose – intense mixed feelings where love and resentment coexisted. Out of all my immediate family members, my relationship with Andrew was the most intense and complex. I loved Andrew. And *still* love Andrew. Despite his shortcomings – many of which I share – he remains the single biggest influence and inspiration in my life. We did have a lot of great times and laughter together. I was lucky to have shared an incredibly creative childhood that just would not have been possible without him. There were many times when I was young when he gave me pep talks when I was feeling down – and he could be incredibly kind and sensitive. He was also one of the most perceptive people I've ever known. I genuinely valued his opinions and insights. He was the closest person in this world to me in terms of taste in music, books, films and humour. But he suffered from depression on and off for years, had a dark side and could lash out and be spiteful. And we had some vicious fights. Andrew often used to say he was 'born two pints shy', and certainly, when sharing a few rounds of real ale with him at a local pub he could be the best company a person could wish for – funny, kind, profound, insightful. I was at Andrew's bedside when he died. Holding his hand, crying and praying for him. It was a privilege – if that is the right word – to be with him at the very end. It was a bright and sunny winter's day in January, clear blue skies and sunshine bathing him on his death bed. Most days I think about all the members of my immediate family who have passed away.

JW: I can't imagine how that must have felt as you were obviously such a close family. To refocus on more positive memories, what other places did you live in your childhood?

MJ: We moved to the village of Great Wratting, Suffolk, and from age 7 to 9 years old I went to the Cangle, a school in nearby Haverhill.

JW: And were you happy there?

MJ: I was actually, but my happiest school memory of all is the school I went to next – Chalkstone Middle School, between 9 and 10 years old. It was brand new at the time – we were the first pupils to go there. But even that has since been demolished. Then unfortunately we moved to Ongar (Essex).

JW: Ongar is where the truancy started?

MJ: It was.

JW: Did you have close friends at Chalkstone?

MJ: I did. Though most were at Great Wratting. Back then there was more greenery between Haverhill and the neighbouring villages. Lots of fields. We used to have to take the school bus as Great Wratting felt quite remote. But Haverhill is starting to spread in every direction. And this is happening all over the country – endless over-development and destruction of the green belt. It reminds me of 'Going, Going' the poem Philip Larkin wrote for the Department of the Environment.

We went from the Two Puddings – and a very urban existence where we weren't allowed out because of the traffic on Stratford Broadway – to the tranquillity of the Suffolk countryside. It was as if our childhood suddenly switched from black and white to technicolour. Suffolk is quite flat and the skies seem huge in summer – suddenly we were playing beneath them in endless, golden corn fields, overwhelmed by new sights and sounds. We became fascinated by the various machinery the local farmers had, the combine harvesters and tractors in different colours: red for Massey Ferguson, green for Claas and blue for Ford. We'd spend hours down at the nearby river fishing for minnows and sticklebacks or capturing frogs and toads to keep as pets. I received a little Raleigh bicycle for my seventh birthday – metallic red and blue with fat, white tyres. My dad taught me to ride it in London on what we used to call the Promenade.* Of course, I couldn't ride it anywhere apart from the yard at the back of the Puddings but suddenly I was cycling around the empty lanes of a Suffolk village.

JW: Did you find that you never felt really entirely comfortable away from London and the urban sprawl?

MJ: Not really because we were always going back to see relatives and the Two Puddings anyway so we had the best of both worlds. Since my time living in Suffolk as a little boy I've always loved the countryside. It's the suburbs I don't like.

Now, I may have spoken sometimes about the importance of having a 'thinking place'. Have I ever spoken to you about thinking places?

JW: You have. The grave of William Blake.†

MJ: Well, that is one and I've got a couple of dozen thinking places sprinkled around the world.

JW: You've also got your desk, where you write.

MJ: Yes, that is a very important thinking place for me. The concept of a thinking place was introduced to me by my oldest friend Nick Freeston when we were kids and living in Ongar, Essex. He can't remember this but I do as I have a very good memory. His family had just moved from a little flat above a greasy spoon on the high street to a house that had fields behind it. One day he said, 'Matt, I've found this lovely tree in the field behind the house that I go to most days and I just climb the tree and sit and I think.' I said, 'What do you mean?' He said, 'Well, it's just good to have a

---

* This was the elevated walk along architect Joseph Bazalgette's Northern Outfall Sewer, created after the 'Great Stink' of 1858. It was rebranded as the 'Greenway' in the nineties.
† William Blake (1757–1827) was an English poet, artist, and visionary whose illuminated books and prophetic writings profoundly influenced Romanticism and later countercultural movements.

thinking place where you can reflect on life and that's what I do in this tree.' I then realised I'd already had my first thinking place but hadn't given it the name or the concept. It was at the end of a long walk from the cottage in which we lived in Great Wratting – past the river and across fields. I would always go there to think if I had problems, if I wanted to make life changes or just fancied a bit of time by myself. I would go there and just think. Even after we sold the house and moved on I would still go back there whenever I could and I would sit and think. These days people do not spend enough time thinking – especially young people. My own kids are always staring at screens. It drives me mad as it is really screwing up their brain chemistry and hormonal systems. We *all* need to spend more time sitting and doing nothing but breathing and thinking.

JW: Can you recall any particular, life-changing moments in your thinking place?

MJ: I remember when my mum died in 1999, I went over there and just sat for hours by myself trying to somehow communicate with her. I still go to that thinking place. I love people but I enjoy my own company too. It must be awful to be lonely but it is also a real luxury to have time alone to think. It's good to have the contrast.

JW: Where's your thinking place in Mallorca?

MJ: Primarily the small terrace of my mountain cottage. It's the closest place to heaven I know. There are a few others – a mountain walk close to my home there where I sit on a favourite rock amongst the pine trees and just think. I also have thinking places in the grounds of the old Arab Baths and the cathedral in Palma.

JW: Göteborg?

MJ: I have some there too. A favourite is Järntorget – 'Iron Square' in English. There used to be a lovely little cigar café called Cigarren.

When I lived in Göteborg and Jack was a little boy at school I'd often sit outside there, drinking coffee, writing in my notebook and watching the world go by – either in the morning or late afternoon amongst the sunset shadows. It always felt so 'European'. Obviously, it is in Europe, but there was something exotically, typically European that was hard to put my finger on. What's strange is that – completely coincidentally – when Jack grew up, he also started sitting there drinking his coffee, writing in his notepad. He had no idea I'd done the same when he was a little boy. Sadly, Cigarren has now changed location and also there are now tall buildings springing up around Järntorget changing the atmosphere. No escape from property developers!

JW: New York?

MJ: There are a few there too. Certain benches in Union Square and Washington Square Park; and a square in Chinatown. Certain churches. Public places you can just sit and think and that do not appear to be in danger of being removed and redeveloped.

I have specific bars and restaurants too but sadly many of my favourites have disappeared. The most important thing about a thinking place is that it's somewhere you can go back to repeatedly across many years and decades – where you can sit and think about your life and compare where you *were* to where you *are* and then think about where you *want* to be.

JW: Do you feel fortunate to have lived in London, Göteborg, New York and Mallorca?

MJ: Very lucky. I feel very grateful to have had a certain amount of luck and opportunity. Yes, you do create your own luck to a certain degree but you can't take anything for granted. I've been very lucky to have known many wonderful people in my life who have helped me. There are countless hardworking, talented people in life who just don't get the rub of the green.

JW: Box Hill (Surrey) was just about drivable from London. That was my thinking place. John Lydon sang about it in 'Flowers of Romance': 'I've got binoculars, on top of Box Hill.'

MJ: What about your current thinking places?

JW: I'm not sure I have one at the moment. I like to sit in my music room at my house.

MJ: Yes, well, that's what I was thinking. Are you happy with that?

JW: I love it, I love to sit in there with my records.

MJ: My first thinking place was (and still is) a large hole in the ground in a field in Suffolk, cratered by a bomb during World War Two. I discovered it when we were children and we'd play over there – fashioning little slides from trays and cardboard boxes and whizz from the top edge to the bottom. Especially in winter if there was snow. There were no trees then so it was much deeper but I suppose over the decades silt and vegetation have gradually filled it in.

JW: After Suffolk, what are your memories from Ongar in Essex?

MJ: Well, I became a teenager there. So, there are lots of memories. I remember a wonderful youth club called The Haunt. It was run by volunteers and on Thursday and Friday evenings they organised discos. They hired a DJ who would bring his decks, oil lamps and strobe lights – but also his girlfriend – who was very scantily clad and a sort of sexy go-go dancer – which was odd considering we were little kids! The pair of them seemed quite old to me though they were probably only early twenties at most.

He'd mainly play glam rock: Bowie, T. Rex, Sweet, Alvin Stardust, Roxy Music, Gary Glitter but also Tamla Motown, soul and rock'n'roll. It was fantastic – one of the highlights of our week. We all learned to do 'The Bop' – an old-fashioned rock'n'roll dance from the fifties that came back into fashion in the early seventies. We all used to wear shoes with stacked heels, and later on those shoes called 'wedges' that had a thick crepe sole. We loved our clothes and dressing up. But I never had a girlfriend – I did develop crushes on a few girls at The Haunt but I was just too shy and too young to know what to do about it.

JW: This is where you formed your first band. Did you play gigs in Ongar too?

MJ: Yes, at the Budworth Hall on Ongar High Street. Nick and I did our first 'gig'. I say gig but all we had were cardboard boxes as drums and elastic bands wrapped around tissue boxes as guitars! We weren't even invited – we just showed up and made a lot of noise. They kicked us out after a while: 'Look boys, you can't be in here making all this noise and disturbing everyone!'

JW: Did you bill yourselves as something?

MJ: No, we just showed up. I don't know what we were thinking.

JW: How old would you have been then?

MJ: Eleven. It was actually Nick who suggested we form a group. The pair of us were obsessed with pop music and addicted to buying singles. We used to hang out at each other's homes listening to the latest releases.

JW: That is very young. What was it you were playing?

MJ: Just our own stuff initially. Things we made up. Eventually we did get some halfway decent gear, a few extra members and started doing cover versions: some Beatles songs, Bowie's 'Rebel Rebel', 'Johnny B. Goode' by Chuck Berry and 'All Right Now' by Free. We even did cover versions of Deep Purple: 'Smoke On The Water' and 'Black Night'. There's a nice synchronicity because I now work with Gillian Glover, Roger Glover's daughter.

Nick always had much more gear than me. I had barely anything but he had one of those little orange or red Bontempi organs, a Stylophone, a nice drum kit and maybe some other bits and pieces from Woolworths. I think the brand name they used for their in-house equipment was Audition.

JW: What were the reasons for moving to Ongar? You moved into another pub, The King's Head?

MJ: Yes. I lived there between the ages of 10 and 16. My parents became the landlords even though we still had the Two Puddings in our family. The Two Puddings was so busy in the late sixties that my parents thought they could sort of retire early to Suffolk and give their kids the idyllic childhood they wished they'd had – and that my dad might start seriously writing and establish a new career as an author.

It turned out to be a pipe dream though because shortly before we were due to move there was a gangland-style shoot-out at the Puddings which made the front page of the *Daily Mirror*. My dad had his phone tapped by the police because they were convinced it was related to his connections to the Krays and their arrest the previous year – but it was nothing to do with that. My dad was always annoyed by that story in the paper and claimed he was misquoted by the journalist in order to make a more dramatic story. The journalist had repeatedly phoned him up, pestering and asking the same question until he got the answer he wanted: 'It's a bit worrying. I can't think why this could have happened.' My dad thought it made him sound weak – and 'face' was everything in the East End in those days. My dad and uncles actually knew who the culprits were and got the matter dealt with. But shootings were very rare in London in the sixties and the consequence of all the hysterical publicity was that trade dropped off a cliff as people became too frightened to go there. Anyway, after three years living in Great Wratting – and with the takings from the pub not improving much – my parents were running out of money. They didn't want to move us all back into the small flat above the Two Puddings but the brewery – Watney's

– had asked them if they fancied becoming licensees of The Kings Head in Ongar.

It was originally built as a 17th-century coaching inn, and had lots of old out-houses and a lot of land – though the woods behind, that stretched down to the little river at the back, were completely wild and overgrown when we lived there. My truanting began a year or two after I started going to Ongar Comprehensive School.

It eventually got so bad that when skipping school my friends and I would just get on buses and head off to other towns for the day. Back then you'd take the 175A to Romford, the 339 to Brentwood or the 32 to Chelmsford. Or we'd go to one of the fields behind The King's Head, past the little river and far off in the distance. We'd build little dens in the hedgerow where we'd keep our stashes of comics, sweets, cigarettes, cider. And we'd hunker down for the day. Francis lived above Senners, the newsagent directly opposite The King's Head. Nick's parents ran the greengrocers. We'd all steal what we could from our respective family business. It was quite tight knit. There was also 'Haggis', Simon Jones, David White and a few others. The little river there was the inspiration for 'Down By the Frozen River'.

JW: What made you think back to that to write the song?

MJ: I wrote it as a poem years ago but lost it. I always wanted to write about truancy, because I have strong feelings about the British education system and the way working-class kids just slip through the net. I was useless at school but I cannot remember a single teacher who ever expressed interest in helping me. I was destined to be one of those invisible kids who just end up either on the dole or trapped inside a mindless job until retirement age. But I am one of the lucky ones because I found music. Or music found me. And yet the number of intelligent young people that don't have that luck and end up getting involved in drugs or crime and living deeply unfulfilled lives because of a lack of encouragement is shocking. Many slip through that net not because they're stupid, but because of a combination of circumstances. We were a very mischievous little gang – regularly tormenting the neighbourhood playing 'knock down ginger', breaking into and vandalising empty buildings, smoking and drinking, having gang fights with fireworks ('Bangers' and 'Air Bomb Repeaters') and getting into trouble with the police.

JW: And how did the past in Ongar begin to encroach later on your creative process?

MJ: I have clear memories of walking through muddy fields with damp shoes clogged with ice amidst blankets of snow and the sound of the crows cawing in the cold winter air. And I remembered that somewhere I had a typewritten poem I'd written about it – it wasn't on a computer file and I couldn't locate it. When it did eventually turn up I made some minor changes and additions.

Part of me regrets being a truant and not – for instance – studying music and its theory. Yet, there is a deeper part of me that understands music didn't start with people sitting around contemplating scales, keys, intervals or counterpoint. It started with the raw need to express the inexpressible and by banging, blowing or beating on anything that early humans could lay their hands on.

The benefit of being unburdened by academic expectations or achievement is that you can float freely; become a genuine free thinker. I know that today's orthodoxy will be laughed at in a hundred years' time, just as we laugh at what people passionately believed a century ago. So, I've tried to maintain that outsider perspective, to look at things sideways or in reverse or upside down. Being a nobody from nowhere can be quite liberating.

JW: Do you know what happened to any of the people that you truanted with?

MJ: I keep in regular contact with Nick Freeston. He's my oldest friend and has always been very supportive. The Freestons were a kind family who've also had more than their fair share of tragedy. Nick's younger brother Russell died in a car accident at just seventeen. He used to operate my cassette recorder for me during Road Star rehearsals. He was a lovely lad.

I lost touch with most people I went to school with. Some got jealous or resentful, others just disappeared. But Nick has always been one of my biggest supporters. He's a lovely man. A West Ham fan, like you.

JW: And what does Nick do?

MJ: He's a successful greengrocer. He took over the family business I mentioned earlier. I lost touch with most of my other truanting buddies after we left school.

Nick and I recently listened to some recordings of Road Star – our first band. I need to have them digitised because every time I play them they break because they're so old. I recorded them on my little Amerex cassette recorder but didn't have much money to buy fresh cassettes so I would just keep re-recording over the top of old ones. Boots, Philips, AGFA and BASF were some of the makes I owned and they came in various lengths: C30, C60, C90 and C120. The latter were so thin it would twist up around the pinch wheel and snap. It was always a false economy.

JW: Your passion for the physical media side of music obviously flourished here.

MJ: Andrew and I became addicted to 7-inch vinyl singles in Ongar. There wasn't an actual record shop here but a toy shop, called Toy Fayre, that had a small counter at the back that sold singles. You could order them if they didn't have them in stock. It seemed like a golden age to us. Some of the singles we collected – and which still sound great to my ears include: 'Hot Love' by T. Rex, 'Silver Machine' by Hawkwind, 'Starman' by David Bowie, 'Layla' by Derek & The Dominoes, 'Popcorn' by Hot Butter, 'School's Out' by Alice Cooper – and of course Sweet, Mott The Hoople, Lennon, McCartney, Harrison, Ringo Starr solo singles, Gary Glitter, Chicory Tip and tonnes of others.

Like the Two Puddings, The King's Head had a jukebox but this time – as we were older – we'd got friendly with the man who changed the records each month. They were well used by the time he came to switch them over but rather than chuck them away he gave them to us. Having access to all those old records off the jukebox gave us an unfair advantage over our mates when it came to building a big singles collection! But Andrew, Nick and I – all of us – were addicted to 7-inch singles... Addicted to the point that Andrew and I would even steal money from the pub to feed our habit.

We used to hold little play-back parties on a Friday or Saturday night in the front room above the pub when our parents were downstairs working. We would change the lightbulbs to red and Andrew, Nick, Eugene and I would dress up in glam outfits, mime guitar on old tennis rackets and crank out our singles collection on the old GEC radiogram at high volume. We'd spend hours dancing around the room. It was fantastic! One Christmas Andrew got a little National Panasonic cassette recorder and we started recording our own little music shows, playing our favourite singles and also creating little plays with different characters for which Andrew, Eugene and I would do the voices.

JW: Can you remember your first album purchase?

MJ: *Ride A White Swan* by T. Rex (1972) was the first LP I bought with my own money – from the local Co-Op. It had been released on MFP Records – the budget imprint of EMI – as a compilation of earlier recordings. The first single I bought was a re-issue of a sixties hit: 'Nut Rocker' by B. Bumble & The Stingers.

Although I loved *Ride A White Swan* an even more significant album for me was the soundtrack to a film called *Stardust*, starring David Essex. My Uncle Kenny bought me the double-cassette album of the soundtrack the same Christmas I received my trusty little Amerex cassette recorder. But it wasn't the original soundtrack music on the second cassette that fascinated me – it was the selection of sixties songs on the *first* cassette. It was the first time I can remember properly hearing Jimi Hendrix, Jefferson Airplane, Lovin' Spoonful and Procol Harum. Four tracks in particular blew my teenage mind: 'All Along The Watchtower', 'White Rabbit', 'Summer In The City' and 'Whiter Shade Of Pale'. I just couldn't stop playing this little cassette. Over and over again. I've never liked guitar solos much but Hendrix's on 'All Along The Watchtower' remains my favourite to this day. I couldn't believe the expressiveness and sensuality of his playing – far above and beyond anything the glam-rock groups were serving up. I couldn't stop listening to it.

I had become so obsessed with vinyl I even signed up to one of those mail-order record clubs whereby you paid a subscription but never knew what was going to arrive in the post each month. The first LP that arrived was *Snowflakes Are Dancing* by Isao Tomita, which I absolutely loved and which further cemented my love of electronic soundscapes.

JW: Apart from stealing, how did you and your brothers get the money to buy singles? Did you do odd jobs?

MJ: As kids we were given chores in exchange for pocket money. Going to the greengrocers with a list from my mum on Saturday morning was one. Some of the others I had to do were sweeping the yard and 'bottlin' up'. All of us boys had to do it. It involved taking a notepad, going through the pub shelves and writing down what was needed for the next session: 17 x bottles of pale ale, 12 x bottles of brown, 25 x lemonades etc. But before replenishing the shelves you'd first have to remove all empties from the skip – which was full of broken glass and dregs and stunk – and fill the empty crates up for them to be recycled. Then you'd go over to the bottling shed to bring across fresh bottles with which to fill the shelves. It was a good system as the brewery and soft drinks companies all re-used their glass bottles. Not recycled but *re-used* – they cleaned and re-labelled them and put them back into use – far better for the environment than the recycling of today. In fact, thinking about it, we had electric milk floats which delivered the re-used milk bottles too. Far more efficient and effective than all the nonsense 'greenwashing' corporations use to manipulate us and thus earn a fortune.

Anyway, to make the bottlin' up chore less tedious – and to stave off boredom – I'd devise competitions in my head between companies like Schweppes, Britvic and Cantrell & Cochrane etc.

as to who was selling the most. I even created personalities for different brands of drinking vessels, for instance Ravenhead dimple pint mugs seemed more characterful to me than their Dema Crown rivals. We'd each get paid a weekly amount for this daily chore and – of course – all monies earned would instantly be splurged on the latest 7-inch vinyl.

JW: How did you alight on Road Star as a band name?

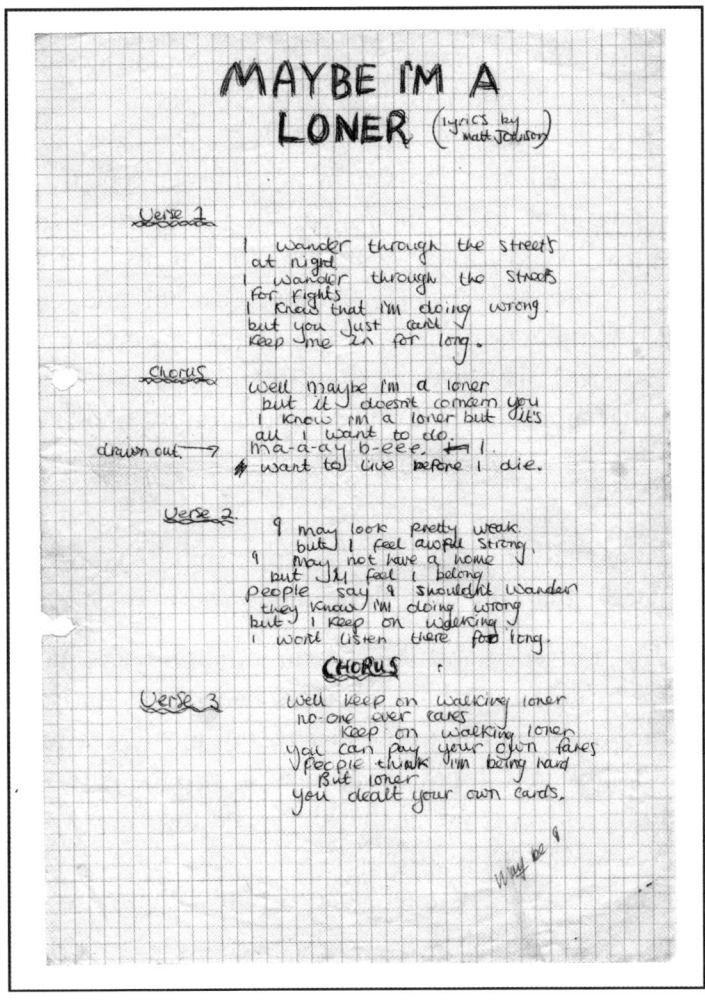

MJ: Probably because it was quite glammy. We weren't a bad little group really but in our minds our rivals were Flintlock, a band on children's TV featuring boys around our age. Road Star began with Nick and me and a lad named Russell Ball on acoustic guitar; but the definitive line-up was when we added Mark Bratby on bass guitar and Brett Giddings on lead guitar. Brett was clad in faded denim and wore patchouli oil. He was in the year below us at school but somehow seemed more sophisticated. He introduced us to the joys of Led Zeppelin and also the sickly liqueur Southern Comfort. His older brothers were also in a band and kindly allowed us the use of their Sound City 120 amplifier and SG copy guitar. The Giddings were another kind family who were also hit by tragedy when one of the brothers died in a road accident. The Johnsons, Freestons and Giddings all shared similar sadness over the years.

I barely owned any equipment and desperately wanted my own little amplifier. I saw one for sale in a used music gear shop in Stratford – an old Elpico AC88 for £15. But my dad wouldn't give me the money, so I sat in my bedroom and cried. My wonderful, empathetic mum must have heard my crying and came in to sit with me. She gave me the £15 and off I went to buy it. I still own that amplifier to this day and recently had it restored. They sell for about £500 these days.

JW: The King's Head is still open as a pub isn't it? Were the living quarters larger than the Two Puddings?

MJ: Yes, it is still open and the accommodation was much larger. It was nice to no longer have to share bedrooms. Andrew and I went from sharing punch ups to sharing our musical tastes. Above the door to my old room there was a strange little painting – possibly an old portrait of the king. The top floor was where mum, dad and Gerard lived.

Thinking about The King's Head is reminding me of this little game that Andrew created to play by himself. It was called 'Dice Football' and he'd write out the names of thirty-two teams in the format of a cup competition. Scores would be decided by the throw of a die – a team could score between one and six goals. I then – foolishly – took up this game myself. But I went quite a bit further than Andrew by creating fantasy football teams and players – some based on actual British teams and some completely made up. I'd create names and characters, draw their likenesses, design their kits and organise transfers between clubs.

But then things started to get completely out of control as fantasy really took hold and I started developing backstories about their lives, personalities, character flaws, imaginary newspaper headlines, scandals, comebacks and redemptions. It is incredible how our imaginations can run so wild. I used to also be in the yard of The King's Head pub kicking a football around – against walls – imagining I *was* these various footballers. I'd spend hours and hours in that yard. It kept me fit I suppose, but the problem is that as I have such an addictive personality the number of teams and players involved started to grow to absurd proportions. It became a full-time job keeping up with it all! I had notebooks full of drawings of all the players, the kits, the results of all the competitions the teams were in – Europe as well as Britain – plus there was international duty to deal with too! I had to gradually train my mind not to think about them at all. It really was like coming off an addiction. It was like an early – purely imaginary – video game I suppose. I can understand how kids get so addicted. Even now – many decades later – if I dare to think about these characters they quickly come roaring back to life.

I don't think Andrew realised what chain of events he'd set in motion by inventing that game! He was always very creative and he soon started sharing our dad's office so he could set up his own little printing press. He'd always been a big fan of American comics, especially illustrators like Jack Kirby and Steve Ditko, and was a regular at Comics Conventions in the seventies. At one he even got to meet and spend some time with the legendary Stan Lee, the writer, editor and publisher of Marvel Comics who helped transform the comic book industry and co-created many of the most famous superheroes of the 20th century. Lee gave him a personally signed copy of *Silver Surfer #1* and Andrew came home so inspired he saved up and bought a Gestetner duplicator (a mechanical stencil duplicating machine) and started illustrating and publishing his own comics. He was so hard working and so ambitious he was an inspiration to the whole family. He soon had a few comics and fanzines on the go simultaneously.

He created one called *TARDIS* in 1975 but passed it on to someone else to run after about a year. It continued for about twelve years in its original form, until 1987, when it was merged into the Doctor Who Appreciation Society's magazine *Celestial Toyroom*. Andrew was featured in the *Evening Standard* under the headline 'The Teenage Tycoon' and was even invited onto BBC Radio 4's daily morning programme for an interview with Libby Purves who, by a strange quirk of fate, also interviewed my dad when we were promoting *Tales From The Two Puddings* in 2012. Our family had been getting into the habit of appearing on national media – a year or so earlier my mum, dad and Gerard had featured on *Nationwide* (a hugely popular current affairs and magazine programme on BBC One at the time) as Gerard was the first British person born on 1 January 1973, the first day of the UK's membership into the European Economic Community.

JW: A lot seemed to be happening for you as a family when you were living above The King's Head. Was it an inspiring place to live? Atmospheric?

MJ: The pub was actually haunted. There is a book from the seventies titled *Haunted East Anglia* by Joan Forman that mentions The King's Head. There were a lot of strange things that happened there. Doors would suddenly be locked from the inside when no one was in the room, mirrors would fall off walls and tragedies happened. A lovely little boy who was a friend of Gerard's died there. It devasted our family and my parents could no longer bear to live there. Once, Andrew, Eugene and I were playing hide-and-seek in the lounge at the back of the pub when it was closed and we all saw a figure moving. It wasn't Andrew, wasn't Eugene and wasn't me. No one else was around and we didn't know who or what it was.

The Tudor Lounge was a small hall at the back of the main pub that was initially used by members of the Rotary Club for their own events. Our dad managed to get rid of them and with our mum turned it into a restaurant instead. They also started promoting folk music nights at weekends and some of the regular performers included Ralph McTell, Sean Buckley, Jasper Carrot and others – including the aforementioned Jake Thackray. Occasionally, if they were playing multiple nights, the folk musicians would leave equipment set up, like amps, microphones and mini PA systems. I'd sometimes shove a mic down the back of the old piano, put it through the little PA system and turn it into a kind of electric keyboard. That's where I learned to play piano. But I must have been making a hell of a racket. My dad – who would be trying to take a nap during afternoon closing hours – would sometimes shout down the dumb waiter, 'For God's sake Matthew! Stop making all that noise! You just keep playing the same thing over and over again!'

That's a charge that has been levelled at me many times over the years by family members and girlfriends. But what most don't understand is that when I'm writing, each time I play something on an instrument I'm hearing it differently because I'm trying different ideas out in my imagination. It is all to do with what you might call our internal playback machine. Now, we all have this but for most people it only kicks in when they have an irritating ear worm. But for me – and I assume most musicians – it is a system I control. So, for instance, I will playback a song I'm working on in my imagination dozens – maybe hundreds – of times, trying out different arrangements or overdubs – and this can either be with an instrument or without.

JW: And you taught yourself to play piano?

MJ: Yes. I'm not a great piano player and primarily play around the keys of F# and G#. There was a boy at school playing a boogie-woogie tune in F# and I sneakily watched over his shoulder to memorise it and then tried it out on the pub piano when I got home that afternoon. I taught myself from there.

JW: It all leads back to Jools Holland!

MJ: It does! Back then the Tudor Lounge was all mock Tudor with red velvet curtains, red carpets and dark red lampshades. When I was playing the piano down there by myself as a young lad I used to vividly imagine I was performing at the Royal Albert Hall. I just seemed to know I'd be performing at venues like that. There was no doubt at all in my mind.

JW: Which of course you later did.

MJ: Even though my school reports were terrible and I was continually being told how useless I was by everyone and that I'd get nowhere, there was something inside me that – even as a young boy – seemed to know I'd be okay.

JW: Let's talk about Ongar Comprehensive, the school you attended there. What was it like?

MJ: It was a huge, sprawling site of old and new buildings. A massive school. I was surprised they knocked it all down.

JW: I know you weren't academic but did sports offer any salvation?

MJ: Football did. But I liked playing football with my friends *outside* of school not *for* the school. Our sports teachers were horrible – not unlike the one played by Brian Glover in Ken Loach's *Kes*. They only encouraged the bigger kids who were already very good at a range of sports and who were pets of the sports teachers.

JW: Were you in the school team?

MJ: I was only picked for the school football team once.

JW: Sport for me was a salvation because if you weren't good at sport and you weren't clever you were nothing. It's the only reason I didn't get bullied.

MJ: I can understand that. I fell in with a gang of kids who were smoking, misbehaving and truanting. I gravitated to them because academically I was failing.

JW: Did your school have corporal punishment? The cane etc.? I went to a school where there was caning in front of everybody at assembly by a teacher called Mr Fletcher.

MJ: We were hit over our knuckles with rulers.

JW: School apart, it was a happy time for your family?

MJ: Yes, and we had some wonderful holidays when we were kids. There were holidays all over the UK and Ireland – often driving to Wales, Scotland and Cornwall. It was usually always raining of course and with the car often breaking down. When we lived at the Puddings we once travelled by ship to Portugal and – unusually for the time as it was behind the 'iron curtain' – we visited Bulgaria too.

But the most memorable holiday of all for me was the first time I ever went to America. It was 1976 – their bi-centenary – and I was 14 or 15. We flew on a Pan-American Jumbo Jet, which was an experience in itself. Our holiday was spent in a large camper van travelling through California, San Francisco, along Big Sur, touring Disneyland and Universal Studios in Los Angeles, and seeing the surreal neon glow of Las Vegas in the desert. I loved the look and sound of the beautiful big trains, became obsessed with those huge American cars from the sixties and seventies. We even went to drive-in movies. I found the people there so warm, friendly and welcoming and with a wonderful positivity that was a sharp contrast to the moaning and groaning of dreary, grey Britain. I fell in love with its contradictions.

I cannot deny the incredible impact and inspiration American culture has had on my life in the decades since. So many charismatic public figures: the stories of Hemingway; poetry of Plath and Whitman; the films of Lumet, Lynch, Scorsese, Coppola, Kubrick, Brando and Woody Allen; the sporting genius and social conscience of Muhammad Ali; the compassion of Martin Luther King Jr; the music of Howlin' Wolf, Nina Simone, John Lee Hooker, Hank Williams, Bob Dylan, Woody Guthrie, Billie Holiday and The Doors; the paintings of Edward Hopper and Georgia O'Keefe; photography of Diane Arbus, Ansel Adams and Robert Frank; the architecture of Frank Lloyd Wright – and on and on it goes, countless men and women whose impact radiated all the way across the Atlantic.

That trip – sleeping in a camper van, travelling from place to place, city to city – planted the seed for my love of touring – and embedded a deep affection for America. In later years I found myself travelling the length and breadth of the US on tour buses, falling in love with the incredible architecture of many of the great American cities, often staying in legendary hotels like The Drake in Chicago, the Chelsea and the Gramercy Park Hotel in New York, the Chateau Marmont in LA – places where history and myth blurred. That family holiday opened so many doors in my mind. I always knew I would live there after that trip as it created a deep, abiding affection for 20th-century America.

CHAPTER TWO
The Desire Of The Moth For The Star

Though still living above the family pub in Essex, a job at the famous De Wolfe Music publishing company and recording studios enables Matt's access to London culture and also leads to a sharpening of his musical skills and acumen for operating equipment. See Without Being Seen *is born amidst squats and the Scala cinema. The post-punk DIY ethos provides spiritual sustenance and broadens a pool of contacts, friends and collaborators.* Burning Blue Soul *simmers on 4AD whilst Some Bizzare's Stevo moves into Matt's orbit.*

JW: So, you decided to leave school early and get a job?

MJ: I left school at 15. I could not wait to escape. I had some wonderful friends and a good social life but I hated school. The ages of 15 and 16 were a lonely time for me. My mum would not let me have a moped – there had been some accidents with kids being knocked off and badly injured and she was a worrier. Now, as a parent, I fully understand her worries. But at the time it was very hard for me as all my best mates from school suddenly went around on their little mopeds, buzzing off to neighbouring towns and villages. I was left behind with no one to talk to but myself. I went into a state of deep introspection for the first time in my life.

JW: And how did you respond to this change of circumstances in your social life?

MJ: By spending more and more evenings and weekends in relative isolation, I managed to start breaking through the feelings of loneliness and melancholy and almost enter a state of bliss – just being in my own company and thinking. I started to sense and see things I'd never noticed before. Through a certain amount of loneliness and intense introspection came a slow realisation that we really inhabit a sort of shadow world; that a greater, more intense reality exists just outside our five senses – just out of reach.

I determined to educate myself by reading more. I started deepening myself emotionally, started having extremely vivid dreams. Colours became more intense and I could hear things I couldn't previously. I started to become my own teacher and borrowed books from my dad's shelves at his recommendation: Somerset Maugham, Siegfried Sassoon, Evelyn Waugh, Anthony Powell and Kingsley Amis I enjoyed – but his suggestions of George Orwell, Graham Greene and Ernest Hemingway resonated much more. Also, the biographies he had of important contemporary figures such as Malcolm X and Fidel Castro made an impact. That relatively short period of eighteen months remains one of the most important periods in my life. It was the making of me really.

I was also given pep talks by both Andrew and our cousin Jackie about what to do as far as work and career. And in fact, Jackie gave me the money to buy a book that literally changed my life. It was written by a famous television personality and songwriter of that time, Tony Hatch, and was titled *So You Want To Be In The Music Business* (1976). It contained lots of great advice for young people wishing to get their foot onto the first rung of the music business ladder – including writing to record labels, recording studios or music publishers for the job of tea boy.

I wrote to virtually every company in the back pages of that book – studios, record labels and music publishers. There were pages and pages of them – and all I received was rejection after rejection. All apart from one music publisher who offered me an interview. I hadn't even told my parents what I was doing and so the first they found out about it was when I told them I had a job interview in Soho! Dressed in my smartest shirt and jacket – and accompanied by my dad – I took the Central Line to Tottenham Court.

We went up the stairs at 80–88 Wardour Street and into the reception of De Wolfe Music. I had never been to a job interview before. I didn't even have a CV! I'd just sent in a handwritten letter expressing my passion for music and desire to start a career in the music business. I was interviewed by a lovely man called Gary Thomas. He was only about 24 at the time but seemed like a proper grown up to me. He must have taken a shine to me as I was offered the job within a few days without even a follow-up interview. I'm forever grateful to Gary for giving me that chance. Although I didn't end up staying at De Wolfe for more than a couple of years, the experience of working in Soho as a 15-year old was transformative.

JW: How long would it take you to get from Ongar to De Wolfe in Soho? Would you go in weekends as well to do social stuff?

MJ: Door to door it would take me about two hours. So, in effect, it was a twelve-hour day and I got paid just £18 per week. But I loved what I was doing. Thank God that train line was operational when I was a youngster. It was my lifeline to civilisation.

Sometimes I'd go in at weekends to De Wolfe to do some stuff with my colleague and friend Colin Lloyd Tucker. He would be given the keys and so if we were working on each other's material I'd go in. The wages were low but one of the perks of the job was that we would be allowed into the studio during down time. The studio was modestly equipped but had good-quality gear and some nice keyboards including a Minimoog, Clavinet, Fender Rhodes, Hammond Organ and a Prophet-5 which belonged to in-house composer Simon Park.

JW: Would you also go round central London record shops?

MJ: There were some lovely old record shops between Shaftesbury Avenue and Chinatown that I used to visit but they were demolished around 1980 I think.

JW: And what was Soho like then? I knew it in the mid-seventies/early eighties. It was vibrant.

MJ: Working in Soho from 1977 was exciting and slightly nerve-wracking as it was Britain's most infamous red-light district in those days. On occasion – when navigating the underlit back streets on my way to deliver cans of 35mm film or boxes of tapes to post-production suites – I'd get accosted (at one time even pushed up against a wall in a dark alley) by sleazy characters involved in the porn industry, aggressively trying to persuade youngsters to earn extra pocket money by performing in front of the lens. It was slightly unnerving for a 15-year-old. I never mentioned this to my parents as I didn't want to worry them.

Apart from porn the main industries were film and music. There were a lot of film editing suites and distribution offices as well as recording studios. There was also the nightclub scene – a residue from earlier decades – and a few music venues, like the Marquee, which was next to De Wolfe's offices. I spent a huge of time in there and saw everyone from Pere Ubu to very early Human League and even U2.

There are not many places I knew from those days left. Bar Bruno is still there – though that was called Pick & Chews back then. Maison Bertaux, Lina Stores, Bar Italia and some pubs: The Ship, Dog & Duck, De Hems, the French House, the Blue Posts, Coach & Horses are still hanging in there but many shops, cafes, restaurants and pubs have long gone.

I used to love walking around Soho and central London during lunchtimes. Martin Brand – a fellow tape-op – and I would often wander down to Downing Street and sit and have our sandwiches opposite Number Ten. These days it's gated with heavily armed guards surrounding it and you can't get close, but back then you could literally just walk into Downing Street. Incredible how much the world has changed in the last few decades.

Often in the evening – after leaving De Wolfe and whilst waiting to go to a gig – I'd sit down in front of the fire exit door at 10 Soho Square, next door to Église Protestante Française de Londres. I used to stare up at the neon-illuminated 20th Century Fox logo on a rooftop opposite. Somehow it seemed to connect to my fantasies of the music career that may lay ahead. I had a sense Soho Square related to my ambitions but wasn't sure how. A few years later I signed to CBS – a few doors further along Soho Square on the corner building.

JW: And what was the day-to-day working environment like? Tell me more about the equipment you were learning on. What sort of musicians worked at De Wolfe's studio?

MJ: It was a friendly environment, lots of chatter and laughter. An indication of its family atmosphere is that many of the people I worked with stayed there until they retired. There are still a few of my old colleagues there like Steve Rosie, who was tea-boy between Colin Lloyd Tucker and me. Soon after I started working as tea-boy Mr De Wolfe had to have a quiet word with me in the kitchen because my tea wasn't deemed strong enough. He demonstrated how to squeeze the tea bag against the side of the cup with the teaspoon to provide the desired strength. Mr De Wolfe was very charismatic, always immaculately dressed: dark suit, white shirt and tie, tanned, smelling of expensive cologne. He was well-spoken and slightly distant, though not unfriendly.

There was a large crossover between the London jazz scene and the film and library music world in those days. As a tape-op I'd often be sat at the back of the smoke-filled control room operating the large tape recorder whilst jazz musicians who were legends by night would be jobbing by day to earn their crust. It was a fascinating world on which to eavesdrop and much of the music that was casually written and recorded off the cuff actually stands up just as well as – sometimes even better than – work that was painstakingly crafted with the benefit of time and money.

I've always been a gear-head and I loved suddenly being surrounded by all this recording technology. I loved the smell of electrical equipment and tape and the way it mingled with the aroma of coffee and tobacco smoke. There was something deeply comforting about that to me. The staff at De Wolfe took the training of youngsters seriously and you had to practise on these old green

Ferrograph tape machines before you were allowed anywhere near the newer slicker Ampex machines. I remember the chief engineer there, the late Les Saunders, teaching me editing and how to measure lengths of leader tape when positioning it around your shoulders – for 15ips [inches per second] he'd say, 'bollock to bollock' and for 7.5ips it would be, 'tit to tit'. After a few weeks on the Ferrographs I was then taught how to properly clean, demagnetise and line up the Ampex machines – which was something we would do every Monday morning. Another of my tasks was relabelling what seemed like hundreds of old tape boxes. So, I had to quickly learn to type too. In fact, I typed the words 'Copyright Music De Wolfe London' so many times I could literally do it with my eyes closed. Which I often did!

JW: What age were you when you left Ongar?

MJ: I was 16 – nearly 17.

JW: Although you hadn't received much academic guidance what self-discoveries did you make about how you needed to live your life?

MJ: After leaving school I realised I had to become my *own* teacher. I started seeking out self-improvement books and rolled up my sleeves to make something of my life. Much of this was about positive thinking and creative visualisations about who I wanted to become and where I wanted my life to go. Of course, this was many years before the self-help industry and its countless gurus became ubiquitous. In those days it was hard to find these types of books. But I did find one – *23 Steps To Success & Achievement* – that recommended reading the classics and becoming self-disciplined; to connect one's mind to great thinkers and writers and hope some of it might rub off. So, I started heading off into bookshops by myself, exploring the works of André Gide and Jean-Paul Sartre amongst others. Of particular inspiration at this time were also the American late-19th-/early-20th-century New Thought movement – writers like Ralph Waldo Emerson and

William Walker Atkinson. There was an interesting bookshop called Watkins* on Cecil Court – off Charing Cross Road – that I used to visit during my lunch hour at De Wolfe. It dealt more with esoteric and occult titles but I picked up some interesting books.

It was during this time that I began my journey of self-improvement in earnest. Although it didn't really bother me at the time I now began to feel a certain stigma at having left school at 15 with zero qualifications – not even a single CSE. So, I decided to teach myself how to become more disciplined and orderly in my thinking and in my life generally. I also determined that my learning would be mainly based upon Camus' philosophy of personal experience – to 'eat life before it eats me'. So many people educated in the university system that I met back then seemed to come across as quite arrogant on one hand yet naive on the other. Seemingly content to live life second-hand through university teachers and recommended textbooks, rather than going off to humbly explore the world themselves and experience life through the heart and the soul instead of just the ego and the intellect.

JW: After leaving Ongar where did your family move to?

MJ: We moved to Loughton, Essex. I never really spent much time there to be honest. I didn't know anyone or have any friends there. The building that used to house The Crown pub that my parents took over is now some sort of restaurant.

JW: So, your family went from the Two Puddings—

MJ: —to the cottage in Great Wratting, to Ongar and The King's Head, then to Loughton to take over The Crown. I was still working at De Wolfe and had formed THE THE by the time I was 17 whilst living above that pub.

---

* Watkins Books is still open and specialises in spiritual and esoteric books.

JW: So, you were a commuter?

MJ: Yes, I was still commuting to Tottenham Court Road via the Central Line. Actually, I always liked the tube station in Loughton, it's a Grade II listed structure from the 1940s. I'd also occasionally drive in. My first car was a little white Vauxhall Viva that my Uncle Freddie helped me buy at a car auction. I passed my test aged 17. First time. Although they say the better drivers are the ones who fail their test a few times.

JW: From your driving today, I was imaging you had never actually got your full licence!

MJ: Well, I did write off three cars before the age of 21! I was a speed freak as a kid.

JW: And you were all living above a pub again?

MJ: Yes. It was during my time living there that I left De Wolfe. But I didn't tell my parents for some time. Not sure why.

JW: Did you leave or were you fired?

MJ: I was *about* to be fired because I was quite mischievous. They were very nice employers and treated staff fairly but they gave me a couple of warnings because I was skiving and doing my own thing. They warned me once, then a couple of months later warned me twice. It was three strikes and out so I thought, sod it, and left so I could devote myself full time to THE THE. After a while my parents found out I'd left and my mum was a bit annoyed: 'Well, you can't just lie around here all day long doing nothing!'

JW: You and Andrew were now sharing a bedroom again?

MJ: This was the weird thing about moving there. The pub was big but the flat above was so small. Gerard and Eugene shared a bedroom. And yes, Andrew and I had to share one again too. Consequently, we had a couple of vicious fights. Full-on fist fights. I remember one: I'd borrowed one of his sweatshirts – we'd sometimes swap clothes – and he walked past whilst I was speaking to a friend on the phone and just grabbed and pulled the collar of the sweatshirt really hard. I remember calmly thinking, 'Right, when I finish this phone call I am going to punch him full in the face.' So, when I put the phone down, I went over to where he was sitting and punched him full in the face as hard as I could. Then of course he punched me as hard as *he* could, so then we were really going at it. Gerard was only a little boy and started crying. He buzzed down to our dad in the pub to tell him. He was a big man our dad. Six foot three and sixteen stone. So, he came upstairs and picked us both up. Me in one hand, Andrew in the other. Shook us hard and really told us off. We had a couple of fights like that whilst living there and each time we didn't talk to each other for six months despite sharing a small bedroom. Six months! We were obviously both very stubborn.

JW: It must have been difficult in such confined spaces.

MJ: It was, but most of the time we got along very well. By this point, Andrew was doing his foundation degree at Loughton College – before going to Camberwell for his BA – and I was out much of the time heading into London, to gigs, staying with friends or sleeping at squats. But we still spent a fair amount of time together in that little room. We had an old record player in there and used to sit for hours together listening to music.

Andrew was actually one of the original punks. Long before it became mainstream. He was in the audience at the legendary Sex Pistols gig at the 100 Club. He was always out at gigs – always discovering new music. And he would bring it home and play it to me. I wasn't a fan of punk so much. I liked some of the punk stuff he played – he had an original copy of *Spunk*, the Pistols' bootleg album – and I remember really loving that version of 'Submission'. I liked The Clash too but most punk left me cold musically – though I appreciated the energy and intent behind it.

He'd also bring back copies of the punk fanzine *Sniffin' Glue*, edited by Mark Perry, who soon formed his own band, Alternative TV (ATV).

Soon he was bringing home albums by American artists that I found far more powerful than British punk: Iggy Pop's *Raw Power*, Television's *Marquee Moon*, Patti Smith's *Horses* and many others. His taste was so eclectic that he might play Captain Beefheart's *Clear Spot* one minute followed by Nick Drake's *Bryter Layter* the next. I remember in our bedroom one evening we listened to an interview John Lydon [Johnny Rotten] gave to Tommy Vance on his Capital Radio show in 1977. We were both impressed by Lydon's emotional honesty and his great taste in music. We instantly fell in love with Tim Buckley after hearing 'Sweet Surrender' as well as Doctor Alimantado & The Rebels, Kevin Coyne and Augustus Pablo. I remember one night – it must have been on John Peel's BBC Radio 1 show – we heard The Residents for the first time. I was blown away by them. Loved it. The next day Andrew came home with a copy of *Duck Stab* for me. He could be extremely thoughtful.

Andrew was also in a band of his own, called Camera 3, with his friends Graham Weston on guitar and Paul Miller on bass. I would sometimes record their rehearsals for them. I thought they were great live and Andrew had a strong presence as a singer. I even wrote the music for their first and only single 'Russians In Space' but cheekily wasn't credited.

JW: Did the creative exchange and sense of shared endeavour continue?

MJ: Apart from sharing a bedroom, Andrew and I also shared a studio space. The Crown was a sixties building and had a large cellar with relatively high ceilings and was laid out in a sort of U shape. At one end was the cold room with the kegs of beer as well as our dad's little office. Along the main section was the pub's stock – endless boxes full of beers, spirits, soft drinks, cigarettes and bar snacks piled high. At the far end Andrew and I set up our little studios. He had a large desk with his pens, brushes and arts materials laid out – around this time he'd started drawing illustrations for the music weeklies *Record Mirror* and then *Sounds*. I'd set up my little music studio next to his. I was down there a lot. I'd get home from work and go straight down to the studio in the cellar. I was either in the West End going to gigs and seeing friends or down in that little studio. *See Without Being Seen* was largely recorded there, though I did take the tapes into De Wolfe to tweak them. Often Andrew and I would be in our studios together, working away on our projects, sneakily pilfering stock, drinking endless cans of Foster's lager and puffing our way through packs of Dunhill fags. We'd get drunk together down there, playing music and discussing ideas.

I remember one strange evening when our parents, Eugene and Gerard were away on holiday. Andrew had been left in charge of 'running' the pub and locking up each night. He had a group of close mates he was always in the pub drinking with (including Mark Wallinger – later a Turner Prize-nominated artist). They'd usually get roaring drunk. I was often recording in the cellar quite late but my dad would normally tell me when he was locking up the pub so I could go up. On this occasion, I just happened to realise it was well past midnight and the pub was already closed. I went upstairs to the eerily dark and silent pub and realised I was locked in. I tried calling Andrew on the extension phone in the flat above. No answer. I tried again – and again. I was getting worried as I didn't fancy sleeping in the pub. So, I started screaming up the dumb waiter. No answer there either. It slowly dawned on me that the only way to get to the flat was to empty out the little dumb waiter of its stock and shelves, climb inside and pull myself up by the rope inch by inch. It was extremely dark and claustrophobic and I was worried that if let go of the rope I'd go hurtling down to the ground. By the time I'd reached the kitchen at the floor above I was furious as I thought Andrew was playing a prank. When I tried to go into our bedroom I couldn't even open the door. I managed to force it open and found Andrew so paralytic drunk that he'd accidentally barricaded himself in and could barely wake up even after I started screaming at him.

There was another more worrying incident when Andrew was

extremely drunk at The Crown. I was woken in the early hours one morning – around 3 a.m. – by very faint cries of 'Help me … help me'. It seemed to be coming from outside the bedroom window in the car park. It took me a while to wake up and – at first – I thought it was someone from the neighbouring Indian restaurant that shared the car parking area. I looked out the window and was horrified to see Andrew in nothing but his underpants, with his limbs contorted this way and that. He was so drunk that – thinking he was going to the toilet – he opened the window by mistake and fell straight down – onto the tarmac. He'd broken his arms and ankles and I remember the ambulance crew being convinced he was on LSD and had been trying to fly! He was in terrible agony and though still very drunk and slurring did his best to convince them otherwise.

JW: It strikes me as quite something that a working-class family would produce so many artistically minded children.

MJ: I thought you were going to say drunken children! It is unusual, yeah, very unusual. The funny thing is that I think our chosen professions could have been interchangeable. If Andrew had chosen music I might have chosen film. Or Gerard might have chosen music instead of film. Sibling rivalry determined we'd follow different paths but I think each of us could have done a reasonable job in each other's professions. Eugene was also artistic. Quite a few of our cousins are creative: Kenny's daughter Annabel is an accomplished ceramicist.

Both our parents were encouraging but a lot of that came from our mum's side. She'd say, 'I just want you to be happy, whatever you do. I want you to choose something you love. It doesn't matter about the money.' Obviously, she wanted us to be able to pay our way, support ourselves and be responsible but more than anything she wanted us to follow our dreams. She was very proud of us. Our dad was also encouraging but he provided more of the literary and political side I suppose. He was very well read. Talk at the family dinner table revolved around films, books, politics and music as well as the usual family gossip, winding up and bickering! It was an interesting combination but there was always a general love of culture.

JW: My dad's background meant he had no access to culture but he grew to love films as he got older. My brother was and still is really interested in culture. But he was expected to follow my dad into the building trade.

MJ: Children are often expected to follow their parents but there was no way I was going to become a publican!

JW: Did you help out at home during your teenage years?

MJ: Well, Andrew and I would often be horizontal on the sofas in the flat above the pub nursing hangovers, watching daytime telly or old films we'd taped with the VHS recorder. Our dad would occasionally come upstairs, shout and holler about what lazy bastards we both were and Andrew and I would just look at each other, shrug and wonder what his problem was. Eugene, on the other hand, was a much bigger help to our parents. He was energetic, kind and thoughtful and would be tidying up and trying to make things nice for our parents. Although it certainly *appeared* as though I was just on the dole and lying around watching telly my parents were not yet convinced music was the full-time job I already considered it to be.

JW: Did they encourage you to find another job?

MJ: There was an insurance company in the same building as The Crown – Walrond & Scarman. Some of their staff drank in our pub at lunchtimes. Unbeknownst to me, my mum asked if there were any jobs available for one of her sons. They said yes, a position had become available in the post room for a city runner. I was not happy about this but felt manoeuvred into it. I was only there six months before I intentionally got the sack. I loathed it. During my short tenure, there was a merger/takeover. It was my first awareness of such a thing – all of a sudden, strange new faces appeared in the office with people temporarily doubling up on each other's jobs whilst a general sense of insecurity permeated; everyone nervously wondering where the axe might fall. The best thing about this job were my bi-weekly trips into the City. I'd usually take the Central Line from Loughton to Liverpool Street. But I'd often sneak off and wander into Shoreditch or the back streets of the City and pretend my work duties took longer than they did. If I drove I'd come back via Forest Gate to have a cup of tea with my Nanny Sue and tell her my plans for my music career – which she listened to eagerly. We'd often chat about ghosts and otherworldly matters too.

W&S had an office at 36 Spital Square and from there I'd walk to the City Document Exchange and visit various other buildings to drop off and pick up important papers. I remember passing the Lloyds Bank building at the junction of Threadneedle Street and Bishopsgate. I'd often see the same man lovingly polishing the large brass Lloyds Bank plaque on the front entrance. It was always gleaming. In the years since, whenever I pass this building, I notice how dull and neglected this plaque has become. For me, it's become symbolic of the cost-cutting and general lowering of standards within the City and the country as a whole. The lack of care that permeates so many layers of British life these days.

The hours I had to spend in the post room were unbearable. There was one old man in the main office I couldn't stand. His face always looked like he'd been sucking on an unripe lemon. I tried to be nice and smile but he never smiled back once. My Uncle Kenny had worked for the same company many years earlier when they were located somewhere else and confirmed to me that this man was a spiteful bastard back then too. I liked to leave on time so I'd keep on top of the post all through the day, regularly doing my rounds, asking everyone if they had any post for me. Most would always hand it over upon asking. But this man always said he had no post throughout the day until right at the very end – just as I was about to leave – whereupon he would hand over a massive pile for the franking machine as if to say, 'You are *not* leaving.' I couldn't bear him. At the end of my last day there I shoved a potato up the exhaust of his pale blue Vauxhall Cavalier and bent his window wipers back. It was raining heavily as I watched him try to drive off. Bastard! Though I kind of feel bad about it now.

We may age physically and intellectually yet it seems harder for us to mature emotionally, doesn't it? You often come across old people like that – still full of piss, vinegar and spite. Who wants to take that with them into the next world?

JW: It sounds like an extremely tedious, soul-sapping job. Luckily music came to your rescue. How did THE THE come into existence? How did you find like-minded souls?

MJ: What my generation used to do when we wanted to form a band was place a classified advert in the back pages of *Melody Maker* or *New Musical Express (NME)*. The first advert I placed in early 1979 was in *Melody Maker*, citing my influences as The Residents, The Velvet Underground, Syd Barrett and Throbbing Gristle. For some odd reason I received replies from jazz funk musicians who were not only far more technically accomplished than me but who also had completely different taste in music! It seemed bizarre as I'd clearly stated what sort of music I liked. Maybe it was just the sort of people who read *Melody Maker*? But I did receive a reply from Charlie Blackburn, a lad from Hull who was also a big Syd Barrett/early Pink Floyd fan like me. Unfortunately, Charlie seemed to enjoy drinking beer more than actually playing music so we just spent many nights getting drunk and *talking* about music rather than actually playing it. I suggested the name The Marble Index for our prospective band – inspired by the Nico album of the same name – but we only had two rehearsals before I realised it was going nowhere.

I decided to place my next advert in *NME*, citing my influences again but this time with the caveat, 'Enthusiasm more important than ability,' as I wanted to avoid the jazz–funk musos. I received four replies, one of whom was from Steve Parry of the band Neu Electrikk who just wanted to get in touch with a kindred spirit. I arranged to meet the other three at The Ship pub on Wardour Street – a few doors along from De Wolfe. Keith Laws was one of the three and there was a female drummer called Janice and another chap – a would-be violinist called Peter. We had one rehearsal as a four piece – which didn't work out. Then one gig as a three piece – which also didn't work out. So, Keith and I decided to proceed as a duo. I'd liked Keith instantly. An East London working-class lad like myself I found him very perceptive and funny. He was also a real culture vulture and had been going to the same underground gigs as me, such as the Final Solution-promoted concerts for the likes of Throbbing Gristle. We were also both Cockney Reds so had a lot in common.

I really liked his family too, who were always very welcoming. Keith and I were out together all the time, going to various gigs and events, after a heavy Saturday night out we'd usually pick up the night bus from outside Centre Point and back to his. We'd often sit up into the early hours in his bedroom smoking fags, listening to music and discussing philosophical ideas. It was Keith who turned me onto a lot of krautrock, including Kraftwerk, Neu! and Faust. The following morning his mum would usually invite me to stay for the Sunday roast. I remember his dad used to love his old vinyl collection and would spend Sunday afternoons with his feet up listening to old Bobby Darin LPs. We were inseparable for a couple of years and real partners in crime. During his time with THE THE his day job was in the civil service as an accountant I believe, but it was no surprise after he left THE THE that he went on to excel as a research psychologist as he was always a deep thinker and ambitious beyond the confines of the music business.

JW: It does sound like Keith played a very important role in helping you get the group of the ground. I found a very early *NME* interview with you ('THE THE: The Definitive Article', Chris Bohn, *NME*, 9 October 1982) where you spoke about the fact that the name THE THE enabled you to put a barrier between people and yourself. You also mentioned that the name of a solo artist on a record can put some people off. What interested me most however was the below quote: 'THE THE allows me more flexibility, styles will constantly change, anything can happen actually...' Does this still strike you as an apt depiction of the importance of the name THE THE?

MJ: Yes. The name always felt like a blank canvas that didn't suggest a particular style or type of music. I'd always loved the concept group idea of the Plastic Ono Band, something amorphous that couldn't really be pinned down. It was Keith who suggested the name to me. Though he'd actually got it from Tom Johnston, the wonderful Fleet Street cartoonist from Northern Ireland who became our first manager. He was introduced to us by Keith's brother, Darren. Tom had badges printed with the name THE THE on them as a parody of band names in general. We'd been mulling over names for weeks. I'd suggested The Dead Beats plus also Insect Fear – which was suggested by Andrew. There were a few other names in the mix I've since forgotten. One evening Keith telephoned and made the suggestion. I liked it instantly but wanted a couple of days to think about it. Whilst mulling it over I mentioned it to a friend, a Bohemian, hippyish girl, who said, 'Oh, are you a fan of Wallace Stevens?' I had no idea who that was but she explained 'the the' were the last two words in one of her favourite poems, 'The Man On The Dump'. 'Where was it one first heard of the truth? The the.' After reading the poem myself there was no hesitation.

JW: THE THE was gigging as a four-piece at one point. I think you were playing tracks like 'Controversial Subject', 'Perspective And Distortion', 'What Stanley Saw', and you were working with Colin Lloyd Tucker. I've got another track here, but I think I've written it down wrong: 'Ex Mar Boo'?

MJ: Yes, for a while THE THE comprised of myself, Keith, Tom (our manager) on bass guitar and photographer Pete Ashworth on drums. Apart from 'Controversial Subject' we weren't playing those other songs live though. That is the correct spelling of 'Ex Mar Boo'.

JW: Were those other songs from your 1979 album *Spirits*?

MJ: Yes, but I'll need to rewind to provide context as there were just so many things going on simultaneously. I was still working at De Wolfe in Soho plus I'd built my first little recording studio in the cellar of The Crown. I was a very ambitious teenager and wanted to learn about recording techniques and start releasing my own records – but it was difficult as it seemed you had to be signed to a major label or one of the indies to gain access to this world. This was years before the Internet of course so it was harder to find information in those days – De Wolfe had subscriptions to magazines like *Studio Sound* and others – maybe *Sound International*.

There was also a fanzine I came across once or twice called *Contact* which dealt with the avant garde. I remember reading articles somewhere about the influential experimental recording studios in Britain, Europe and America. In London you had Electronic Music Studios (EMS) and BBC Radiophonic Workshop but all around the world there were similar places: Studio d'Essai and Groupe de Recherches Musicales in Paris, WDR Studio für Elektronische Musik in Cologne, Studio di Fonologia Musicale in Milan, Columbia-Princeton Electronic Music Center in New York, the San Francisco Tape Music Center in California and the Moscow Experimental Studio of Electronic Music in Russia.

I also saw photos of American composer Raymond Scott in his home studio that looked incredible. Those old experimental recording spaces seemed half-art studio, half-science laboratory. Rooms with oscillators, tape recorders, test tone generators, reverb chambers, filter banks, splicing blocks, chinagraph pencils – tape loops strung across rooms like cobwebs, fluorescent bulbs humming overhead. It fascinated me and working in the 'Transfer Bay' at De Wolfe surrounded by lots of analogue equipment inspired my own fantasises of having a 'sonic laboratory'. Funnily enough – thinking about musique concrète* – the name of the German side of my family was Stockhausen – though they changed it to Stock after World War One due to anti-German sentiment.

---

* Musique concrète is a genre of experimental electroacoustic music that uses recorded sounds as its raw material.

I learned a lot about analogue recording techniques between the ages of 15 and 17. Colin Lloyd Tucker, a singer–songwriter colleague at De Wolfe and friend to this day, helped by showing me the tricks of the trade with tape manipulation: looping, flanging, phasing, reversing, vari-speeding etc. I started to realise I didn't really *need* a band to make records. Around this time Thomas Leer released his single 'Private Plane', which I'd hear at many events and gigs I was attending and I fell in love with it. The reason that record was so influential for me was that I found out Thomas had created all the music by himself in his bedroom so it confirmed I was on the right path. Cabaret Voltaire, The Normal, The Residents and early Human League were also influences on my early recording experiments.

JW: Let's talk about your memories of recording *See Without Being Seen* in 1978.

MJ: I was 16 when I bought my Akai 4000DS MK2 tape recorder in 1978. It cost me £147 new and I saved up for a year to pay for it. It arrived when we were still living above The King's Head. Unboxing a piece of equipment has never given me such pleasure. This was a couple of years before the first 4-track cassette Portastudios came to market and the Akai used a system called 'Sound-On-Sound', which meant you overdubbed as you went – but couldn't remix. It was the poor man's Revox and just about affordable for someone like me. I still own it and had it refurbished to transfer and digitise the original recordings I made on it. I also had an old Shure Unidyne microphone I got from the Two Puddings, a pair of headphones and some simple effects: Electro-Harmonix Muff Fuzz, Memory Man, Y-Triggered Filter, Small Stone Phaser and a Rhythm 12 drum machine (borrowed from my brother's band Camera 3) plus a Colorsound Tremolo and Cry Baby Wah-Wah. I'd also bought an old Crumar Roadrunner piano I found in the *Exchange & Mart* and a few other bits and pieces – including a Telecaster copy I borrowed from Charlie Blackburn. I loved my little recording studio but in my imagination it seemed far more impressive than it really was.

I'd play around the key of F# on the keyboards but I couldn't play chords on a guitar yet so I'd tune all strings to the same note to play 'drone-chords' through the delay pedal. Then Charlie Blackburn showed me the moveable E barre chord and I just took it from there. I hadn't learned any instrument in the 'traditional' way as that didn't fit the 'non-musician' post-punk ethos that was guiding me at that time. It's something I sometimes regret as learning to read and write music would have proven useful later. Then again, my songs and recordings wouldn't sound like they do if I'd just followed the same well-trodden path as everyone else. I had limited use of synthesizers, the Minimoog and Prophet-5 at De Wolfe. There was also a Roland CR68 drum machine I might record some drum patterns on though they were designed as accompaniment for organists with pre-set rhythms such as bossa nova and samba.

I'd been learning on the equipment at De Wolfe but there was a lot of trial and error – which is as it should be to an extent. I'd hear a sound on a recording and wonder, 'How did they do that?' and try to re-create it. So, there was a lot of experimentation and getting things wrong – especially levels and setting up optimum signal chains. I didn't have compressors or equalizers so I'd record to the Akai quite hot – to get natural tape compression. Analogue is quite forgiving compared to digital and can soak up a lot of level, but even so, things would be distorted at times. This was all done over six or seven months. I'd spend countless hours writing and recording in my cellar–studio, often late into the night and then take the quarter-inch reels into De Wolfe and – during lunchtime or after work – edit, EQ (equalisation) and loop. For some reason the management at De Wolfe had very kindly given me my own little studio, which was a small room at the top of the building with amazing views over Soho. I think they were trying to motivate me because I was a naughty kid – always being told off for being late or being cheeky. I did actually do all the work I was supposed to do for De Wolfe but obviously spent some time on my own stuff too.

There were numerous recordings I worked on during this period including my debut album. *See Without Being Seen* was first released as a DIY cassette album in 1979 and we re-released it forty years later in 2019 for Cassette Store Day* through Cinéola. We later released it as a CD with a few extra tracks from the period. Although it was rudimentary I put a huge amount of time and effort into it and took it very seriously.

Obviously, at the time I couldn't afford to manufacture on vinyl – and CDs weren't even invented yet. I also couldn't afford to mass manufacture cassettes either. But I designed the little cassette sleeve and used the Xerox machine in the De Wolfe accounts department to create multiple copies. I then duplicated the recordings onto several dozen C45 cassettes and sat and assembled it all. It was really exciting, like having my own pocket-sized indie label – albeit much more DIY than even the most hardcore indie bands. I then took the cassettes to various underground gigs to sell – plus I'd take them to the offices of various indie label bosses I was getting to know. I think you'd be very hard-pushed to find a more fully independent release in the true spirit of the post-punk ethos than *See Without Being Seen*. It was even distributed by hand!

JW: Can you explain the origins of the cover for the reissue of *See Without Being Seen*?

MJ: Most of the sleeves of records I've released since Andrew died feature his artwork. It is important for me to sustain our creative connection. I was looking for a cover idea for *Seen Without Being Seen* and – flicking through some of his old sketch books – came across a drawing he'd done of me. It was actually done slightly later than the period the album represents but it just felt apt. The period photographs of me were taken by Darren Laws, the younger brother of my former bandmate, Keith. The little doodles are mine as are the photos of some of the original recording equipment used on the album. There's also the original cassette sleeve I'd

---

* Cassette Store Day (now Cassette Week) is an annual celebration of cassette tapes as a music format. Begun in 2013, many bands release limited editions of previous albums on cassette.

created entirely with Letraset.* We've worked with the excellent designer Martin Lewis for many years now and he helped bring everything together.

JW: You have spoken about some of the sounds on the record but where were you lyrically?

MJ: I'd started writing lyrics from the age of 11 or 12 when I was the singer in Road Star. My lyrics until *Burning Blue Soul* were understandably very naive and on *See Without Being Seen* the lyrics were teenage fantasy and quite obscure, taking inspiration from some of the vintage sci-fi comics I was addicted to at that time. I used to collect black-and-white reprints of old American comics, published in Britain by Alan Class Comics – they included titles like *Creepy Worlds, Suspense, Sinister Tales, Secrets of the Unknown* and *Astounding Stories*. I loved those comics and some of the titles of the songs contained in *See Without Being Seen* – such as 'Spaceship In My Barn' – I took from these magazines. Even the title 'What Stanley Saw' from *Spirits* was taken from a story in one of these comics.

The master tapes of *See Without Being Seen* were missing for years and they took a while to locate as I have extensive archives at various locations. We found them but due to a condition afflicting certain old tape formulations called 'sticky tape syndrome', we first had to dehydrate them. Mark Allaway – who manages Studio Cinéola for me – worked on this. Once he dehydrated the tapes he played them back on my restored Akai 4000DS MK2 and digitised them.

What was invaluable to us when preparing this release was that Steve Parry from Neu Electrikk still had his original copy of *See Without Being Seen* – one of very few still remaining – and kindly lent it to us to compare. There were only seven tracks on the original cassette but when we re-issued for Cassette Store Day we added three extra tracks. But it still wasn't mastered. For the CD version I wanted to master it properly and add more extra

---

* Dry transfer lettering sheets.

tracks from that era. They all sounded pretty good and I can't recall why they didn't end up on the original cassette. But they are all instrumentals, which suggests I never got around to finishing the lyrics. Matt Colton from Metropolis engineered the mastering.

'Sugar & Spies', 'People On Sight', 'Let's Do It Again' and 'Empty Night Train Home' were all also additional tracks. The title of that last piece no doubt inspired by my long train journeys back to Loughton at night – quite often tipsy. I was a very impatient teenager, anxious to get going on my career in music and with *See Without Being Seen* I think I made a decent start.

I'd been in bands before of course – primarily Road Star, and then I played bass in a punk band for a couple of months with Nick Freeston called Anti Establishment. Looking back, I consider *See Without Being Seen* my first album. It's crude and naive but I worked incredibly hard on it and tried my best. It's a moment captured in time – a teenage diary.

The next set of tracks I was working on would've been for the *Spirits* album, including 'Ex Mar Boo'. I can't remember what that name meant. I did hear the track recently – we're planning to finally release *Spirits* so we're digitising the tapes. 'Ex Mar Boo' sounded pretty good. The lyrics are a bit anxious – as you'd expect from a teenager – but I thought sonically it was good. Colin engineered some of those sessions for *Spirits*, including 'Uncoiling Love's Amphetamine', 'What Stanley Saw', 'Perspective And Distortion' and others.

'What Stanley Saw' was the only one released commercially. I licensed it to Cherry Red Records as part of a 1981 compilation album featuring an interesting line-up of left-field artists: Thomas Leer, Virgin Prunes, Lemon Kittens, Robert Fripp, Lol Coxhill, Kevin Coyne, Mark Perry (AKA Alternative TV) and Eyeless in Gaza, amongst others. Funnily enough, that compilation ended up being called *Perspectives & Distortion*. I'd played Mike Alway (the A&R man at Cherry Red Records) some of the tracks from *Spirits* and he said, 'Look, we'd love to license 'What Stanley Saw', but could we also use the title *Perspectives & Distortion* for the name of the compilation? We'll give you a tenner for its use.'

Actually, I'd borrowed the title from a painting my brother Andrew was working on. I'm not sure if I ever gave him a cut of the £10! My track 'Perspective And Distortion' is along the lines of 'What Stanley Saw' – sonically quite dense and similarly featuring drum machine, synthesisers and guitar.

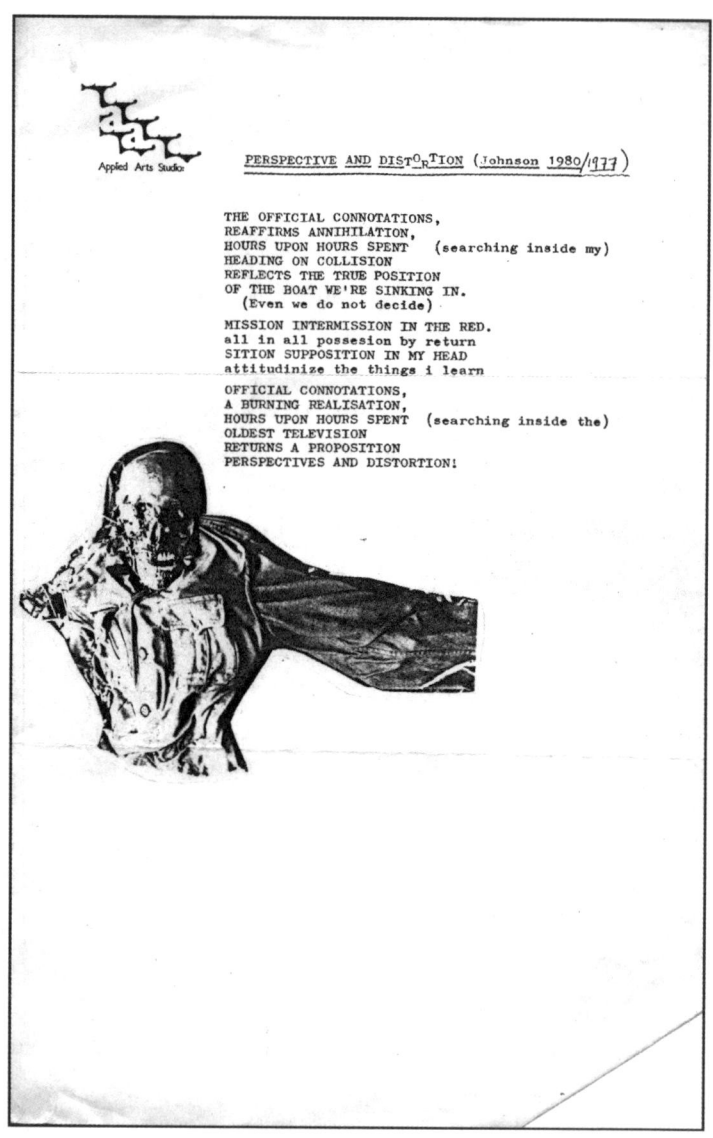

JW: You discovered a love of musique concrète around this time. There was a book that was dear to you.

MJ: Yes, I'd recently bought Terence Dwyer's *Composing with Tape Recorders* (1971) and was learning new tricks and techniques from that. I've still got my original copy. Apparently, the film director Peter Strickland was also influenced by that book when he created *Berberian Sound Studio* (2012), which I loved. From a gear fetishist point of view my two favourite films are that and *The Conversation* (1974). Incidentally, one of those additional tracks on *See Without Being Seen*, 'White Stone On Earth', was one of my first attempts at musique concrète. I made quite a few recordings in that style subsequently but that's the only one I've released so far. I'd enjoyed the work of Luc Ferrari, Tod Dockstader and Raymond Scott but the original inspiration would really have come from 'Revolution 9' from The Beatles' *White Album*. That album remains one of my greatest creative influences – lyrically and musically. As kids, 'Revolution 9' used to fascinate and terrify Andrew and me in equal measure. Being exposed to a recording like that as a child was fascinating. It was dark and disturbing yet also cinematic. The Beatles' experiments in musique concrète helped open my mind musically at a very young age.

JW: There are similarities with your later work in the way these early recordings use sound texture. There is less narrative but they contain the same interest in the structures of sound, which has always been a very big element of your work.

MJ: Like many kids my age I had a fascination with tape recorders. Sitting in my bedroom messing with my family's old Cossor reel-to-reel tape recorder – which I'd sneakily commandeered. I'd record and play back half speed, double speed, reverse, overdrive the inputs for distortion etc. I found the plasticity of sound fascinating – looping, playing with time, creating unusual atmospheres. It was almost a way of bringing one's dream world into waking life.

At the time I'd been listening to a lot of the music Andrew

introduced me to; plus, I found a lot by myself visiting post-punk clubs and gigs. Some of what I was listening to influenced what I was doing – some didn't. Colin at De Wolfe turned me onto The Velvet Underground at age 15. I actually smoked my first joint one lunchtime whilst listening to them for the first time – 'What Goes On'. He also turned me on to Bowie's *Low,* Eno's ambient music and even Al Bowlly! I had a coterie of people I'd go gigging with – individually or as a group: Andrew, Colin, Charlie, Keith, Tom Johnston, Chris Wilson and a few others. We drank cheap lager, ate cheap food at places like Pollo or Stockpot in Soho or at a Pizzaland or Spudulike outlet. We all wore old military clothing too.

We went to tonnes of gigs – the number of bands and musicians we saw was mind-boggling looking back: The Pop Group, Wire, Scritti Politti, Suicide, Devo, The Slits, The Monochrome Set, Cabaret Voltaire, Throbbing Gristle, Patrick Fitzgerald, Spizzoil, Fad Gadget, The Durutti Column, This Heat, The Red Crayola, 23 Skidoo, Magazine, Echo & The Bunnymen, Clock DVA, Swell Maps, pragVEC, Alternative TV, Subway Sect, The Normal, The Fall, Joy Division and Thomas Leer & Robert Rental. I would have seen most of these multiple times – plus, that's just a short list off the top of my head! There were countless others. Not sure how I afforded it really as I had such little money. But there were ways of sneaking into gigs as the live music scene was more relaxed and less corporate or security-conscious then. There were so many amazing venues in London. Some of the ones I frequented included the Music Machine, Rainbow Theatre, Lyceum, Acklam Hall, ICA, Diorama, Heaven, Hackney Collective on Beck Road, Dingwalls, Roundhouse, Vortex, the Bridge House, Clarendon Hotel Ballroom, the Fridge, Metropolitan Wharf, the Nashville, the Electric Ballroom, Hope & Anchor, 100 Club, 101 Club, Rock Garden, The Venue in Victoria. I also performed at most of them.

I was out multiple nights of the week and because the journey back home to my parents' pub in Essex was so long I'd often crash over at people's places – sleeping on sofas, on floors, in squats – sometimes even in derelict buildings. I was a sociable lad and found it pretty easy to meet people and make new friends – boys and girls. If I wasn't at a club, venue or cinema I'd be in the pub.

I especially loved those old centrally located Victorian gin palaces like the Princess Louise in Holborn, the Viaduct Tavern on Newgate Street or The Salisbury on St Martin's Lane. In those days they didn't play muzak – it was just the sound of people talking and laughing so it was like going back in time.

I often went to the old Scala Cinema on Tottenham Street to their all-night screening events where bands might also be playing. I'd often go with Jim Thirlwell*, my friend 'Italian Alex', Keith or others. I used to also spend a fair amount of time at the London Film-Maker's Co-Op in Camden Town and would often head off to parties with people I'd met there.

I remember these really opulent squats where we'd go to all-night parties and sometimes sleep over – huge old John Nash-designed stucco terraced houses on Park Square between Regent's Park and Marylebone Road. They were derelict and the electricity was cut off so partying was strictly by candlelight and battery-powered cassette players. Certain friends would often be there with their cheap speed – sulphate which tasted and smelled like Ajax cleaning powder! They were incredibly atmospheric gatherings – like something from the party scenes in *La Dolce Vita*. You'd be hard pressed to find a squat in an area like that now as I imagine they've all been fully restored and sold off for many millions to oligarchs.

These were my formative years and I consider myself very lucky to have been intimately involved in this extremely fertile time in music history. I was excited to be part of this new, hidden world as I was fascinated by underground music and art scenes. Because it was the pre-Internet age you'd have to find things out via word of mouth or underground fanzines. The information always seemed murky and mysterious – often more rumour than fact.

I still think this 'post-punk' era was one of the most fascinating periods in British music – its sheer variety and inventiveness – and all as a consequence of the 'Big Bang' or 'Year Zero' ushered in by punk.† None of the bands I've mentioned above sounded

---

* Known professionally as JG Thirlwell, AKA Foetus.
† 'Year Zero' refers to 1976, when music journalists generally agree British punk began. It saw a rejection of mainstream rock, leading to a new DIY attitude and cultural shift.

at all alike yet there was a shared ethos and independence of spirit.

The music of punk itself was boring to me and I found that the herd mentality was most evident amongst those who vociferously declared themselves 'different'. How many punks simultaneously dressed in the same clothes, listened to the same music, had tattoos and piercings and dyed their hair a similar colour whilst opining they 'just want to be different'? Yet they clearly wanted to be 'different' – together. The desire to fit in with the herd is powerful.

This next wave of bands was more esoteric and meaningful to me and I feel grateful to have been part of it. It was a small scene but I finally felt like I'd found a place I belonged, even though I was younger than all the people I was meeting. I got to know a lot of those involved quite well; Jim Thirlwell, Wire, This Heat, Throbbing Gristle, Thomas Leer, Cabaret Voltaire amongst many others. Though of course post-punk was really only a 'movement' in hindsight. In reality it was just lots of individuals doing their thing at a particular moment in time.

Apart from the post-punk bands I was regularly watching I started discovering experimental recordings from international artists from the previous generation. For instance, I'd found some old Tod Dockstader vinyl in one of the record shops in Soho I used to visit, albums like *Eight Electronic Pieces*, *Luna Park* and *Quatermass*. They were mind-blowing to me. If you listen closely you can probably hear some of Dockstader's influence in my soundtrack work all these years later. Many musique concrète and early elektronische musik pieces sound more vital than much of today's electronic music, because they weren't tethered to dance floors, algorithms or commercial demands. They bypass 'music' as we usually think of it and go straight to a kind of sonic unconscious – almost like hearing our world through an alien ear. The results were often eerie and dreamlike.

I'd also been hearing through the grapevine about mythical experimental music cooperatives such as Zodiak Free Arts Club in Germany, San Francisco Tape Music Center in America. Pre-Internet it was hard to find detailed information about stuff that was so left field. We take so much for granted these days but it was all word-of-mouth or vague rumour back then and you had to be a bit of a sleuth. By the time I'd found out about them both had long ceased to exist. I was intrigued about experimental collectives and gatherings of creative souls and yearned to find something similar in London, which is why I became quite obsessed with post-punk music and felt so drawn to it.

> Dear Matt,
>
> I have enjoyed listening to your record. I wish we were in the financial position to work with you. Our limited funds are already spoken for.
>
> Thanks for sending your tape and allowing us to hear your taped ideas and music.
>
> Sincerely,
>
> Hardy Fox
>
> RALPH RECORDS
> 444 Grove St.
> San Francisco
> 94102

Although I was only a teenager, I was confident and ambitious but also impatient. I'd been in bands since I was 11 so felt I should really be putting more recordings out by now. So, I'd be travelling all around London on the tube with my dog-eared *A-to-Z*, beating a path to the offices of the various independent record companies I knew, Ivo Watts-Russell at 4AD or Mike Alway at Cherry Red Records – hawking my latest recordings from *See Without Being Seen* to *Spirits* and making a general nuisance of myself. I'd sometimes go and see Geoff Travis at Rough Trade Records who – though turning me down three times – was at least encouraging and made me feel hopeful. I'd send cassettes to every obscure record label in the US or Europe I could find an address for. I did receive a few encouraging replies. Ralph Records, The Residents' label in the US, also took time to reply – albeit turning me down. I'd become friendly with Rod Pearce at Fetish Records. He'd re-issued Throbbing Gristle's *The Second Annual Report* – which Andrew bought – and was also working with Clock DVA and 23 Skidoo – both of whom I liked. Rod was always encouraging and told me – when I gave him a copy of *See Without Being Seen* – that I represented the 'true spirit' of punk and should feel very proud of myself.

JW: You were doing some work with The Gadgets around this time, and also with Peter Greenaway,* the film director.

MJ: Greenaway was a client at De Wolfe. I didn't know him well – I was only a junior – but I'd receive notes from the librarian working with him, copy the required music and take his tapes to where he was working. I had no creative involvement but he was affable and a regular at De Wolfe. This would have been for his corporate job – making films for the Central Office of Information (COI)† – rather than his own films.

A lot of interesting people visited De Wolfe. I had been put in

---

* Peter Greenaway is a film director, screenwriter and artist. His films include *The Cook, the Thief, His Wife & Her Lover* and *The Draughtsman's Contract*.

† The COI was the UK government's marketing and communications agency from 1946–2011, designed to handle public information campaigns and shape cultural attitudes.

charge of the sound effects department there for a few months because the woman who ran it left on maternity leave. One day a guy came in who was looking for the sounds of cranes and general dock noises. I sat with him playing tapes – 'Is this good?', 'How about that?' I managed to help him find what he was looking for, and when he left a colleague – who had been hiding around the corner – suddenly squealed, 'Do you know who that was!?' I said, 'No.' He said, 'Peter Gabriel!' I didn't recognise him. I also met Henry Cooper, the late British heavyweight boxer. He was dressed in a smart navy suit, white shirt, tie – broken nose of course – he was huge. We did lots of post-production work for adverts, TV and film so you'd have all sorts of characters from all walks of life coming in to do their voiceovers.

Concurrent with the early years of THE THE, The Gadgets were purely a studio band between myself, Colin Lloyd Tucker and another chap at De Wolfe – who we ended up falling out with. I was involved in three albums – *Gadgetree* primarily but much less so with the follow-ups, *Love, Curiosity, Freckles & Doubt* and *The Blue Album*. But, importantly, it meant I'd *finally* released my first vinyl record. We'd worked out a fair arrangement with De Wolfe that if we could use their studio for the recording sessions – and retain rights to the sound recordings – we'd then sign over the publishing to them for no advance.

As I had a lot of contacts in the post-punk world it was left to me to find a label for its release. It ended up being through Final Solution who were starting a record label. Colin Faver and Kevin Millins were known mainly as promoters rather than record label execs – in fact, they promoted many of the underground gigs I used to go to in old crypts, warehouses and other unique spaces. They even organised the live music events at the original Scala Cinema on Tottenham Street I mentioned earlier. They had one particular event which, in my opinion, was the high-water mark of post-punk: four nights in August 1979 in the basement of the YMCA on Tottenham Court Road, featuring most of the great and good of the post-punk scene. We didn't perform, sadly, but Keith and I attended every night with some other mates and we all loved it.

Gadgetree (1980) was actually Final Solution's first release – as well as my first release on vinyl. Some time ago Cinéola* put out *Official Bootleg 003* – via our website – which features just The Gadgets' tracks I wrote and sung on, plus a previously unheard version of a Gadgets track by Colin Lloyd Tucker, and an interview between Colin and me from 2010, talking about our time at De Wolfe and learning our trade. I'd always enjoyed working with Colin. We'd work together, go to the pub together, go to gigs together. He was a mate and very encouraging. I was a couple of years younger than him and he turned me on to a lot of interesting music. He's a talented, eccentric and prolific musician who should have received more recognition than he has. He remains a dear friend and we still have a laugh.

JW: You also collaborated with some bands of this era.

MJ: Wire had taken us under their wing and produced THE THE's first single 'Controversial Subject'/'Black And White'. They also invited us to support them for their two London shows at the Notre Dame Hall at Leicester Square, which was a very big deal for us. In fact, I was quite anxious about these gigs as I was only 17. So, to cancel out my nerves I arranged to have my driving test on the same day as the first concert. I sort of double-bluffed myself and then nervelessly passed my driving test first time – and also felt very relaxed for the shows with Wire too.

Around this time Keith and I had also become friendly with This Heat. They invited us to their rehearsal/recording facility at Acre Lane in Brixton called Cold Storage. It was a large, former industrial refrigeration facility they shared with various artists – including David Cunningham of The Flying Lizards. Charles Bullen recorded and prepared our backing tapes for our live performances on their Teac 4-Track. They also used to let us watch them rehearse. To my young ears This Heat were exceptional musicians and mesmerising to watch – whether rehearsing or live

---

* Cinéola is Matt Johnson's independent record label, production and publishing company.

in concert. They were very kind, lovely guys and quite hippyish looking back – they loved their pints of real ale and roll-up fags. Charles even helped set me up for a job at Townhouse Studios with a friend of his who worked there. I went for an interview and would have got the job if it wasn't for the absurd commuting times between Loughton in Essex and West London.

THE THE's first gig – promoted by our manager Tom Johnston – was supporting Scritti Politti and pragVEC at the Africa Centre on 11 May 1979. It was the week Margaret Thatcher got elected. Keith and I had seen Scritti's first gig – at Acklam Hall, Portobello Road. By their third gig we were supporting them. They seemed to have so much more experience than us even though they'd only performed two gigs more!

JW: What about your relationship with record label 4AD?

MJ: THE THE were one of Ivo Watts-Russell's first signings for 4AD. My relationship with him started with 'Controversial Subject'/'Black And White' – our double A-sided debut single. Tom Johnston had actually paid for that to be recorded out of his own pocket. Tom introduced Keith and me to Bruce Gilbert and Graham Lewis from Wire and they soon became involved as our producers. In the late seventies Tom worked for the *Evening Standard* as a cartoonist and had an office in Covent Garden where he would let us rehearse and sometimes sleep. The area then was in stark contrast to the overcrowded tourist hub it has since become. It was quiet and run down – even a bit derelict – as the fruit and flower market had recently vacated the site. It was very atmospheric and quite eerie in the evening. Tom was sociable and knew a lot of people, a few of whom drank in The White Lion pub on James St, including Bruce and Graham.

I was a big fan of Wire's newly released album *154* and respected them. They had an interesting method of working in the studio – cerebral, open-minded and experimental. 'Controversial Subject' did pretty well – it was played and championed by John Peel and featured in the indie charts the music papers used to publish as their alternative to the main singles charts. Shortly after this release that particular line-up disbanded and I went back to recording *Spirits* as a solo project. I played those tapes to Ivo but rather than release those he suggested I go back into the studio with Gilbert and Lewis as producers to start on a completely new project – which would become *Burning Blue Soul*.

Around this time Pete Ashworth and I had played a gig or two as a duo, so I invited him to be part of the recording process. Pete was a good drummer but was primarily known as a very successful music photographer. He had great taste in music and had introduced me to German experimental rock band Can. He was very influenced by the drumming of Jaki Liebezeit – and his wonderful, man-machine, polyrhythmic style. So, we went into the studio but unfortunately Pete and Graham Lewis didn't get along – weird chemistry. Pete – quite naturally – was used to creating rhythms between all the elements of his kit. But Graham was convinced Pete's kit was 'squeaking' and that he must therefore break his drum kit down to its component parts and overdub one drum at a time for a cleaner, more precise sound. Pete was incredibly uncomfortable with this as he had a particular style of playing. Tensions mounted. It wasn't a productive session.

Then Ivo – after hearing the somewhat-confusing results – said, 'Why don't you just go back in with Bruce and Graham by yourself?' So, I did and we recorded 'The River Flows East In Spring' and 'Time (again) For The Golden Sunset'. They turned out well and we were all happy. Unfortunately, due to a clash of schedules, Bruce and Graham weren't involved in any more recordings on the album.

I was writing a lot of material at that time and it was agreed with 4AD that I could go back in the studio alone. There was a studio opposite my nan and grandad's flat in Forest Gate called Stage One Music. I worked there with the house engineer, Pete Maben, who was quite dub-influenced, great to work with and very creative. I liked working closely with an engineer like that and credited him with co-production on the songs we worked on together.

One of the most memorable sessions was with Ivo co-producing when we recorded and mixed 'Another Boy Drowning' and 'Icing

Up'. We drove to Spaceward Studios in Cambridge in his little blue Peugeot and took our sleeping bags so we could have a full day's recording, sleep on the floor in the live room, then get up very early the next morning to start work again. It's what you did in those days – made every second count – as recording sessions in proper studios were like gold dust to young musicians like me.

Burning Blue Soul was a bit mix and match – patchwork really – as it was created over several months in different studios with various people and with a shoestring budget of £1,800. Five recording sessions with two songs recorded and mixed per session, as I recall. But that was part of its charm; and it didn't sound like any other album at the time. Meanwhile, those earlier recordings for *Spirits* were then put in the freezer and forgotten about – apart from 'What Stanley Saw'.

JW: Ivo was important. 4AD was such an influential label. I get the sense that the artists that were on that label were quite close-knit. I think around this time you may have even played with The Birthday Party.

MJ: When Ivo was thinking of signing The Birthday Party he invited me to go see them perform at the Moonlight Club in West Hampstead. On the drive there he excitedly told me, 'Their singer is like a wild, young Elvis Presley!' So, he ended up signing them and at some point, arranged for us to play together at The Rock Garden in Covent Garden. Officially, they supported us, although it was simply the result of a coin toss – because we were both starting out at a similar time on 4AD and neither of us wanted to open for the other. So, Ivo being the fair-minded fellow he is, said Nick Cave and I should decide by the toss of a coin. Which we did. I liked The Birthday Party – nice guys and very talented. Some of the other acts on 4AD were interesting too – I liked The Cocteau Twins musically and personally. Colin Newman from Wire was also on the label at this point and Bruce and Graham were releasing projects with Ivo too. Bauhaus released an album with him; and I loved Ivo's This Mortal Coil collaborative project. He had a clearly defined aesthetic, not only with regards to the kind of music he wanted to release but also how the albums would look too, with Vaughan Oliver creating the visual identity.

JW: We need to talk about the cover of *Burning Blue Soul* – you mentioned Vaughan Oliver – and about the fact that the album came out as Matt Johnson originally.

Firstly, I want to talk about some of the tracks because you mentioned that you'd started listening to Can. I think I read that you were listening to French composer Erik Satie, and you were reading the musique concrète book you mentioned. When I was playing the record, it really had the feel for me of the World Service or a shortwave radio where you'd flick through and get little snippets – you might get a little bit of something from Turkey, and you'd flick through and get something from somewhere else in the world. *Burning Blue Soul* has that feel to it. Sonic globetrotting. It is the opposite to insular. Looking outward at all the music that's out there floating in the airwaves. It is reminiscent of Brian Eno and David Byrne's *My Life In The Bush Of Ghosts*.

MJ: The record that was most inspirational to me as far as shortwave radio was Holger Czukay's solo album *Movies*. Pete Ashworth first played it to me upon its release in 1979. Do you know that album?

JW: Brilliant record, yes.

MJ: It's gorgeous. He used a lot of shortwave radio, with old-school editing, looping and layering. 'Persian Love' I found particularly inspirational. I loved the atmosphere of Can generally. Jaki Liebezeit's drumming was mesmerising and I also loved Michael Karoli's guitar playing. In fact – along with The Residents' Snakefinger – he was my favourite guitarist of that era and made a major impression on me; the simplicity of his playing, as opposed to a lot of western rock music where they're playing too fast with too many notes. I remember a quote about his playing – attributed to Czukay I think – something like, 'The reason other guitarists play so many notes is because they cannot find the right ones.' So true! I also loved Popul Vuh, amongst other krautrock bands. I came to them via word of mouth in the post-punk scene as a lot of British bands were inspired by krautrock. I enjoyed the way we all used to discover new music: word of mouth and trying to join the dots up. I really miss that element of culture, the investigating and finding of clues. I have mixed feelings about the dawn of the search engine because so much is now spoon-fed to us – and with AI it's only going to get easier and easier and make us lazier and lazier. We'll all end up like the characters in Disney's *WALL-E* if we're not careful. It was an exciting feeling going on a cultural hunt and discovering things not many other people knew about. These days so much is just ripped out of the underground and absorbed into the mainstream too early and easily.

The album which was my biggest influence – I've spoken about it before – was the *White Album* by The Beatles. From when I was about 6 or 7 years old my brother Andrew and I would just listen to it over and over again. From simple, gorgeous melodic tracks like 'Sexy Sadie' and 'Happiness Is A Warm Gun', to more aggressive tracks like 'Yer Blues', 'Helter Skelter' and the musique concrète-inspired 'Revolution 9'. As a result, I understood at a young age that many disparate elements could work together. I loved the merging of tracks, segues and pieces overlaid. Some tracks were more like a continuous piece, rather than having distinct start and end points. So, with parts of *Burning Blue Soul,* you're never quite sure when one track ends and another one starts.

JW: That's what, again, reminds me of shortwave radio but also reminds me of the film soundtracks you've been doing. Particularly 'Red Cinders In The Sand' – it's largely instrumental and you're thinking, this is different. It's ambient. But you can also see a pop element coming in, because it has a terrific THE THE-style guitar riff, which comes into it. For me, *Burning Blue Soul* feels like you're bringing together *Spirits* and *Seeing Without Being Seen*, but there is an emerging idea that although the songs still need to be experimental and exciting, that they need to have (if you forgive the term) 'hooks'; something people can latch on to. This is what really emerges for me when I listen to it again. Were you thinking along those lines when you were creating it?

MJ: It was more intuitive, really. I was just experimenting, doing what felt good. There was – as you can tell by the cover – a nod to psychedelia, though the irony was, at that point, I'd never done any psychedelics at all. It was six months before I'd even experienced ecstasy for the first time but a love for sixties experimental music was definitely in the background.

JW: Strangely, some of the record is also very tranquil. 'The River Flows East In Spring' starts off with an instrument on it – it sounds Japanese – and then it goes somewhere darker. It really reminds me of Tom Waits' album *Swordfishtrombones*. There's something about *Burning Blue Soul* which is so unclassifiable that I think makes it stand the passage of time. You listen to it, and it doesn't sound like a record from thirty, forty, or whatever years ago. It sounds like something that you'd make now. Which is why, I think, when you're reissuing things like *Spirits* and *Seeing Without Being Seen*, they sound interesting because they sound so contemporary.

MJ: Funny you say 'The River Flows East In Spring' has a Japanese element to it as the title was actually inspired by a Chinese film I saw at the NFT in the late seventies called *The Spring River Flows East* – which was essentially about the Japanese war against China. I think a big mistake many bands make when starting out is trying to copy other artists. So, by the time their records are released they already sound dated. But if you're drawing inspiration from larger life – above and beyond fashions and trends – trying to deal with subject matter that underlies the human condition, including things which really resonate with your own personal truths and experiences, what you create will never go out of fashion.

Sonically I wasn't trying to copy anyone. I was just trying to get the sounds I was hearing in my mind onto tape. That's probably why the recordings still sound pretty fresh. As you mentioned, people wouldn't necessarily associate those recordings with the time period in which they were released. There was a lot of music from that period that sounds trapped in that time. Not that that's a bad thing in itself – it is what it is. If you listen to certain film soundtracks from films in the eighties they often have that slightly cheesy synthesiser sound and a snare drum with lots of compression and reverb on it. Everyone was copying each other, and it pigeonholes certain sounds and textures to certain periods. It sets in stone a moment in time. I think it's always important – I know it sounds corny – to recreate what you're hearing and feeling within your own mind, rather than what everyone else is doing. Don't be afraid to be unique.

JW: When you look at the song titles on *Burning Blue Soul*, there is an interest in nature. Something like 'Time (again) For The Golden Sunset'. But the lyrics to this are much darker – and centre around a theme you still return to: the dichotomy between happiness, joy and love on the one hand, and pain and doubt on the other. There's a duality.

> I thought I loved you
> But I think I must be wrong
> There's another feeling in my heart
> This sense of pride
> Is silencing my sorrow
> I find it hard to come alive
> When I'm hollowed out
> From the inside

It begins to set this – I don't want to use 'template', that's not the right word – but a lack of fear to be soul-searching. The title, *Burning Blue Soul*, suggests turmoil. The lyrics are beginning to touch on that, aren't they?

MJ: The title *Burning Blue Soul* was actually suggested by former bandmate, Keith. It was during the writing of the album that my breakthrough as a songwriter happened. 'Another Boy Drowning' is the first time I really felt I was digging deep and expressing something intensely personal. I cried during the writing of that song. It was therapy, a rite of passage, a definite sense of life about to change irrevocably. And, related to that – if I think about my first single for 4AD, the double A-sided 'Controversial Subject'/'Black And White', the lyrics on those are a bit gobbledygook and intentionally obscure.

As a lyricist, it was John Lennon who had the biggest impact upon me. The maxim I ended up trying to live by as a songwriter was his simple words of wisdom: 'Tell the truth and make it rhyme.' (Although truth is subjective and what is mine might not be someone else's, of course.) With *Burning Blue Soul*, I tried to put that into practise for the first time. Of course, I was just a teenager, an angst-ridden insecure young lad, but it was an honest expression of how I felt at that time. It felt like I'd finally found my voice with 'Another Boy Drowning' and my passion for songwriting really started to blossom then. Periods of loneliness and melancholy created a compulsion to try and express the inexpressible and connect with like-minded souls. This creative process became my therapy. But it was also, if I'm being completely honest, a way I thought I could attract girls, earn decent money and avoid getting a proper job!

JW: With this record there's the lyrics that look at your personal anguish. But in '(Like A) Sun Risin' Thru My Garden', you sing:

> The sky is glowing with anticipation
> And casts a shadow across the nation
> A dust is rising from the heat of the sun
> I'm drinking... for the thirst to come

These lyrics show you looking at the world from a personal point of view, yet also on a more collective level.

You mentioned 'Another Boy Drowning'. That track really coincides with the coming to power of Thatcher. The lyrics deal with civic unrest:

> There's people on the streets
> Throwing rocks at themselves

> Because they ain't got no money
> And they're living in hell
> But there's animals down the road
> Adding fuel to this heat
> It never did take much guts
> To be a sheep

You're focusing your gaze not only inward, but outwardly on what's happening in Britain. You're surveying the landscape and really crystallising what's going to be much more than a cold spell ahead; a very dark spell ahead in the UK, in fact.

MJ: I was becoming increasingly politically aware around this time. Though we'd often have political chats around the family dinner table I'd never been on political marches or directly engaged. I met a lad called Martin Brooke – a colleague of Charlie Blackburn's from their time working together in the Selfridges packing department. He was extremely political and invited me to join him on political marches. He also took me to see Tony Benn give a lecture, who I found very impressive. It was a real eye opener for me – the difference between the 'Red Benn' caricature demonised by the tabloids and this softly spoken, compassionate man energising a packed-out hall. Martin also introduced me to Sylvia Plath – who became a favourite poet for a time.

But, I digress. 'Another Boy Drowning' was written shortly after the riots spread across the UK in places like Brixton, Toxteth, Chapeltown etc. And we're back to those dark days now, aren't we? I've been doing phone interviews the last couple of days for Germany and Austria, and every single journalist said, 'Your lyrics feel like they could've been written today.' I answered, 'As a father I really wish that wasn't the case! I wish we lived in a happier world. I'd love it if all those old lyrics and songs were completely out of date, that the world was now in a better place.' But human nature doesn't change. Now as throughout history we've got a very powerful ruling class – or rather predator class or parasite class – dominating and exploiting the majority. It's part of the human condition; and whilst it may change its form superficially, from generation to generation and as civilisations fall and rise, the aggressive, fascist, dominating, totalitarian mindset is never far beneath the surface within the minds of those predators who seek power over others. It could be considered a disease of the soul.

JW: I've been thinking about that lyric, 'It never did take much guts to be a sheep.' When you *do* question things and *do* speak out, it's okay when you're rallying around something that everybody feels incensed about – most people with any soul or heart were anti-Thatcher. But when you start doing it against things that some people hold dear, that not everyone concurs, you put yourself in quite a difficult position and make yourself a target, as I think you've found recently.

MJ: You certainly can. Cancel culture has become so prevalent now, and it's intriguing to watch. You've got a generation of young people terrified of saying anything – and we're all now starting to self-censor to a degree. There are certain things we might like to say but then we wonder, oh, is it worth it? Is it worth all the misunderstanding and the flak? This is the situation we now find ourselves in. And it is not accidental but part of a sophisticated campaign of social engineering – control borne out of decades of research by think tanks and behavioural scientists. For instance, you can clearly see techniques informed by experiments like Asch Conformity* – amongst others – in use on social media platforms, through devices like echo chambers and filter bubbles, where 'public opinion' is created through the *illusion* of consensus with the use of 'likes', bots, and 'trending topics'. Thousands of fake accounts flood platforms with identical messages or hashtags. This creates a false sense of majority opinion. How to have a democracy in name only where the general public are less and less involved with the policies and decisions that affect their lives? We can discuss this in more detail later.

---

* The Asch conformity experiments, conducted by psychologist Solomon Asch in the 1950s, showed that people often conform to obviously incorrect group judgments due to social pressure.

JW: There's an interesting lyric in 'Bugle Boy':

> The country's riddled with social ills and aches
> But my heart is calmed by her embrace

Then you mention an incident that happened, where a young child saw you with a guitar and asked you to play. That's one of the rare instances in one of your lyrics, which is very specifically autobiographical, isn't it? It's a direct reference to something that happened to you, with this boy asking you to play your guitar. What's the story there?

MJ: It was in the car park of The Crown in Loughton. I was just putting the guitar in the back of my first car – my little Vauxhall Viva – and there was this kid who said, 'Hey, mister, play us your guitar.' I said, 'No, I can't.' I put the guitar in the car and drove off. I do remember thinking, why didn't I just take a minute to play a couple of chords for him? I was probably in a rush or something but it did stick in my mind and that's why it ended up in the lyric. Also, in 'Bugle Boy' I mention the girl I was trying to chat up at the music club in Victoria, The Venue. I was tipsy, she was an attractive girl, and I suppose I was trying to be clever. I don't remember what I was saying, but she wasn't very impressed with me, obviously, and just said I was pretentious and walked off.

JW: I don't think that's a charge that could be levelled at you. We've spoken about the record musically, lyrically a bit. I know we've spoken about some of the engineers you've worked with. I just want to be clear; this is the album where everything was played by you. Is that right? On other THE THE albums there are other musicians.

MJ: Yes. I keep thinking I'd like to do another song-based album like that. I play a range of instruments on the soundtrack albums and it gives a certain sound and feel if you play everything yourself. On the other hand, working with other musicians – particularly very good ones – gives another kind of energy and takes things to a different space. On *Burning Blue Soul* it was drum machines, tape loops, guitars, keyboards, messing around with voices and effects. Percussion. Lots of stuff. I played a lot of instruments. Even a cowbell – literally an old bell taken from the neck of a cow – not the percussive instrument.

One thing I do wish is that the multitrack tapes of *Burning Blue Soul* still existed – I could've remixed it. I'd love to have had that opportunity, but 4AD had such little money back then that they used to record over their multitracks – I think a Dead Can Dance album was recorded over the *Burning Blue Soul* multitrack.

JW: That's incredible.

MJ: Yep. That's what they did at 4AD in those days.

JW: The sleeve – you mentioned the psychedelic element. Was that designed by Keith Laws?

MJ: No, but Keith did suggest the *idea* of the sleeve – based upon *The Psychedelic Sounds Of The 13th Floor Elevators* album cover – and his younger brother Darren took the photo (of my eye). Although he was no longer part of THE THE, Keith was incredibly supportive during the making of this album and was a great sounding board for me as I trusted his opinion. I then asked Andrew to design the sleeve – and he did try but he was in a rush and it didn't work out very well to be honest. So, we ended up using the painting Andrew did of me on the back, but Ivo asked designer Neville Brody to do the actual artwork.

There have been three sleeves for this album. The first was the large psychedelic eye, with black and red swirls. The second was the photo of me with a Tim Buckley hairstyle in front of industrial buildings. The third is a painting Andrew did, in yellow hues.

JW: I haven't got the original psychedelic one. I've got the '83 reissue with the industrial backdrop and the '93 one with the cover painting by Andrew, which I think is the first time the record came out as THE THE. Prior to that *Burning Blue Soul*, as with *See Without Being Seen*, was released as Matt Johnson but now they're both THE THE.

MJ: I made the decision to re-release them as THE THE simply because I wanted everything racked in the same section in record shops. If I could go back in time I'd probably have all my records under the name Matt Johnson rather than THE THE – this name has proven a nightmare as people can't find us online much of the time. There were no Internet search engines when I chose this band name. But it has ensured a certain amount of anonymity and led to it remaining a cult band forever I suppose.

JW: I was looking back at the original reviews of *Burning Blue Soul*. There weren't that many, but when the album *was* reviewed it was positive. When it was reissued as THE THE, the acclaim and the coverage it got was much more widespread. That's probably partly attributed to the fact it was now credited as THE THE, but I also think that there's the sense that when it came out originally it was probably ahead of its time for some people. Do you think that's true?

MJ: Well, it's not much use being 'ahead of your time'. Better to be 'on time'! I don't know… people didn't know what to do with it when it was released because it didn't fit into any category. Ivo did the best he could at the time and we did get some decent reviews but it was a strange record and therefore hard to categorise. And you know what some music journalists can be like, they often like to categorise: 'It's like this band… or… it's like that one.' They don't quite know what to write when an artist doesn't sound like anyone else.

JW: Also leading on from Ivo and signing with 4AD, how did Stevo* become a presence in your life? He was managing other

---

* Stevo Pearce is founder of Some Bizzare, an independent record label and management company.

acts, and he was quite keen to work with you and manage you. How did that relationship originate?

MJ: It's quite a funny story. I was becoming involved with 4AD and Some Bizzare simultaneously and there is a certain amount of overlap between various projects and releases – I was working on THE THE, The Gadgets and my solo work concurrently, so it's impossible not to jump around as I answer your questions. I work like that to this day – with multiple projects on the go! I was still living above The Crown with my parents and my dad thought it quite odd I was getting all these phone calls: 'Who are these blokes called 'O' that keep phoning up all the time? Is it some sort of cult?' Apart from Ivo – and now Stevo – I'd also recently started working with Theo Chalmers at Cherry Red. I got to know Theo as I was often up at their offices in Kensington Gardens Square visiting Mike Alway. Cherry Red had a few interesting artists at the time: The Monochrome Set, Eyeless In Gaza, Dead Kennedys, Ben Watt and Tracy Thorn – who later teamed up to become Everything But The Girl. Anyway, Theo was under orders to sign young post-punk songwriters by the bucket-load – on cheap advances with lopsided terms in the company's favour. Awful deals in retrospect. I was just another kid on the dole queuing up for the privilege of being exploited. I didn't even ask a lawyer to give it the 'once over' I was so naive. I found out the hard way what 'in perpetuity' meant. An expensive mistake, but I learned from it going forward.

My favourite Cherry Red memory is being at one of their Christmas parties when Ian McNay (the owner) introduced me to Jim Thirlwell. I knew Jim by sight as we both attended the same underground gigs. And he was actually in the front row of THE THE's first ever gig at the Africa Centre and reviewed it for a fanzine. Jim had an amazing green-and-black bouffant hairdo in those days and Keith and I used to whisper to each other on stage, 'Look who's here again – Chickenhead!' Jim and I quickly became close friends and have remained close friends ever since. I love that man.

Anyway, back to Stevo. The singer from the band Naked Lunch,

Tony Mayo, warned me in advance, 'He's a complete and utter nutter! Watch out!' Stevo was certainly colourful and also younger than me – and I was very young myself – he was also an East Londoner. But he had this mischievous sense of humour which quite appealed to me. He was also very passionate about what he was doing and very persuasive too, a force of nature and one of those individuals who made things happen wherever they went and certainly not a bystander or passive observer of life.

I received my first phone call from him out of the blue. I don't even know how he got my number. We'd never met but he was very direct and just said, 'I want THE THE to support Cabaret Voltaire!' I really liked Cabaret Voltaire but the gig was miles away, near Nottingham at the Porterhouse Club in Retford. I said, 'Okay, how much are we getting paid?' But there was no money on offer so it was basically just doing Stevo a favour. In the end Keith (at that time still a member of THE THE) and I got paid a crate of beer to share. I liked Cabaret Voltaire musically as well as on a personal level. I used to go and see them perform regularly anyway so I enjoyed it just from the point of view of playing with them. From then on Stevo became more of a presence. Phoning up constantly.

He was DJ'ing a lot at that time. The Chelsea Drugstore was one of his regular gigs – and a club near Tottenham Court Road station. Someone labelled him (or possibly he labelled himself) a 'futurist' DJ. There was a futurist electronic scene going on at that time that was sort of a spill-over from the Blitz Club and the New Romantic scene I suppose.

The 'futurist' scene was not my thing to be honest: THE THE were part of a sub-movement in the post-punk days known as 'The Long Mac Brigade'. Whenever going out together – as a band or with friends – we used to wear these long, dark green army surplus trench coats, often carrying pretentious books, wandering around with serious expressions, attending secret, experimental gigs in church crypts and disused warehouses. A sort of UK indie version of the cowboys from the Clint Eastwood film *Pale Rider*! My brothers and I would purchase our outfits from Silvermans, the army surplus warehouse on Mile End Road. It's still there. Whereas the futurist bunch were more closely related to the New

Romantic gang though slightly less flamboyant in their clothing; slightly less 'pantaloony'.

Stevo had been compiling his own 'futurist' chart – his favourite new electronic singles – in the music weekly, *Sounds*. He'd included 'Controversial Subject' which was a cult hit at the time. Having his own chart – and a growing profile – led to him assembling an album of his favourite up-and-coming electronic artists. This became the first Some Bizzare compilation album. He asked Keith and me if we could contribute. We had a track we'd just recorded called 'Untitled' so we decided to license that to him. He gathered up recordings from various artists and signed the album to Phonogram. Not sure if he received an advance or any royalties for it but we didn't get paid a penny – neither advance nor royalties.

The *Some Bizzare Album* generated a lot of interest in the British music press; consequently, the major record companies began sniffing around. Around this time we did a gig supporting Soft Cell up in Nottingham at Rock City. They were developing quite a cult following. We also met Rusty Egan there, who was an early and big supporter of Stevo, Some Bizzare and THE THE. But it was B-Movie – also on the compilation album – that Phonogram *really* wanted to sign. Stevo told them, 'Yes, you can sign B-Movie but only on the condition you also sign Soft Cell.' As we know, Soft Cell quickly became a world-wide phenomenon whilst B-Movie pretty much disappeared.

It was shortly after the release of this compilation album that he expanded Some Bizzare into a management company and production company/record label. He would sign artists to Some Bizzare and then try to license to a major label. Soft Cell and B-Movie provided the template after both were licensed to Phonogram. As soon as a new artist had a big hit all the major labels would instantly try to copy it. There are not many original thinkers running major record companies! Stevo wanted to follow the same formula for THE THE. So, we recorded a new single, 'Cold Spell Ahead', which ended up being released independently and distributed by Pinnacle because every single major label in the UK turned it down.

JW: I want to ask in more detail about 'Cold Spell Ahead'.

MJ: 'Cold Spell Ahead' was a song I'd been working on for some time. It was inspired by an unrequited infatuation with a girl that left me achingly bemused. The B-side was a more experimental track called 'Hot Ice'. We recorded them both at Stage One. I've mentioned the excellent in-house engineer there, Pete Maben, who'd also worked on a few tracks on *Burning Blue Soul*. It was an interesting session because, although Keith was still technically in the band, I ended up playing everything myself. In my little studio at home I'd learned to play lots of instruments and knew how I wanted things to sound. Keith was providing moral support in the studio but there was no point in me showing him what to play when I could easily just play it all myself. I really liked Keith – he was inspiring to spend time with as he was a very thoughtful person – but he didn't stay involved in music for much longer and soon went back to studying.

'Cold Spell Ahead' is actually the embryo of 'Uncertain Smile' but there is another part of that song's outro which I call 'Touch of Experience'. I always loved that outro, and it was very, very tricky to pull off because it involved a tempo change – and this was pre-MIDI and computers – so we'd have to change tempo manually, on the fly. During a certain point both Pete and I had to physically press buttons on the drum machine and sequencer simultaneously to make it feel seamless. It took a few passes to get it right. These days it's simple to do something like that. Funny enough, Daniel Miller – from The Normal and Mute Records – had been in the night before our session producing Depeche Mode and had left some of his gear set up. It was a bit naughty but we used his ARP 2600 synth, APR 1601 sequencer and his drum machine. Daniel was such a lovely man and always very supportive and encouraging to all of us younger bands so I'm sure he wouldn't have minded.

Stevo then did the rounds and played the new recording to many record companies. But all of them turned their noses up – *including* Annie Roseberry who was A&R* at Island Records at the

---

* A&R stands for Artists and Repertoire, a division of a record label responsible for discovering new musical talent and developing artists.

time and would later be my A&R person at CBS. When Stevo got bored taking the recordings around the labels I started taking them myself. Ironically, I even took the tapes up to CBS. Howard Thompson, an A&R man there, actually turned the cassette off halfway through and dismissively said, 'Well, this is not very good is it!?' I was only a teenager and felt humiliated by the experience. This was in stark contrast to playing tapes to say, Geoff Travis at Rough Trade, who would at least have the grace to listen all the way through and say something like, 'You're not quite there yet, Matt, but it's sounding good so keep going.' Which is exactly the encouragement you need when you're a kid. Rough Trade had signed a lot of artists I liked and I'd been keen to join them at one point but it didn't work out.

JW: You did a residency at the Marquee Club, didn't you?

MJ: Yes, in 1982, after the release of 'Uncertain Smile' but before the release of *Soul Mining*, I agreed to a month-long residency at the old Marquee Club on Soho's Wardour Street. We performed every Thursday. For these shows I decided to form two THE THE 'supergroups': one aggressive and one mellow. To glue the identity together I insisted all members wore black. This wasn't too hard as most of them did anyway. Amongst our ranks were JG Thirlwell, Thomas Leer, Colin Lloyd Tucker, Simon Fisher Turner, Jean Marc Lederman (AKA Kid Montana from Belgium), Peter Ashworth, Steve James-Sherlock, Zeke Manyika and Edwyn Collins from Orange Juice, Stephen 'Mal' Malinder from Cabaret Voltaire, and Soft Cell's Marc Almond.

The shows were great fun and each performance ended with all members on stage together, all now wearing a black balaclava too and strumming, thrashing and banging guitars in an open chord tuning of E to create a massive cacophony, a wall of sound to envelope the audience within a deafening drone. Like a cross between Terry Riley's 'In C' and Glenn Branca's 'The Ascension'. Not that we really knew what we were doing at the time. But the show contained everything *including* the 'kitchen sink' which Jim and I had found on the street and dragged along to the Marquee to use on stage as a percussion instrument.

This was all great fun except on the final night of the residency some half-wits in the audience decided to hurl bottles and glasses at the stage. It was dark and hard to see where the missiles were coming from. After being hit in the head several times the band decided to roll up our collective sleeves and fight back. At least I thought they did. But all of the members had scarpered backstage apart from just two. On one side of me was Jim Thirlwell and on the other was Marc Almond. The three of us piled into the front row of the audience – boots and fists swinging. Marc had actually taken off his guitar and was swinging it like a golf club aimed at the row of heads in the front. After the crowd sensibly scattered away from the stage the lights came on and security intervened.

Back in the dressing room the rest of the band looked quite sheepish. I was a bit annoyed they had mostly run away.

Then, all of a sudden, a few audience members staggered backstage, dripping with blood. One was a hardcore Soft Cell fan who Marc had bludgeoned. The look on this poor fan's face! All he could say was, 'Why Marc, why?' Marc had calmed down at this point and was incredibly apologetic. It turned out the people in the front row were entirely innocent and we'd attacked the wrong people. It had been some cretins in the back row who'd started all the trouble and then left everyone else to deal with it. But Marc is certainly a good person to have beside you in the trenches when the going gets tough!

JW: But what a line-up! Mal is one of my favourite music artists – I think he's a genius.

MJ: Mal is wonderful. So, this was 1982, a few months before we started recording *Soul Mining*. After these shows I decided which musicians to bring onto the sessions.

JW: Like a football trial.

MJ: Yes, I suppose. Jim, Zeke and Thomas. There were other musicians and guests on the album of course but I'll come back to that.

As far as 'Cold Spell Ahead', we decided to release independently through Some Bizzare with Pinnacle distributing it. It came out in 1981 – the same year as *Burning Blue Soul* – and did quite well critically, generating a fair amount of interest. Stevo, who had a strong relationship with Phonogram and Decca, persuaded them to take a chance and fund me to re-record the single with the red-hot English producer at the time, Mike Thorne, who was based in New York and still basking in the glow of the massive worldwide success of Soft Cell's 'Tainted Love'.

I flew to New York in May 1982 to record the freshly retitled 'Uncertain Smile' with Mike, who had also produced my favourite Wire album, *154*. I was only 20 years old and was blown away by Manhattan. Stevo and Marc Almond both told me all about it as they'd been back and forth many times over the last few months. But it far exceeded even their descriptions. I'm not sure whether it was the American comics we read as kids or all the films we'd seen that were set in NYC but the strange thing was that I instantly felt at home and just knew I would live there one day. It's a cliché, I know, but those silhouettes of huge water towers perched on top of buildings, the steam escaping from manhole covers, the famous old Checker Cabs and the astonishing art deco skyscrapers – I was smitten and loved every minute of being there.

We recorded at Mediasound Studios, a former church on 57th Street. Mike was a gracious host, encouraging me to try pastrami on rye and Tropicana orange juice which – believe it or not – was then something of a delicacy to an Englishman as it was unheard of in the UK at that time. Mike also took me to Manny's, the legendary music store on 48th Street. Whilst wandering around in there a tongue drum* caught my eye. I purchased it and used it for the famous intro to 'Uncertain Smile' – although Mike didn't hand it back to me at the end of the session, which was a bit cheeky.

---

* A tongue drum is a rare African percussion instrument.

I'd been booked into The Mayflower – the famous old rock'n'roll hotel on Central Park West – which was New York's equivalent to one of my favourite London hang-outs, the Columbia Hotel in Bayswater. But – on my first or second night – I ended up getting picked up by an older woman (well, maybe four years older than me) at the legendary Mudd Club and dragged back to her place on East 3rd Street. That area was run down in those days and part of the infamous Alphabet City. Her apartment was directly opposite the local Hell's Angels Club House – apparently, they kept some semblance of order in the neighbourhood compared to the adjacent streets. She turned out to be an intense character to say the least. Upon arrival she brought out a large biscuit tin, opened the lid and passed it to me. But it didn't contain cookies – it was filled to the brim with various drugs, pills and paraphernalia, including little green Christmas tree-shaped things which I found out later contained dextroamphetamine. She said if I didn't fancy anything in the tin, how about some heroin? I declined but she quickly whipped out a tourniquet, wrapped it around her arm and was injecting herself in no time. Her eyes rolled back in her head as she slumped backwards – her face soon wreathed in the most blissful expression I'd ever seen. I was intrigued and enjoying the intensity of my new surroundings. It was like wandering into a scene from an Abel Ferrara movie! I ended up taking a Quaalude* and moved in with her and her cat for the duration of my trip.

Whilst in New York I made sure I paid my respects to John Lennon. I went and stood outside The Dakota building for a while – and realised I'd seen it somewhere before – *Rosemary's Baby*! I then wandered to the nearby Café la Fortuna for a coffee as apparently it was one of John's favourite local haunts. There were photos of him all over the walls. As it wasn't even two years since his assassination I imagine the place hadn't changed too much and it made me feel closer to him. His death impacted me intensely – as it had millions of people around the world.

As a big fan of *Taxi Driver* (1976), I also felt obliged to wander

---

* A Quaalude is a powerful sedative/hypnotic.

the streets around Times Square. This was many years prior to its 'Disneyfication' so it didn't seem much different to the scenes I'd watched Robert De Niro as Travis Bickle skulk around in. It was edgy, heavy and didn't disappoint. Andrew had been the first to see *Taxi Driver*. He was blown away and encouraged the rest of us to go see it too. Gerard, our cousin Peter and I were all equally affected. De Niro's performance had electrified audiences with the same intensity Marlon Brando's had in *A Streetcar Named Desire* a generation earlier.

There were some amazing clubs and bars in Manhattan back then. Danceteria was my favourite but I also visited Downtown Beirut, Holiday Cocktail Lounge, Cedar Tavern and CBGBs amongst others. Two pieces of music remind me of that trip: 'Wordy Rappinghood' by Tom Tom Club was always being played at Danceteria but the other piece that instantly transports me is the 12-inch version of the original 'Uncertain Smile' with Crispin Cioe's beautiful saxophone. I'd constantly listen to the rough mixes on my Walkman whilst riding to and from the recording studio in a Checker Cab – often at night. It was an extremely intense and enjoyable trip all paid for by London Records, which was part of Decca, which was part of Polygram* – all now part of Universal.

When I returned, I discovered that Stevo had pulled off a devious sleight of hand by conning Decca/London Records into paying for the recording of this 'demo' – an *extremely* expensive demo in New York City with a top producer – without any paperwork that confirmed they owned it. I don't know how he did it, but he did. It was such a successful recording session that when we brought the tapes of 'Uncertain Smile' back to England every major label was suddenly fighting over themselves to sign THE THE. So, Stevo started a bidding war which – of course – CBS went on to win.

It was a big story in the tabloid press at the time with Stevo and the head of CBS, Maurice 'Obie' Oberstein, meeting in

---

* Polygram was a Dutch conglomerate which owned multiple record companies including Phonogram, Polydor, Decca and London Records, amongst others.

Trafalgar Square at midnight, to sit astride the lions and sign the deal. I managed to avoid this 'ceremony'. It was Obie who was responsible for signing me. As mentioned earlier, I'd been rejected by their A&R man Howard Thompson – and by Annie Roseberry when she was A&R at Island Records, and she'd recently been recruited to CBS.

Obie was a legendary character in the music industry. He was a THE THE fan so he overruled his entire A&R department to sign me. He was completely eccentric – sometimes wandering the corridors of the record company dressed in what looked like a monk's costume. I think he had some sort of medical condition, where his voice would randomly jump an octave halfway through a sentence – as if it had never broken – before returning to normal pitch... which could be disconcerting. He'd also insist his dog, Charlie, attend meetings. I recall one occasion, when I was asking him if we could have extra money for something or other when he decided to confer with his pet, 'What do you think, Charlie?' Charlie reacted with a noise Obie must have found agreeable. 'Charlie says he likes you! So, I'll agree to it.' Ironically, despite me ribbing her about turning me down at Island Records Annie turned out to be the best A&R person I ever had during my years with major labels. The situation was certainly ironic though as CBS could have signed me for a fraction of the fee they eventually paid if Howard Thompson hadn't turned down an earlier version of the same song.

I remember at the time discussing my move to a major label with Ivo. Now, Ivo doesn't recall but I clearly remember telling him, 'I may be moving to CBS,' and him replying, 'You're too young. It's too early in your career. You can do that later on.' So, he advised against it. I respected Ivo but obviously ignored his advice. Should I have stayed on with 4AD? I don't know. But at the time I was feeling impatient that my life hadn't changed at all after the release of *Burning Blue Soul* and I suppose I was seduced by the siren call of a major label.

Upon its release *Burning Blue Soul* received positive reviews but I didn't receive an advance so still had no money. I was still living with my mum and dad and by this point had left De Wolfe and was on the dole. Unlike my older brother Andrew, I didn't go to college but like many of my contemporaries in those days I considered the dole an 'arts grant'. I've certainly paid back the meagre amount of money I received many thousands of times over with the amount of tax I've paid over the years!

But Stevo's promises of a major label deal represented an opportunity that I could finally earn a decent living from music. I could come off the dole, get major backing to create more ambitious projects, work in better quality studios with quality musicians and make records that were aggressively promoted. It was a very seductive thought for a 20-year-old working-class lad on the dole.

In those days, CBS was a powerful, highly respected record company. They seemed to really support singer-songwriter album artists over the long term: Johnny Cash, Leonard Cohen, Bob Dylan, Bruce Springsteen and Paul Simon were artists of theirs I admired. They had The Clash too. For me, as a kid just out of my teens, signing to CBS was what it must feel like being a very young footballer and signing for Manchester United.

JW: Or West Ham…

MJ: Hmmm, not sure about the Hammers! But you can see why it's often said to a young footballer, 'Look, it's better if you go to a lower division side to play regularly to prove yourself, rather than go straight to a big club where you may just become a fringe player.' There are strategies to slowly build a career. But it was glamorous signing for CBS. They were a great label in those days with more gravitas than PolyGram in my eyes and I really liked the people I met at the label. Even their lawyer at that time, John Kennedy – who became a good friend – seemed more excited about signing me than the A&R people at PolyGram did. It was exciting.

Stevo at that time was extremely energetic with amazing ideas. Unorthodox in his methods and very effective, but he did upset a lot of people. He was an East London lad who was dyslexic but highly intuitive – plus he had good taste in music. He was building a record label which, by the mid-eighties, became the most exciting independent label and management company in the UK. Various artists on the roster were licenced through Some Bizzare to major labels. For instance, Soft Cell to Phonogram, Cabaret Voltaire to Virgin Records, THE THE and Psychic TV to CBS. There was a close relationship growing amongst everyone on the label.

JW: It feels to me that with the development of your career and where it stands now, the thing that has stood you in good stead is the fact that you are an autodidact. You developed a passion for music and you taught yourself how to use the equipment. I know you were working at De Wolfe, but you were largely self-taught. Similarly, as a musician – and I mean musician not lyricist – you can play pretty much anything. That came out of the fact that you were having to do it off your own back, working-class background etc. It put you in good stead down the line that you could do it all, that you knew how to operate things, that you knew how to record yourself, you knew how to engineer.

MJ: In a way yes. I don't consider myself a great musician – I can't read or write music for instance and rarely practise – I'd be unemployable as a session musician on a THE THE session! But I have a knack for being able to get *something* out of any instrument I pick up. I have my own style and feel. But I've always considered myself first and foremost a songwriter who plays instruments rather than a musician who writes songs. Bear in mind that I came of age in the era of the 'non-musician'. I think another important thing that shaped me – because it was very tough at the time – is getting turned down by every single independent and major label in the country, not once, not twice, but about three times! I got so many rejection letters I could have wall-papered my bedroom with them. But instead of putting me off it just made me more determined.

The key thing was building inner strength. This relates to my time at school – being told by teachers I was useless, that I would go nowhere and end up as nothing. Instead of discouraging me it actually made me more determined and perversely more confident too. This mindset has proven invaluable when dealing with any negative reviews that might come my way. There are lots of musicians I've known over the years – many well-established – who crumble and go to pieces when faced with a negative review from a critic. I think my experiences with schoolteachers and record companies toughened me up and gave me a deep belief in my own convictions.

CHAPTER THREE

This Is The Day Your Life Will Surely Change

Matt moves to Highbury, a new logo is created for THE THE and Soul Mining *introduces his unique sound and thematic concerns to a new and growing audience. There is newfound confidence as a songwriter as well as the clear development of a distinct aesthetic direction involving Matt's artist brother, Andrew (AKA Andy Dog).*

JW: The 1983 album *Soul Mining* evolved out of your decision to abort *The Pornography of Despair*. Can you talk about that?

MJ: Shortly after releasing *Burning Blue Soul* and 'Cold Spell Ahead' I started working on *The Pornography Of Despair* but I wasn't sure at that point if it was going to be released through 4AD or Some Bizzare. At the time I'd recently left home and was living in a bedsit in Aubert Park, Highbury, with my friend 'Italian Alex' Sartore and her Japanese flatmate Akane. I moved into what was a broom cupboard-sized room. Yet, I somehow managed to set up a little studio in there. I'd saved up and upgraded by investing in a Fostex A-8 – a brilliant little ¼-inch 8-track multitrack recorder recently brought to market – and a Studio Master desk. I also brought all my cellar studio equipment from The Crown. I set it up in that tiny room and that's where I wrote and recorded most of *The Pornography Of Despair*. I knew someone who'd just bought the brand-new LinnDrum and they let me use it for a few hours to record backing tracks onto my A-8. I then begged, stole and borrowed time from various studios to overdub more vocals and instruments.

Initially, I was sleeping in the broom cupboard too, but it was so claustrophobic that Alex must have felt sorry for me and let me share her bedroom. She probably regretted it though as after I vacated the cupboard I took over large parts of the flat and tended to lay out all my gear – recorder, mixer, foot pedals, keyboards, guitars, speakers and cables – as well as pencils and paper – all over the floor. Plus, I'd also be lying on the floor myself! So, they had to play hopscotch to get from one side of the room to the other.

I possessed tremendous vim and vigour in those days and was working flat out on many projects simultaneously. When I signed to CBS they'd obviously loved 'Uncertain Smile' and were convinced I was going to be the next big pop sensation. That wasn't in *my* mind, but it was certainly in *theirs*! 'So, let's get you underway on an album,' they said. 'What else have you got for us?' When they heard *The Pornography Of Despair* rough mixes they were nonplussed. 'Erm... this is all a bit dark and weird!' So, at their request I re-recorded some of those tracks. What I did was transfer my original 8-track recordings across to 24-tracks and replaced many parts with fresh overdubs. Although, quite a few of the original vocals recorded in my bedsit remained.

That original version of *The Pornography Of Despair* is raw and experimental and a natural progression from *Burning Blue Soul*; but the new versions I recorded were neither one thing or the other, and were certainly not commercial enough to satisfy CBS. Some of these re-recordings made it out as B-sides on forthcoming singles and on the cassette version of *Soul Mining* but I'd already started getting bored with the tracks by this stage so I started writing new ones.

'This Is The Day' took the new album project into a completely new direction. *The Pornography Of Despair* – as the title suggests – was dark, lo-fi and 'psychedelic' – a bit claustrophobic too, maybe because it was written and recorded in a broom cupboard! Only one song from *The Pornography Of Despair* ended up on *Soul Mining* and that was 'The Sinking Feeling'. There was also 'Perfect', which was called 'Screw Up Your Feelings' originally.

Although my first single 'Controversial Subject' had been played by John Peel on his BBC late-night Radio 1 show, 'Uncertain Smile' was taken up enthusiastically by daytime DJs Kid Jensen, Peter Powell and Janice Long. BBC Radio 1 was very powerful back then compared with today as there was no Internet and less choice or competition. Audience numbers were far higher and for young artists of my era it was incredibly exciting being told your record was going to be played on Radio 1. To be informed it was being 'playlisted' – receiving regular rotation through the day on various shows – was like winning the lottery. As a youngster I'd sit around the radio with my family, listening excitedly as my songs were first played on air. They were moments of real joy for me as my parents and relatives felt very proud too. 'Uncertain Smile' picked up a lot of plays and the second single 'Perfect' did too. The equivalent these days is my records being played on Radio 6 Music by Marc Riley, Steve Lamacq, Chris Hawkins, Matt Everitt, Lauren Laverne, Stuart Maconie, Gideon Coe, Mark Radcliffe and others. I'm still very grateful for any support received.

JW: 'Perfect' was the first single of yours I bought! You then decided to become more involved in production yourself and around this time you started working with Paul Hardiman.

MJ: Oh, was it? The original 7-inch was good, I loved that.

How I started working with Paul Hardiman is a bit of a long story. Stevo was an abrasive character. I got on very well with him in those days and we became close friends but I think certain people in the music industry – who were older, more middle class maybe – couldn't cope with him, just didn't know how to deal with him.

I had a good – albeit brief – relationship with Mike Thorne and the recording sessions in New York for 'Uncertain Smile' went extremely well. That was in May 1982. I went back in October 1982 to record 'Perfect' and 'The Nature Of Virtue' (another track from *The Pornography Of Despair* that we'd re-record to end up as a B-side).

Then (how old would I have been – 21?) I got completely out of it for these recording sessions. A combination of ecstasy, Hawaiian grass and Quaaludes. I went crazy and didn't know what I was doing in the studio. Wandering around in a daze – bumping into things. Highly unprofessional and naive. I've since become extremely professional by the way! But I was a kid and I'd always been quite mischievous. So, to me it was perfectly in keeping with my character – at that time – to smash up hotel rooms and mess about in the studio. Mike wasn't amused, understandably. I've never seen him since to apologise but I felt bad as I liked him, he seemed a decent chap just trying to do his best – albeit a bit straight and uptight.

Now, Mike had a very expensive sampling keyboard called a Synclavier which had cost him a fortune – tens of thousands of pounds – the price of a house at that time. To claw back some of the money from his investment he'd insist it be hired for all of his recording sessions – and would charge the hire costs to the artist. This used to enrage Stevo so he suggested I show up with my £200 Omnichord and use that instead of the Synclavier. So, when I arrived back in New York I said, 'No, Mike, we're not using *that*, we're using *this*.' Mike wasn't happy about that at all as it was lost rental revenue. Ironically, the Suzuki Omnichord has since become a famous cult instrument still used to this day whereas the Synclavier is now a museum relic. I used the Omnichord to write and record 'This Is The Day', 'Perfect', 'The Nature Of Virtue' and – later on – 'I Want 2 B U'.

Anyway, the sessions quickly deteriorated and went south. Whereas Stevo and I went north and embarked upon our infamous drug-fuelled, *Fear and Loathing*-style trip to Detroit via Niagara Falls. CBS naturally became alarmed at this highly expensive, out-of-control trip – like a football club signing a young player at great cost who then has a breakdown and goes off the rails! They're like, what the hell have we got our hands on here? This guy is uncontrollable! Though I think they soon realised it was actually Stevo more than me. Of course, I went along with it and was certainly partially to blame but I think I was the more reasonable one out of the pair of us. Mike and Stevo then had a very bad falling-out – I don't think they'd ever liked or respected each other anyway.

An interesting aside is that although I was back in New York to record the second single for CBS – who I was signed to for the UK and rest of the world – I was actually signed to Sire in the US at that point. They were a cool label in those days – founded and run by the eccentric Seymour Stein. Soft Cell were with them and had great success so Stevo felt I should be there too. During that trip I was invited to meet Seymour for the first time. As he was parading me around Sire's offices he excitedly introduced me to another young singer he'd recently signed – who was also being paraded around. He whispered in my ear, 'She's going to be HUGE!' She and I awkwardly shook hands at Seymour's behest and exchanged some pleasantries. She seemed friendly enough – confident if reserved. Seymour's faith – in her at least – was soon to be spectacularly rewarded. It was Madonna!

After a few months, CBS informed us they wanted to buy out my contract with Sire so I'd be signed to them exclusively worldwide. Stevo and I thought it made sense at this point but Seymour didn't agree. So, we decided to play a horrible joke one night when he was visiting London by dragging him into Trident Studios and blasting him with 'Dumb As Death's Head' (a highly uncommercial, unreleased track from *The Pornography Of Despair*) and insisting *this* was going to be the follow up single to 'Uncertain Smile'! Shortly afterwards he agreed to CBS buying out my contract.

Back in London, Stevo suggested, 'Look, how about working with Paul Hardiman instead? I want you to meet him.' Paul had been Mike Thorne's long-term engineer and had not only worked on 'Tainted Love', but also – of particular interest to me – Wire's *154*, my favourite album of theirs.

JW: Wire keep recurring.

MJ: Yes, there was that connection. Stevo arranged for me to meet with Paul and I warmed to him instantly. He was very down to earth with a sense of humour that cracked me up. I felt comfortable in his company straight away. I thought, I'd definitely like to work with this guy. The first thing we worked on was remixing 'Perfect', from the aborted session in New York. Mike had actually mixed it in my absence but I found his version too weak and gutless.

Paul recently reminded me we remixed it over Christmas '82 at SARM East studios in London and it had nearly ruined his marriage because he wasn't at home with his wife and kids! But in spite of that it went really well. I really liked Paul's sound as it was tougher and I enjoyed our sessions. That was the trial to see if we would work on an album together. Of course, *Soul Mining* didn't have a name at this point but I'd started writing fresh songs and decided to junk *The Pornography of Despair*.

Around this time, I'd also got together with Fiona Skinner, my first long-term girlfriend. We'd met briefly at *Top Of The Pops* when she was there with her boyfriend at the time – Billy McKenzie from The Associates – and I was there as a guest of Soft Cell. We met again at the Camden Palace (which had just changed its name from the Music Machine) and that's really the first time we connected.

JW: I used to go to record fairs there.

MJ: It was a great venue wasn't it? I was down there all the time. I remember one night chatting with George Michael. We'd both just signed to CBS and someone introduced us. A deeply tanned George advised me, 'Before you start doing any photo shoots and videos, you've got to make sure you get yourself onto a nice sun bed. It makes *such* a difference!'

It was strange suddenly finding myself in the company of artists like Annie Lennox, Boy George, Clare Grogan, George Michael and other budding pop superstars – either at nightclubs or backstage at TV shows. They were all very friendly, likeable people – and we were all working towards our first 'hit' records – yet I was being pushed into a world I wasn't part of and didn't *want* to be part of. I'd been happy enough to take the record company advance to buy my first flat so the debt must be repaid I suppose. I'd always considered myself an 'album artist' when there was such a thing – and part of the post-punk world – so I was definitely feeling like a fish out of water. However, it was an interesting experience suddenly being on the inside looking out rather than the outside looking in. I was now straddling two worlds and probably one of the few people chatting with Genesis P-Orridge one day and George Michael the next.

JW: And you were also now in a new relationship?

MJ: Yes. Fiona's relationship with Billy was on-off. I'd met him a few times with her and really liked him – a great singer – but they split up and she and I went on our first date. Straight after that I flew to New York, and of course, no texting or e-mails back then, but I telephoned her a few times – even during the infamous trip to Niagara Falls and Detroit. Then we had our second date when I got back, which was 5 November, over at Battersea Park for the fireworks. We fell in love. I was still living in the bedsit in Highbury with 'Italian Alex' and Akane.

When I met Fiona, she was living in Braithwaite House on Bunhill Row opposite the historic Bunhill Fields – burial place of William Blake. Her flatmate at that time was a nice chap called Alan McDonald, who was very friendly though the first thing I noticed when I visited was that he was drawing giant penises and assorted gay erotica all over the walls. He had an interesting technique I suppose – feverishly scribbling with black and gold felt pens in a Keith Haring style. He had lots of friends over – all the time – a little gay mafia including designer Judy Blame, shoe designer John Moore and a few others involved in fashion and the arts. That was Fiona's gang at the time. Most of them are dead now sadly. Fiona would serve drinks and cook for them and described herself as a bit of a 'fag-hag'. The atmosphere was always noisily animated with lots of laughter as they would endlessly gossip or discuss the latest fashions. I'm not sure what they made of me – generally dressed in old Levi's and Dr. Martens boots, sitting in the corner reading about politics or listening to experimental music with headphones on.

Eventually Alan moved out and moved on. Fiona has always been incredibly kind, giving and supportive of her friends – often to her own detriment. People sometimes take kindness as a weakness though and I thought she was being taken advantage of at times. I used to tell her it was a bit unfair she was often lending money to her flatmate and his friends without getting paid back, etc. But at heart Alan and his entourage were a decent bunch – some even went on to become well-known figures in the fashion and arts world, featuring in exhibitions about that particular slice of London life in the early 1980s. The new flatmate who suddenly appeared was at the other end of the scale. She was very quiet and drank vodka for breakfast. She was mysterious and had an air of Greta Garbo about her – even the way she did her hair. I think she may have also been secretly in love with Fiona at that time, so I must have been quite an irritant. But she was an intelligent person and a good photographer and has since gone on to become a successful painter in New York. She was the one who first suggested I go to visit William Blake's grave in the nearby Bunhill Fields.

Fiona introduced me to many things in the early years of our relationship including: art deco, the Bauhaus movement, Anaïs Nin and ee cummings as well as her favourite restaurants, bars and shops. She was artistic, creatively driven and a source of incredible support and encouragement, happy to listen to a new musical or lyrical idea regardless of how late at night or early in the morning it might be. I'd often wake her up in bed strumming on my guitar but she never complained. I could always rely on her to give honest feedback on the songs I was working on, which she did throughout our relationship.

Fiona also created the definitive logo for THE THE. It was about the third of fourth version. Even legendary graphic designer Neville Brody tried his hand at it, but his didn't really work for me.

Fiona was working in the graphics department at Thames TV at the time and she created lino cuttings of an entire alphabet and then experimented with distressing it before placing the letters in various configurations. As soon as I saw it I was happy. It looked like an ink stamp, with a timeless, vintage feel but also had a certain heft. It has endured and I'm still very happy with it. Ultimately, I suppose a logo is only as effective as what it represents but I immediately thought it suited the type of project I was trying to build.

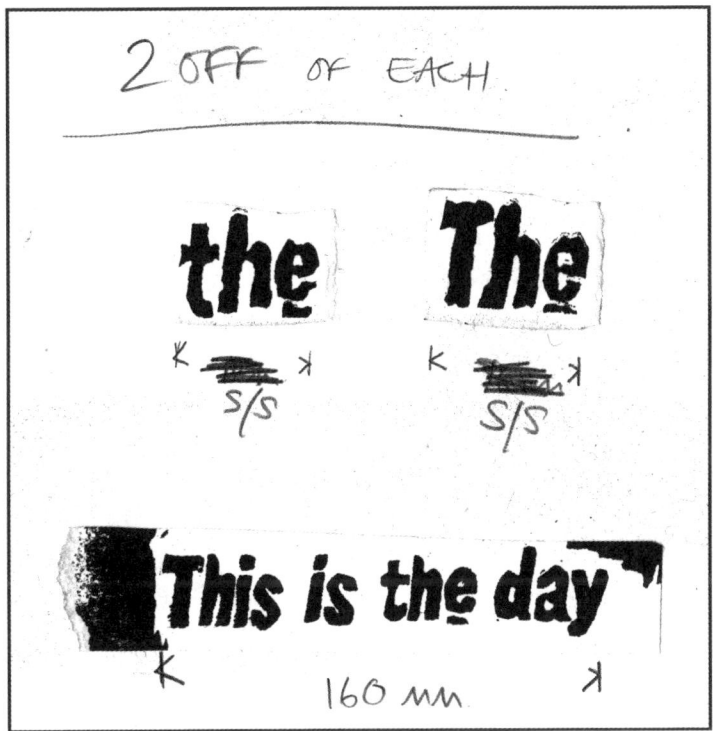

Around this time, I also bought a 4-track Portastudio. I needed something more portable than my 8-track system as I was also sometimes working at Braithwaite House whilst Fiona was at work. That's where I completed writing 'This Is The Day'. I remember crying when I was writing it. With a lot of my best songs or what I think of as my best songs, I can get quite emotional as I'm writing them. 'This Is The Day' has ended up – by far – being my most successful song to date. As I was writing it I knew I was creating a special song.

Paul and I then re-recorded 'Uncertain Smile,' plus 'The Sinking Feeling' was brought over from *The Pornography Of Despair*. Then I wrote some more new songs. 'GIANT' is another of the more successful ones from that era. It became a huge track in the club scene and is still played regularly to this day – more than forty years later.

JW: 'GIANT' is amongst my favourite of your songs. It's got an African feel to it.

MJ: Yes, that would be Zeke Manyika's influence. I also wrote 'I've Been Waiting For Tomorrow', which became the album's opener; the track 'Soul Mining'; and probably the most unusual track on the album, 'The Twilight Hour', which was written in the early stages of my relationship. I remember writing the lyrics to that at Aubert Park. I can't recall exactly which point I moved into Fiona's place, I was back and forth for a bit. Her place was a maisonette on the fifteenth floor, with amazing views across London. I'd be showing up, hanging out and was sort of tolerated by her gang. I was a rough-and-ready East Ender and not a big fan of fashion to put it mildly. But, you know when you get into a new relationship and you have the odd sleepover, which turns into three or four nights per week and before you know it you've moved in!

It was a very sociable period and I was out at parties all the time, at squats or nightclubs. It's odd looking back now how many of the people I'd bump into during the course of an average week have gone on to become well-known figures – even posthumously. There was recently a big exhibition at the Tate Modern about the late Leigh Bowery and he was someone I'd often see at a squat party and have a little chat with. He always seemed in good humour.

There were always lots of interesting people dropping by and hanging out – both at Bunhill Row amongst Fiona's gang of friends – and back at Aubert Park. Jim Thirlwell would often be over and Thomas Leer and Johnny Marr would crash over sometimes too – this was when Johnny was in London having his meetings with Geoff Travis, negotiating The Smiths' deal with Rough Trade.

Matt's paternal grandparents, Nanny Ginny & Grandad Charlie, 1930s.
Courtesy Johnson Family Archive.

Matt's maternal grandparents Grandad Joe & Nanny Sue, early 1960s.
Courtesy Johnson Family Archive.

Matt's mum, Shirley, 1950s. Courtesy Johnson Family Archive.

Matt's dad, Eddie, with his brother, Kenny, 1950s to 1990s. Courtesy Johnson Family Archive.

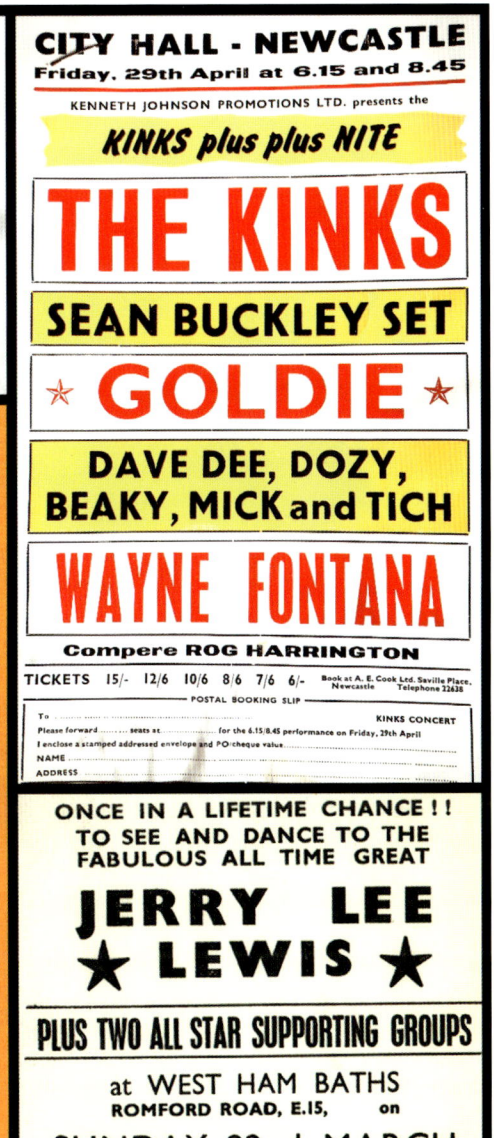

A selection of Uncle Kenny's concert posters, 1960s. Courtesy Johnson Family Archive.

The Two Puddings in the 1960s. Courtesy Johnson Family Archive.

Daily Mirror

5d. Saturday, March 8, 1969. No. 20,279

PUNTER'S PARADISE

CALLING all racing fans, and anyone who fancies a little flutter.

Turn to PAGE FIVE right away for full details of PUNTER'S PARADISE, the greatest-ever FREE competition for racing fans.

It costs you nothing to enter but the prize is FIFTEEN £1 CROSS-DOUBLES on the first six winners EACH day of the opening meeting of the Flat at Doncaster.

Three days when all your Double-dreams can come true.

Think of all those lovely outsiders romping home!

Don't be pipped by the post. Closing date is next Tuesday. Turn to PAGE FIVE and get your entry to Punter's Paradise off TODAY.

CAR BANDITS FIRE ON FOUR POLICEMEN

Mrs Castle acts in the Ford crisis

By ALAN LAW, Industrial Correspondent

PRODUCTIVITY Minister Barbara Castle intervened in the Ford strike last night immediately after learning that the emergency peace talks had collapsed in anger.

She ordered her top aides to contact the union leaders and Ford officials and ask them to come to the Ministry for talks at the earliest possible moment.

Early this morning it was announced that both sides had agreed to go to the Ministry today.

Top Ministry peacemakers will meet Mr. Leslie Blakeman, Ford's labour relations chief at 10.30 a.m. Then they will meet four union delegates.

The two-week-old strike is bleeding vital export earnings to the tune of £1,000,000 a day.

More than 30,000 of Ford's 47,000 workers are now out and all production of cars, lorries and tractors has been halted.

Storming

Last night's two-hour meeting between Ford and union negotiators ended with both sides storming out.

After the meeting at the Charing Cross Hotel, Mr. Blakeman said: "The union's demands were quite unacceptable."

Mr. Blakeman was obviously very angry and upset.

Mr. Jim Conway, for the unions, looked equally annoyed.

He said: "Ford had nothing to offer except a return to work." Asked why the talks had collapsed Mr. Blakeman said: "We were placed in an impossible position."

"The unions wanted to tie our hands behind our backs before they would even discuss a new peace formula.

"They wanted us to withdraw all legal action, withdraw all penalty clauses from the new package pay deal, and increase the rates of pay above what had been offered in the original deal."

Mr. Blakeman said that Ford had offered to withdraw the legal action and suspend the controversial pay agreement on condition that the men returned to work.

VAUXHALL assembly lines are likely to start rolling next week following a plan last night to settle the dispute at the Ellesmere Port plant in Cheshire.

NEW PEACE TALKS TODAY

'KISS ME QUICK' SUSAN

ACTRESS Susan George, above, will have a good reason for saying "Kiss me quick" to her boy friend, Benny Thomas, today.

The couple haven't seen each other for months and were hoping for a big reunion.

Then 18-year-old Susan found that she has to leave Heathrow Airport for New York to work on a film just one hour after Benny, a singer, flies in—from New York.

They will hardly have time to say hello.

Picture: DOREEN SPOONER

By TOM TULLETT and ALAN SHILLUM

A CHICAGO-STYLE shotgun gang fired on four policemen last night from a car cruising past an East London pub.

The gunmen attacked after the policemen had answered a 999 call from the pub, where a fight had broken out earlier.

Early today all police cars in London were alerted in a search for the gang's car—a dark blue Ford Zephyr.

The drama at the Two Puddings pub in Stratford Broadway began after closing time while licensee Eddie Johnson was clearing up.

Suddenly shots blasted through the window of the saloon bar.

Mr. Johnson dialled 999. Two policemen from nearby West Ham police station raced to the pub.

Shotgun

They called by radio for assistance and two detectives in a patrolling Q-car joined them.

As the four policemen stood talking to Mr. Johnson in the pub's doorway, a blue Zephyr cruised past slowly.

A shotgun blasted out from the car's rear window and the policemen dived for cover as pellets splattered across the pavement.

One of the Q-car's crew, Temporary Detective Constable Gordon King, was hit in the ear by pellets.

The Zephyr made off at high speed chased by the patrol car. But the gunmen got away at Bow Bridge flyover, about two miles from the pub.

The policemen were unable to get the number of the Zephyr because its rear number plate was folded down.

Police believe that there were three men in the car.

Constable King, 22, was examined by a doctor at West Ham police station. But he was only slightly hurt and did not need treatment.

Police had been called to the Two Puddings just before closing time to deal with a fight in the bar. They cleared the pub.

Mr. Johnson, 35, said after the attack: "It's a bit worrying.

"I can't think of any reason why this should have happened."

Apollo boosts Moon hopes

From ARTHUR SMITH in Houston, Texas

TWO brave men aboard a tiny, spidery, Spacecraft gave a tremendous boost to America's Moon hopes yesterday.

For almost six hours they flew alone through Space in the frail, untested Moonbug, up to 113 miles from their Apollo 9 "mother ship."

And the huge success of the seventeen-ton craft's tests means that it is all systems go for man to take his first step on the Moon in just four months' time, when Apollo 9 is due to touch down.

Danger

Yesterday's test flight by astronauts James McDivitt and Russell Schweickart was one of the most complex ever carried out.

Five times they fired the engines of the four-legged Moonbug—the same operation which men will use to land on the Moon.

The flight was filled with danger. For if they had failed to rejoin Apollo, the Moonbug could not have returned.

◆ **Continued on Back Page**

Shoot-out at the Two Puddings, 1969. Courtesy British Newspaper Archive.

Name	Matthew Johnson	Music	REPORT

Form 1R

Teaching Group .....

D	5

Comments:

Matthew does not pay very much attention to his work. If he did it would improve.

Teacher's Name A.M. Cooke

Matt's outstanding music report from his first year at secondary school, 1973.

But outside school, music was a full-time passion with his band Road Star. A compilation of meticulously recorded sessions and hand-drawn cassette covers, 1973-76.

My flatmates were very tolerant of me and my behaviour – if a bit irritated at times – because I'd often get home very late at night – probably still on sulphate! Sleeping through to mid-afternoon whilst they would have got up early for work. A lot of *Soul Mining* was written with me lying on the floor at Aubert Park with all my gear and cables and paper and pencils spread everywhere, my little stove pot espresso maker burbling away in the background.

When we came to start work on recording the album, Paul and I looked at a few different studios but primarily recorded it at The Garden in Shoreditch – owned by musician John Foxx at that time.

JW: John Foxx was a pioneer of electronic and synthesiser music.

MJ: Yes, John was ahead of his time. And it was an unusual studio, because it had a very big control room for its time. Prior to that, control rooms tended to be quite small spaces. They would house the engineer and the producer but the band weren't really encouraged in there. We saw a bunch of studios but fell in love with The Garden. It quickly became one of my all-time favourites. I had no idea, of course, that I'd later buy the studio for myself. We recorded most of the album there – but we also did some at Advision Studios, on Gosfield Street, off New Cavendish Street. I remembered Advision from when I worked at De Wolfe as I used to have to take tapes and equipment there if there was a session booked in.

So, *Soul Mining* was primarily recorded at The Garden, and also at Advision and SARM East, where we'd worked before. We ended up mixing at Genetic Studios – which was owned by Martin Rushent, who sadly passed away in 2011. He was the producer of The Human League, The Associates and the Buzzcocks amongst many others. His studio was in Berkshire and I remember staying at Paul's house – also in Berkshire – when we were mixing. We drove back and forth daily in Paul's little souped-up Ford Fiesta. Genetic was very well equipped and we mixed on an SSL* if I recall correctly. Martin came in one morning to have a listen to

---

* Solid State Logic (SSL) is a manufacturer of professional audio equipment.

the early mixes of *Soul Mining*, loved what he heard and gave us a big thumbs up. That was very encouraging as he was probably the UK's most successful producer at that time.

JW: *Burning Blue Soul* had been an independent success. And around the time you were making *Soul Mining*, there were the independent charts but also the mainstream charts, which were very bland and boring. I get the sense that with this record you didn't just want to be in the independent charts. You wanted to make something which was uncompromising and very much you, but perhaps would reach ears beyond the kind of independent clique?

MJ: That was the whole point of signing to CBS. If you look back and think *Burning Blue Soul* was a success, well it wasn't at the time – at least not commercially. Yes, it did get good reviews but it cost peanuts to make and didn't sell much at the time. I didn't get an advance – or even have any significant royalties from sales in the pipeline. I was still on the dole and broke and quickly realised, 'Okay, this isn't going to get me very far financially.' Trying to be a functioning full-time musician was tough. Now, Ivo from 4AD was lovely, I've nothing but good things to say about him. A lovely man, very supportive and kind. But then Stevo appeared in a puff of smoke and started making outrageous promises. Sign with me and you will *own* – not rent – your own flat in just a matter of weeks etc. I also became friendly with Soft Cell at this time – Marc and Dave were very nice guys – and seeing close-up the success they were starting to enjoy I thought, I wouldn't mind a bit of that. Remember, I'd been in bands since I was a kid of 11 and had been inspired by T. Rex and various glam-rockers as well as The Beatles. So, I suppose I fancied a bit of rock star success.

JW: Also, if you're making things, you want people to experience them. If you're a writer and you write a book, you want people to read it. If you're creating something, surely the idea is that you want as many people as possible to have access to it.

MJ: Absolutely. So, when I started out as an 11-year-old in my little garage-band Road Star – literally rehearsing in garages, playing cover versions, performing gigs in village halls and birthday parties, it was all very much inspired by glam-rock. My bandmates and I would dress up in platform shoes and dance around, fantasising about being rock stars. But, from my mid-to-late teens I drifted towards the experimental music world – for instance musique concrète – whilst working at De Wolfe and learning about tape manipulation and electronic music. I was, of course, also feeling inspired by the many post-punk pioneers I got to know personally – and who themselves had probably been inspired by krautrock or whatever – such as Cabaret Voltaire, This Heat, Wire and Throbbing Gristle. There was always a duality though in that I loved this experimental music world but I also loved simple, great song writing. I was very inspired by singer–songwriters like John Lennon, Bob Dylan, Hank Williams and Robert Johnson. I also loved soundtracks too of course. I wondered how I could achieve a combination of these three elements. Reaching a bigger audience whilst maintaining artistic integrity?

I think Mal from Cabaret Voltaire once described Stevo as a sort of prophylactic – a condom between the music industry and the artist. Which was true in a way. He was ferocious in terms of his dealings with record companies and defending his artists against them – as the story earlier illustrates when he got Decca/London Records to pay for my recording session in New York when they didn't even have the right to use it (see page 100). Stunts like that. And Some Bizzare artists *did* feel we were protected somehow, that we were this small, alternative enclave existing inside the major labels – a sort of Trojan horse – and that we could maintain complete artistic integrity yet reach huge audiences. That was part of the Some Bizzare philosophy. Naive I suppose.

My musical tastes were very varied so it's not like I only listened to experimental music or only listened to pop or rock. I listened to everything, including jazz, classical, soundtracks and music from around the world. I think that eclecticism percolated through *Soul Mining*. Its instrumentation was varied. I'd never felt limited in terms of what instrumentation I could or couldn't use. I didn't feel obligated just to use guitars, bass and drums. I said, 'I want marimbas. I want melodicas. I want accordions, harmonicas, strings, cellos, double basses – congas!' All these beautiful instruments. I just felt, why should I be pigeonholed as being either pop or alternative or experimental? That's probably why over the years it's been impossible for people to categorise THE THE because it changes all the time. My taste is like that.

JW: And how was *Soul Mining* received?

MJ: *Burning Blue Soul* received good reviews but was a slow burner; *Soul Mining* received great reviews but was also a slow burner. It's only over the decades since that some of its songs are considered classics. 'This Is The Day' has been an incredibly successful song and is continually used in feature films, TV shows, adverts and has also been covered by many artists. If you could condense all of the plays it's had – and copies it's sold – over the years it would have been a number one single for weeks… but its success has been stretched out over decades – what is known as a long tail. The album only reached number 27 in the charts upon release.

JW: It was an improvement on *Burning Blue Soul*…

MJ: Yes, and it was a critical success at a time and a big step forward from *Burning Blue Soul* commercially.

Going back to the making of it, for me the decision to co-produce with Paul Hardiman was the right one. Mike Thorne was an old-fashioned type of producer in a way and liked to tightly control how his recording sessions went; I was always keen to be more experimental and hands-on myself – and my personality type is that I don't like being told what to do. So, my ideal situation is always being one of the co-producers with a great engineer. Paul was a great engineer and we worked well as a production team. He'd come up with ideas, I'd come up with ideas – the sound of that album is our collaboration.

I worked with a lot of good people on *Soul Mining*, but the single most important collaborator was Paul. We worked very closely together throughout the whole process and had a lot of laughs. He was very funny and talented and *Soul Mining* was also a big step on the road to him becoming a successful producer in his own right, the critical acclaim of that album opened a lot of doors and he went on to produce people like Kate Bush, Chris Rea, Lloyd Cole & the Commotions and many others. So, it was a mutually beneficial situation. In terms of the musicians on the album it was a combination of friends I respected – who I think helped give it an edgy feel – plus the odd special guest and some very talented session musicians. Amongst these friends was Zeke Manyika, whose presence is strongly felt on the album as both a drummer and singer. He plays drums on 'I've Been Waitin' For Tomorrow (all of my life)', 'The Twilight Hour' and 'GIANT', as well singing on the latter.

Technically, this was just pre-MIDI*. Sequencers back in those days were synced by control voltage and tended to be part of large, expensive synthesizer setups I couldn't afford. There were some new, affordable little sequencers on the market – such as EDP's Spider – but these were hopelessly unreliable and unsophisticated. So, the way we had to create tracks like 'Waiting For Tomorrow' and 'GIANT' was that I'd say to Paul, 'Right, I want to record this bassline over and over again, so we'll have six minutes of that. Then we'll have six minutes of this syncopated synth line. Then this piano or guitar part for six minutes.' So once all these parts were recorded onto the multitrack we would create the arrangement by using the mute buttons on the desk. People automate this on their DAW† software these days. They'll take a loop, cut and paste sixteen bars of that, twenty-four bars of this. It is now common practice and easy, but in those days the way we were working was very unusual.

We would have to look at each other, both put our hands on

---

* MIDI stands for Musical Instrument Digital Interface and is a technical standard that allows electronic musical instruments and equipment to communicate and exchange information about music. It does not transmit audio itself, but sends data such as note pitch and duration which allows for the control, sequencing and synchronisation of instruments and software.
† DAW stands for Digital Audio Workstation.

it: 'You mute those four buttons; I'll mute these four buttons. Ready? Cut! Now bring those ones in.' That's how we created the arrangements for 'Waiting for Tomorrow' and 'GIANT'. We had twenty-four tracks full of great parts and great sounds, but if we just left all the faders at equal levels it would be a complete mess. We had to sculpt the arrangements out of it. I played many instruments myself on that record – guitars, synthesisers and keyboards, marimbas too probably – but decided to get in some mates and some excellent session players. So, Zeke being a very good drummer was prominent and on 'GIANT' his voice is also featured. We wanted to have big, strong vocal chanting at the end as that was always intended to be the album closer, although lyrically it's quite introspective – some might say miserable...

JW: It's celebratory, isn't it, 'GIANT'?

MJ: Yes! There's a duality. I try to combine uplifting music with poignancy in the lyrics. The music itself expresses joy and optimism and 'GIANT' was the track I wanted to end with – on a very high, joyous, positive note. It was very important to me that after the introspection of the lyrics had finished that the music would rise up, take over and lead the listener off into the sunset somewhere hopeful.

JW: Do you think there is a dichotomy between the music of 'GIANT' which is celebratory (and we'll talk about some of the African influences) and the lyrics? You used the word 'miserable'. That's not the word I'd use, but they *are* questioning. They're not afraid to deal with issues: 'I'm scared of God and I'm scared of hell and I'm caving in upon myself.' The lyrics are introspective and existential. Working in counterpoint to that you've got this incredibly celebratory piece of music. Did you intend for the music to take the listener somewhere different than the lyrics?

MJ: Yes. I've always tried to do that, with songs like 'Perfect', 'This Is The Day', even 'The Beat(en) Generation', the lyrics are quite dark but combined with a singalong, whistling tune. If you have uplifting music with saccharine lyrics it's a bit unbearable – that's what much of the music we hear on the radio is, which I don't care for. Conversely, if you have dark, melancholic music with dark melancholic lyrics, it's just too depressing. I think it's more powerful to have a combination. Sweet and sour, yin and yang. To have people tapping their foot whilst singing along to intense subject matter.

Talking of 'GIANT', there's an unfortunate story with the multi-track. I would have loved to be able to do some remixes of that track – it would be great to get a variety of people to remix – and to remix it myself. I love the mix we have on the album, but it would've been great to play around with it in later years. Anyway, record producer/remixer Arthur Baker was supposed to do it. He was very much the 'man of the moment' when it came to remixes in those days. So, I flew all the way to New York with the multi-track to meet him at his studio. I arrived on time but he kept me waiting in reception for over half an hour – which I thought a bit rude. Then, during our meeting as he was talking to me, Arthur had his hands down his sweatpants most of the time scratching his balls! I always think manners and politeness are important – it was the way I was brought up – so this was quite disappointing. Arthur eventually got back to us telling us he was declining the offer to remix 'GIANT'. I found out later that the multitrack that was given to me to handover was the *original* as – stupidly – they had not made a copy. It was then 'lost' at his studio and never seen again – which really upset me. A couple of years later when *Infected* was released, and featuring heavily on MTV and radio, I bumped into Arthur at Nell's – a cool nightclub on 14th Street I used to frequent. He was very chatty and friendly and asked if he could do a remix of 'Infected'. I politely declined his offer.

JW: Whilst we're on 'GIANT' – you mentioned a big Zeke influence. I think Jim Thirlwell is on it too and Thomas Leer. It's a funky track. 'Funky' is not a word I like to use, but it *is* a funky track! But, also, as you mentioned, it's got that great tribal chanting at the end. Were you listening to a lot of African music? I know that your influences are quite wide and disparate. I think – and I might be wrong – you had plans at one point to do a record which incorporated more of that?

MJ: I've had plans, many plans. I am a man with plans. I wanted to do albums of hymns, big band music, acapella, many different genres – so yes, that would've been somewhere in the plan of projects that never happened, unfortunately. I'm a fan of Nigerian musician Fela Kuti – I probably would've first seen him play around then. I also discovered Baaba Maal around this time too. It's so long ago now, I can't really remember how it all came about, but I remember we recorded the 'Yeah, yeah, yeah'-type chant at the end with Paul, Zeke and myself singing it multiple times to build up the size and try to make it vast… and Zeke suggested the counterpoint. He was amazing during those recording sessions – he's Zimbabwean and moved to Glasgow to study many years ago, and then came to London where he remained for many years. He's so passionate about his roots, so connected to that culture. He's got a beautiful, rich voice and his drumming – the drumming that he did on 'GIANT' in particular was the best drumming on the album. Fantastic. Zeke's presence is very much felt on that track. We're still very close friends; we were texting yesterday winding each other up about football! During the time of *Soul Mining* we were very close and spent a lot of time together.

I do remember though, the first time I was going to work with Zeke he was *three days* late! It was to play drums on 'This Is The Day' but we ended up using Andy Duncan because Zeke went AWOL. Paul, who hadn't yet met him said, 'Your fucking mate, when is he ever going to show up!?' There were no mobile phones so you'd leave messages on answer machines and hope to hear back. 'Where is he?' And then he finally shows up, 'Hey guys, it's African time!' With his big smile and lovely vibe it is always well worth the wait as he's wonderful.

Also, the sound of the drumming on *Soul Mining* is also the sound of The Garden live room. It was a wonderful room, designed by Andy Munro – who became a well-known studio designer after that. That was his first studio I believe and he designed it especially for John Foxx. It had unusual angled ceilings, hard walls and a wooden floor. It was very lively and had a particular sound. You'd close-mic the kit but also place microphones further away to pick up the sound of the room – and then heavily compress and gate.* That's how you'd get that vicious sound that was popularised originally by John Bonham and then by the likes of Peter Gabriel and Phil Collins with Hugh Padgham using the Stone Room at Townhouse Studios. They would create massive, heavily compressed, gated drum sounds which were popular back in the eighties. But The Garden had its own particular sound that we loved. So, we went down that route on 'Waiting For Tomorrow' and 'The Twilight Hour'.

On 'GIANT' we also mixed in a little bit of Simmons, which were these electronic drum modules – quite primitive electronic technology compared to these days. You'd take the signal from the drums and trigger electronic sounds from these modules – you could either do it live or off of the tape recorder. You can hear it on 'GIANT' – they're being triggered by Zeke's patterns on the toms. You hear the Simmons sounds being slowly faded up behind the acoustic drums.

We also start the track off with a drum machine – I can't remember what drum machine I would've used in the recording – I did have a little Roland TR-606 Drumatix and an E-mu Drumulator but it was probably a LinnDrum that we used. I wrote the bassline on a little Yamaha CS-01 but then got Thomas Leer to play it on a Roland Juno-60 I think. I wrote all the parts when I was writing the song and recording the demos. Again, it was all very syncopated, with sequence-type parts and synthesisers but all actually played by hand. It does sound sequenced but it's actually not – it's all live and very organic.

Jim Thirlwell played the wonderful percussion solo on 'GIANT'. What was brilliant was that Jim being Jim – not a trained musician

---

* An audio compressor smooths out volume by controlling loud and quiet sounds. A noise gate reduces or mutes sound below a set threshold to remove unwanted noise.

but very instinctive and incredibly creative, a wonderful producer and ideas man – said, 'Ah, I've got an idea.' He went into the kitchen and brought out various pots, pans and trays, set them all up in the live room and said to Paul, 'Just put me into record during this section.' We were wondering what he was cooking up – no pun intended! 'Right, now go again,' he said, and over four or five different passes he created this wonderful syncopated section of percussion. Again, nowadays it would all be simply sampled and sequenced but this was all intuitively constructed in his head and purely spontaneous. So, there's this very organic approach across the recording of this album that I think explains why it still sounds very contemporary and fresh.

JW: It's very clear with *Soul Mining* – and I've obviously been listening to all these records again, intently, in preparation for doing these interviews – is how well it hangs together as an album. It seems to me that when you decide on the track order, you want the listener to go on a journey. You've mentioned the idea of 'GIANT' being the final track, as a celebratory end point. That is obviously very clear on the copy of the record I've got. But the Americans added an extra track, 'Perfect', which has got a musician on it – one of my favourite British jazz musicians, a guy called Harry Beckett. He was one of the guest musicians that came in. What was your reaction when CBS added the extra track, after you'd carefully determined the track order?

MJ: 'Perfect' *was* originally supposed to be on the album. It was a hangover from *The Pornography Of Despair* but had been released as one of my first singles on CBS. For some reason we decided to change it. I don't know why as I really liked the original 7-inch with former New York Dolls singer David Johansen on harmonica, who had been introduced to me by Mike Thorne. It's tough sounding and urgent, whereas the later version was too laid back and had a bit of a calypso vibe. When I'd finished re-recording it I realised I didn't like it as much.

Harry Beckett was a gentle, nice man. I'd wanted to try a different instrument on the new version and had wondered how do you replace a legendary harmonica player? With a legendary trumpet player!

JW: He was a brilliant musician. Beckett did three incredible solo records: *Flare Up* (1970), *Harry Beckett's Warm Smiles* (1971) and *Joy Unlimited* (1975).

MJ: He was a lovely man. I was just never happy with that particular version. Something about the rhythm and the vibe, I couldn't work out where to place it on the album. I think it just went on too long. So, we thought, 'Let's make this a 12-inch in its own right, or maybe a double A-side with whatever the next single was going to be.'

It was odd, neither of the first two singles – the original 'Uncertain Smile' and the original 'Perfect' – were on the *Soul Mining* album. Everything was back to front and upside down. Not what you would call best practice, let's say. But the third single *was* on *Soul Mining* – 'This Is The Day'.

JW: And how was your relationship with Stevo during this period?

MJ: Stevo and I quickly became 'partners in crime'. Two working-class lads with a daredevil streak. On our way to or from promotional tours in the US, Australia and Europe we'd often take detours and find ourselves in places like Bangkok, Jamaica, Singapore or Mombasa. At times it was like skimming through the pages of one of the encyclopaedias I had as a child.

One bizarre week in particular stands out. Within the space of just a few days we were standing on top of the Empire State Building, then standing in front of the Leaning Tower of Pisa, then in Rome clamberbing around the Colosseum and then – whilst waiting at the airport in Rome to fly back to London – Stevo suddenly said, 'Hey, why don't we go to Egypt instead of England?' It seemed like a good idea to me so we quickly made a change of plans and jumped on the next flight to Cairo. I remember phoning my parents after we arrived and explaining I wouldn't be visiting for dinner tonight as I was now in Egypt! We'd met a young lad there who had some horses he would rent us and promised to show us around the pyramids. The following morning, we woke very early and were riding horses around the Great Pyramid at dawn before climbing inside all the way to the top and into a little chamber that was dimly lit with a low-wattage red lightbulb. Seems like a dream now and I doubt you'd get that close these days. There was a real sense of glee to all this globetrotting.

JW: Were there any disasters on the trips?

MJ: There was a time – just post *Soul Mining* – that we headed to Kenya for Christmas. We landed in Mombasa and stayed for a couple of days whilst en route to the small island of Lamu. We'd been forewarned to be extremely careful about drinking water from questionable sources. The night before we were leaving Mombasa we were wandering some desolate, under-lit backstreets. It was sweltering and we were thirsty when we came across a filthy little bar. I ordered a bottle of beer *without* ice – whilst Stevo insisted on ordering a pint of tap water *with* ice. I said, 'Stevo, I really don't think that's a good—' But with a Cheshire cat grin, he clinked his glass against mine, said 'Cheers!' and quickly guzzled the lot. A day later – on Lamu Island – Stevo was awkwardly running back and forth to the toilet every ten minutes, tears rolling down his face, crying, 'I've got dysentery!'

He'd never learn though. I'd bought plenty of sun cream and mosquito repellent for that trip because we'd been warned about the intensity of the sun, heat and insects. Stevo dismissively said that cream for sun and insects was for wimps and refused to put any on. Within two days he was boiled red as a lobster, covered in painful bites and lying motionless and silent beneath his mosquito net – apart from the occasional, gentle sob.

JW: And did *you* also screw up on these trips as a result of youthful exuberance?

MJ: Well, what sort of person would go scuba diving off the coast of Africa before learning to swim? Me! I didn't properly learn to swim until I was 27 – a couple of years later.

Stevo managed to score some very strong grass and would go off scuba diving completely stoned out of his head. Somehow, he managed to convince me to go too even though I couldn't swim! It was Christmas Day and we piled onto a small motorboat with half a dozen other people and headed off to sea. The scuba instructor gave me a quick ten-minute verbal lesson before we all jumped into the water. This was highly unprofessional. It soon turned into a nightmare. I had a faulty buoyancy control device, the wrong amount of weights on my belt and an ill-fitting face mask. I was soon really struggling in the deep water. The rest of the group – including Stevo – swam off and I was left alone with a mask filling up with water, sinking deeper and deeper into the depths.

I really thought I might die but it turned out to be one of those pivotal moments in life where you allow something inside to just take over. I realised I had to stay very, very calm, think clearly and stay positive. Despite having lost all visual contact with the instructor and the rest of the group I managed to get myself out of that situation and back to the boat in one piece. A horrible situation that could have turned fatal if I'd panicked.

JW: It feels as if the combination of Stevo and yourself had the propensity for mischief and disaster.

MJ: I've always been partial to cars made between the mid-sixties and mid-seventies – obviously due to the era of my childhood and teenage years. Whilst in Los Angeles I'd head to a car rental place called Rent-A-Wreck. In those days – the 1980s – they had an incredible selection of classic cars from my favourite era. I remember one occasion when we were in LA promoting *Soul Mining* and had some days off. We went to Rent-A-Wreck and I picked out a huge 1972 Cadillac Eldorado convertible in baby-blue metallic with a cream hide interior. After floating off the car lot it seemed obvious to us the only thing to do was point it towards Tijuana. Its nose gently rose as I pushed down on the accelerator and off we zoomed. I've long had a soft spot for mariachi bands and thought whilst there we could search for some authentic

Mexican musicians to use on some recordings for the next album.

But – Stevo being Stevo – a quick visit soon turned into a few days of mayhem and debauchery. We'd wander from seedy bar to seedy bar – drinking endless slammers, getting drunker and drunker. By the end of each night the pair of us would end up slumped unconscious in the corner of some dodgy establishment. A vivid memory is that each place we went to seemed illuminated only by very dim red lightbulbs. It was like being trapped inside a David Lynch film. We never did find any musicians. I'm amazed we even got back in one piece. I couldn't drink Tequila for years. Even the smell of it would make me heave.

JW: And how were things going with the US promotion of *Soul Mining*?

MJ: It was going very well and was a lot of fun *until* we showed up in New York for a second time on the promo tour. Stevo and I took the trip to the very corporate CBS offices in Midtown Manhattan, way up inside this forbidding, monolithic skyscraper known as 'Black Rock' – it looked like the Dark Tower of Mordor! Oh, there was one other thing, the US company had an issue with the UK sleeve artwork – the painting by Andrew of one of Fela Kuti's wives (see page 131). They said, 'If you've got an African woman on the cover its going to look a bit weird. It gives the impression it's an African album or a Reggae album.' They wanted to use an image of me, of my screaming head that Andrew had also drawn. I thought, okay, as long as the colour scheme stays the same, so that it looks part of the same family as the original sleeve. So, I wasn't being unreasonable.

When I got to their offices, I looked at this alternative sleeve, thinking, 'Oh, okay. It looks alright.' But when I turned it over and looked down the track list on the back I saw there were now eight tracks, not seven. What!? 'Perfect' is now track eight. I showed it to Stevo and he and I both went ballistic. Who the fuck has done this? What's going on? We found out it was the A&R man. A&R man!? He wasn't *my* frigging A&R man! A fellow called Bob Feineagle, I think his name was. I'd never met him before. He wasn't a nasty person, just a bit dopey I guess. He simply said, 'Oh, hey man, I just thought it would make it better value for the consumer.' I hate that word, 'consumer'.

JW: They didn't even think to ask you?

MJ: Nope! Never asked, just stuck it on. I hit the roof. I was livid – I made it quite clear in all the interviews. I said, 'It's so fucked up!' It's like an author writing a book and the publisher secretly – sneakily – adding a discarded chapter as the final chapter. It took years, twenty-odd years, to get it removed from the US version. I was incandescent. Very, very upset. It caused big rows.

CBS never really knew what to do with me in America. Though to be fair I was my own worst enemy. I refused to tour, I'd only agree to very limited amounts of interviews, I'd turn my nose up at TV performances. I really was not an easy person to deal with back then. Like one of those maverick footballers in the seventies who's got the talent but misbehaves continually and so keeps getting dropped.

JW: My favourite was QPR's Stanley Bowles.*

MJ: Yes, I liked Stanley. He was a heavy gambler, wasn't he? Smoker and drinker too probably.

JW: Yes, but he also got offered money by adidas and Gola to wear their football boots, so he'd go on with one of each! He took the money from both. That's funny.

This falling-out with CBS led to Stevo saying, 'Look, both parties are not happy. Why don't you release us from the contract?' A figure was mentioned of £60,000 to be released – what happened there? Because they didn't, did they?

---

* Stanley Bowles was an English professional footballer who played for Queens Park Rangers and earned five England caps. He is remembered for his irreverent, nonconformist attitude, as much as his talent.

MJ: No, they were playing around with us. It was them who actually said to us that if we were so unhappy they would tear up the contract if we gave them £60,000. They tried to bluff us. They thought we'd be too frightened and cave in but we instantly replid, 'Yes, please!'

JW: So, Stevo would've picked up the phone, rang other record companies?

MJ: Yes, we'd have easily got the money, but they went back on their word. It was becoming a complicated relationship with CBS. There were a lot of good people there who I really liked personally – some I'm still in touch with – and so I look back on that time fondly. They were very supportive in many ways.

The Americans particularly just didn't know what to do with me. Because THE THE never fit into any category they didn't know how to 'position me in the marketplace' – all that marketing spiel nonsense. So, there's that problem on the one hand; but on the other I wasn't very cooperative as I didn't much care for the way they were trying to market me at the time.

JW: You didn't want to tour?

MJ: No, I didn't want to tour in those early days. There was a *lot* of pressure on me. The head of the company would continually try to arm-twist me, and I'd simply say, 'I don't want to.' Some of the promotional stuff they used to try and force bands to do – appearing on little kids' shows and things like that – I actually did some of that in those early days. You'd go to Europe – arrive in France, Germany or Italy for interviews and then someone would say, 'Oh, we've arranged a TV show for you to appear on,' and you'd be whisked off in a car to a TV studio and find yourself on a stage miming – or singing live over a backing track. And there'd be all sorts of bizarre things going on around you – weird stage sets, clowns, odd people with strange clothes prancing and dancing inches from you whilst you were trying to sing – with cameras stuck in your face.

JW: There's some great footage of Public Image Ltd on a kids' show.

MJ: Yes, lots of bands found themselves in these strange situations. You just didn't know where you'd end up. You were trusting – at first. But that's why we had to get stricter – the equivalent of a rider would be sent across before my promotional trips. No kids' shows, no this, no that. But, unfortunately, that had the effect of dampening the enthusiasm of the record company, because they just thought, 'Hang on a minute: we've got all these other young bands happy to do everything they're told to help us recoup our investment; and then we've got this—'

JW: —difficult Londoner.

MJ: Yes, misbehaving and causing problems.' Their enthusiasm cooled, naturally. They just thought, why bother putting all our effort into this ungrateful individual? I couldn't blame them really, looking back.

JW: You mentioned the album's sleeve. The cover on the record that I've got, the UK version, is obviously Andrew's work. It's of one of Fela Kuti's wives? It seems to fit the record, but it's a very specific thing to use as well.

MJ: She's smoking a joint too. Well, Andrew and I were close – if we weren't sharing a room I'd often hang out in his bedroom chatting or he'd come to my bedroom. I was often looking at the work he was doing, or he was listening to songs I was working on. Anyway, sometime after we'd both left home I was visiting his studio – I can't remember where he was living at the time – probably his digs whilst he was studying for his degree at Camberwell College. We were talking about sleeves – the 'Uncertain Smile' and 'Perfect' ones were sort of caricatures of me and we were trying to find artwork suitable for *Soul Mining*. I came across his painting of one of Fela Kuti's wives. I can't recall the reason Andrew chose her as a subject, but I just loved its atmosphere, so vibrant and full of life. The colours were beautiful aquamarines, golds and blues. I thought, this will work. Then he obviously worked on it some more, finessed it to get it right, did some of the other illustrations, the little details and doodles on the back and inner sleeve.

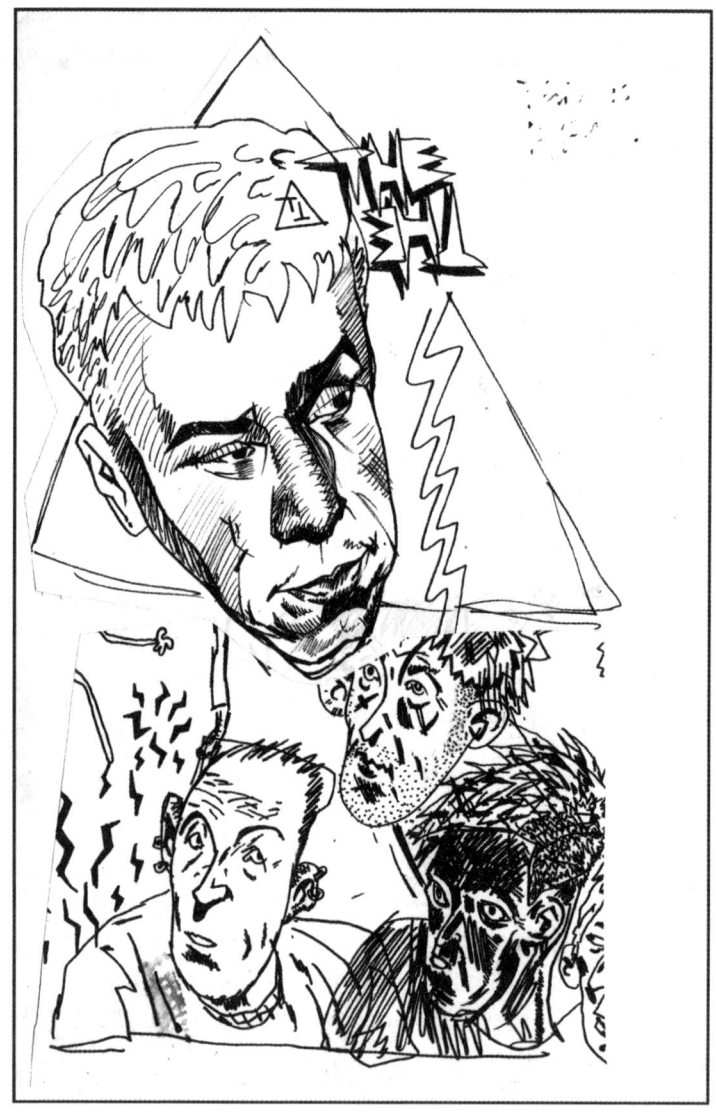

JW: You look at that sleeve and think, 'I want to listen to this record.'

Now the other thing I wanted to ask was you mentioned Fiona Skinner working at Thames TV in the graphics department and creating the THE THE logo. Was *Soul Mining* the first time it had appeared on a record?

MJ: I think so. On 'This Is The Day', we used Fiona's typeface but with a different layout, so *Soul Mining* may have been the first place we used the definitive logo.

My first manager, Tom Johnston – or his girlfriend Judy – created the first logo and we had little badges made up. Later we asked Neville Brody to have a go, and he came up with the one used on the original 'Uncertain Smile' single sleeve and its related posters. I was never fully convinced about that design though.

JW: Brody did a lot of the Cabaret Voltaire sleeves.

MJ: Yes, he was an excellent designer and nice chap but I was not happy with his design. Of course, Fiona was also an excellent graphic designer – so I asked her to have a go.

It started with her new handcrafted font, which Andrew used for the 'This Is The Day' single sleeve, however with the letters in a different arrangement to later iterations. Fiona refined it and designed the definitive version for us: with small and large 'The's, the larger one capitalised. Reproduced again and again over the years, it has subtly evolved. Some slightly fatter, some slightly slimmer. But it is her version. I've loved her logo from the moment she created it and we still use it.

Also, when we write the band name in regular text now, it is always fully capitalised as THE THE. It's not that we're trying to shout at people off the page: the problem is that when you see it written out partially capitalised, 'The The', it sort of disappears. We all have an 'auto-correct' function in our brains. For instance, have you tried writing out sentences with the vowels missing and observing how your brain quickly auto-corrects and fills in the gaps? We were having the same problem with the band name in that it often disappeared within text as peoples' brains auto-correct the second 'The' out, thinking it a mistake. So, we made the decision a few years ago to always write it fully capitalised, so it pops out. It's been hard enough as it is over the years having a band name that is un-Googleable! In the early days of search-engines we pretty much vanished – became invisible. It has damaged us massively commercially but I suppose I've got used to it – in some ways it is like going back to the old underground music days I grew up in and so it's quite novel to be hiding in plain sight in this overexposed digital era.

JW: We spoke about 'GIANT' already (see page 119) but I want to talk about a couple of the tracks on *Soul Mining* in more detail.

'I've Been Waitin' For Tomorrow (all of my life)', the opening track, contains some of your very early political lyrics: 'I've been filled with useless information / Spewed out by papers and radio stations'. It seems that this commentary on media and propaganda was a continuation of some of the political lyrics on *Burning Blue Soul*.

MJ: Yes, on *Burning Blue Soul* there were political songs, like 'Song Without An Ending', and in 'Another Boy Drowning':

> There's people on the streets
> Throwing rocks at themselves
> 'Coz they ain't got no money
> And they're livin' in hell

JW: On *Soul Mining* it felt like the first time it would've connected with a wider audience? You spoke about not necessarily wanting to make a commercial record but wanting to maybe broaden the appeal.

MJ: Possibly, although 'Perfect' was also political: 'Bodies queue for nothing / For it is to nothing they belong', so in my mind I don't see *Soul Mining* as the start of my political lyric writing but just a continuation.

JW: Because 'I've Been Waitin' For Tomorrow' is the first song, you straight away think that it is setting the tone for the rest of the album.

MJ: It was important to do that. The album could've opened with 'This Is The Day' for instance, but I wanted to open with a strong, strident song. As mentioned earlier, there's always been this duality between the more experimental, aggressive side and the more melodic, structured side of my music. I felt – probably because I'd gone with relatively soft singles ('Uncertain Smile' is a gentle song) – I felt the need to reassert the more experimental side and begin with 'Waitin' For Tomorrow'. Though it may not sound so aggressive with what is happening musically forty-odd years later, it was a vicious opening track in its day compared to what most of my contemporaries were doing. What sets this song apart is Zeke's powerful drumming and the way we used The Garden's live room by cranking up the volume and compression. It was quite vicious-sounding, lyrically hard: 'The cancer of love is eating out my heart,' and 'My mind has been polluted, my energy diluted.' It was intentional to open with a hard-hitting track, knowing there were also these beautifully melodic, commercial songs still to come on the album. I suppose part of me didn't want to give the impression this album was just an easy ride, but was going to be a journey of ups and downs.

JW: Musically *Soul Mining* is an eclectic record because of your interest in texture, how songs are put together and your use of technology. There's a jazz element, there's an African element and 'This Is The Day' has a kind of folk element. You've got these bittersweet, pensive lyrics; and then the fiddle and accordion which can often be quite melancholic, but on this they don't *feel* that way. They feel slightly – you won't like the use of this word – jaunty. There's a kind of up-beat-ness to it. You said earlier that it's one of your most enduring and popular tracks.

MJ: I love accordion. For this recording we brought in a very interesting guy, Wix – Paul Wickens – a brilliant keyboard player and very talented musician. His name was probably suggested by Annie Roseberry. I'd already written the main accordion theme for 'This Is The Day' on my melodica for the demo. Wix played that wonderfully but he improvised the solo and it was virtually all first-take as I remember. A beautiful solo. We were very happy with him. He actually performed on *Mind Bomb* too and we had wanted him to come on tour with us for the Versus The World Tour – but do you know who quickly nabbed him by making him an offer he couldn't refuse? Funny enough, he's still with him to this day.

JW: No, I don't.

MJ: Paul McCartney! Wix has been his musical director and keyboard player ever since. Anyway, a good man, brilliant musician and highly professional. He appeared in the video for 'This Is The Day' and on some TV shows with me too.

I also love fiddle so we got Paul Boyle in too. Another good guy and I love what he played. I really wanted joyousness from the fiddle and the accordion because although the lyrics do have a sweet sadness – I mentioned earlier I cried whilst writing it – I wanted the atmosphere that lingered after the song finished to be one of hope, that each day contains the possibility of change.

Interestingly, during The Comeback Special Tour in 2018 I was asked how it felt to be performing 'This Is The Day' again after all those years. I replied that it actually means more to me now than it did back then. I was only 21 but to write: 'You've been reading some old letters / You smile and think how much you've changed,' I was just a kid, really and it was written beyond my years. Now, when I read old letters and realise how much my life has changed, I think about all of the people I've loved and lost as well as all the amazing things that have happened to me in the intervening years – it has imbued the song with more power for me.

Also, when I think of the original video we made for that song – though I didn't like it at the time – all of my immediate family are in it. Most of them have now passed away, tragically. Furthermore, singing it live now – to audiences that grew up with it – it may well mean more to them too. When a song is new, it hasn't yet had time to become part of the soundtrack to events in peoples' lives. Over the years that song has taken on many meanings for people. There is a poignancy to it but I think of it as an optimistic song. 'Your life will surely change.' I am by nature an optimist, although some people might be surprised by that. I still get excited about the possibilities of each new day, when you go to new places, meet new people. Life is always pregnant with possibilities isn't it?

JW: I think that comes across in the lyric as well, doesn't it?

MJ: I hope so. Some people have asked, 'Were you just being ironic?' I say, 'No.' Melancholia and joy can coexist. It's what I often think of as a sweet sadness. I'm not talking about depression. Depression is a disabling state. But melancholia is a wistfulness that can be triggered by the smell of nature after fresh rainfall, looking at the sky in a certain light or time of day, unexpectedly running into an ex-lover, listening to a specific piece of music or sensing a long-forgotten fragrance that stirs something deep inside; it's life-affirming.

JW: I think melancholia is the sense that there is the possibility of happiness. Whereas depression is the sense that there is no possibility.

MJ: Exactly. It's a totally different thing. It's a bittersweet song, but ultimately one of hope. That's how I think of it. And the instrumentation was meant to reflect that, to be uplifting.

JW: Can you expand on another lyric: 'I'm just a symptom of the moral decay / That's gnawing at the heart of the country'? It's personal, political, everything. It's in 'The Sinking Feeling' – which has a great guitar solo on it.

MJ: That was me. I don't often play lead guitar.

JW: Is it you? It's a great guitar solo. It's quite atonal, isn't it?

MJ: I suppose it is. But to your point about the lyrics: Thatcherism was really starting to bite. This song was a hangover from *The*

Pornography Of Despair, so this lyric – and this album generally – is darker than *Soul Mining*. The reality of Thatcherism was beginning to be revealed. The privatisation programme and the asset stripping were underway and unemployment levels were shooting up. The pure contempt for the old British culture and way of life and the British working class was becoming apparent, the inexorable rise of the right and the neoconservatives (see page 165) – and they would basically proceed to take over the country and carve it up for private profit and greed. So, this was the early days of that process; and being aware of what was going on – as a young songwriter – I felt compelled to try and put it into my songs.

JW: You re-recorded 'Uncertain Smile' for the album. I think the Jools Holland story is quite well-known, but I don't think we could do this book without mentioning it. He would have been in Squeeze at this point, is that right?

MJ: I think it was post-Squeeze.

JW: Jools Holland wasn't actually in Squeeze for very long. He was a founding member in 1974 but he left in 1980. So yes, this was post-Squeeze.

MJ: Again, it was Annie Roseberry who suggested him. Annie was always supportive – though even *she* wasn't allowed in the studio when we were recording. In fact, all the record company were banned – and Stevo helped enforce this ban. It wasn't personal but I can't make records by committee and when people come to the studio they can't help but try to justify their jobs by giving advice – even when it's not sought. Stevo was like a Rottweiler in this regard. But then I wouldn't even allow *him* in the studio either! It was Paul and I. We had the close working relationship, and would bring the musicians in and out. So, we re-recorded 'Uncertain Smile' for *Soul Mining*, even though we could've saved money and just put the original New York version on.

JW: It's very different, though.

MJ: It *is* different. We could've used the original versions of both 'Uncertain Smile' and 'Perfect' but Paul felt quite strongly that the album would then feel too much like a musical patchwork by featuring production from different engineers and producers. He'd rather, as co-producer, be involved in every track so that it would be a whole album project we'd done together. I thought he was right.

With the re-recording of 'Uncertain Smile' I played acoustic guitar instead of the Rickenbacker electric 12-string I'd played on the original. Overall it has a less electronic feel to it, more organic and acoustic. Instead of the Roland TR-808 drum machine on the original we used Andy Duncan on drums. We recorded a long version of the song because we thought it could then be turned into a 12-inch – as the original was – without having to elongate via edit sections. In those pre-digital days, you had to chop tape around. So, we thought we'd record extra-long just in case. When the backing track was recorded we then had this long outro, rotating through the chord sequence. We sat around, pondering – what can we put on top? Of course! It was staring us in the face – sitting in The Garden's live room was a beautiful Yamaha C3 baby grand piano. We hadn't used it much up until this point apart from when I played it on 'Waitin' For Tomorrow' but it was a good-sounding, bright, well-maintained piano. 'Do you know any good pianists?' we asked each other.

Thinking about it now, of course Wix could've done it but I'd only just met him and thought of him as an accordion player. I didn't yet know what a great all-round keyboard player he was. Though I don't think Wix – or anyone else for that matter – could have done as good a job as Jools ended up doing. Anyway, I'd spoken to Annie, asked her advice and she'd immediately replied, 'Jools Holland!' Then, the rest is history of course. I've told this story many, many times so I'll keep it short.

Jools showed up in his full motor bike leathers on a swelteringly hot summer's day, sat down at the piano and proceeded to play the best piano solo on a pop record in the last forty-odd years

JW: He likes his bikes and cars, doesn't he? He always struck me as a very nice man.

MJ: He *is* a very nice man. I like Jools very much. I spoke to him recently and he put me in touch with a mechanic to work on my old Rover.

Anyway, as Jools hammered out this stunning solo Paul and I just looked at each other and smiled knowingly, 'We've fucking got something here!' It was a spontaneous first-take with one small drop-in – all made up on the spot by Jools. Interestingly, Jools has a very different memory of that session. He remembers playing over a shorter, instrumental section – like a middle 8 – repeatedly and that we just edited it all together. But that is not how I remember it at all. I'll have to ask Paul one of these days how he remembers it. But anyway, Paul and I were absolutely thrilled. So, thrilled in fact that we asked Jools if he'd like to join us for dinner at a local café – just a cheap, little greasy spoon called Gina's that Paul and I went to most early evenings because there was nothing much in that area at that time. Jools ended up paying for his own food – which I still feel embarrassed about. What a couple of cheapskates Paul and I were! But to be fair we were both broke.

JW: We've almost gone through every track but I feel that 'The Twilight Hour' – which is brilliant – is one of those lyrics that is very emotionally bare. It's quite a despairing view of relationships.

MJ: It is in some ways, yes. My relationship with Fiona was very new – it was the first proper relationship I'd had. Sometimes deep insecurities float to the surface when beginning a new relationship – particularly when young and inexperienced. For instance, if the phone doesn't ring when you expect it to and you can start succumbing to all sorts of paranoid fantasies. It must be even worse these days I suppose – the era of mobile phones, social media and people 'ghosting' each other or obsessively monitoring each other's social lives. Horrible.

Anyway, the song was about that sort of intense, disorientating insecurity at the start of a relationship. I loved the lyric – it still makes me chuckle – sung with irony of course, 'You're relying on her for your independence.' It sums up that early insecurity. On a personal note I quickly got over that negativity and our relationship thrived as we were together eleven years. We had our ups and downs during that time, of course, but overall it was very good. So, that song was written about the very early stages of a relationship when I was very young. I doubt I'd write so emotionally naked these days.

JW: I was going to ask you that, because *Soul Mining* is confessional. When you write a track as lyrically open as something like 'Soul Mining' or 'The Twilight Hour', people may read the lyrics or listen to the song, and it could give you problems couldn't it? Because it's explicit in what it's detailing. Was there ever a consideration of, 'No, I don't want to write that because once that lyric is out there there's no putting it back'?

MJ: Not really. But there certainly is now – there's a lot of stuff I wouldn't write these days; back then I was less sensitive, more arrogant, ambitious and slightly intoxicated with a feeling of artistic license – to do whatever it takes regardless of others' feelings and that art should be the ultimate arbiter of your decision-making, rather than considering the impact it may have upon personal relationships and friendships. There's certainly a lot of things I wouldn't do now that I did then. Some people may think that type of brazen behaviour is artistic fearlessness but it's more selfishness. The songs are not all autobiographical though – some may be or they may instead be composites drawn from others' lives or situations.

JW: In these interview sessions I don't intend to ask you to retrospectively rate or review an album. I think that's firstly because this book is quite an organic thing; but it's also because I see you as someone who's very much still striving to do *interesting* work, and I don't think you're somebody that *does* necessarily look back. It's one of the things I like about you.

Some people rely on past glories; I think you do a project, and you move on, because you're always thinking of the future. But *Soul Mining* was such a transitional moment in your career for a number of reasons. Is it something that you think took you to another level – professionally and commercially? It feels to me like a moment where you went from being one type of artist to being another type of artist.

MJ: Yes, definitely. It was the first time I'd collaborated with other musicians to that degree. On *Burning Blue Soul* and *The Pornography Of Despair* I played everything myself and this was the first time I had a decent budget and was allowed to take my time working on good studio equipment. I had a great engineer and co-producer in Paul Hardiman, some top musicians – good friends who were very talented and also superb session players. Also, having the muscle of a major label to then lift it up and promote it properly helped massively whereas, though *Burning Blue Soul* was a strong debut album, it proved easier to ignore, being released through an indie label with limited firepower.

JW: The independent charts versus the real charts?

MJ: Yes. But *Soul Mining* didn't chart particularly high upon release, nor were the initial sales that great at the time. They were respectable.

JW: It's the longevity.

MJ: Exactly. It's an album that continues to tick over. Decade after decade. And internationally too. It did pretty well all over the world. America, Australia, Germany, France, New Zealand, Canada and elsewhere. This longevity is what I always really wanted. It's far more valuable – to me – to have an album that's still being bought and played many years after its release than having a number one album that is forgotten within three years.

JW: Which is what records do now. They go in at number one and then they're gone.

MJ: I'm very proud that it is now considered one of the great albums of its era. It was a job well done, I think, from Paul and myself. We put a huge amount of work and love into it. We worked long hours and each sound was carefully crafted, each part worked out painstakingly. Everyone involved worked very hard.

JW: You can hear that in the record.

MJ: I did feel at the time that it *might* stand the test of time – it's what I hoped for at least.

CHAPTER FOUR
I Was Trying So Hard To Be Myself
I Was Turning Into Somebody Else

Politics on a global scale and the brutalising effects of Thatcher on the British working class are placed front and centre as subject matter. Matt recruits another post-punk figure to record with: Rip Rig + Panic's Neneh Cherry. Rather than tour, a film is commissioned for each song and Tim Pope and Peter 'Sleazy' Christopherson also join Matt's coterie of collaborators. Infected *is a critical and commercial success.*

JW: We spoke about the success of *Soul Mining*, and I just wondered if – before we talk about *Infected* – you could talk about the period in your life after *Soul Mining*. You were in a relationship with Fiona Skinner, you'd moved into a new flat in Carysfort Road in Stoke Newington and you were seeing a lot of Stevo at his place in Hammersmith. I know that you've mentioned Mal of Cabaret Voltaire, but you were hanging out and listening to lots of loud industrial music. Is that a fair summation of where you were?

MJ: That's just a tiny slice and there was a lot more going on. There were a lot of people in our social life and we were out all the time at late-night parties or at clubs and bars like Café de Paris, Wag Club, Bat Cave, Zanzibar, Le Beat Route, Heaven, Limelight, Kettner's, Dirt Box evenings. It all gets muddled up in my mind as I was probably quite tipsy much of the time. Or we were round each other's houses – not only Stevo but mates like Zeke, Ian Tregoning, 'Italian Alex' (Sartore) and 'Blonde Alex' (Kerr-Wilson) and lots of others. Paul Webb too. He and his partner were a big part of our social scene.

JW: Paul was a member of Talk Talk?

MJ: Yes, and is now known as Rustin Man. We're still good friends. A funny story regarding Paul is that he and I – probably inspired by Ken Russell's film *Altered States* – used to go inside these sensory deprivation tanks every Saturday afternoon after our weekly run around Victoria Park. We were using the effect of the tanks to try and boost the effects of the ecstasy we were taking! I had a lot of other close friends – men and women – that I was hanging out with, as well as my label mates at Some Bizzare, of whom Mal was one.

That *Soul Mining* period was characterised by a lot of ecstasy use, when it was being written – from about the age of 21. The first time I took it was New Year's Eve 1981 at our good friend's flat in Knightsbridge – which was a fair few years before the late-eighties 'Summer of Love' and its sudden discovery by the mainstream. This was because of the connections with Some Bizzare, through Stevo, Marc Almond and Dave Ball – their friend from New York would bring it over. The timelines all start to merge and muddle to be honest as there was so much going on in those few years. There were lots of parties, including at my flat on Carysfort Road – Paul Webb actually lived a few doors along on the same road.

Also, bear in mind that Some Bizzare (still representing me as management) had also been rapidly growing into the most exciting independent label in the UK: Soft Cell, Marc & The Mambas, Cabaret Voltaire, Psychic TV, Coil and Test Department were now colleagues. I brought in Jim Thirlwell with his Foetus project and he in turn brought in Einsturzende Neubauten, Wise Blood and Swans. There was a lot of hanging out and late-night partying with all these bands, often at Stevo's mad house in Hammersmith or at the Some Bizzare office in St Anne's Court – which then moved to New Cavendish Street. I really liked all these people and – apart from the split in Psychic TV which led to the creation of Coil – I don't recall any artists having any sort of tensions or fall out – which was remarkable I suppose given how many egos were involved.

Around this time, I built a new 16-track studio in my spare room. I'd been using my little Fostex 8-track recorder. But I upgraded to a Fostex B16 tape machine, Allen & Heath System-8 1616 mixing desk, BEL BD80 Digital Delay, Lexicon PCM60 Digital Reverb, Drawmer DS201 Noise Gate, Urei 1176 Compressor and assorted microphones. I bought the entire little studio from Martin Westwood at the professional audio equipment supplier HHB. Plus, from Syco Systems I'd recently purchased a PPG Wave 2.2 synthesizer and – last but not least – a brand-new Emulator 2 – one of the first in the UK. This is where I would write *Infected*. It was composed over a couple of years, 1984–1985. The lyric that took the longest to write – eighteen months on and off – was 'Heartland'. A real labour of love. I worked really hard on that. Not that I hadn't worked hard on lyrics before but I'd never worked on lyrics over such an extended time period before. Again, I'd often be lying on the floor with my pencils, pens and notepads writing and rewriting.

JW: It seems you had developed a habit of writing on the floor?

MJ: Yes, I did. My bones ache too much to be on the floor too much these days! But when younger, I'd often be on the floor. As a kid I remember me and my brothers – especially Eugene – would lie on the floor with the TV inches from our faces – literally hypnotised, I've realised many years later. I always liked being on the floor, playing with my toys as a kid – I suppose the habit stuck. Anyway, I'd write and rewrite – with piles and piles of paper with scribbled out lyrics all over the place. Nowadays all my rewriting and correcting tends to be done on the laptop. Better for the environment I guess; though, sadly, I no longer have all the paper trails which show the evolution of the lyrics.

JW: There was a relatively short gap between *Soul Mining* and *Infected*.

MJ: Yes, compared to later years. It's really the length a gap between albums *should* be. It is ridiculous the length of time I started to leave between albums later on.

JW: Do you think that was because of the success of *Soul Mining*? You'd achieved some of the things you wanted to achieve – a broader palette of music and songs that were lyrically quite dark and dealt with emotional issues; but the music in contrast was sometimes lighter. So, there is a sense that you had a newfound confidence in yourself as a songwriter and composer?

MJ: Yes, definitely – I felt vindicated. *Soul Mining* was selling fairly well over an extended period of time – not a huge commercial hit but critically acclaimed nationally and internationally. But, even at the start of the *Infected* project, the record company were already nagging me, 'Okay, with this next album you've got to go on the road.'

I wanted to continue working with a wide range of musicians – but new ones. I liked to keep moving forward – not looking back. Let's think… who was on *Infected*? Well Zeke was again but he didn't play drums this time – just sang on the title track. As far as drums, I was recently introduced to Dave Palmer – a member of ABC at that time. It was through Gary Langan, who produced 'The Mercy Beat' and 'Angels Of Deception'. Gary had been Trevor Horn's engineer and had worked with Dave when Trevor produced ABC's *The Lexicon Of Love* album. Dave and I hit it off straightaway. He was a phenomenal drummer – at that time one of the best in the UK. He was also a lot of fun to spend time with. Very engaging company and very funny. He quickly became a very important part of that record – my right-hand man in a way.

JW: Why was Paul Hardiman not involved in the follow-up album?

MJ: The truth of the matter is that Stevo did not get along with Paul's manager – who also happened to be Paul's wife. Stevo's negotiating skills were extremely bullish. He took no prisoners and often left a trail of destruction in his wake.

It was ironic as it was Stevo who'd first suggested I meet with Paul after things fell apart with Mike Thorne. Now, Paul's wife Eileen could also be a tough negotiator herself, so when it came to working out a new deal for Paul for a new album at an improved royalty rate the two of them just locked horns and couldn't get along or agree upon anything. She thought Stevo was highly unreasonable and vice versa. Things deteriorated from there sadly. It was really unfortunate. Paul and I liked each other, we worked well together and never fell out, but as our respective managers ended up loathing each other and could not agree a deal, that got in the way. So, it became time to bring in someone else.

JW: You had a lot of loyalty to Stevo.

MJ: I did in that period, yes. We made a good team in those early days. He kept a lot of the promises he made in terms of what we were going to do, and he had these really big, dramatic ideas. During the recording of the album, because I didn't want to go on tour he suggested – I can't remember at what point this came up – that instead we make a video for every song and tour that instead. It was a highly unusual idea, especially back then. Not a cheap one either. CBS (or was it now Sony? I can't remember when the takeover happened) were pressurising me: 'You've got to tour! You have to put a band together!' Our retort became, 'No, we want you to pay for a video for every track on the new album instead of providing tour support.' I promised I would then tour the world with the film.

JW: *Infected* is the first time I remember thinking of an album as not just a record and the first time I can remember the concept of one video for every track. I remember when *Infected* came out, and seeing it launched. You'd call it a 'multimedia project' now, wouldn't you? It really was ahead of the game in that sense. But the concept of the film was also a way for you to resist being forced to go out and tour.

MJ: Yes. All credit to Stevo for that because he persuaded and pushed them. I'm not sure another manager could have done that. He was very impressive in the way he'd harass CBS. Every opportunity, whenever he'd bump into the chairman or MD – which was Paul Russell at that time – he'd nag him. 'Right, you are going to cough up, we are going to do this.' Russell would reply, 'No, you've got to tour!' Basically, he eventually wore Russell down in a war of attrition. 'Look, fund our film project and Matt will do all the interviews you want, he'll travel around the world to promote it for a year. Or you get nothing, and we won't promote it at all.' Anyway, I did keep my promise and I spent month after month flying around the world screening *Infected: The Movie* in countless cinemas – across Europe, America,

Australia, New Zealand – huge amounts of interviews and promotion. CBS/Sony were good to their word and I was good to my word. It was far more effective than a tour anyway as it was so unusual at that time. People still talk about it to this day. Anyway, we're getting ahead of ourselves here…

JW: We'll come back to all the videos. Who did you get in to replace Paul Hardiman?

It was initially Gary Langan – who engineered but was also credited as producer on 'The Mercy Beat' and 'Angels Of Deception'. Gary – again suggested by Annie Roseberry – was also a member of Art of Noise. He was a nice guy, good vibe, excellent engineer. We did those two tracks together but as we were preparing to do more he got a call to work on another project – I can't remember who, some big pop band at the time he saw as too good a career move to turn down. The dates clashed with mine so instead of hanging around for him we swiftly moved on.

I wrote a wish list of potential collaborators. I demoed 'Out Of The Blue' and 'Heartland' at my studio and sent copies to Brian Eno, Holger Czukay and Tom Waits. Eno came back lukewarm, we never heard from Holgar Czukay – though I'm not sure we even had the right address or that he received the demos – and Tom Waits came back very positively, wanting to get involved. I then arranged with Annie – supportive as ever – that I'd go to New York to spend a week with him to discuss the project.

JW: This would have been around the release of Waits' *Swordfishtrombones* 1983 album.

MJ: A bit afterwards but that's what gave me the idea, I loved *Swordfishtrombones* and saw him perform it at the Dominion.

JW: I went to that.

MJ: I was blown away. Loved it. Didn't he do a week of shows there?

JW: Incredible.

MJ: The sound – so organic and unusual and with a beautiful stage production. Anyway, he was very encouraging so I flew to New York for a week to discuss work methods and check out studios with him. At the time he was working on *Rain Dogs* (1985). I even got to meet the great Robert Frank, who was working with Tom for the cover of his new album – I believe he took the back-cover photograph.

We all met up at the Chelsea Hotel, which was where Tom was living at that time. He was having a stressful time though. He wasn't drinking and I think he'd just fired a manager. 'I caught them going through my pockets!' he complained in one of his vivid metaphors. We discussed ideas in depth and even visited one of the last remaining old-school recording studios in Manhattan – that we planned use on the project – it was either Columbia or RCA. He was very much into old technology and atmospheric recording environments.

He also introduced me to the Ear Inn during that trip. It was the second oldest bar in Manhattan I believe; and from the eighties, through the nineties and early noughties, it was my local, my regular hangout. It used to be full of musicians and artists but it may well be full of frat boys and tech gurus now. My good friend, the late Roli Mosimann, was also a regular there – as was my mastering engineer Howie Weinberg. In fact, they named a drink after him called the 'Howie Margarita' which was basically a very strong margarita in a pint glass. Two or three of those and the evening would be over! There was always a nice bunch of people there – including the staff. That was my most regular haunt when living in New York. I was there several nights per week – usually until the early hours.

Anyway, it was whilst sitting in the Ear – Tom drinking bitters and soda and me a Stoli and tonic – that he gave me a most fruitful piece of advice. He pulled out of his back pocket a tiny, beaten-up notepad, tapped it and urged me to do the same and carry one on my person at all times. He said, 'This is your butterfly net. Without it the words may still come but they will all just fly away

– lost forever.' I loved the way he spoke. He had a very poetic turn of phrase.

JW: You got on?

MJ: I really liked him. I was young – only 24 – I guess he was a decade or so older. At that time his wife was also pregnant – or had just given birth – and they were living out of suitcases at the Chelsea Hotel. He was also trying to finish *Rain Dogs*, managing himself, whilst dealing with legal issues with his ex-manager, so he was starting to get stressed. At a certain point – a month or two later – he came to realise he was just spread too thin with various personal and professional commitments.

JW: There's an honesty to that. He probably would've been working with Kathleen Brennan around this time as well. What a great thing to have done… And what was Robert Frank like?

MJ: Very friendly and charismatic. Tom was keen for me to meet him but to be honest, I didn't know Frank's work before our meeting – I felt quite embarrassed about my ignorance. But we got on well – so straight after the meeting I went to one of my favourite bookshops – the Strand on Broadway near Union Square – and picked up a copy of Frank's book, *The Americans*. That kick-started a passion for street photography for me.

JW: He's another one of my heroes, Robert Frank. What a great memory to have. Tom Waits must have really seen something in your work to have given his time.

MJ: He's not really known for being a producer of other people. But he was very encouraging and said, 'Look, your demos are so explicit, just produce yourself. I don't think you really need a producer, just get yourself a good engineer, get in the studio and carry on doing what you're doing.'
    Warne Livesey and Roli Mosimann then got involved with the project as engineers/co-producers. I don't think they actually knew

each other then but they were both introduced to me by my good friend Jim Thirlwell. I didn't work with them at the same time but separately on different tracks.

Warne had worked at Wave Studios – which used to be in Hoxton Square – not far from The Garden. He'd worked with Jim on *Nail* and also with Coil on *Scatology*. We did some demo sessions at The Garden to test our compatibility. The first track we worked on was 'Heartland'. Warne's a lovely guy, talented and conscientious but it took time for me to adjust because whereas Paul was humorous and playful, Warne was more introspective – at least in those days he was – he's a wild man these days! – so it took a little while to establish our relationship. The demo session went well at The Garden but Warne didn't want to continue working there as he preferred Livingstone Studios in North London. I'd much preferred The Garden on every level to be honest – but I agreed to his request as he knew Livingstone well and felt happier there.

I met with Roli around the same time. He was Swiss, a former drummer with Swans and just starting to get into production and engineering. In those days he lived in a beautiful loft on Watts Street in TriBeCa, Manhattan, with his first wife. He had a very original thought process and a great vibe. Very funny – especially after a few drinks! Whilst initially I was meeting with Warne and Roli to find just the one person to finish the entire record with, I found I liked them both so much I just couldn't decide between them, so I decided to work with both but on different tracks. With Roli, there were two tracks: 'Sweet Bird of Truth' – a lot of which was recorded in New York – and 'Twilight Of A Champion'. The four tracks I did with Warne were: 'Heartland', 'Out Of The Blue (into the fire)', 'Slow Train To Dawn', and 'Infected'.

JW: You like a nice working environment, people to relax, you've got a bit of a sense of humour.

MJ: Yes, contrary to what people outside of my inner circle might think, I like working in a playful, easy-going environment. I don't like working with people – or in atmospheres – that are uptight.

The best ideas come when people are relaxed. You have to feel comfortable with people in order to make mistakes without fear of judgement.

JW: You see it with the people you work with now. People you obviously like working with.

MJ: You can't be in an environment where you're frightened of trying things out. If you find yourself in a situation where you're too nervous about making any wrong moves you won't make any *right* moves either.

As far as recording studios for *Infected*, there were quite a few involved. Warne, Roli and Gary all had their favourite studios and I respected their choices. With Gary we'd worked primarily at Air Studios – the original one on Oxford Circus. I loved that studio, one of my favourites. Originally set up by George Martin, it was incredibly well-equipped and well-maintained, beautiful sounding live rooms, wonderful staff, a great location too – right on top of Oxford Circus looking down on the bright lights and busy people. I also worked at SARM West and Metropolis Studios with Gary too.

Warne favoured Livingstone Studios, which was up in Wood Green, North London. I was at that time living in Stoke Newington and used to drive there each day. Back then it was relatively easy to drive in London compared to the nightmare of today with all the traffic cameras, blocked-off roads, draconian speed limits and endless penalties and money traps. Livingstone was a decent studio – nice staff and competitive rates – but too vibeless for my taste. But Warne felt comfortable there and we primarily recorded the four tracks he worked on there and mixed at Comforts Place in Surrey – which was my first experience of a residential studio. A great place, also with good equipment and nice staff.

Roli requested we work at Unique Studios near Times Square in New York as he'd worked there quite a bit and knew the staff well. This was fine by me as I loved recording in Manhattan and it was highly enjoyable being perched above Times Square, peering down at the chaos. Across the various sessions, we did additional work at The Garden plus a few days at a place called the Wool Hall near Frome in Somerset – which was owned by Tears for Fears I believe. Also, Warne and I did some additional recording at Air Studios.

JW: There was another track that you recorded before you did 'Heartland', called 'Flesh & Bones'. That was on a compilation.

MJ: That was with Paul Hardiman. It was post-*Soul Mining* and was supposed to be the start of the new album project. That was a very strong track as far as I was concerned. It ended up appearing on the second Some Bizzare compilation album *If You Can't Please Yourself You Can't Please Your Soul* – but it really deserved to be on a proper THE THE album. That was the last time Paul and I worked together, sadly. That was also recorded in The Garden and featured my brand-new PPG Wave 2.2 synthesizer, which cost me £5,500 – a fortune in those days. I think that was the only recording I ever used it on!

JW: Have you still got it?

MJ: Yes, I do actually but I'm in the process of selling it as it never gets used.

JW: When you sell something like that, you always regret it.

MJ: Hmm, I don't know about that. I'm at the stage where I've got far too many guitars, keyboards and other bits of equipment.
'Flesh & Bones' intentionally shared some lyrics with 'Heartland'. I sometimes reference my own songs in my lyrics – and occasionally other peoples' writings too. So, 'The cranes are moving on the skyline,' reappeared in 'Heartland'. It has become more and more pertinent unfortunately. At one point recently, I counted sixty cranes just from my own rooftop. Sixty! It is tragic what has happened to London.

JW: I remember seeing *The Inertia Variations*, and I don't think that lyric is repeated in the documentary, but that's immediately what I thought of when you're up on your roof and you look out.

MJ: It is out of control. The planning process in London is venal and corrupt.

JW: Was 'Heartland' the first song you wrote for *Infected*?

MJ: Yes. It took a long time to finish those lyrics and they were written across eighteen months. I'm not sure if the phrase about Britain being the fifty-first state of the USA had ever been used before I first wrote down those lyrics in 1984. I'd never heard it said before it popped into my mind but it is quite an obvious thing to state I suppose. It's been fascinating – and disturbing – to watch how easily and completely British culture has been subsumed into America's during my lifetime. Even our most cherished traditions morphed into their American equivalents: Father Christmas became Santa Claus, 'Penny for the Guy' gave way to Halloween's 'trick or treat'. Our language shifted too – birds and blokes all became 'guys'. Even the V-sign – that ubiquitous insulting hand gesture – has been replaced by the American middle finger. Our high streets are filled with American chain stores and franchises, our TV screens are saturated with American imports – essentially an alien culture. We've also imported 'Black Friday' – the chaotic shopping spree dressed up as a holiday tradition. Restaurants in London now offer Thanksgiving dinners. No doubt we'll soon be fully celebrating the 4th of July and Independence Day! Our political interests and foreign policy have been completely re-aligned to match Washington's. The coloniser has become the colonised. Britain and Europe have been under American occupation since the end of World War Two so, I suppose it was inevitable that the local cultures would slowly disappear. As a character in Wim Wender's *Kings of The Road* opined, 'The Yanks have colonised our subconscious!' Is there even such a thing as British culture anymore? Any social cohesion brought about by shared cultural references apart from all watching the same shows on Netflix?

Not far from where I live in London sit the UK headquarters of several big American tech firms and financial institutions. I often see young Americans striding about with easy confidence – a sight that puts me in mind of the days of the British Raj, when a small class of expatriate administrators from the East India Company ruled the subcontinent on behalf of the Crown, living in enclaves of familiar comforts. Today it is Big Tech and Finance that seem to govern the old continent on Washington's behalf, with these bright young American administrators learning their trade in London's digital colony, surrounded by the familiar comforts of Starbucks, Whole Foods and co-working sanctuaries, before returning home to the Empire's true capital.

JW: What was the easiest song to write on *Infected*?

MJ: Lyrically, 'Infected' was probably the simplest song. In fact, I didn't finish the lyrics until we were mixing at Comforts Place! We were due to start mixing it one morning but I still didn't have the bloody lyrics finished. So, I sat up scribbling late at night and early the following morning. Lyrically, 'Infected' was a bit of a knock-off song to be honest. An easy one to write in some ways. It's not one of my best lyrics. But sonically it was very powerful and served its purpose.

JW: It goes back to that idea of something you revisit in 'Dogs Of Lust', that idea of love and desire not being pleasurable, but almost a burden. I think a lot of people saw it as a parable for AIDS, because it was around that time.

MJ: I certainly wouldn't describe love and desire as not being pleasurable, but they're definitely more complex and conflicting than we're led to believe when young. And yes, *Infected* being released at the height of the AIDS epidemic certainly caused the record to 'chime with the times' in more ways than one.

JW: The Wool Hall is where The Smiths used to work, wasn't it?

MJ: I believe so. Roli and I worked on 'Twilight Of A Champion' there. I remember around this time I bought what I call my 'rock star car,' which was a beautiful jet-black BMW 635 Alpina – a Grand Tourer. So bloody fast! Roli and I would drive to and from the studio in that.

JW: My brother had a red one. Just the shape of those cars. Incredible. They're a fortune now, they're so collectible.

MJ: I sold mine for not much money a few years later because, well, that's a long story…

JW: My brother crashed his.

MJ: I nearly crashed mine! Fiona's family are Scottish – live in Montrose – and we'd often go up there to visit. So, I'd just bought this car and we took it for a holiday ride up there. It was lovely driving around the mysterious Loch Ness and the various beautiful villages en route. Anyway, on the way back to London on a fairly empty motorway I'm thinking, let's see how fast this car can really go. So, I put my foot down, up the bonnet rose and in no time the speedometer was reading 130mph and – because it was the Alpina version – it would've gone faster too. Now, when I was younger I was a bit of a mad driver – I'd written off three cars by the age of 21 – I was a naughty boy and I loved speed. So, we're going faster and faster and my palms are starting to sweat – 130mph – but then the weirdest thing happens. In the rear view mirror a car suddenly appears and starts flashing its headlights. I instantly thought it was the police, 'Fuck me, they want me to pull over!' The thing is, when you're going 130mph you come up so fast to someone in front who is only going 70mph – the legal speed limit – it's very dangerous. So, I wondered – for someone to have almost instantly appeared in my rear-view mirror – who the hell were they and how fast were *they* going? I pulled over to the middle lane expecting to see blue flashing lights and being ordered onto the hard shoulder – but instead, it was a woman in a Mercedes estate who simply glided past, fixed hairdo, blank expression, cool as you like – one lady in a hurry. She must have been doing nearly 150mph! I was half tempted to put on a chase to see how fast my new car really could go – but the whole experience made me feel queasy and anxious. My heart was pounding, my palms were sweating. At those speeds you'd have no chance of controlling the car if something went wrong – no chance of surviving a crash. I really didn't like it. That moment totally changed my feelings about driving fast – or even owning a fast car.

The other thing I didn't like was that having a car that was considered quite flash, people would get very jealous – run their keys down the bodywork when it was parked or pull up beside me at traffic lights, trying to stare me out, wanting to race – or at junctions they would just never let me out. It's as if you're some kind of a threat to them. I'm talking about male drivers here not females. Something insecure about boys and their toys I suppose.

JW: There's a lovely line in *The Inertia Variations* where you're in your old Rover and I think you're driving down to your dad's. I think you say something like, 'I'm going to get there at the same time.'

MJ: Yes, that's my old Rover P5B. Shortly after *Infected* came out I owned two cars, the BMW plus an old Rover P5B. I'd loved those old cars since childhood – they were famously used by prime ministers, diplomats and royalty. I've owned a couple over the years – saloon and coupe versions. When I started driving the old Rover I noticed how people would simply smile and wave and let me out at junctions, rather than try to race me or scratch up my bodywork. I could only drive slowly now – of course – but it made the experience so much more pleasurable. I was no longer a threat to other drivers' manhood, just a harmless curio pottering slowly along the road.

JW: Says a lot about people, doesn't it? People treat you nicely.

MJ: It does. I thought, you know what? I prefer this. I'm in an old, understated car that's not capable of racing anyone. Everyone's just waving and smiling. I prefer life in the slow lane. It could be a metaphor for life. Actually, I remember once Andrew and I were driving along a country lane and some impatient driver was trying to overtake. Andrew remarked that all of us think everyone else on the road is driving either too fast or too slow, but that *we* are driving at just the right speed. It's quite a profound thought if you extrapolate it to every other aspect of human life. Most of us think other people's food is too spicy, salty or bland but that *we* add just the right amount of seasoning to our own food. You can apply it to politics too. We all believe our own political views are just plain common sense but that everyone else is either too far to the right or too far to the left. We each have our own truth, shaped by our personal experiences, the era we live in, and the information we've been exposed to.

JW: Exactly. So, you were testing out recording studios…

MJ: Yes, between the collaborations with Gary, Warne and Roli on *Infected* we worked in lots of studios: London, New York and the English countryside. I'd also invested in a lot of recording equipment and instruments for that album, including an early computer sequencer. As I said, on *Soul Mining* there were no sequencers, it was all hand-played but for *Infected* I purchased a UMI-2B sequencer that ran on one of those old BBC Acorn computers. Laughably weedy when compared to the Logic Pro and Pro Tools DAWs of today. But, of course, they in time will also seem laughably weedy.

Those early personal computers were very puny but it was all we had access to. I've always enjoyed being on the 'bleeding edge' of technology and during that period I owned a Sinclair Spectrum, a Commodore 64, the BBC Acorn and then the Atari 1040ST – which was by far the best of the bunch. But for 'Twilight Of A Champion' we used the very, very basic UMI-2B sequencer system

– it was painstaking work and took us forever to program. It would've been easier just to play everything live like I did with the previous album! But Roli took a masochistic delight in programming arcane pieces of equipment. We then decided to record a real brass section on that track and brought in the talented Andrew Poppy to do the arrangement for us. I can't recall how we met Andrew – maybe Stevo or someone else from Some Bizzare knew him – but he was a highly talented up-and-coming classical composer–arranger and did a brilliant job. He also signed to ZTT around this time I believe. As far as some of the other collaborators, there was Tessa Niles, a very experienced backing singer who Warne was friendly with. She provided backing vocals not only on 'Heartland', but 'Out Of The Blue (into the fire)' and 'Angels Of Deception'.

JW: The backing vocals on 'Out Of The Blue (Into The Fire)' are particularly good.

MJ: She was terrific. We also brought in Neneh Cherry to duet on 'Slow Train To Dawn'. That came about because I loved her vocals on *Kill Me In The Morning* by Float Up CP; an offshoot of Rip Rig + Panic, who in turn were affiliated with The Pop Group – who I used to watch live.

JW: Did you work with their drummer Bruce Smith?

MJ: I knew Bruce socially; we'd sometimes bump into each other at night clubs and I always liked him – he was together with Neneh around that time, or they'd recently split up. But yes, Bruce and I worked together a few years later on *Dusk*.

JW: Neneh has gone on to become a really interesting artist as well.

MJ: Yes, she's become involved in films too in recent years, hasn't she?

JW: Yes, she made a film with Mark Cousins titled *Stockholm My Love* (2016). But she's also one of those artists that seems to have been less worried about being explicitly commercial and wanted to make records that she likes.

MJ: Maybe the influence of her dad, Don Cherry, and the uncompromising career he had.

JW: She had that big hit, 'Buffalo Stance', and then she made *Home Brew* (1992), a record involving her partner, Cameron McVey. But then she did records such as *The Cherry Thing* (2012) which includes a great version of Suicide's 'Dream Baby Dream'. Some people knew Rip Rig + Panic, but I think it was 'Slow Train To Dawn' that really brought her wider attention.

MJ: Neneh was fun to work with and I really liked her, a warm and smart person. We had a good time meeting up before we made the record, and also during the recording and the making of the video too. She was definitely game for a laugh.

We had lots of interesting musicians and singers work on that album. The wonderful Anna Domino, Ashley Slater, John Thirkell, Guy Barker and Luís Jardim. Steve Hogarth played the piano solo on 'Heartland' and went on to become the lead singer in Marillion. We even had Jeff Clyne, who'd played the legendary opening bass riff on 'Carter Takes A Train' on *Get Carter*, to perform upright bass on 'Out Of The Blue (into the fire)', itself a comment on the underground sex world and a subtle nod to one of my favourite films.

We had a lot of laughs in the various studios where the album was made. I know some people may find that hard to believe, because I've been assigned the reputation of being miserable and over-earnest.

JW: I don't understand how you got that.

MJ: Well, it's partially lazy journalism but let's be honest, no one forced me to write about the subject matter I do! Now, I mention the following conversation because it seems so pertinent now even though it was many years before the Internet.

When I was about 22 it was arranged for me to have dinner with Leonard Cohen. We shared the same lawyer at the time – Marty Machat. Marty said he wanted 'Lenny' – as he called him – to advise me on my career. So, Leonard spoke about a number of things but one thing that stood out was his advice to try and avoid being pigeon-holed early in my career, because it would cast a very long shadow that would be very hard to escape from. The interesting thing is that he complained that it was as if there was a giant computer filing system somewhere and that every time a journalist typed in the words Leonard and Cohen then up popped a page full of pejorative adjectives; 'gloomy', 'depressed', etc. He was actually laughing whilst he was saying this and said he'd now resigned himself to his fate, but advised me to try and avoid it. Well, the same thing has since happened to me! On many Internet searches the adjectives most commonly attached to my name are now probably 'gloomy', 'melancholy', 'serious', etc. And of course, now I'm the one laughing at the absurdity of it all because anyone that really knows me knows this is the polar opposite of who I really am. But it was interesting how he described the future Internet.

JW: I think there was also a class thing amongst British music journalists as well.

MJ: There definitely were sections of the British music press back then who could be sneery and quite patronising towards many bands – who tended to come from working-class backgrounds. But fast forward in time and nowadays being in a band has become a respectable middle-class career move. They even flock to colleges and universities to learn how to be in a band or how to work in a recording studio. I find it all quite absurd. To me, the most vital, visceral music will always be created under more stressful conditions and by people who do not want to do anything else – or more accurately who *cannot* do anything else – with music being their only escape route in life rather than a safe, sanitised 'career move' their parents paid for and approved of.

JW: Do you think there was also jealousy stemming from the fact you are self-taught?

MJ: No, I doubt it. But a working-class truant who established himself on his own terms possibly did irritate some people.

JW: I think people are sometimes suspicious of that. I've got notes on each song, but I also want to talk – because you mentioned this with *Soul Mining* and it struck a chord – about your increasing political awareness.

You started to talk on *Soul Mining*, in the lyrics, about state propaganda, becoming vessels for information that we're just fed. Obviously *Soul Mining* was written and released shortly after the time of the coming to power of Thatcherism. I think if you ask anybody that's interested in music to name an LP that really deals with the rise of Thatcher and Thatcher's Britain, they would pick *Infected*. You were obviously sensing this disregard for the working classes, Thatcher's wiping out of age-old industries, looking after the people with money and power. You decided to address this – explicitly I think on 'Heartland'. I think that's a song that really paints a portrait of Britain that probably feels like Britain is now, actually.

MJ: With regards to Thatcherism and Tory contempt towards the working class: well, how do you get turkeys to vote for Christmas? You convince them they are *not* turkeys. The Tories convinced the working class to continually vote against their own interests, deluding them into believing they were not really working class at all. Thatcher plugged into people's *aspirations*, not their reality. In certain ways these old songs are depressingly still relevant, and have been depressingly relevant since I wrote them. I'd much rather they be considered relics of a bygone age that are completely irrelevant.

JW: The thing that's terrifying is that they're not, are they?

MJ: As a father I want my children – and everyone else's children – to grow up in a happier and more peaceful country and world. You must feel the same?

JW: Yes, I feel *exactly* the same, as most parents would I hope.

In 'Heartland' you point out the relationship between America and Britain: 'This is the fifty-first state of the USA,' which is obviously a famous lyric you came up with. You must have been angry at seeing what was being done to this country, and as you've said, the thing that's most upsetting about a song like that is that we don't seem to have moved on from it.

MJ: No, we haven't in certain important respects. For decades now – whether the Tories or Labour are in power – UK foreign policy has followed the lead of Washington's neoconservatives*. I was brought up in a Labour household. *Old* Labour that is – not the disappointment *New* Labour became. Brought up with what I would consider simple, common-sense values: humanity, empathy, anti-war, fairness, caring about the society we inhabit together. Nothing radical or extreme. Very moderate in fact. This in comparison to the new world Thatcherism helped usher in – an ideology of 'no such thing as society' and every person for themselves.

JW: In a 1987 interview with *Woman's Own* Thatcher did say: 'There is no such thing as society. There are just individual men and women, and there are familes.'

MJ: Maybe the meaning of what she said has been misunderstood or quoted out of context over the years, but Reaganomics and Thatcherism mid-wifed the birth of neoconservatism in the West. It is an ideology that has since grown more extreme and infiltrated political parties on the right of the spectrum in the US, UK and elsewhere, whilst its twin – neoliberalism† – has infected the erstwhile parties of the so-called left of the spectrum such as the Democrats in America and New Labour in the UK. Now faux left really.

---

* Neoconservatism typically advocates interventionism in international relations together with a militaristic philosophy.
† Neoliberalism typically advocates deregulation, privatisation, monetarism, austerity and globalisation.

JW: It is certainly not the Labour Party we knew from our childhoods. I'm not sure who they really represent anymore.

MJ: No, nor am I. There has been a consolidation of power of the neoconservatives/neoliberals into a sort of 'Uni-Party' which appears to have hijacked many political parties. We all know about the former – and its far-right roots – and the latter is what I'd call the 'extreme centre' or faux left. They have managed to convince much of the electorate that that they are moderate when in fact they are extremists: pro-war, pro-privatisation and completely intolerant of views they do not like. They hide behind the fig leaf of identity politics in order to get a free pass amongst the faux left generation.

This 'Uni-Party' has infiltrated major parties on both sides of the Atlantic. Just think back a few years to when Tony Blair – supposedly a British Labour prime minister – and George W. Bush, an American Republican President, led their respective countries. Their foreign policies were nearly identical as both dragged us into the illegal war against Iraq. A few years later, compare the foreign policies of David Cameron, a British Conservative prime minister, and Barack Obama, an American Democratic president. Their foreign policies were also identical – not only to each other but also to their predecessors – as they involved the West in further illegal conflict, this time against Libya and Syria. The same situation now exists for most western European governments too. They are all taking orders from the same entities – the supranational institutions – above national governments which ultimately control the 'permanent state' of the respective governments of the collective West. So, we see the same playbook followed regardless of which party is 'officially' in government: The Forever Wars,* the Color Revolutions and the regime-change operations, and the pillaging and privatisation of resources of poorer countries continues unabated.

---

* The term Forever Wars refers to open-ended, decades-long military engagements such as Afghanistan and Iraq, sustained without clear victory or exit; as Orwell wrote in 1984, 'The war is not meant to be won, it is meant to be continuous.'

JW: And where do you think Britain in the 21st century fits in with all of this?

MJ: Well, the old institutions in Britain still stand, but their purpose has shifted. It's left the old Britain we remember from our childhood and youth feeling like a museum exhibit. Many grand old buildings still stand in London for instance – a sense of history lingers in the remaining architecture, but the substance behind it has faded. Façadism is a property developer's trick that's grown fashionable over recent decades. In order to circumvent conservation rules, a few inches of the frontage of a historic building are left standing whilst everything else about it is demolished and replaced by something entirely different and new. The physical skyline of London is now symbolic of the neo-liberal chaos that has infected the country and you can see it in many of its institutions too, including the NHS, the BBC, Royal Mail and others. Britain may *seem* the same in many ways, in that many of the old structures *seem* to remain, but the original purpose has been stripped out of most. Britain as a country has been 'façaded'.

JW: Yes, it does seem like that. The Britain that has been revealed in recent years does not seem to be the Britain any of us voted for.

MJ: I think there is a sense of powerlessness amongst the electorate, because, in reality, we're living through times where the public are being phased out of the democratic process, which has devolved into a type of corporate oligarchy, where elections are little more than staged pantomimes with pre-selected candidates, the winners of which go on to do the bidding of their donors. This illusion of choice is maintained to allow the public to periodically let off steam, to vent their anger at Government A or Government B. But, aside from some cosmetic changes, policy remains fundamentally unchanged regardless of who wins. Democracy is the lie we have been told to stop revolution. I've met quite a few local and national politicians over the years. Many are good, decent people who got involved in politics to really try to make a positive difference. But unfortunately, the system is so rigged that those who try to stick to their principles can find themselves marginalised whilst the morally flexible may find it easier to ascend the greasy pole of power. Some call the unseen force behind governments the 'deep state', but I think it is more accurately described as the 'permanent state'. No matter who you vote for the State always wins! And – as for certain politicians – it's not so much that power *corrupts* but more a case that power *attracts* highly corruptible people. And highly corruptible people are easier to blackmail and control. Psychopaths seem to dominate global power structures just as short people dominate horse racing and tall people dominate basketball.

JW: We might actually be better off with jockeys and basketball players in charge of our government!

MJ: I actually think you might be on to something! They couldn't do much worse, could they? But what can you do? Protest seems a bit pointless these days, I still sometimes go on marches even though we all know deep down it no longer makes much difference and that it's just another of those façades – those pretences – that we are still living in a free society that values freedom of speech and expression. I suppose going on a march is still a good thing to do from time to time – even if just for the sociable aspect and the exercise!

JW: It's a good thing to do for your own understanding that you still believe in something.

MJ: Maybe. My dad went on marches up until he couldn't do them anymore. A couple of years before he died he was still going on them. It made him feel that he was amongst like-minded people and trying to do *something*. Although that reminds me of a funny story about my dad. He loved his food and on one march – which happened to be heading along Piccadilly – he broke away and sneaked into Fortnum & Masons for some afternoon tea and cakes as the march carried on without him. It made me and my brothers chuckle.

Thinking about the eighties again, there were other songs around that time that also provided a snapshot of Britain under Thatcherism, notably 'Ghost Town' by The Specials and 'Shipbuilding', the Elvis Costello and Clive Langer song performed by Robert Wyatt.

JW: Again, Elvis Costello was someone that really skewered what Thatcher was about, songs like 'Tramp the Dirt Down', from *Spike* (1989). But 'Shipbuilding' along with 'Heartland' are *the* songs about broken Britain, aren't they? The dichotomy becomes clear if you were tp listen to 'Heartland' without the lyrics. It's got the guitar—

MJ: —the piano and harmonica solos.

JW: It's quite a folk song.

MJ: Yes, I suppose it is. Talking of the instrumentation, I was always very happy with the strings on that track. A notable technical aspect of writing/recording *Infected* was that – as mentioned earlier – I'd bought an Emulator 2, one of the first in the UK, that cost me a small fortune at the time of £9,000. That really shaped the sound of the album. I wrote the string parts for 'Heartland' on the Emulator 2, Warne arranged them and we then brought in a real string section to play them. Owning that machine – one of the first 'affordable' samplers – helped give the album quite a widescreen, cinematic feel, because I could suddenly create ambitious demos in my own little studio. I also knew we had the budget to hire real string and brass sections to help bring the album to life.

The 1980s is a decade I look back upon with mixed emotions – there is a lot I hated about the '80s in general, but for me personally it was a spectacular decade. I was in a happy relationship, earning good money for the first time, had bought my own flat, owned nice cars, was travelling the world and starting to establish a successful international career. But that didn't take away from my feeling that much of the rest of the country was being fucked. I felt saddened and horrified about what was happening towards large sections of the population – the working class, public servants

– all the lies endlessly repeated as the country was being prepared for asset-stripping.

JW: That goes back to upbringing, doesn't it?

MJ: Yes, it does.

JW: If you're proper Labour you care about your fellow humanity, don't you? You don't just think, I've done alright.

MJ: Exactly, and that's really bothered me. Particularly with the working-class Tories.

JW: That's why we've got Brexit.

MJ: The Brexit conundrum is more nuanced though as there was – and is – a lot of anger from many ordinary people towards both the unelected elite in Brussels – who do seem self-serving and unaccountable – as well as towards the self-serving and unaccountable elite in Westminster. Actually, I hate the term elite – more like parasite class! Part of the problem is that the working class were deserted by New Labour, who took their vote and support for granted and who – under the likes of Blair – set about seducing the middle class instead. The working class were deserted and consequently felt ignored and betrayed. There are many layers to this going back decades and the rise of the working-class Tories, the followers of Thatcher and readers of *the Sun* – all coinciding with Murdoch's ruthless grip on media power and convincing working people to vote against their own interests – convincing people there's no such thing as community, that it doesn't matter anymore about your neighbours or the community you live in.

JW: I think that was the worst thing with Thatcher, actually – this idea that community doesn't matter.

MJ: Yes, horrendous. But now, the governments and oppositions we're saddled with are so uninspiring that one almost ends up pining for the bad old days of Thatcher. At least you knew where you stood. Many of the West's contemporary political figures seem less like independent leaders and more like quislings for unaccountable networks – such as the World Economic Forum's 'Young Global Leaders' programme* – acting as administrators, or gophers, for Establishment interests. Take Sir Keir Starmer: his past professional connections, including those to the security world and organisations like the Trilateral Commission,† raise questions that, to me, the mainstream media shows surprisingly little curiosity about. It seems plausible he was cultivated by Establishment circles as a future prime minister. After all, receiving a knighthood at such a relatively young age could be interpreted as recognition for services rendered – or perhaps for services expected.

JW: I was talking to my wife about this. Thatcher was evil, but at least she actually believed in politics and she believed in what she was doing, right or wrong. The politicians we've got now, they're just crooks.

MJ: I don't get the impression any current leaders of the West really believe in anything at all but power and profit – both for themselves and for those they *really* represent – which doesn't appear to be the populations they are elected to serve. Going back to the British governments of the 1980s there were some members – some of the old Tory wets – that at least had a bit of humanity.

JW: Michael Heseltine turned out to be relatively human.

MJ: There were a few of those that in retrospect don't seem too bad, What annoyed so many about the Matt Hancock affair – the former Health Secretary during the COVID-19 pandemic – was

---

* The World Economic Forum's Young Global Leaders programme brings together promising leaders under 40 from business, politics, and civil society to collaborate on global initiatives and public policy.
† The Trilateral Commission, founded by David Rockefeller, is a non-governmental forum promoting cooperation among North America, Europe, and Asia on political and economic issues.

that he should have resigned months earlier. By then, widespread reporting had already highlighted serious conflicts-of-interest concerns, questionable procurement decisions, and a series of pandemic measures that many saw as confused, heavy-handed, or damaging to public wellbeing. On top of all that, he was only forced out because he was caught having an affair.

JW: Doesn't that say something about this country? The thing that forces him to resign is the fact that he's caught having an affair, not his political failures. That's the worst.

The other thing with 'Heartland' is, I think it was the first single from *Infected*, and it was a hit.

MJ: It was the second single. 'Sweet Bird Of Truth' was the first but that was instantly banned by BBC Radio 1 because of the outbreak of violence in the Middle East happening at the time of its release. 'Heartland' was also initially banned but then we did a radio edit to remove the word 'piss' from the lyric 'piss-stinking shopping centre'.

The odd thing with 'Heartland' is that it could've been top 10 – it scraped inside the top 30 – but at the time of its release CBS was in dispute with many high street record chains – some distribution argument and complication – so you could only buy it in selected outlets. It was all a bit of a disaster for that release. It received a huge amount of radio play and interest and lingered in the charts for weeks. But I was destined to be an album artist not a singles artist, which is fine by me.

Also, I think 'Heartland' should've probably been called 'The 51st State' because people were referring to it as that rather than its actual title so that created confusion. Anyway, I made mistakes and its release was cursed by bad luck.

JW: I remember the first time I heard that track it was in conjunction with the video. You were a good-looking boy back then, you had your Levi's on and your white shirt; there's a bit of a reference to Bruce Springsteen's 'Born In The USA' in the video. Even though it didn't do as well as you hoped, it was a successful single. But it was also an indicator of deep politics on the album. Because *Infected* doesn't just look at politics on a national level, it really looks at it on a global level. It talks about Reagan and the bombing of Libya. It feels to me that this is a record where you're also writing about love and desire, but you're writing about politics on a wider scale.

MJ: That's because of the realisation Britain had essentially become a vassal-state of Washington. So, then you start to tug on this thread: where is this all leading? This was all pre-Internet of course and access to information was limited, and obviously I'm not an academic or an economist, just a working-class songwriter trying to figure out what the hell is happening in the world and who or what is the real power structure behind the façade of our elected governments.

I looked at the policies that were formulated out of the Washington think-tanks at that time – also from the Chicago School of Economics* and the likes of Milton Friedman† and the free-market economic theories that basically were the bedrock of the neoconservatives, Reaganomics and Thatcherism. They tried it in places like Chile first before rolling it out across the West. Two decades after *Infected* was released Naomi Klein wrote a book *The Shock Doctrine* (2007) which detailed this. You realise: not only are they doing this around the world against other populations but they are now doing it against their *own* populations too. Politics is no longer national but supranational and there are multiple layers of control way above the paygrade of the politicians we supposedly vote into office to act on our behalf.

The UK and US, bound together in a weird, lopsided 'special relationship', actually both seem less like nations these days and more like cogs in a larger, supranational machine – one that operates with a kind of ruthless, psychopathic detachment.

---

* The Chicago School denotes a University of Chicago tradition advocating free-market economics and limited state intervention (UChicago Economics Dept.).
† Milton Friedman (1912–2006), a leading figure of the Chicago School, advanced theories of monetarism and argued strongly for deregulation and market-driven policy (Friedman, *Capitalism and Freedom*, 1962).

I started taking more of an interest in politics generally around this time – on local, national and international levels – and of course you soon start to realise the level of corruption is big even on the local level. National level too, of course; but on the international level, it's even more massively corrupt. Democracy is a façade. If you were alive during Roman times and living somewhere in the Empire your eyes would be looking towards the capitol for answers, towards Rome. In our day and age all roads lead to and from Washington, DC and the various think-tanks and foundations that formulate foreign policy that are based there. There are many of these of course, with the most visible ones probably being the Council on Foreign Relations, the Trilateral Commission, the RAND Corporation and the Brookings Institute.

Over in the UK we've got Chatham House AKA the Royal Institute for International Affairs amongst others. These numerous secretive foundations and think-tanks are what dictate western foreign policy – or rather the vast international financial institutions, entities and individuals behind them. All of this is going on behind closed doors of course, plans being drawn up for countries but without involving the populace at all. Then we hear the usual marketing spiel of the benefits of policies like 'public-private partnership', which is just a euphemism for getting the public to pay for everything whilst it is then all privately owned – and all by the same entities who fund the politicians to enable this parasitical legislation to get passed in the first place.

JW: Agreed! So, with 'Sweet Bird Of Truth', did it give CBS, especially in America, cause for concern?

MJ: The single was withdrawn soon after release even though – at that point – 9/11 obviously hadn't happened and terrorism hadn't gone completely off the scale. The first time I came across media sensitivity with my songs in America was when I was hosting a show on MTV called *120 Minutes*. I was given the opportunity to play *Infected: The Movie* in its entirety – and discuss my political thoughts in between the videos. I was sat in a chair, talking direct to camera. I was making statements about certain aspects of US and UK foreign policy and its negative impact upon the rest of the world and possible consequences but, as it was being broadcast, there was a banner running across the bottom of the screen: 'The views you are hearing are not the views of MTV.' But at least they allowed me on to say such things. Nowadays I probably wouldn't be allowed as censorship across the board runs so deep – including on social media. I might even be cancelled.

But anyway, 'Sweet Bird Of Truth' was the first single from *Infected* and we wanted to make a quick video using real news footage from the war in the Middle East. Fiona was working for ITN at this point and had contacts with people who were gathering footage from Beirut and elsewhere in the region. So, one evening I was up at the ITN news offices reviewing some of this footage – very dramatic and shocking, of bombings etc. and they were going to give us permission to use some of it for the promotion of the single. It is obviously an anti-war song but then – literally that week – there were a couple of events that changed everything. Reagan and the US bombed Libya* – talk about life imitating art! And there was the awful kidnapping of John McCarthy.† He was a journalist who worked for an international news agency and it sent shockwaves through the media. The people at ITN who were going to give us permission to use the footage then basically said, 'No, this is just too much of a hot potato now. We can't allow you to use any of this stuff.' The topic was becoming too delicate and the BBC banned 'Sweet Bird Of Truth'. There are no swear words in it or anything, but the subject matter just became too sensitive as emotions across the region were inflamed. CBS were even advised by the security services to remove the American flag that was on the roof of their London Soho Square offices.

---

* The United States carried out air strikes, code-named Operation El Dorado Canyon, against Libya in April 1986 in retaliation for the West Berlin discotheque bombing ten days earlier, which US president Ronald Reagan blamed on Libyan leader Muammar Gaddafi.
† John McCarthy, a British journalist, writer and broadcaster, was working for United Press International when he was kidnapped. He was the longest-held captive in the Lebanon hostage crisis, imprisoned for more than five years.

JW: I used to constantly play 'Sweet Bird Of Truth'. 'This is your captain calling.' I love the way you used vocal distortion. It's obviously the voice of a pilot, and there's a narrative. I love that telling of a story. A bit like Bowie I suppose with *Space Oddity* (1969).

MJ: The human voice is so expressive and I've never understood why it shouldn't also be put through effects like guitars and keyboards. Since *Burning Blue Soul* I've often played with creative equalization – sometimes sculpting mid-range sounds, then adding distortions and delays. I've found on tour that rather than have our front-of-house engineer change the sound on one microphone, it's more interesting to use three – it creates a more dramatic visual effect and is easy to switch between from my end.

JW: Obviously, in that song, you're writing from the perspective of a pilot. You philosophically deal with religion in some of your songs and the lyric 'I ain't ever been to church or believed in Jesus Chris / But I'm praying that God's with you when you die' sends shivers down the spine.

MJ: I was at a party in the US a couple of years after this was first released when I got introduced to a young American Air Force pilot – and this stuck in my mind – he'd recently returned from a tour of duty, flying combat aircraft in the Middle East, and he said, 'I just want to tell you that I listen to your song 'Sweet Bird Of Truth' all the time.' He'd actually been in a similar position to what I was trying to write about.

JW: It also deals with the inevitability of death, putting someone in the position of having to accept their fate.

MJ: I tried to convey that internal conflict; how much do you really believe in what you are being asked to die for? Evidently, many young service people are well-prepared to kill – particularly in this age of remote-control drone warfare. But how many are really prepared to die, especially on behalf of the greed of others?

I remember some key turning points when writing the song.

Firstly, finding the right chords for the chorus – I actually wrote this song on guitar – and once the chorus chords slipped into place then the melody soon followed. Secondly, I had all the lyrics strewn across the floor – as usual – but I couldn't seem to get them connected in the right order. I was really… stuck. Just staring endlessly at the words, trying lots of different variations but nothing felt right. I realised I needed to change mindset so I dropped half an ecstasy tab and within an hour all the words had magically fallen into the right place – line by line.

JW: Magically fallen into the right place line by line? We might have to try the same technique to help edit this book!
Tell me about Anna Domino.

MJ: Anna is a very talented American singer–songwriter in her own right. During the promotion of *Soul Mining* I started asking people about female singers as I knew I wanted to use some on the next album. Anna's name came up a few times but people weren't sure if she was Belgian or American. Actually, she was a New Yorker who happened to be living in Brussels as she was signed to the Belgian label, Les Disques du Crépuscule. We arranged to meet and we had some crazy nights in Manhattan. She became a friend and we used to hang out. I really wanted her to sing on 'Sweet Bird Of Truth' – she created those beautiful harmonies for the backing vocals on the choruses. Very unearthly and eerie.

JW: There's also that great, scratchy guitar. It goes back to that post-punk sound.

MJ: My roots. Post-punk. Obviously, that was a big influence on me, many of the bands of that era. But the technology was changing. *Infected* was my first digital album, whereas *Soul Mining* was completely analogue. I think, looking back, there are changes I would make to the production. Maybe it's a bit too brittle at points – but bear in mind, this is very early digital technology, 16-bit, 44.1kHz with those early, relatively primitive convertors. Also, the ubiquitous use of SSL desks at that time meant there could be a tendency to use compression and noise gates on every track, just because they were there. I think the temptation to use them proved too great and consequently controlled the sound too much rather than allowing it to breathe. In fact, one of the reasons SSL desks became so popular was due to their computer recall function. Many A&R departments insisted bands made their records on them as it was then supposedly easier to get mix tweaks – bass drum up by a decibel in the chorus etc. A pain in the backside.

JW: We've mentioned the engineers and producers working on different tracks, and we've mentioned some of the specific tracks. 'Angels Of Deception', which Gary Langan produced. That seems to deal in part with Greenham Common*.

MJ: There is a small reference to that yes, 'He's stuck his missiles in your garden'. There are also many other elements mixed up in those lyrics, like the Chicago school of economics – 'And his theories down your throat'. Also, what was that game show with Leslie Crowther called? *The Price Is Right*. His catchphrase was, 'Come on down!' – which was very well known in those days. So, I added, 'The devil's in town' I sometimes reference my own lyrics or other songs, books or cultural catchphrases to add a bit of colour.

JW: What about the production and instrumentation of 'Angels Of Deception'?

MJ: We had Tessa Niles provide some great backing vocals, Palmer on drums, Luís Jardim – with some excellent percussion. I wanted it to feel quite unusual with the instrumentation so we used Jeff Clyne on upright bass and added strings too. My favourite part of the song is the intro and first verse. The word 'cinematic' comes to mind again. I think it was Johnny Marr's favourite song on this

---

* Greenham Common Women's Peace Camp was a series of protest camps established to protest against nuclear weapons being placed at RAF Greenham Common in Berkshire, England.

album – he loved it so we played it on the Versus The World Tour. It has quite a joyous outro, which meant it worked well live. But I've not played it live since. It's not a song that gets talked about much, but I do love the opening atmosphere and lyrics. It's quite humorous: 'Well, it's high noon at the UK Corral,' just using Wild West imagery and the idea of riding through the FM stations on a journey across the country – a bit like that old British indie film *Radio On*.* Of course, we had Reagan, this cowboy president, and these sinister theories being pushed forth by shadowy institutions. And the UK as Air Force One.

There's also an occult element to the lyrics too, of course, with the suggestion of fallen angels and an inverted, upside-down reality where nothing is really what it appears to be. To be honest, how can the fruits of western foreign policy – and the murder, maiming and displacement of millions of people in the last few decades alone – be described as anything but demonic? It is all deception and inversion. The slogan 'Freedom & Democracy' is now so threadbare and little more than a convenient advertising slogan, a kind of fig leaf upon what is, in reality, a vast, violent and unaccountable power structure. And yet, people still tend to listen more to what politicians *say* than to what they actually *do*. Take Barack Obama, for example, and the irony of him being awarded the Nobel Peace Prize at the start of his presidency. He soon increased US military spending and significantly expanded drone warfare and targeted assassinations – including operations that killed American citizens. Many analysts noted that the scale and reach of his administration's bombing campaigns exceeded even those of the Bush era in several theatres. Yet because he was telegenic and a skilled orator, people seemed not to notice – or at least not to mind

Anyway, I always felt 'Angels Of Deception' was a companion song to 'Heartland' as I had the two together in my mind as I was writing them; but 'Heartland' has since completely overshadowed it. 'Angels of Deception' was recorded at the same time as 'The Mercy Beat' which also alludes to the idea of demonic forces

---

* *Radio On* is a 1979 influential British road movie directed by Christopher Petit.

controlling from the shadows. They were both recorded at Air Studios and SARM West with Gary.

JW: I know we spoke about 'Slow Train To Dawn', mainly in terms of the Neneh Cherry vocal, but can I highlight another one of your lyrics which deals with the emotional burden of desire: 'Sometimes I get so lonesome I could die.'

MJ: That's obviously a reference to Hank Williams'* 'I'm So Lonesome I Could Cry'. My variation is a bit darker! Also, there's a lyric that appears in 'The Mercy Beat' as well as 'Slow Train To Dawn': 'I'm just another western guy / With desires that I can't satisfy.' That pretty much summed up how I was in those days. Drugs, sex and alcohol.

JW: The Holy Trinity! And what about 'Twilight Of A Champion'?

MJ: Or 'Twilight Of A Champignon' as Roli and I used to jokingly refer to it at the time. You know where I got that title from? Remember the old Sunday newspapers and their supplements? When they were worth reading (I haven't read them for decades) I used to buy the *Sunday Times* and *Observer* for their magazines – they used to be good, didn't they? The magazines at least, with incredible photography, investigative journalism and in-depth features. Well, there was a photo of Muhammad Ali on one of the covers – in his post-retirement years. The title on the cover was 'Twilight of a Champion'. Ali was one of my favourite people growing up. I loved him alongside John Lennon – both for their talent and their political courage. Anyway, this story was quite poignant as his powers were obviously fast draining away. But I squirreled away the title and thought, 'I'll find some use for that.'

Lyrically this song really dealt with the notion of personal corruption: at what point does it start, and where does it end? For

---

* Hank Williams was an American singer, songwriter and early pioneer of country music, regarded as one of the most significant and influential musicians of the 20th century.

me there was a certain amount of guilt coming from – not a poor family by any means – but a working-class family. I had a good childhood, we went on foreign holidays, we didn't want for things, we had toys. We weren't rich but, for certain periods of time, particularly in the 1960s when the Two Puddings was so successful, we were relatively comfortably off. But my parents never lost their working-class values and humility.

So, there was a bit of unease for me suddenly getting hold of money after years on the dole and maybe feeling a bit undeserving and conflicted about it. There was also the sense that I could definitely start to feel this newfound fame – and its financial rewards – starting to corrupt me a bit. Less-pleasant sides of my personality starting to reveal themselves. So, that interested me, this process of corruption. What are our individual thresholds? Are we all potentially corrupt and susceptible deep down – whether it relates to money, power, sex, drugs or a combination of all? Is there an event that happens personally that suddenly – almost like a break in a seal – allows all sorts of dark things to seep in and change a person permanently? With the opening lyrics I wanted to create a dramatic opening scene: 'The rising moon faces the sickening sun / And the lights in the tower blocks go on one by one'. I've always loved cityscapes and big skylines, the lure of the big city – its sense of destiny, its dreams, its nightmares, its corrupting influence.

JW: I think you said that this was partly inspired by a painting?

MJ: Yes, Chicago Skyline. It's by Federico Lloveras from 1962. It was in my home as far back as I can remember. As a little boy I would just sit and stare at it. You can see the old Chicago skyline as it was in the early sixties. The Prudential Building – and Marina City – I got to know all these buildings from staring at this painting. Maybe the Drake Hotel where I stayed in many years later? The skyline looks completely different now but as a little boy I used to stare at this painting for hours. I also have prints of some other Federico Lloveras' paintings. He's my favourite water-colourist, considered one of the greatest in Catalonia.

JW: And this inspired the track?

MJ: Yes. Well, at least its atmosphere: 'A big-shot overlooking this black iron skyline / Sits back in his new leather chair'. At that point I'd also just bought this lovely, black leather sofa from Heal's on Tottenham Court Road. Cost me a lot of money!

JW: It's very good that you remember all these lyrics.

MJ: Thank you.

> Ripped off the back of some unfortunate beast
> I'm smiling through my teeth
> Anybody can be a millionaire, so everybody's
>   gotta try
> But by the laws of this human jungle
> Only the heartless will survive

That's a comment in 'Twilight Of A Champion' on Thatcherism and Reaganomics and the 'greed is good' ethos.

JW: You spoke about unpleasant aspects of your personality coming out and there is this lyric in the song:

> I sold my soul, to pay for my dinner
> My stomach grew fatter, but my heart grew
>   thinner
> I ain't foolin', I'm fallin'
> I wasn't wicked, just weak
> I ain't lyin', I'm dyin'
> Crippled by deceit

You have mentioned you admired Robert Johnson,* who supposedly did *the* deal with the devil for success. How were you coping with success?

---

* Robert Johnson was a great American blues musician (the first ever rock star, according to The Rock and Roll Hall of Fame). Legend has it that he sold his soul to the devil at the crossroads in exchange for success.

MJ: I'd say I just became more selfish, awarded myself an artistic license to be a selfish idiot, really, and it was harder for the people around me. But I was very young – only 24 or something. You have to cut people a bit of slack – cut *yourself* a bit of slack. I wasn't intentionally treating people horribly, but for a few months of my life I became a bit cocky and arrogant. That first burst of fame and celebrity is actually the most toxic and you just have to hope you can immunise yourself against it as soon as possible – which I hope I did.

JW: But the thing is, you pulled it round. If you'd carried on in that vein...

MJ: I didn't carry on in that vein. But shortly after *Infected* came out, Fiona left me because of my bad behaviour. It was six months of contrition really, and she came back. I had quite a period of self-reflection and I really did try to change.

JW: For someone that's made a career from scratch, created their success, and now has the things they might not have expected – the money, the accolades, a certain amount of adulation – it must be harder to cope if they're not from that world and perhaps weren't pegged as someone who would go on to have that success. It must be more of a mind fuck.

MJ: I ended up becoming a bit of an overachiever – as I've spoken about many times before, I was a chronic truant. I even failed my CSEs, though I saw that as a badge of honour at the time. I was skipping school and had officially left by the age of 15, but then I went through quite a traumatic period of self-reflection. I managed to get that job at De Wolfe in Soho, thankfully, which was a real a lifesaver for me. Suddenly finding myself in Soho every day I had to grow up very quickly.

I suppose, it echoes my dad – his education was very broken because of the war and its aftermath, but he developed a love of literature and self-discovery. Personally, I think education really begins when you leave school. Or at least it should. There was an amount of insecurity for a number of years – if I'd come across someone who was university educated I might feel a bit of a chip on my shoulder. But over time I came to realise many of the brightest people I'd meet were actually self-educated or had left school early. Conversely, I started to realise some people are literally over-educated to the point of stupidity – to quote a recent lyric of mine – and have little worldliness, intuition or common sense.

JW: It's a lack of life experience, isn't it? That's what it often comes down to.

We haven't talked about 'The Mercy Beat' that much. You've mentioned some of your demons. This seems to be a track dealing with a love of the drink?

MJ: Fiona and I were both drinking quite a lot. Vodka and tonic mainly in those days. You never feel there's a problem when you're young. At that age I didn't feel there was – but I was hung over every morning and it became normalised. I remember one occasion when my brother Andrew came around to our flat in Carysfort Road and he pulled me to one side because on our mantlepiece and around our fireplace were stacked dozens and dozens of empty vodka bottles. We didn't throw the vodka bottles away. They were like trophies. They were everywhere. We were drinking a *lot*. Fiona loved her vodka and tonic – she was the one who got me into them! But Andrew said, 'I think you're drinking a bit much. Maybe rein it in a bit.' It stuck with me – especially as Andrew loved a drink even more than me! At the time I was young, mid-20s, you feel invincible, don't you?

Anyway, onto 'The Mercy Beat'. Lyrically, I can detect the influence of my close friend Jim Thirlwell. We spent a lot of time hanging out together. Though he had now moved to New York, I was over there quite a lot or he'd see me on his visits back to London. We drank a lot and misbehaved together, played each other new music we were working on, swapped notes and ideas.

Jim has been one of my closest friends in this life. We've obviously known each other since around our late teens and have had some wild times together over the years. Obviously, we've calmed down since. But I remember one night in the late eighties at a concert at the Ritz in New York, when we both happened to be highly intoxicated. Jim suggested we should become 'blood brothers' – which seemed to make perfect sense at the time – so we found a blade of some sort, sliced the tops of our thumbs, let the blood dribble out and did the deed. But then, unrelated to our little ceremony, we happened to be recognised by someone involved in the show and, somehow, they persuaded the pair of us to clamber onto the stage to say hello to the audience. So, up we went and whoever it was that invited us up there then started trying to interview us. Neither Jim nor I could give much of a coherent answer. Jim then demanded the audience express their appreciation of us by throwing money – and the audience obliged by pelting us with nickels and dimes. Jim had the last laugh though as he scoured the stage and picked up every last cent so we could spend it all on booze later that night. There was a surprising amount of money! As you can imagine it was all a bit surreal, but that was the sort of mischief he and I used to get up to.

Anyway, when I listen to 'The Mercy Beat' certain memories come up and I can definitely detect Jim's influence in some of the imagery I used – but again, it ties in with the overarching themes of *Infected*: biblical metaphors to illustrate the eternal, internal spiritual battle between good and evil. But with this track I also tried to update a timeless theme into a late 20th century cityscape – like a sort of *West Side Story* drama condensed into one song, with big sound and big drama.

In terms of the music, the main guitar melody may have been a hangover from *Pornography of Despair*. There was a track called 'Leap Into The Wind' that had a very similar guitar motif. One of those things I would automatically play whenever I picked up the guitar, so I needed to get it recorded. That would've been the starting point for that song. There were also these syncopated keyboard parts which I worked up in my 16-track studio. I wanted to make a big, epic track. It was always going to be the finishing track on the album. Remind me of the opening lyric…?

JW:

> There's a high wind blowin'
> And the stars are shining bright
> Oh, what a night this is going to be
> I think I'll let the world sleep without me

Again, it's quite nocturnal. 'I got one eye open and one eye closed / And my thin body's trembling beneath the bed clothes'. You've written quite a lot of songs that are about night-time.

MJ: Yes, and I've always loved driving, so cars and driving feature quite heavily in some lyrics too. Again, the biblical aspect, the battle with temptation. Not that I was brought up religiously, but I'm certainly aware – having ingested a certain amount of hallucinogenics – of the archetypal imagery that seems to continually reappear. It makes you wonder: if the use of symbolism came about through transcendent states, did people in those states see this imagery and bring it forth into the material world? Or was it imposed over millennia and seared deeply into our collective unconscious and DNA? I think there's something to be said for them already existing and we somehow experience them or access them through certain altered states, whether drug-induced or through meditation or revelation.

The struggle between light and dark has long fascinated me, and it seems to be prevalent in the world at the moment, even more so than when I wrote this song. We're living through strange, dark times and – like I said earlier – inversions are everywhere, there seems to be occult energy at play from the shadows. This song was an example of trying to write about that, and using a certain amount of metaphor. It is intentionally cartoon-like and humorous at times but it's pretty straightforward in terms of what it is about.

JW: Also, all of the lyrics on *Infected* (and I've mentioned the fact that they're about politics on a national and global level) are about the subjects that have always been of interest to you: for example, existential battles or desire. But these feel like lyrics by someone who's really coming into their metier now. Using metaphors, creating lyrics that are very smart, but also quite poppy, They're not just politics for numbskulls.

MJ: Thank you, Jason.

JW: *Soul Mining* was the record that changed your career; *Infected* was the one that cemented it, I think.

MJ: It ruffled quite a few feathers when it came out. But it received amazing reviews. Because no one else was doing anything like it at that time. The record itself was one thing, but with the powerful videos and the imagery, it was a very big project in a lot of ways. A lot of people performed on it, the videos were filmed all over the world, Tim Pope and Sleazy Christopherson...

JW: We'll come on to that later. *NME* described it as an 'angry' album, but they didn't mean that as a criticism – I think they meant that constructively. But as you said, the first three singles, 'Heartland', 'Sweet Bird Of Truth' and 'Slow Train' were all banned, weren't they?

MJ: There were four singles: 'Sweet Bird Of Truth', 'Heartland' and 'Infected' were banned, but 'Slow Train To Dawn' wasn't.

JW: But the video was quite explicit...

MJ: For its time. *Infected: The Movie* received an 18 certificate from the BBFC but nowadays it would be considered quite tame. It was shown on Channel 4 in its entirety twice, which was quite a coup.

JW: The interesting thing is that I always thought of *Infected: The Movie* as being all Tim Pope.

MJ: It was during the making of *Infected: The Movie* that I first got to work with Tim. He directed two tracks in Manhattan, 'Out Of The Blue' and 'Twilight Of A Champion'. He also directed 'Slow

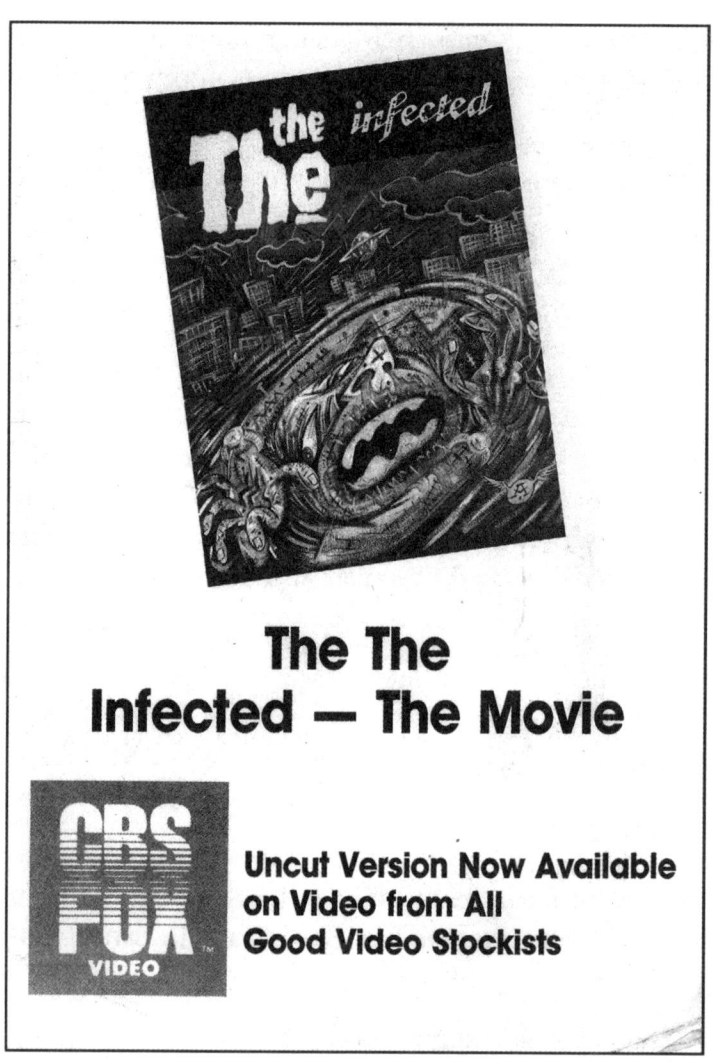

Train To Dawn' at an old steam train museum in the Midlands (UK).

We'd actually met a few years before in a Chinese restaurant in Soho at a luncheon with Marc Almond. Tim has since gone on to become one of my closest friends. I love Tim. He is one of the most loyal people I know. We go on holiday together with our families and we're God parents to each other's children. But when we first started working together we would often clash. He is very tall but in those days he also had very long hair and would wear these handmade velvet suits with pantaloon trousers that stopped about five inches above his ankles. He looked quite dandyish but also had a very waspish tongue and could be extremely passive-aggressive. As this was at the height of my 'method songwriting' period – when I was full of testosterone intensity – we'd often wind each other up terribly. But the most important thing was that I really enjoyed working with him as he had such a fertile imagination and always assembled a top-notch team around him: producers, cinematographers, make-up, assistants, etc. Tim only directed three of those eight videos but his – all shot on 35mm – were the most cinematic in my opinion. When he's working he's incredibly focused and you can almost see the ideas fizzing around in his head, whilst his legs endlessly fidget and move. Tim has always had a quick mind and a very cinematic imagination and he should have made more than the single feature film he's so far made.

JW: So in addition to Tim Pope directing parts of *Infected: The Movie*, tell me about Peter 'Sleazy' Christopherson?

MJ: Sleazy did three: 'Infected' (in Iquitos, Peru), 'Mercy Beat' (in La Paz, Bolivia) and 'Heartland', at the old Beckton Gas Works in East London.

JW: Where Stanley Kubrick shot—

MJ: Yes, where he shot *Full Metal Jacket* (1987). I can't say I knew Sleazy well before we became label mates at Some Bizzare but I was obviously aware of Throbbing Gristle (Sleazy's band) from when I was a teenager and used to go and see them perform – often with Andrew. I knew Genesis (P-Orridge) and Sleazy vaguely from around that time and always found them friendly and approachable. London seemed quite small back then – if you were into experimental music or hanging out at certain gatherings, you'd bump into the same faces.

Sleazy was an interesting character as apart from Throbbing Gristle and Psychic TV he was also involved with the design group Hipgnosis. Their album covers were legendary and they were branching out into video. Sleazy was very much at the heart of that. It was Stevo's idea to do a long-form video album for *Infected* and I had a vague notion of wanting to film somewhere exotic and dangerous.

It was Sleazy and his partner at Hipgnosis, Aubrey 'Po' Powell, who suggested Peru and Bolivia. Once we were actually there the reality of the place seeped into the fabric of those videos: the military curfew, soldiers in streets, political protests, drugs, prisons, danger, the unpredictable atmosphere and sheer volatility of the environment – you couldn't script it. I may have come up with some of the themes and images but Sleazy was brilliant at spotting the accidents, the little bits of chaos that happen when you're out in the world, and folding them into the narrative. His gift was not only in visualising them but in seizing the accidents, the encounters, the moments of chaos, and weaving them into something that made sense on screen – even though so much of what ended up being filmed was pure chance.

One notable thing about Sleazy was that, despite his hardcore creative life – and his work with Throbbing Gristle, Psychic TV and Coil *was* incredibly hardcore – he was an extremely gentle, warm and polite man on a personal level. Slightly reserved but easy to talk to and spend time with. As a director, he was patient and meticulous and open-minded to my ideas – certainly no insecure egotism. Yet he never lost sight of the bigger picture.

The last time I saw him I was living in New York. I was waiting for my suitcase at the baggage carousel at JFK when who should come over to say hello? Sleazy and his partner Geoff (AKA John Balance). The last communication I had with him was via e-mail when he was living in Thailand. It was shortly before he died in 2010. We were humorously comparing notes about some long-standing issues with Some Bizzare. I was shocked when I heard he died.

JW: Then 'Sweet Bird Of Truth' was directed by Mark Romanek, who would go on to make *Static* (1985) and *One Hour Photo* (2002).

MJ: 'Sweet Bird Of Truth' was shot in a disused aluminium factory in Brooklyn.

Alastair McIlwain – an animator – created 'Angels of Deception' in London. Andrew provided a lot of drawings, sketches, motifs and ideas and they were brought to life by Alistair.

I can't remember in which order all the films were made but 'Heartland' (directed by Sleazy) was first.

JW: 'Heartland' is the one I remember. But I was going to ask about the toll the project took on you. You put yourself through it for the videos.

MJ: Yes, it was quite exhausting but I was young – only 24 years old – I doubt I'd have the energy to go through all of that now. I remember at one point of the shoot – for 'Infected' itself – I was on the upper deck of a boat and strapped into this chair-cage contraption. There were these two local Peruvian guys who were instructed to pick me up in this cage and rush me to the edge and sort of pretend to throw me off...

JW: You were obviously strapped in.

MJ: Yes, totally strapped in. Couldn't move my arms or legs. So, they would pick me up – the top of the deck was a bit wet and slippery and they were both barefoot – and they would pick me up and rush me – inside the cage – right to the very edge and pretend to throw me over – take after take! Not very pleasant, but to be honest I was probably quite high so wouldn't have cared! You can imagine what the cocaine was like in Peru and Bolivia.

JW: I imagine it was pretty good.

MJ: Very good, very cheap, very plentiful – and very dangerous! So, everyone, the crew, me – and everyone else – was high all the time. That, and in La Paz at least, sipping coca tea to deal with the altitude sickness.

JW: The video for 'Out Of The Blue' (directed by Tim Pope) was shot at a Spanish Harlem brothel next to a crack house. That video also has the real ring of danger. I've always loved the start, where you leap into the car – you don't bother opening the door.

MJ: It's what you do, isn't it? When you're driving a big old convertible Buick in Harlem at that young age. I wouldn't fancy it doing it at my age now though. I might fall off the side!

JW: That video dripped with seediness and authenticity.

MJ: As mentioned earlier, I was having what I would call my 'method songwriting' phase. Having been a fan of films like Schrader and Scorsese's *Taxi Driver* I found that area of life fascinating and in my early to mid-20s I'd sometimes go to Times Square, Alphabet City or the Bronx just to hang out. Those areas were *very* different in the early eighties – before gentrification. I liked what I considered to be its authenticity. Tim was the perfect director to capture that atmosphere as he liked similar films to me plus really understood the cinematic nature of my own music productions. In later years I realised – of course – that you can be just as authentic in a little country village in England as you can in Alphabet City, but in your early 20s, you're more taken in by a lot of that stuff. Reading books like Hubert Selby Jr's *The Demon*.

JW: Brilliant. Everyone thinks of him for *Last Exit To Brooklyn* but *The Demon* is a better one.

MJ: A dark and twisted tale.

JW: Did you go straight from recording and mixing the album to doing the videos? It must have been exhausting and it must have started to take a toll on you mentally.

MJ: Yes, and I'm surprised I did it, really, because after *Soul Mining*, I was extremely run down and lost my eyesight temporarily. They couldn't figure out what it was despite my spending a week at the Hospital for Nervous Diseases in Maida Vale. I underwent a battery of tests – including a lumbar puncture – but all they could come up with was that I may have picked up a virus in Africa when I was over there. I still suffer a bit from whatever it was to this day. It was brought on by overworking, meddling in drugs and overworking again. And then I went and did it all over again with *Infected* but on an even bigger scale! But when you're young you've just got this boundless ambition – and energy.

JW: Was there a period where you just collapsed with exhaustion?

MJ: No, I just kept going right until the end. The whole process – writing it, recording it, filming it, then travelling around the world promoting it – was a very long project. And by the end I was going out of my bloody mind and behaving like a spoiled brat, travelling around the world, throughout Europe, Australia, New Zealand – all across America – showing the film in cinemas everywhere – night after night after night. And there I'd be, propped up at a nice table in the corner sipping my vodka and tonic like a little prince, having people come up to greet and praise me.

JW: 'Would you like anything, sir?'

MJ: Yes, it was a bit like that. 'Some more mashed potatoes, please!' It even got to the stage where I would throw a fit if my hotel suite wasn't luxurious enough. It's fascinating what effect travelling around the world like that can have on a youngster – in a bubble whilst having your ego continually massaged. All highly unpleasant behaviour really, which, thankfully, I quickly grew out of.

JW: I saw the film at the Electric Cinema, London.

MJ: It was way too loud that night though, do you remember that?

JW: It felt like a real event. Shortly after *The Inertia Variations* came out in 2017, Nico Marzano, the curator at The ICA got permission to screen *Infected: The Movie* again. It is very hard to get permission to screen. I know it was shown on Channel 4, but there's never been any Blu-ray or DVD. Is that something that could happen?

MJ: Unfortunately, there are lots of complications with Sony which means it's unlikely. They could do better trying to persuade me by renegotiating the old crappy deal I am on. It's an old story. A very boring story.

JW: Could you not do it yourself?

MJ: I do actually want to see if I can license and release it through Cinéola.

JW: That would be an amazing thing. Because when we did *The Inertia Variations* at HOME, everyone that came said, 'Why can't you show *Infected: The Movie*?' The whole thing, the *Infected* album, the singles, the film, the relationship with Tim Pope that spawned a lifelong—

MJ: Friendship, yes.

JW: It was a huge endeavour. How do you see *Infected* in terms of where it took your career? *Soul Mining* took you into a more commercial area without sacrificing your principles; but this was the next level.

MJ: It took me into a more political area – in some ways each album was more successful than the last but this one did take a toll on my personal life and on my relationship.

JW: Success does do that.

MJ: I've seen it many times since with others; and that was my moment to be tainted by fame. I was only 24 or 25. On the other hand, it was an incredibly fertile, ambitious project with so many talented collaborators involved. We had a lot of fun, it was incredibly successful and we achieved what we set out to achieve. It was critically acclaimed internationally – as well as in the UK.

JW: How was your relationship with Stevo at the end of the project?

MJ: Well, it was starting to become a big problem. He was absolutely superb in those early stages of the project, persuading CBS to dig very deep to support the project with a lot of money. He helped set things up with the various directors and was incredibly passionate about the entire project. *Infected: The Movie* would not have happened without Stevo. But, as it progressed, things just became more and more… deranged. There was stuff going on.

JW: I wasn't going to use the word 'deranged', but…

MJ: Certain things happened – I won't discuss in detail, but there were several foreign trips where I'd actually have to leave Stevo and travel to the next city alone. It happened three times. So, I was starting to travel alone more and more, and having to manage myself more and more.

JW: I think it's good to have those periods in some ways, because you become self-sufficient.

MJ: Yes. I couldn't imagine having a manager now to be honest – though I've had seven over the course of my career. Most were very nice, none were really right for me.

So, it was on these foreign promotional trips that things started to careen out of control – sometimes the record company would call and talk to me about the fact Stevo had disgraced himself in some way, and I'd have to take control, calm things down and apologise. It was like role reversal. As if he was the unhinged artist and I was the responsible manager. This went on and on and it got more and more tiresome and draining. He had his issues – going on live radio for an interview whilst apparently on LSD and then being removed whilst on air – it was endless. He was a good friend at that time and I was very fond of him. I would repeatedly sit down and plead with him, 'Look, if this carries on we're going to have to split up. I can't take much more of this.' And it would happen again... and again. Then he finally did something that was so beyond the pale that I still don't even discuss it publicly. I had to be good to my word – otherwise you end up repeatedly trampled.

By the time it came to the next album his management had effectively ended. Although on the *Mind Bomb* sleeve it said Some Bizzare, that was just a contractual obligation, but he had nothing at all to do with my career post *Infected*. I found the whole thing deeply sad and depressing because we'd been good friends and had worked well together but what can you do when someone is not only spiralling out of control but just point-blank refuses to receive any help or listen to any advice you give them?

JW: Did you stay in contact with him?

MJ: No.

JW: It strikes me he was the last of the line of—

MJ: —Those old maverick music biz managers? Yes.

JW: The old mavericks, exactly. Andrew Loog Oldham, Brian Epstein, and then you had Geoff Travis, Malcolm McLaren and Stevo was probably the end of the line.

MJ: Yes, because the record industry – like most industries probably – was being taken over and run by corporate lawyers and accountants. There was no longer room for the old music moguls and mavericks; people who would sign stuff on a hunch, just trust their gut because they knew when something was good. Instead, it became all about the bottom line, quantifiable and accountable to the shareholders. It became a very different industry.

JW: The only thing we haven't spoken about is the sleeve of *Infected*.

MJ: Have you got the photographic album cover where I'm covered with blue marks?

JW: Yes.

MJ: Okay, so, there was a problem. The four single sleeves Andrew did for the *Infected* project are my favourite sleeves he did for me. I love those. They are fantastic. The images Andrew was creating for the album sleeve I was never totally happy with – and he was running late – that's why I think the first 100,000 copies or so were the film still of me. It's the so-called 'torture' sleeve – me bare-chested and grimacing – but with marks and motifs Andrew drew over the top.

JW: I've got one of the first ones? That's good.

MJ: Yes. That's a still from the 'Out Of The Blue' film. We had to use it as Andrew was so late with the cover deadline and he let me down, really. It ended up rushed and caused a lot of friction between us.

I felt the single sleeves were the best. They were outstanding, those four, in their contrasting background colours: The rich blue of 'Sweet Bird Of Truth', the vivid red of 'Slow Train To Dawn', the pure white of 'Infected', the deep black of 'Heartland'. They're beautiful. They're my favourite sleeves out of all the ones Andrew did for me. But the album sleeve? Whilst working together on it I was probably looking over his shoulder: 'That's not right, that's not right,' and he ended up missing the deadline. It caused a fall-out between us which is why he didn't do the *Mind Bomb* sleeve. He actually told me he didn't want to do it.

JW: Was the *Mind Bomb* sleeve purely because of that fall-out or was it the record company?

MJ: No, it had nothing whatsoever to do with the record company.

JW: So, *Infected* was critically and personally a highlight. I think it was in the charts for thirty weeks?

MJ: Yes, it sold enough to go platinum in the UK and picked up great reviews across the board. So, nothing to complain about really.

JW: Did it create pressure for you? Did you immediately feel pressure to create more music?

MJ: No, I never really felt that pressure because if I have an idea and I want to go off in a new direction then I'll do that – I don't care if everyone else wants me to go somewhere else. I just follow my instincts regardless.

JW: Do you ever listen back to the old records?

MJ: Not often. I did for The Comeback Special Tour (in 2018) though, just to re-orientate myself.

JW: When I've spoken to other musicians they rarely listen back. Green Gartside of Scritti Politti can't stand to.

MJ: I don't have a phobia of listening back, though I will sometimes hear my mistakes – or rather think how I could have improved it. Often when I do listen back it is a pleasant surprise, because I hear there's an honesty there. I tried as hard as possible to do the best I could. All the sleepless nights, working so hard to make a record I love, not for someone else but ultimately for myself. If I can make a record that makes *me* cry, that gives *me* goosebumps and gives *me* a charge of energy then there is a decent chance some others may be similarly affected by it too.

JW: I also think there's a real integrity to the lyrics. I think that's why, if you were a certain age and you were interested in music and interested in the world, you had to own records like *Soul Mining* and *Infected*. There's this period where Johnny Marr was in The Smiths, and everybody of that generation would have every Smiths record. I think *Soul Mining* and *Infected* were the same. Everybody *had* to have those records. I won't put this in the book, but listening to *Infected* is really how I started to get political.

MJ: Put it in the book!

JW: I was at that age where I was starting to realise that music wasn't just an escape. I feel the same way about films and books. With music, like any art, you don't necessarily escape the world, you engage with it. Specifically, 'Heartland' was the song that politicised me.

MJ: I've always questioned authority and the relationship between the powerful and the powerless. I've long wondered about the tensions that are continually being whipped up between different groups too. It's really a class issue more than anything. It's the fuckers that own everything against the rest of us. It's the old divide-and-rule, the oldest trick in the book that still works a treat. They do not want a populace that is united and consequently has the power to fight back. That is why the unions were destroyed and why they are continually creating more and more subdivisions, so you have everyone fighting each other. You've got feminists pitted against the trans community or Black people pitted against the Asian community or against White people. That's exactly what they want, and people still fall for it. Every time! All at each other's throats. But it has always *really* been about top versus bottom, rather than left versus right or black versus white. It's the parasite class, the predator class, the ruling class – whatever you want to call them.

CHAPTER FIVE

Through The Ether And The Mists Of The Mind

There is controversy over 'Armageddon Days Are Here (again)', a song dealing with the impending clash between Christianity and Islam and record execs go into panic. Johnny Marr joins the fold. Sinéad O'Connor becomes the latest collaborator. A new album with the familiar themes emerges. THE THE becomes a formidable touring outfit.

JW: What was your intent when creating *Mind Bomb*?

MJ: I was in my mid-to-late 20s – it's a long time ago and hard to remember my exact mindset. I obviously wanted to make a very strong follow-up to *Infected*. I recall my working title for the album was actually *Psychonaut* – which made sense at the time I suppose because of the meditation I was doing and magic mushroom tea I was drinking.

On the opening three tracks I tried to explore themes of political unrest, religious extremism and the biblical notion of End Times: the battle between good and evil. St Paul wrote: 'For we wrestle not against flesh and blood, but against principalities, against powers, against the rulers of the darkness of this world, against spiritual wickedness in high places.' All cheerful stuff, though I'm not sure how I ended up in that mindset really. I was reading a lot, experimenting a bit with hallucinogenics – not for recreational purposes but creative purposes – along with a strange, 'purifying' diet of distilled water and organic grapes, plus meditating each morning and evening.

I was also dream journaling at that time too. What is strange is that once you have the *intent* to start memorising your dreams and writing them down immediately upon awakening, it's surprising how much you really *can* remember. It is as if the subconscious mind or higher self really is actively trying to communicate. I remember one vivid dream in which I was advised to purchase and read books by Walt Whitman, Carl Jung and Nietzsche! How strange is that? But, looking back, I can't remember how I morphed from the excessive hedonism of *Infected* into this spiritual – almost perversely evangelical – mindset for *Mind Bomb*.

Before I start any new album, I'll have a set of criteria – lyrically and musically. The subject matter is always really the same for me: love, sex, war, life, death, politics, God and religion. Musically, it's how I want an album to sound, who I'm going to collaborate with, what equipment and instrumentation to use etc. For this album I knew I wanted to co-produce with Warne and Roli again. This time, four tracks each. Again, working separately with them although they would share an engineer – the talented Felix Kendall who Warne introduced us to – so there was some sonic consistency between the tracks. I also had a few names written down in terms of the musicians I wanted to work with.

JW: Islam features quite strongly on the album. Of course, the album was written before the invasion of Kuwait and Salman Rushdie's *The Satanic Verses* controversy in 1988 and subsequent fatwa in 1989. You focused on the subject quite some time before it became a very popular subject to consider.

MJ: Look, if you flag something up too early you'll be condemned as mad – or a 'conspiracy theorist' – but like many people I'd long found the Middle East fascinating and disturbing. And I could sense something dark heading towards us. A lot of the violence and radicalisation we've seen in recent decades had been triggered by long-standing policies of the West towards the region. Tensions go back centuries of course but (the obvious Israel–Palestine conundrum aside) in the post-World War Two world there was the overthrow of Iran's elected prime minister, Mohammad Mossadegh, for instance – who became popular largely because he nationalised the nation's oil industry. The British had controlled it for decades and didn't want to give it up so MI6, as part of Operation Ajax* with CIA assistance, overthrew and charged Mossadegh with 'treason' and installed the hated Shah – which of course led to the increasing unhappiness and consequent radicalisation of large parts of the population with the Iranian Revolution of 1979, the hostage crisis and the return of Ayatollah Khomeini.

I wonder how relations between the West and Iran might have turned out otherwise. But it's a highly complex, explosive issue and it was hard *not* to pick up a sense of a big storm brewing. On one hand there were radicalised elements of Islam; on the other, some Christian fundamentalists in America who believe in biblical End Times and Gog and Magog; and then the Zionist fundamentalists who believe in the red heifer and the third temple. It is a highly explosive, frightening mixture. As Voltaire observed: 'Those who can make you believe absurdities can make you commit atrocities.'

I had also just read *Armageddon Essays 1983–87*, a book by Gore Vidal, which dealt with this in part; but as far as I recall a lot of my interest in the subject stemmed from reading outside the mainstream – something I've always tried to do. I do keep an eye on mainstream media – BBC, *The Guardian*, *The New York Times*, *The Washington Post*, *Russia Today*, *Daily Mail*, CNN etc. to check the propaganda du jour. I've always been curious about world affairs and trying to find out what's *really* going on behind the pre-prepared headlines.

In fact, you can't help but wonder about the veracity of some of our history books too. History is written by the victors – of

---

* Operation Ajax was the 1953 CIA–MI6 covert operation that overthrew Iran's democratically elected Prime Minister Mohammad Mossadegh and restored the Shah, reshaping Middle Eastern politics for decades.

course – and so we never really get to hear the other side of the story. A certain amount of history is really just past distortions and lies permanently pickled in aspic. But, as George Orwell wrote in *1984*, 'Who controls the past... controls the future: who controls the present controls the past.'

When you're young you assume the news is like the weather and that it just – sort of – happens. You trust what you see, hear and read on the likes of the BBC as we are brought up to believe that we have 'The News' whilst other countries – particularly those deemed unfriendly – just have propaganda. But as you get older you start questioning what 'The News' actually is and who gets to decide which handful of stories – amongst the millions of events happening daily across the world – are deemed worthy of being promoted across every mainstream media channel in the western world – generally in lockstep. Who *really* owns the three main news agencies that provide the majority of these stories – Associated Press, Reuters and Agence France-Presse? Whose agenda is *really* being pushed across the media and for what purpose? Often the drums for further wars are being busily beaten.

The West has this habit of framing its conflicts in the same way time and again. There is always a clear villain: Castro, Saddam, Chavez, Gaddafi, Putin – scarecrows dressed up in Hitler costumes in the minds of the public and cast as the next great dictator who must be stopped at all costs; that our very way of life is under threat. And – just like the 'Two Minutes Hate' depicted in Orwell's *1984* – many members of the public do respond to such levels of propaganda with visceral hatred.

Anyway, I digress. There is a lyric in 'Armageddon Days': 'They've forgotten the message and worship the creed', and I think there *is* a lot of common ground between the fundamental inspirations of the major religions but much seems to have been lost as religions became ossified and institutionalised over time. I have friends from various religious backgrounds and its obvious there is much common ground. But our world suffers the endless tragedy of misunderstandings between religions being whipped up into hatred and violence for nefarious purposes.

JW: You got flak for 'Armageddon Days Are Here (again)'.

MJ: 'Armageddon Days' is not an anti-Islam or an anti-Christian song. It is an anti-war song. It was supposed to be the first single from *Mind Bomb* but there was such a febrile atmosphere around the publication of Rushdie's book that it was withdrawn. We went with 'The Beat(en) Generation' instead. You know, I don't think 'Armageddon Days' has ever actually been played on the radio. It was unfortunate because it represented the overall tone and atmosphere of the album more accurately than 'The Beat(en) Generation', which was a bittersweet pop song whose lyrics were hard and acidic but in terms of melody and sound were dipped in sugar-coating.

The single led to my first appearance on *Top Of The Pops* though, so did its job to help promote the album – which reached number four. The third single was going to be 'Kingdom Of Rain', but that didn't happen because of issues revolving around Sinéad O'Connor. There was another song, 'Jealous Of Youth', that was recorded at the same time and was *supposed* to be on the album, and I regret now that it wasn't. I put on 'Gravitate To Me' instead. Johnny Marr – who was now part of the band – always wanted 'Jealous Of Youth' on the album – it came out later as part of an EP but I think Johnny was right.

JW: Did *Mind Bomb* feel like a band album? THE THE is often seen as *your* thing.

MJ: Absolutely! I knew I wanted to put another band together and perform live again. The catalyst for this was a couple of shows I performed with Zeke Manyika as part of the ill-fated Red Wedge* Tour and its attempt to help elect the Labour Party into government and Neil Kinnock as prime minister. Those small shows – one at Acklam Hall, the other at Islington Town Hall – were the

---

* Red Wedge was a collective of musicians formed in the UK in 1985 who attempted to educate youth with the policies of the Labour Party leading up to the 1987 general election in the hope of ousting the Conservative government of Margaret Thatcher.

first shows I'd performed since the Marquee residency a few years earlier (see page 96). But I got the taste back for being on stage. So, I started thinking about what sort of band I wanted and gradually put together what was considered by many at that time a sort of 'alternative super group': Johnny Marr, the guitarist from The Smiths; David Palmer, the drummer from ABC; and James Eller, the bass player from Julian Cope's band. In my mind each of them was the best on their respective instruments in the country. We quickly grew into a very tight band and developed a close friendship. It felt like we were on a real mission for that album and tour. There was a wonderful camaraderie. It may not come across on the recordings themselves but the sessions were full of laughter, pranks and warmth. After studio work finished we'd often continue hanging out socially, listening to music, unwinding or going to gigs together. One night we all went to see Prince and were suitably blown away.

I'd obviously known Dave Palmer for a number of years having been introduced to him by Gary Langan during the making of the *Infected* album. James Eller was introduced to me by Warne Livesey, who'd told me he knew of a superb bassist who would fit right into what I was trying to do. James was instantly likeable as well as being a supremely gifted player. He is also a gentleman and a very kind man. I love James.

I suppose it's a hangover from younger days when I was addicted to the fantasy football game I'd mentioned earlier – where I'd create imaginary teams. But, in my mind, putting together a band is like putting together a football team. The drummer is the goalkeeper, the bass player the central defender, keyboard player the central midfielder, lead guitarist is the winger and the singer – obviously – centre forward. In my mind Palmer was Peter Shilton, Eller was Bobby Moore and Marr was George Best. I'd worked it all out in my mind and just knew it would work.

The situation with Johnny raised a lot of eyebrows at the time – with him quitting The Smiths and switching to THE THE. But what most people didn't know was that Johnny and I had known each other from when we were in our late teens – *before* he was a member of The Smiths. We'd met in Manchester in 1981 through a mutual friend, Pete Hunt. I'd actually met Pete at a nightclub or gig one drunken night in London. As mentioned earlier I was always out and about, very sociable and meeting new people. We must have got along as he invited me to come up to Manchester. I went up a few times, meeting more of Pete's entourage and going out to a few nightclubs. Anyway, on one of my trips he said, 'You have *got* to meet my friend Johnny! Johnny's a star! You and Johnny are *really* going to hit it off!' So, Pete arranged for us to visit the clothes shop Johnny was working at.

I remember our first meeting vividly. He was such a positive person, incredibly warm and enthusiastic. I could see why Pete thought Johnny was going to be a star as he had an easy-going charisma. We hit it off immediately and Johnny suggested he bring his guitar over to where I was staying later that evening. So, he showed up with his green Gretsch or Rickenbacker (I can't recall which). There was another guitar there that I picked up and we started jamming, swapping chord shapes and riffs. He asked me to show him riffs from *Burning Blue Soul* and he showed me some of his. We kept in touch after that and even discussed the possibility of him joining THE THE. But it was not feasible at that time as he was settled in Manchester and we were just too far apart.

Sometime later he told me he'd formed his own band and asked if it would be okay to crash over at my place in Highbury whilst he held discussions with Geoff Travis at Rough Trade. Whilst negotiations progressed he stayed over two or three times. But we lost touch soon after as I was now off promoting my albums around the world and The Smiths exploded into the British music scene.

Several years later we bumped into each other backstage at an Iggy Pop gig. I think I would have been there with Tim Pope, who was a friend of Iggy. Johnny was still in The Smiths at this stage but Iggy said to us, 'You guys should work together.' Johnny and I agreed it would be an interesting idea but I didn't think anything more about it until sometime later when the news broke he'd quit The Smiths. At the time I'd already started recording *Mind Bomb* and although I'd already recorded my electric guitar part on 'Armageddon Days' I was having trouble with 'The Beat(en)

Generation'. The part I was playing was just not hitting the spot for me. I couldn't seem to nail it. As soon as I heard about Johnny's decision to quit his band I made my move.

He came over to my loft in East London in the early evening and we were still in a very animated discussion by the following morning! I think sometime in the night we'd even gone to Heaven – the nightclub in Charing Cross – as that was one of the few places you could get a drink in the early hours in London back then. But as dawn broke, it was decided Johnny would become a member of THE THE. During his time with my band he was so committed and brought such energy and positivity. We'd be on the phone for hours at a time, multiple days throughout the week discussing whatever it was we were working on at the time. He's also incredibly funny and would have me in stitches with his mimicry and impersonations. He's one of those rare people in the industry you never hear a bad word about. I think that's because he genuinely likes people and is very present in the company of whoever he happens to be with at the time. He tends to give people the benefit of the doubt, though doesn't suffer fools.

JW: I wanted to ask about the album track order. 'Good Morning Beautiful', 'Armageddon Days' and 'The Violence Of Truth' are very weighty and political. Then we have 'Kingdom Of Rain' which feels more intimate and relates to love and sex.

MJ: If side one of the vinyl had consisted of 'Kingdom Of Rain', 'Beyond Love', 'August & September' and 'Gravitate To Me' it would have been considered a 'love' album, but because of the running order – and the surly photo of me on the cover – it was viewed as more aggressive and political. Maybe I made a mistake? We did play around a lot with the running order, depending on themes, tempos, keys and relative minors, etc. The attention played to the running order on an album began to change with the advent of CDs and the loss of that old rhythm between the sides. It used to be so important, not only which track opened each side but also – for instance – the second-to-last track on side one, or third track on side two etc. On vinyl, each position in the running order has a certain dynamic but, of course, it's become less relevant with the rise of streaming. So many people don't even bother listening to full albums anymore. It's a shame. Sequencing a running order feels like a lost art. We'd spend hours trying out each permutation in order to find just the right one.

Thinking about 'Good Morning Beautiful' reminds me I'd actually gone back to some old techniques I used on previous album openers – 'Red Cinders In The Sand' (*Burning Blue Soul*) and 'I've Been Waiting For Tomorrow' (*Soul Mining*) – where I created the music by playing a certain keyboard or guitar motif repeatedly on the multitrack for several minutes, building up the instrumentation around it and then sculpting a structure out of it by mutes and edits.

In the instance of 'Good Morning Beautiful' it was that simple piano riff. I'd been playing it over and over for months. I loved its simplicity and its slightly menacing but poignant atmosphere. So, I put that down as a guide and then we added Dave's drums and James' bass. A combination of the tightness of the rhythm section with Warne's and Felix's engineering gave me just the feel and sound I was after – understated yet relentless and powerful. We then overdubbed the other elements, percussion and brass and, of course, Mark Feltham's treated harmonica and Johnny's electric guitar.

There's a story I've told before about working on this track. Warne was off for a few weeks as he'd suffered some sort of nervous breakdown – actually, he was the third person on this project to suffer a nervous breakdown but that is another story! So, it was Felix at the controls and we were at Wessex Studios for this session. Johnny and I hadn't worked together before and were both probably feeling a bit anxious about whether it would work or not. The session was starting to feel a bit muted and vibeless for some reason so I arranged for some ecstasy pills to be delivered to liven things up. Soon enough we were all flying and everything started to make perfect sense again. When Andrew and I were kids he had an illustrated Bible that contained a powerful image of Jesus's temptation – after his forty day fast – by Satan in the desert. It frightened me as a child but always stuck in my mind.

So, the main direction I gave to Johnny for his playing on 'Good Morning Beautiful' was simply whispering in his ear, 'Jesus meets the Devil', and he instantly got it and started playing those amazing parts you hear on that recording. I absolutely loved it!

I continued working on the lyrics of the track as the general atmosphere of the recording was developing. We set out to build an epic, cinematic soundscape and I always knew this would be the opening track. I actually took the title from one of the last shots in *Infected: The Movie*, from 'The Mercy Beat' video, where you see a carton of eggs in a fridge with the slogan 'Good Morning

Beautiful'. This track was always intended to be a follow on from 'The Mercy Beat'.

JW: Has the directness in your writing ever backfired?

MJ: Looking back, I was young and naive with *Mind Bomb* and – I suppose – a bit evangelical too. I'd been on this intense personal journey, through meditation, hallucinogenics and dream journaling whilst creating that album. I felt a strong sense of what might be coming down the road and just wanted to share it.

My first three albums received positive reviews in the UK but as is the nature of Britain, no matter who you are or what profession you're in, after a while people just get bored with you and decide to take you down a peg or two. It's a British national pastime. A bit like pulling the legs off spiders really. Although *Mind Bomb* had picked up enthusiastic reviews internationally – *Time* magazine in America even devoted an entire page to it – it got attacked by certain elements in the UK. Some said I'd gone mad by writing about an impending clash between Christianity and Islam.

Also, there were elements in the UK press who really had it in for Johnny for 'breaking up' The Smiths and seemed to hate the fact the pair of us teamed up. We found out later that a continuous stream of lies and spiteful attacks in *NME* had been orchestrated by the editor at that time. I can't recall his name – I'd never even met this person so didn't have an opinion about him one way or the other. Apparently, his dislike of me stemmed from the fact I'd been friendly with his predecessor at *NME*. So, because this current editor despised the previous one, anything the latter supported during his tenure was going to be ridiculed under the new regime. It was the sort of behaviour one might find in a school sixth form magazine really. There were continual snide comments about Johnny and me which used to make us both chuckle as they seemed so absurd. It's too long ago to care about but – bizarrely – a couple of the journalists involved apologised to me about it thirty years later and spilled all the beans on the erstwhile editor and his antics.

Matt in the 'Transfer Bay' at De Wolfe Music, 1978.

THE THE with Keith Laws and Matt at the Bridge House, Canning Town, 1981. Photo by Alessandra Sartore.

Portrait of Matt's late older brother Andrew (AKA Andy Dog).

The American edition of the *Soul Mining* sleeve. Artwork by Andy Dog.

Single sleeves from the album, *Infected*. Artwork by Andy Dog.

Film stills from *Infected – The Movie*, 1986.

Photos from the 'I Saw The Light' music video shoot, 1995.

THE THE Versus The World Tour graphic designed by Andy Dog.

THE THE circa 1989: James Eller, David Palmer, Matt Johnson, Johnny Marr. *Mind Bomb* promo image for CBS/Sony, designed by Fiona Skinner. Photo by Andrew Macpherson.

Fiona Skinner & Matt on his 30th birthday in 1991, hours before his surprise trip to New York. Photo by Anne Brosseau.

Matt's late younger brother Eugene, 1989.

Lonely Planet Tour line-up: David Palmer, Keith Joyner, Matt Johnson, Jared Nickerson, DC Collard, Jim Fitting. Photo by Chris Buck.

Naked Tour line-up: including Spencer Campbell, Earl Harvin, Eric Schermerhorn, Matt Johnson.

Look, if you have a career that spans multiple decades of course you're going to have ups and downs and you're going to go in and out of fashion. You just have to take it all on the chin. But I certainly wouldn't want to be a young songwriter starting out today. We're now in an age and culture of extreme self-censorship where many people receive terrible abuse – or cancellation – for just expressing the 'wrong' opinion. The lexicon has been warped and weaponised and things often intentionally taken out of context to provide justification for the most repugnant personal attacks. Cancel culture is toxic. Would I write *Mind Bomb* in this climate? I'm not sure. Would a major record company support a record like this? Possibly not. We're living in a very different world to the one in which this album was created.

Our world has now become so Orwellian that over recent decades even the bombing of other countries has been sold – and accepted – as a moral duty, with euphemisms like 'humanitarian intervention' or 'responsibility to protect'. As if war is really an act of kindness. It is straight out of *1984*.

Those who ask too many questions are often ridiculed and accused of 'going down the rabbit hole', but I think that is viewing things from the wrong end of the telescope. It is the majority of the population who are already 'down the rabbit hole'. Those questioning and researching are actually trying to get *out* of the rabbit hole – and into the sunlight of truth. It reminds me of Plato's cave*, where the prisoners mistake the shadows cast on a wall for reality because they've never seen the world outside. As Schopenhauer† stated, all truth passes through three stages. First, it is ridiculed. Second, it is violently opposed. Third, it is accepted as being self-evident.

---

* Plato's cave is an allegory in *The Republic* describing people mistaking shadows for reality, illustrating how ignorance persists until one turns toward truth and philosophical understanding.
† Arthur Schopenhauer (1788-1860) was among the first philosophers in the Western tradition to share and affirm significant tenets of Indian philosophy, such as asceticism, denial of the self, and the notion of the world-as-appearance.

JW: When you look back at *Mind Bomb* now how do you feel about it? Did it express and achieve what you hoped? Do you have a favourite song on the album?

MJ: I have a few favourite parts. 'Good Morning Beautiful' has just the brooding atmosphere I wanted. Warne and Felix did a great job engineering – in fact *Mind Bomb* was even awarded a prize for the best engineered album of that year by George Martin. Also, it contained some of the best drumming Palmer ever played for me. Mark Feltham was incredible, the way his distorted, delayed harmonica and Johnny's effected guitar spun off each other creating this ominous web of sound.

Lyrically, 'Beyond Love' and 'Armageddon Days' stand up. Dave's drumming on 'August & September' is also some of his best playing for me and lyrically it's one of the most powerful love songs I've written to date, though 'Kingdom Of Rain' runs it close – Sinéad's singing on the second verse is also a highlight and still gives me goosebumps.

Wonderful bass playing throughout by James Eller, of course, and Wix – who had previously played accordion on 'This Is The Day' joined us again to play some beautiful piano and organ. And, finally getting to work with my old friend Johnny Marr was a major highlight in recording that album.

As I've mentioned, I really don't listen back to my old albums very often. During the COVID-19 lockdowns I did a few of Tim Burgess' Twitter Listening Parties which were highly enjoyable – but when it came to preparing for them I realised I didn't even own many of my own records, so I had to download them!

JW: The recording of yours and Sinéad's voices on 'Kingdom Of Rain' is really beautiful.

MJ: I thought our voices worked really well together. She was a powerful singer, great to work with and fast in the studio – very intense and focused. It only took two or three takes and she interpreted the lyrics so well. Warne and I were very happy.

I hadn't thought about Sinéad for many years until I heard the shocking news of her untimely death.* Reading how desperate her last few years had been; her struggles with loneliness, physical and mental health issues and the tragic loss of one of her children really affected me. Brought me to tears. I think of the losses in my own family and what it's like for a parent to lose a child. The same for Sinéad.

The story behind her appearance on *Mind Bomb* is quite interesting. In spring 1987 I was in the Boston offices of CBS/Sony working my way through phone interviews promoting *Infected*. MTV was on a screen in the corner, with the sound muted. Whilst chatting to a journalist my eyes were drawn to the screen. A young woman occasionally appeared – then disappeared. It was the video for 'Private Revolution' by World Party. Even though I couldn't hear her backing vocals there was *something* about her. So, I made a mental note to investigate further.

Back in the UK I discovered her name was Sinéad O'Connor and that she'd just signed to Ensign Records. I repeatedly tried to contact her but was told by both her management and record company that she was either too busy working on her first album or about to give birth.

Several months later I found out she'd appointed John Kennedy to represent her legally. He also represented me and was a friend so he sent me a promo copy of her soon-to-be-released debut album *The Lion and The Cobra*. It blew me away. I knew my intuition was right. John arranged for me to see her perform at Sadler's Wells in London a few months later. She was one of the most powerful female singers I'd seen live. Her intensity was perfect so I started writing a duet with her in mind.

A couple of weeks later she arrived at my East London HQ. When I opened the door, I was surprised at how small and delicate she was. Wearing jeans, a T-shirt and Dr. Martens, sporting a freshly shaved head – a beautiful tomboy, quite shy but with a wry sense of humour and nice smile.

We drank numerous cups of tea, spent hours discussing a wide

---

* Sinéad O'Connor died at home in her London flat in 2023, at the age of 56. The coroner said she died of natural causes.

range of subjects and got along very well. She said she was relieved to find I wasn't as menacing in real life as the person she'd watched on TV running through the jungle in *Infected*! I played some rough mixes – 'Armageddon Days', 'Good Morning Beautiful' and 'The Beat(en) Generation'. She liked what she heard and said she'd love to collaborate. I said I'd send a demo of 'Kingdom Of Rain' soon.

One night, a month or so later, she arrived at Air Studios in Oxford Circus. She was highly professional, had learned all the lyrics and melodies but then injected her own nuances and dynamism into each line. Watching through the control room window as she brought my lyrics to life with her beautiful voice made the hairs on the back of my neck stand up.

We met about half a dozen times – over several months either side of recording 'Kingdom Of Rain' – visiting each other's homes, meeting for drinks, swapping books on poetry and spirituality and having philosophical conversations. I remember her once saying she considered singer–songwriters like Dylan, Marley and Lennon modern-day equivalents of old-testament prophets, sent to convey messages of truth regardless of any price to be paid.

JW: So, what happened to prevent 'Kingdom Of Rain' being released as a single?

MJ: Well, a serious misunderstanding arose. As I mentioned, 'Armageddon Days' was dropped as the first single from *Mind Bomb* due to recent controversies and replaced by 'The Beat(en) Generation'. So, we needed a new second single. CBS/Sony suggested 'Kingdom Of Rain', which seemed a fair idea.

I was travelling across America as part of the Versus The World Tour when it became apparent Sinéad's record company were against us releasing 'Kingdom Of Rain'. I thought it best to speak with her direct so I called her from my New York hotel room. I found her in a strange, cold mood – *completely* unsympathetic to the dilemma I was in. She claimed my record company were trying to 'exploit' her and was adamant she *didn't* want 'Kingdom Of Rain' released as a single and that she *wouldn't* appear in any video we might make. I found her tone harsh and paranoid.

The phone call took an even more bizarre turn when she suddenly started comparing our singles chart positions! I replied I was an album artist – a protest singer. Chart positions were irrelevant as I never had hit singles. Bearing in mind this was six months *before* 'Nothing Compares 2 U' turned her into a pop superstar and that my previous album, despite three of its four singles being banned from radio, *still* went platinum. I just thought this was nonsense. 'Sinéad, c'mon, it's me you're talking to. You know I wanted to sing with you before you even released your first record! If I wanted to exploit a singer for a high chart position I'd have asked Madonna.' (Actually, I might have agreed with her if this was six months *after* 'Nothing Compares 2 U' became a global number one – but it wasn't.)

I just found it impossible to reason with her and we couldn't come to an agreement. We ended the call frustrated and irritated with each other. Her tone of voice was odd – maybe I'd inadvertently offended her in some way? Maybe her record company – or manager – were jealously guarding their investment and pissing in her ear? Even our shared connection John Kennedy was unable to help sort out the mess. I found the whole situation quite irksome to be honest.

Consequently, 'Kingdom Of Rain' never was officially released as a single – although we shot a video in New York with Tim Pope (without Sinéad, of course) and promo 7-inch editions were sent to radio stations. Subsequently we created a radio-edit for 'Gravitate To Me' – and shot a third video with Tim – releasing that as the official second single instead. 'Armageddon Days' *was* eventually released as the official third single further down the line – after the initial furore had died down – but by that time momentum had been lost.

JW: Did you repair your relationship with Sinéad?

MJ: Matters between us were never satisfactorily resolved. That phone call was the last time we spoke directly to each other. As time passed she began speaking publicly of her struggles with bi-polar disorder and other mental health issues. Perhaps she was going through a low phase at the time of our last phone call? Also

– I know from personal experience – the first flush of success can be quite toxic and cause all sorts of insecurities and paranoia and end up damaging relationships.

A few years later – whilst I was touring *Dusk* in America – Sinéad reached out to my management saying she wanted to collaborate again and would I be interested? But I didn't get the message until sometime afterwards. My manager during that album/tour cycle – Steve Rennie – was an aggressive American rock manager. Steve was a decent guy and hardworking but a mismatch for me and had an exasperating habit of doing business behind my back and informing me about it sometime later. Without my knowledge he told Sinéad that yes, I *might* consider working with her again but *only* on the condition she appeared on stage with THE THE in LA to sing 'Kingdom Of Rain' for our upcoming concert there! Not surprisingly, she declined. His clumsy attempt at negotiation really embarrassed me. I was livid. I'd never bargain with another artist like that. The truth is, I *would* have been interested in collaborating again as I didn't bear a grudge and I'd never bad-mouthed her. I think we could have created something even better together as we were both stronger singers by that stage of our careers. But instead, another awkward situation arose and the moment for reconciliation – with her extending an olive branch – passed and that was that.

The last message I received from her was in the mid-noughties, asking if I'd give her permission to include 'Kingdom Of Rain' on her *Collaborations* compilation album. It was ironic really. Of course, I said yes.

JW: And how do you think this album fits with your discography?

MJ: *Mind Bomb* does have an obsessiveness about it. It deals with difficult subjects and involved seeing things in my mind's eye during the making of it that I didn't really want to see; quite dystopian and apocalyptic. I wouldn't want to go back there anytime soon. Music is a powerful stimulant regarding memory and nostalgia but some listeners would obviously have a completely different relationship to that album than I do.

Soul Mining, *Infected*, *Mind Bomb* and *Dusk* exist as a quartet in my mind; the London Town quartet. That's what we named the boxset when they were reissued back in 2002. They are inextricably linked and I'm proud of each. Everyone involved worked so hard and so much thought and passion went into each. They were all intense to make and took a lot out of me personally – but maybe I'm doing something wrong? Should writing and recording albums drain their creator and cause chaos in their personal lives!?

JW: Can I ask about the *Mind Bomb* artwork? The record cover signalled a departure from your work with Andrew...

MJ: As mentioned previously, because he was late delivering the artwork for *Infected* the first 100,000 or so copies went out with the photographic cover – a film still of me from the video for 'Out Of The Blue (into the fire)'. We fell out over it and he said he didn't want to do the next sleeve.

JW: Are those the only ones with photos of you on the cover?

MJ: Apart from the *Burning Blue Soul* reissue yes. Do you know whose idea that was? The *Mind Bomb* cover? Johnny's!

JW: Was it?

MJ: Yes. He said, 'Why do you always put your name at the bottom of the musician credits – as if you're hiding? Get it out there! Put your name in its proper place! Put your face on the cover!' He encouraged me to do it. I probably shouldn't have done, looking back. It meant I was being recognised more when I was out and about, which I didn't particularly like. Then again, my face was in the bloody videos too so I don't know what I'm complaining about!

Apart from the previously mentioned *Burning Blue Soul* my photo had never been on any artwork. But it comes with the territory I suppose – being on television and in the press and even doing books like this. As I've mentioned many times, I've always felt conflicted about fame and celebrity and – to be honest – that has probably held my career back commercially compared to many of my contemporaries because I never fully embraced that aspect of it. I've always been one foot in and one foot out.

JW: For *Mind Bomb* and on the tour, you went the 'Kevin Rowland' route, from Dexys Midnight Runners: dressing everyone in a uniform. The white T-shirts, the jeans.

MJ: I wasn't aware of any Kevin Rowland route but it was very intentional to dress the same, have a group identity. More like a football team I suppose.

JW: I liked that. *This* is what we're going to look like.

MJ: We had a very strong band ethic around *Mind Bomb*. But from the old days of my residency at the Marquee in 1982 I'd decided THE THE would wear all-black when performing live on stage. Partly due to having an ever-changing line-up, it meant that whoever was in the band – and on stage at any particular time – it would always look like THE THE.

The album and singles sleeves for *Mind Bomb* were designed by Fiona and also featured the work of a talented photographer by the name of Andrew MacPherson who I became quite friendly with. He was a hugely successful fashion photographer at that time. We wanted to create – and I hate this bloody word – an iconic image, something classic, simple. For the album cover, we used my face. For 'The Beat(en) Generation' single sleeve we wanted to create something along the lines of *Meet The Beatles* featuring our four faces, and that image ended up as the cover for 'The Beat(en) Generation' single. I was trying to make the idea of this new band tangible by featuring this photo on sleeves and adverts.

JW: Did the record company have any particular views on it?

MJ: I don't think so. I didn't take *too* much notice of their views to be honest although I got along well with many of them personally.

I was quite happy at CBS/Sony but I didn't want them getting too involved in the creative process so they had no input on any of our record sleeves.

JW: And the back cover?

MJ: That was obviously a direct reference – a steal in fact – from the anti-war poster by photomontagist John Heartfield. Titled 'Never Again' it was designed after the horrors of World War Two as both a lament and a warning. The image is of a dove impaled on a bayonet. It did upset some people when the album came out. I'm still passionately anti-war, in fact it's the main thing I still have in common with myself at that age.

JW: I have a question about preparing for the 1989–90 Versus The World Tour. How difficult was it to prepare the songs from *Soul Mining* and *Infected* with the new band members from *Mind Bomb*?

MJ: Well, I was very lucky because I had a brilliant band with which to interpret all the songs. We were joined by DC Collard on keyboards – who I still work with to this day. Actually, his name is David Collard but as we already had Palmer in the band I thought we can't have two Davids! So, to avoid confusion, I dubbed him DC and he's still known as that to this day. Anyway, he's a highly accomplished musician and worked incredibly hard preparing for the Versus The World Tour. He did an amazing job making that tour viable – in terms of recreating the earlier albums – with his use of samplers and sequencers.

When choosing which musicians to work with I tend to rely on instinct and intuition. Obviously a musician needs to be a decent player to begin with but a lot of it is also down to personality and sense of humour. With DC I'd arranged to meet him at my private club near Trafalgar Square. I'd already heard a recording of his playing so wasn't worried about his technical ability. It was his personality I needed to see close up. I'd made my decision to work with him within a couple of minutes. He's a very likeable person – funny, charming, direct and extremely talented. I've often said with DC he's the sort of person you can both take round your aunty's for a Sunday roast or to the sleaziest little bordello you can imagine. He's very content in either place! DC is also the musician I have worked the most with throughout my career.

In terms of preparations for the Versus The World Tour we needed to use samplers and sequencers to be able to recreate what we had done in the studio. Because remixer Arthur Baker seemed to have mislaid or lost the multitrack tape to 'GIANT', we had to redo all the chanting: myself, Johnny, James, Dave and DC. We re-recorded all the chanting by overdubbing, overdubbing and overdubbing. We then sampled and used that for the live shows in place of the lost original.

We've often changed the arrangements of my songs quite dramatically from tour to tour, but on that first tour we tried to keep it faithful to the original records. I had never toured before so Johnny (in particular, because he'd toured extensively with The Smiths) was invaluable, giving me so much useful advice about what to expect in certain circumstances or at certain venues.

It was a very exciting tour for me as there were countries I'd never visited before. Japan, for instance, was the most 'different' place I'd ever been at that point. As with many western bands at that time, as soon as we arrived at a hotel we were overwhelmed by dozens of young girls proffering gifts: books, CDs, pieces of art. They were extremely shy and polite and would hang around our hotels hour after hour – just waiting.

Due to the street and shop signs all being written in Japanese I found it hard to navigate when off wandering by myself. So, I'd do a sort of Hansel and Gretel thing – obviously not with physical pebbles, but mentally put images in my mind in a certain order that I could then retrace: a yellow building on the first corner, a broken streetlamp on the second street etc. One morning in Kyoto I got up in the early hours, wandered the streets and came across a Zendō (meditation hall). The experience of meditating at dawn in such a beautiful location was so powerful that I left the hall feeling too spaced-out and took a wrong turning. It took me many hours to find my way back to the hotel – no mobile phones in those days of course – and I nearly missed my first set of press interviews.

The concerts themselves were highly unusual too. For the auditorium we played in Tokyo I remember we were picked up at the hotel for show time with each band member being allocated his own, personal limousine, so we were driven convoy-style to the venue. During the concert itself – although sold-out and packed – it was extremely quiet. We'd finish a song and there would be silence. 'Security ushers' would be patrolling the aisles to make sure the audience stayed seated, using enormous, long poles with foam-padded ends to gently bash people on the head from a distance to remind them to sit down. At one point, Johnny wandered over and whispered to me, 'The only thing that could make this concert any weirder is if we had no clothes on!' I've since realised the cultural norm in Japan was to listen attentively and applaud only at appropriate moments, for example after a set or at the very end. It reflected broader Japanese values of respect, harmony, and not disturbing others' enjoyment. Apparently, in the decades since, it has become far more westernised, which is a shame.

Versus The World was a successful tour – a long one too. One hundred sold-out concerts I think. We played seven shows in London alone – what we called our 'Four Points Of The Compass' London Tour: Kilburn National, Brixton Academy, Town & Country Club (Kentish Town) and Hackney Empire – on consecutive nights – plus later in the tour coming back to perform three consecutive concerts at the Royal Albert Hall. I had all the house lights changed to red and we lit large bowls of frankincense an hour or so before the audience came in. I wanted to create a unique atmosphere for those nights. Not sure if Health & Safety rules would allow it these days. I've enjoyed all the tours for different reasons but that one remains special because it was my first. The guys in that band were true bandmates – incredibly supportive.

Since I began touring I have always lived by the motto, 'Don't just rehearse until you get it right. Rehearse until you cannot get it wrong.' Before we head off on the road I like to over-rehearse but then dial it back a bit – don't play for a few days, so we get an edge back.

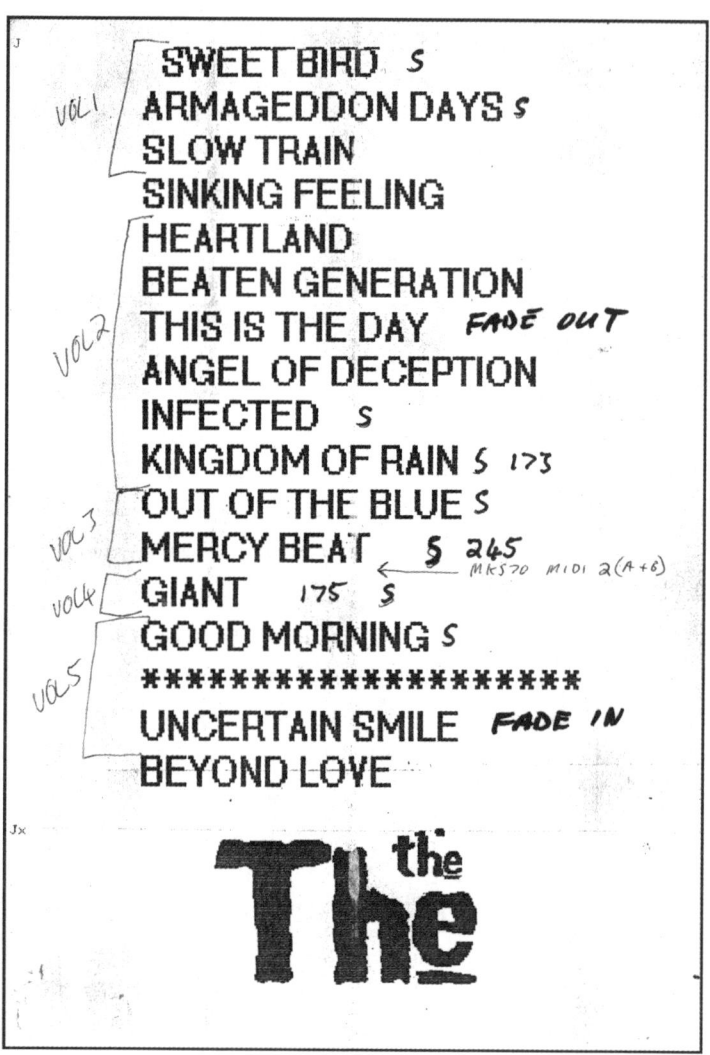

JW: With *Mind Bomb* did you spend more time writing and recording compared to your other albums?

MJ: They were all similar in a way. It's hard to remember. For instance, some songs came easy. 'The Beat(en) Generation', is one of those songs that just poured out almost instantly – compared to something like 'Heartland' which was written over eighteen months. 'August & September' was another one written over a longer period of time. It depends how dense the lyrics are. 'Heartland' and 'Armageddon' are similar in density of lyrics, whereas 'The Beat(en) Generation' is simpler. I can't remember off-hand which album took the longest.

JW: You've worked with a wide range of people throughout your career. Who's had the most significant impact on the songs as you were producing them?

MJ: The most intense relationship during the making of an album is with my co-producer and engineer. I'm with them all the time in the studio throughout the recording process whereas the musicians themselves come and go. Sometimes they may hang around a bit but more often they'll have finished their parts and leave.

Generally, I don't like to have a separate engineer and separate producer – although we did on *Mind Bomb* with Felix Kendall. I like to co-produce with a good engineer. The most important relationships I've had in this regard are with Paul Hardiman on *Soul Mining*, Warne Livesey and Roli Mosimann on *Infected* and *Mind Bomb*, and Bruce Lampcov on *Dusk*, *Hanky Panky* and *NakedSelf*. These relationships tend to be quite intense as you're working together from an early stage of the recordings, through second-stage demos, right the way through to the mixing and the mastering. You're working together pretty much every day and night for a prolonged period. These were all intense working relationships that became good friendships.

JW: I am interested to know how you ordered the songs. You said earlier that 'Good Morning Beautiful' was always going to be the first track on *Mind Bomb*. I wanted to observe that the most hopeful of the songs, 'Beyond Love', being last, leaves the listener with a feeling of hope. Was this intentional, after the heavier, more political material?

MJ: It wouldn't be my intention to leave people feeling depressed or hopeless. But I didn't think the album version turned out as well as some of the demos we did though. It's a known problem that plagues musicians – 'demo-itis'. You record a demo that has a certain energy or mystique but you can never quite recreate it, no matter how hard you try. On *The Comeback Special* we radically reworked 'Beyond Love' and I was pleased with that new direction musically. I was always happy with the lyrics though, particularly the lines:

> The drops of semen and the clots of blood
> Which may one day become like us
> With outstretched hands reaching beyond love
> And up to something above

That song and 'Love Is Stronger Than Death' tie together somehow. Certain songs in the catalogue naturally gather together to become little families. You could say the same of 'Perfect', 'Flesh & Bones', 'The Beat(en) Generation', 'Pillar Box Red' and 'Heartland'.

JW: All of these lyrics could be written today.

MJ: Maybe.

JW: Is there anyone you're listening to now you'd recommend?

MJ: There is just so much great music out there. Let's see. My eldest son, Jackson, sends me lots of wonderful music from around the world and from different eras. What do we have on this playlist he recently sent me? 'Ma Be Ham Nemiresim' by Googoosh, 'Wede Harer Guzo' by Hailu Mergia, Dahlak Band, 'Cracking' by Crumb, 'Timbuktu Fasso' by Amine Bouhafa and Fatoumata Diawara and hundreds of other tracks.

I've got a nice hi-fi system and crank things up through my big old Tannoy York speakers. I often have collaborative DJ sessions with friends around at my place, a game where we will pass a phone around from one to the other, and each person has to play a track the others have never heard but have to guess what it is. I've heard some great tracks that way. Barrie is very good at that game and always pulls out brilliant tracks I haven't heard before. Gillian often plays interesting music in the office I haven't heard before. Gerard plays good music too. He played a brilliant track one session, 'Nànnuflày' by his friend, the late Mark Lanegan from

Screaming Trees, in collaboration with Tinariwen and Kurt Vile. This track has become a regular for me when the night moves into the early hours. But let's check on my phone what I've been playing recently: 'Journey in Satchidananda' by Alice Coltrane, 'Coffee Cold' by Gait MacDermot, 'Ruby' by Ali Farka Touré, 'Hétérozygote' by Luc Ferrari, 'Spoonful' by Howlin' Wolf, 'Her Eyes Are A Blue Million Miles' by Captain Beefheart, 'Baltimore' by Randy Newman, 'The Lone Ranger' by Betty Davis, 'I'm Your Boogie Man' by KC & The Sunshine Band. There is just so much great music out there. Old, new, local, international. It is impossible to keep up with it all. My taste is very eclectic: jazz, blues, ambient, African, Latino, electronic and I do love classical and Baroque. I find myself repeatedly returning to Bach who – to me – was the greatest composer who ever lived.

To be honest, some of the things I love listening to the most are the sounds of nature: birds, the wind soughing through the trees, the sound of water flowing.

JW: How about the title *Mind Bomb*? How did that come about?

MJ: As mentioned earlier, the working title was *Psychonaut*. The recordings were finished, the album was mixed and I was starting to think about the sleeve. But then I changed my mind about the title.

Mind Bomb came about because I was reading Timothy Leary's *The Politics of Ecstasy* (1968) whilst on holiday in Mallorca with Fiona and there was a sentence Leary used that contained the phrase 'mind bomb'. It jumped out as it seemed quite apt at the time. Looking back, I do prefer *Psychonaut*. I might even use it for a future album.

JW: What else was happening in your life around this time?

MJ: I'd sold my flat in Stoke Newington and used the money to purchase a small cottage in the Mallorcan hills not far from Deià. It was another place where I'd caught the 'fag end' of an era. That part of Mallorca was brought to the attention of Bohemian types by the poet Robert Graves. He moved there from England following WW1 and the publication of his memoir *Goodbye To All That*. Lots of poets, painters, musicians and writers followed in his wake over the next few decades and established a kind of artists' colony. It evolved into an intriguing mix of Mallorcan and hippy culture with children of the creative types being born there, mingling with the local kids. But places like that don't remain secret for long and with increased tourism – and aggressive estate agents sensing opportunity – it had the effect of attracting a more affluent, business-minded community – eventually pricing out locals and artists alike. There are still remnants of the old way of life here and there if you know where to look. I often have working trips there with bandmembers before albums or tours.

CHAPTER SIX
The More I See The Less I Know

Tragedy strikes deep at the heart of the Johnson family with the sudden passing of Eugene. A new studio in Shoreditch is procured and Dusk *emerges through the fog and confusion of grief. The album is also suffused with lust and addiction and delivers bonafide hit singles. Achieving a UK chart position of number two, it becomes one of the best-selling THE THE albums.*

JW: *Dusk* emerged three years after *Mind Bomb*, in 1993. What state of mind you were in when you approached it, because obviously a lot had happened after *Mind Bomb*. It was written in the wake of the death of one of your younger brothers, Eugene.

MJ: After *Mind Bomb* was released we embarked on the lengthy THE THE Versus The World Tour. During a pause in the tour – just prior to the American leg – I received devastating news, whilst at my house in Mallorca, that Eugene had died suddenly. I didn't actually find out until two days after it had happened as I didn't have a telephone at my house. My friend Toby Hogarth managed to track me down to tell me my dad was trying to get hold of me. I went to his house to make the call.

I remember that fateful evening well – and that devastating phone call. My dad had asked if Fiona was with me before informing me Eugene had died. I must have gone into an instant state of shock. I thought he was joking. Why would he joke about such a terrible thing? I just couldn't get my head around it. Thank God Fiona was with me. A few years earlier she'd lost her own sibling – her sister June – so there was nobody more empathetic and supportive I could possibly have been with. I could not sleep at all that night – it was one long, waking nightmare. At the break of dawn, we drove to the airport and arranged to get on the first flight back to England. It was a life-shattering, life-changing event for my family. I feel its effects to this day. It seared itself into my nervous system. I still get anxious with unexpected phone calls from family members.

JW: How did that affect your creative life?

MJ: I hear the effect of that terrible experience in the music of *Dusk*. I don't know if gentle is the right word – but certainly they were the most introspective and philosophical set of songs I had ever written. Possibly the best song I've written to date is 'Love Is Stronger Than Death' – the centrepiece of that album and a eulogy for Eugene. It was the first song written for the album and I wrote it not only as therapy for myself but also in the hope it might help others going through a similar situation. I have my own beliefs about the afterlife and what happens when we leave these temporary, fragile vehicles we call our bodies – let's say I have a positive view and I'm certainly no atheist. I used to laughingly say I was a born-again agnostic but my belief is stronger than that. It's all completely unknowable to us in life – of course – and to try to define what that belief really is you can end up subscribing to philosophies you don't really believe in.

My connection to creativity and songwriting was one of the things that helped me limp through that awful period of bereavement. I'm not sure if transmutation or alchemy is the right word in this context but being able to create something beautiful out of something terrible helped get me though one of the darkest periods of my life. I didn't get through it unscathed, though, as that deep sense of loss and disorientation unleashed some dark and addictive patterns of behaviour that affected me for years.

What I was pleased about with 'Love Is Stronger Than Death' – as a songwriter – was not just the overall expression of emotion but also the way musically the structure mirrors and enhances the development of the lyrics. For instance, the way the bridge leads into the chorus, and the acceptance of how we might evolve through loss – 'Here come the blue skies, here comes springtime', and finally the line, 'When everything that dies shall rise'. Rebirth. It is a positive, hopeful song but also a very sensitive song and one that, from what I've heard after many people have written to me over the years, has really helped them get through difficult situations when they have also lost people they love.

I know that it continues to be played at many funerals. Interestingly – at the other end of the scale – 'This Is The Day' still gets played at many weddings. But writing something that people can keep so close to their hearts and carry through life is such a positive feeling for me. That a song inspired by my beautiful brother Eugene has touched and helped so many people all over the world in their hour of need means so much to me. That song helped me process my own bereavement. And if I am to think of what my true essence as a songwriter is, then that song is it. Forget the transitory trinkets of fame and critical acclaim. A simple song written from the heart that has travelled the world over decades – touching and helping people. That's far more important to me than any chart position, review or industry award.

Going into that album, I knew it would be overshadowed by this massive personal event. Also, I knew from the start – I actually found some old notes recently where I'd written out the parameters before I began – that it would be a stripped-down, melodic and organic-sounding album. No synthesisers, samplers or drum machines.

JW: I think you also said that you wanted there to be a concision to it.

MJ: Yes, absolutely. I was carrying over the band from *Mind Bomb* and Versus The World who were a great group of musicians and good friends: Johnny Marr, James Eller, DC Collard and Dave Palmer.

The other thing was, by this stage I now owned The Garden Studio in Shoreditch, where I'd been working on and off since 1982 – from *Soul Mining*. I'd bought it in 1991. For the writing of *Dusk*, I'd also bought myself a Tascam 688 Midistudio. I remember setting that up with a little Alesis SR-16 drum machine in my loft in East London and writing all the songs on that. The demos were all quite specific yet also left room for the musicians to express themselves.

JW: And you decided to change your backroom team for this album?

MJ: As much as I loved working with both Warne and Roli – and they were both good friends – I just thought it was time for a change, to freshen things up. So, my co-producer and engineer for *Dusk* was Bruce Lampcov. This was the first album we did together, although he'd previously done some recording and mixing for me; he recorded three concerts we performed in Detroit plus mixed the soundtrack to the Tim Pope film of our Royal Albert Hall concert *THE THE Versus The World*. Based in London at that time, Bruce was originally from Detroit. He'd worked his way up through the New York studio system – notably Power Station – and had carved out a great reputation as a world-class engineer. We hit it off well.

I wanted to record *Dusk* in The Garden Studio because I felt very comfortable there. It was a wonderful studio, wonderful atmosphere. It had long been like a second home to me, especially now that I owned it. It was in a basement and had a womb-like atmosphere. I set it up with oil lamps and incense and ensured it was very dark. My wanting to create in a dark, warm environment must have been to do with the fragile emotional state I was still in.

Bruce and I obviously spent a huge amount of time together, mostly down in the bowels of the dimly lit Garden – so when taking a break I would insist we have a daily walk around the neighbourhood. I used to take him to the Kosher Luncheon Club on Greatorex Street almost every day. It was an old-fashioned canteen with a great atmosphere, high ceilings, delicious food and friendly staff neatly dressed in white shirts or blouses and black trousers or skirts. You'd often see interesting characters at different tables: Steven Berkoff* was a regular. It was somewhere my dad used to go to in the sixties and was one of the last eateries of its type to survive in East London. It was already under threat though and Bruce and I signed the petitions to help save it, but sadly it lost its battle with its landlord and closed down shortly after we finished recording *Dusk*.

Stratford Carpenters Road...

Johnny tells a funny story about the contrast between the outside world and this little alternative world I'd created in the studio: how he'd drive in each morning in his new, open-top Alfa Romeo sports car – he had a place in Chelsea at the time. He'd drive over from Chelsea, along the Embankment on beautiful blue-skied sunny days, feeling chipper and cheerful and he'd

---

* Steven Berkoff is an English actor, author, playwright and theatre director. He is recognised for staging work with a style known as 'Berkovian theatre', which combines elements of physical theatre and expressionism.

arrive in Shoreditch, park his car, walk in our front door and down the stairs and into this very dark, very hot space where the intensity would then begin. The incense was burning, the oil wheels turning – Dave Palmer used to call it the 'psychic sauna'. It was a powerful experience working in that environment.

Overall the recording sessions went really well but we did have some issues making *Dusk*. Like all relationships, all bands have a certain lifespan, it may be long or it may be short. For this particular band we had made *Mind Bomb*, which was very intense, then gone on the Versus The World Tour, which was also very intense. For the recording of *Dusk*, I could feel it all starting to gently crumble and break apart. The musicians for the most part played beautifully on these recordings but we were not quite as close as before and I could sense everyone getting distracted by other things and slowly drifting apart. To be honest, I always felt a bit on the back foot and a little spaced-out – not quite myself for many of these sessions. I was still suffering from the depression related to grief and wasn't my usual self. Also, around this time Johnny had just started another project with Bernard Sumner from New Order.

JW: Electronic.

MJ: Yes. And James had been offered a solo deal with Polydor around that time too. DC was absolutely fine and was very dedicated to what we were doing but this was his first album with THE THE. Dave Palmer on the other hand became very unfocused. He was doing a lot of partying back then. It was around the time of Acid House, so he'd wander in – often late – wearing baggy clothes, shouting, 'Aceeed! Aceeed!' It was vaguely humorous at first but when it started affecting his performance it became an issue. He was such a great drummer and had such high standards normally, but his focus was wavering and he was having too many late nights and generally misbehaving. There was one occasion when we'd put him up in a nice flat in Knightsbridge and it got trashed. I loved Dave and he was a dear friend and incredible musician but I'd have to repeatedly take him aside and have words.

By this point it was a couple years after Eugene died, but my mum and dad were still suffering very badly. It was so hard on my family. So, all of this in the background really threw me off. I even remember Dave, a couple of times saying, 'What's going on, Matt? You seem spaced-out and not as focused as normal' I thought it was a bit rich coming from him! I'd usually be so sharp in the studio, listening to every beat, each note. But I may have seemed a bit spaced-out because I was feeling introspective and melancholy. My demeanour had changed. I was less extrovert and, I don't know, 'controlling' is not the right word, but I seemed less 'on it'. I was less physically expressive and demonstrative about what I wanted, but I was very much focused in my head. I knew what I wanted. So, with Dave – after a couple of warnings were ignored – I had to throw him overboard because his misbehaviour was getting worse. He'd even started showing up with some girl he'd just met – and this was something we've never done during our sessions – bringing strangers in. It was very hard for me to fire Dave, because he'd been my right-hand man. We worked together so much and I loved Dave as a person, and as a musician I had so much respect for him. It was very tough, it was dispiriting and really got me down.

Then we had to think: how do we replace one of the best drummers in England? I know, we'll bring in one of the best drummers in America! So, we got Vinnie Colaiuta – Grammy award-winning former drummer for Frank Zappa and Joni Mitchell – to come in and play on a couple of tracks – 'Dogs Of Lust' and 'Bluer Than Midnight'. But Vinnie had limited availability as he was on tour and only passing through town. So, we also brought in Bruce Smith – formerly of The Pop Group. I knew him a bit socially and had always liked his drumming style. He played on 'Helpline Operator' and 'This Is The Night'.

JW: He played with Rip Rig + Panic as well, didn't he? And The Slits.

MJ: He did. Public Image Ltd as well. He was involved with Neneh Cherry for years too and they have a daughter together. A really nice guy, Bruce. I liked him. So, I brought those two in and they both did a great job for us.

JW: You had some other guest musicians. Guy Barker?

MJ: Yes – and Ashley Slater, John Thirkle, David Lawrence and Chris Batchelor joined Guy as part of our brass section. And the great Danny Thompson on upright bass who'd also played on *Mind Bomb*. Plus, my old friend Paul Webb sang backing vocals with Zeke on 'Lonely Planet'. There weren't as many musicians as there had been on *Infected* or *Mind Bomb* – or even *Soul Mining* – as I wanted a more intimate sound.

JW: How different was it working with Bruce Lampcov compared to Warne and Roli?

MJ: It's a very warm-sounding album even though it was recorded using fairly primitive digital equipment. It also sounds more aggressive and live-sounding than for instance, *Mind Bomb*. Bruce did a great job. These were still early days as far as affordable digital recording goes. This was pre-Pro Tools – even pre-Alesis ADAT. But there were these new 12-track digital multitracks from Akai – ADAM – that had just come to market. They were modular so you could tie multiple machines together. I bought two to create a 24-track set-up. They were very big machines compared to what musicians have available today but they were small and considered portable compared to, say, the Mitsubishi X800 or the Sony PCM-3324 digital multitracks we'd used on *Infected* and *Mind Bomb*. I initially bought them for my personal studio but then came the opportunity to buy The Garden so I merged my own studio with it.

Bruce was a superb engineer. One of the best I've ever worked with. He was also a wonderful co-producer too as he knew the sort of sounds I liked, so we developed an effective shorthand. I trusted Bruce to quickly get the sounds I liked. Working down in that lovely environment – it was dark, it was hot – was incredibly atmospheric. Bruce was obviously with me the whole time whereas the band members would come and go. We recorded a lot of it live – well, we did when Dave was still compos mentis! Then we'd overdub different parts. Essentially, the core of the sound of *Dusk* is live, which was the right thing to do because it was such a powerful band. We were able to get decent isolation between the instruments and amplifiers but maintained eye lines whilst performing. I think that's what gives the album a certain vibrancy.

JW: When I listen to the material that you've been releasing recently alongside the soundtrack compositions and the early material reissues, it strikes me how interesting it is in a sonic sense. I'm wondering if that's an element that has been missed by some people. I don't hear a massive difference between the sounds on *Dusk* or *Mind Bomb* – which are commercial albums – and some of your more experimental recordings. But I think you've always had an ear for unusual sounds. I read that in the making of *Dusk* there was even a special room that you would use for effects. There's always something interesting soundwise happening on your records, which goes back to your post-punk DIY background and your origins. I think *Dusk* is a particularly fascinating record in terms of what's happening sonically.

MJ: 'Lung Shadows' fits in very well with the instrumental, atmospheric side of THE THE and could easily be on one of the Cinéola soundtrack releases.

There were always three different threads – which are not mutually exclusive. A part of me loves tape recorder experimentation, musique concrète and experimental music; and another part enjoys classic songwriting, whether it be inspired by the likes of Hank Williams, Leonard Cohen, Robert Johnson, Bob Dylan, John Lennon, etc; and the third part is of course film and television soundtracks.

Three very different aspects but I really enjoy each of them. I absolutely love just sitting around working out songs on my acoustic guitar, having a simple, classic band line-up and production for a song; but on the other hand, I also love pottering around with my esoteric synthesisers and tape recorders on a rainy Sunday afternoon, indulging in sonic experimentation, where no sound is out of bounds.

I've tried to combine those elements and sometimes they don't necessarily work that well but other times they do. 'Lung Shadows' being an example of the latter. It was one of those keyboard parts I used to play to myself over and over when I'd sit at the piano – like 'Good Morning Beautiful' – and then I finally found a home for it. People thought the title was referring to lung cancer but it wasn't. It was actually lung shadows as in disconnected ethereal voices. If you listen carefully you can hear voices very slightly. I phoned up female sex workers, recorded them and we mixed them very low in the track. What you can hear is these ghostly voices of orgasmic – or pseudo-orgasmic – women. I assume they were faking their orgasms!

JW: It feels like a very nocturnal record. It reminds me of your Cinéola soundtracks, especially the work you've done with your brother Gerard. There's also – I don't know if 'noir' is the right term...

MJ: 'Noir' is a good descriptive term for *Dusk*.

JW: On three or four tracks, but particularly 'Lung Shadows' and 'Bluer Than Midnight', there is that aspect. But there's also a nod towards jazz. Was that your thinking behind bringing people in like Ashley Slater who you mentioned, and Guy Barker? To have that jazz influence?

MJ: Well, they are great musicians and we wanted to infuse some of the tracks with an element of late-night jazz. I like 'sonic noir' as a description for *Dusk*, bearing in mind when I was writing that album I was living quite a nocturnal life. I'd often get up in the very early hours – sometimes not even going to bed – and head out in 'Harold' my old Rover P5B saloon, and drive around the empty streets of London. Harold had a decent sound system, though it was cassette. I'd repeatedly listen to the demos of songs I was working on and drive around London at three, four, five or six in the morning. Just driving around the City, St Paul's, up the Embankment to Soho, across the river and down the other side. It was wonderful. I would often get out and take long walks through the dark, deserted London streets.

Remember, London was not the twenty-four-hour city it is now, with tonnes of late-night places. These days it's hard to find any solitude in London at any hour of the day or night but back then it was different. Places closed before midnight and the city was deserted by one in the morning. Nowadays, you get hordes of booze tourists shrieking, squawking and rampaging through the streets at that hour and later due to the so-called 'night-time economy'. But it just wasn't the case then.

So, the kind of nocturnal living I was doing then really informed a lot of the writing. I think of that album as being very much under-lit – by sodium light and candlelight. Very shadowy. As I was writing and recording I'd have very atmospheric lighting in the part of my building I was living in then – the floor with the large loft space. It was under-lit with dark reds and oranges, and with very large floor-to-ceiling venetian blinds, the light from the sodium lights outside cast geometric shapes and shadows across the old wooden floors and high ceilings. It was very noir and I think that comes across on the album.

Obviously, the cover artwork from Andrew utilises similar colours as well. Fiona was very supportive of me – as she always was – during that time and encouraged me to do whatever I needed to do to write that album. That period, spending a lot of time by myself, wandering around London, driving around London in the early hours, was therapeutic for me but also quite romantic when I think about it now because it was a very different world, a lost world, a lost London. You don't realise it at the time of course, just how fundamentally society and life will change.

JW: I think you used a phrase in *Long Shadows, High Hopes*, Neil Fraser's biography on THE THE, describing the album as 'a hymn to the city after dark'. I used to like driving around London too. My favourite journey in London was past the old Financial Times building. It was a glass building, and when they were printing you would see these reams of pink paper. It was just amazing. You don't get things like that anymore. As you're talking it reminds me of the shots of De Niro in *Taxi Driver*, driving his taxi through New York with those sodium neon lights.

MJ: I loved that opening scene – with the Bernard Hermann score and De Niro's Checker Cab slowly gliding through the New York steam and neon lights. Well, it definitely had that feel to it, particularly driving Harold, my loyal old P5B, with his intoxicating smell of leather, wood and petrol and his V8 engine rumbling away. Just the experience of driving a car like that is very evocative and enjoyable. That was a big part of it.

To me – in that period of my life – the darkness was comforting – and the candlelight, the sodium lights and the shadows. Another person might find it a very depressing environment and looking back it was definitely a hangover from bereavement. I just wanted to stay in that dark red, womb-like environment during that period of time. It was comforting on the one hand yet, unfortunately, also allowed some dark thoughts to breed.

JW: There's an anecdote that Johnny Marr got very emotional when he was playing on 'Love Is Stronger Than Death'. It deals with death but tries to do it in a way, as you said, which is spiritual and hopes to find something positive in the process.

MJ: I did want it to be uplifting, and to give comfort primarily to myself, I suppose, as I was writing it, but then hopefully to other people too. The first-time that bereavement strikes is a terrible shock – well, it is terrible *whenever* it happens, and, of course, ideally you don't want it to happen at all, but, unless you die young yourself it *is* going to happen. I'm trying not to compare bereavements, but I suppose when loved ones move on from life in the natural order – pets, grandparents, aunts, uncles, parents, older siblings – it is deeply sad but easier to understand, accept and process – because, let's face it – we all know we're on a one-way conveyor belt out of here. But when people seem to just get plucked at random at such a young age, when they've got so much to live for? It just makes no sense, it's tragic and disorientating and often destroys the lives of those left behind.

Despite writing lyrics that may be construed as a bit melancholic or angry I've always been a hopeful person. I've tried to convey that through the music at least. But when these arbitrary events strike so suddenly and so hard, you just start losing faith in the future. There is an anxiety – a realisation – that each of us are dangling from a very fine thread that can be cut at any time and that random, terrifying events can just strike out of the blue. It makes you frightened for everyone around you, because you don't know when it's going to happen next. You develop this mistrust in life, this paranoia, superstition and sense that even when you're feeling really good about things – does that now indicate something awful is about to happen to balance it out? Like the lyric on 'Soul Mining': 'Something always goes wrong / When things are going right'.

With 'Love Is Stronger Than Death', through all the sadness that my family and I were struggling with I needed there to be a positive message in this song. Based on my own, deep feeling that death is *not* the end, that there is so much more to life and the human spirit and our existence than we're able to detect, as spirits trying to express ourselves through these frail bodies, constrained by the five senses that perhaps keep more of reality out than they let in.

Having been someone who has gone through periods of intense introspections at an early age and has also meditated intensively – and experimented with hallucinogenics – I sensed things at a fairly early age, of subtle energy patterns that surround and permeate us. That we are an intrinsic part of something greater than we can realise in our day-to-day ego-driven lives. That there is a greater purpose for our souls. That we may catch only occasional glimpses of the meaning of our lives from time to time – as when very dark terrain is illuminated by an occasional lighting flash. So, I tried to get that positivity into a song, that death is *not* the end, no matter how hard and painful it is to lose someone close to us.

JW: 'True Happiness (this way lies)' is an interesting track because in the past you have spoken about spirituality and Buddhism and this for me is a track on the album which articulates the fact that life is not always about the destination, but also about the journey *towards* the destination. Was that something that you were trying to articulate in this song? It seems to suggest that there's a search for answers and you might not always get the answers, but sometimes it's the *search* that can lead you to other paths of understanding and knowledge.

MJ: I've always enjoyed singing that track live as I think it's stood the test of time. Just to talk about that particular recording for a moment, I wanted to make it a bit vaudevillian, to have a cartoon-like audience reaction to the words as I was singing them. So, when I played it live in the studio, Bruce and I gathered a bunch of crowd reaction samples and loaded them into a couple of Akai samplers and connected several foot pedals that would trigger different audience reactions. We marked each pedal with tape, upon which was written the different expressions, so one would have 'Aah', another would have 'Ooh' or 'laughter' etc. So, I sang and played the guitar live and pressed the relevant foot pedals to get the correct response from the audience dependent upon the lyric. Also, with the opening section, I was trying to impersonate one of those old American TV voiceovers – do you remember the old sixties *Batman* shows where the narrator would be completely over the top?

I wanted the recording to sound a bit theatrical, vaudevillian, larger-than-life. But the lyrics themselves? I think they're quite profound in a way. 'But when you put your arms around me / Well, I'll be looking over your shoulder for something new'. What's the final line? 'The only true freedom is freedom from the heart's desires.' Yes, there is a bit of a Buddhist message in there. We are born and raised in an acquisitive society, saturated by materialism, by sex on television and in magazines – now obviously the internet too.

If you think of America, for instance, it's probably the most affluent country in human history yet there's a disproportionate level of misery, confusion, depression, and addiction to prescription drugs for mental health issues. It's becoming the same in England of course, but America is a particularly poignant example because a country could not wish to have more on a material level. This vast, beautiful continent-sized country has everything it could possibly wish for, and yet so many of its populace are deeply troubled, depressed and lost. Instead of appreciating what it has got and dealing with its internal problems, its government (suffering from supremacy delusions) cannot resist attacking and attempting to dominate all other countries and cultures. On a micro level, many of us as individuals, are trying to calm our internal turbulence and disquiet through whatever means we can lay our hands on – whether it's through sex, drugs, alcohol or—

JW: Consumerism.

MJ: Yes. Retail therapy is rampant. I am rather partial to that myself! But – as with all addictions – it's like drinking salt water – a temporary quenching of thirst but then the craving increases as it rots us from the inside. So, the only solution is to escape from these incessant cravings, but how do we do that? There's the

Buddhist route, but as we know the real hardcore Buddhist route is not the route a lot of westerners choose when they flirt with this philosophy. To many it just means chanting for material things, new relationships and personal pleasure rather than turning one's back upon materialism. I often add a disclaimer when I sing that song live, with the line, 'I've never found peace upon the breasts of a girl,' because I have to admit I've found plenty of peace upon a lot of breasts – albeit temporary but certainly enjoyable. How old is that album now? 1993? How many years is that?

JW: Over thirty years.

MJ: Yes. I sometimes get muddled up with those old albums, so it's hard for me to go back in time and remember what I was thinking about and why, but the important thing is that I do still enjoy singing those songs, and they still mean a lot to me.

'Bluer Than Midnight' was a tough song to write, probably the most naked, soul-baring song I've ever written – to openly ask why can't love ever touch my soul like fear? And to publicly ask to be saved. It was a dark time for me.

JW: As the title would suggest.

MJ: Another of my favourites is 'This Is The Night'. The twisted sibling to 'This Is The Day'. That's also enjoyable to perform live. The mood I was going for there is a bit 'Weimer Republic', candlelit, small club – there's even a lyrical reference to Brecht. DC added his wonderful piano solo. I actually like that just as much as the 'Uncertain Smile' piano solo, even though it's much shorter. Johnny also performed a great guitar solo at the end. There's a bluesy, jazz influence on this song. There's a demo of an earlier version in 4/4 time – a completely different atmosphere and feel – but it just wasn't working so we changed to 6/8 time.

JW: The mention of the blues is a lovely segue, because I've always been a really big fan of 'Dogs Of Lust' which was the lead single from *Dusk*. In the past you have spoken about your admiration for a lot of blues singers, and you mentioned Howlin' Wolf* – we're both big fans.

There is a blues element to 'Dogs Of Lust', not just from that great vocal falsetto where you imitate a horny dog (how I'd describe it!). I also think that track is a really good microcosm of your work lyrically, because it talks about the dichotomy between spiritual and physical yearning.

I remember really being amused by the Tim Pope video. It makes sense now you've described the dimly lit basement studio where you recorded – you all look incredibly hot and sweaty and uncomfortable. It's such a great video.

MJ: The subtitle to *Dusk* is 'Entre Chien Et Loup', which was translated as the time 'between dog and wolf' by Sophie, the French girlfriend at the time of my friend Toby. She uttered the phrase when we were all enjoying a stunning sunset in Mallorca, and it intrigued me. I already had the title *Dusk* but this gave added meaning for me. One might think of a dog as a symbol of fidelity set against the predatory nature of a wolf. I thought this a perfect metaphor for the subject matter of the album: that eternal, internal struggle and the spiritual/sexual tension that pervades this album. So, 'Dogs Of Lust', now how does that start?

JW: I like the siren sounds at the start.

MJ: On 'Dogs Of Lust'? Because on 'Bluer Than Midnight' you can hear actual sirens in the distance.

JW: Both, yes. At least they sound like sirens to me.

MJ: Oh, on 'Dogs Of Lust' it's a combination of guitars and harmonica playing in unison. I'd always hear police sirens outside my place – still do – and I much prefer the sound of the old British police cars – I never liked the American ones we now have. So, I

---

* Chester Arthur Burnett (AKA Howlin' Wolf) was an American blues musician at the forefront of transforming acoustic Delta blues into electric Chicago blues.

played that riff on guitar – sort of copying an old police siren – and got Johnny to double it on harmonica.

JW: Yes, the old sirens are much better.

MJ: Or those old French ones you might hear in a Jean-Pierre Melville film. When I say 'lovely', they were evocative – and they got the job done. I don't know why we all had to switch to the shrieking American version that feels like a knitting needle being jammed in your ear – but that's another subject.

JW: That's the way the world's gone.

MJ: So, Vinnie Colaiuta played drums on 'Dogs Of Lust'. Working with him was interesting, he was a lovely guy. I remember we initially had some trouble getting him to play 'looser' because he's such a precise drummer. We wanted more 'slop' on the snare so he had to overcome his perfectionist instincts to give us what we wanted but we ended up with a mesmerising drum track. James played bass brilliantly – as ever – and locked in effortlessly. I played some basic electric guitar, and Johnny played harmonica and added a few layers of guitars – beautiful interlocking rhythmic parts that I loved as soon as he started playing them. Gave me goosebumps watching him play those.

I can't recall if we'd taken a little bit of acid that night although I do remember us going around to a pub called The Old Blue Last – now a well-known hipster music pub in Shoreditch but in those days, it was a proper old East End boozer with locals who looked like National Front types. A proper pub with beer-soaked carpets and dark red lighting. It was a bit surreal and threatening. Someone may have even been on the piano playing old cockney songs, 'Knees Up Mother Brown' perhaps, but we had a pint or two – it was quite intense but put us in the perfect mood for 'Dogs Of Lust' somehow. I remember that session well: a night session, just Bruce, Johnny and me. In fact, I think that was the last time Johnny and I were actually in a recording studio together. His overdubs on 'We Can't Stop What's Coming' were done remotely.

Later on, we decided to film the video with Tim Pope in The Garden. I bought some sodium lights – same as actual streetlamps but just the light section obviously not the poles! – to give it that sickly orange look. These lamps are designed to light up entire streets so putting them in a compact recording studio was intense. Then Tim being Tim hired in aircraft hangar heaters – very, very powerful heaters. Johnny brought in what he called 'eggs'. They were strong tranquilisers. We also drank a bottle of tequila between us throughout the filming. We didn't have a drummer in the video. It was just me, Johnny and James, because Vinnie had left on tour. I remember Johnny and I took an egg each before guzzling the tequila. James, wisely, didn't partake. Johnny and I were melting, but were quite okay with it as it felt wonderful and sensual in a way, being that hot and sweaty and singing – high as kites. James was very alarmed about the condition of his bass – his pride and joy – as he could feel it literally melting in his hands.

JW: It was that hot, was it?

MJ: It was sweltering, boiling, like being in a sauna. James was genuinely concerned. He said, 'My fretboard is starting to get sticky! The glue is melting! This is not cool!' We were just saying, 'C'mon, chill out, man.' We got through it though. I loved it. For the 12-inch X-rated version we got this attractive young German lady – Nora I think her name was – to perform a striptease. It was a very sexual song and she was in my loft apartment running around naked. She's then superimposed in blue upon our orange glow. I thought it worked very well and maintained the noir atmosphere of the album. It would be banned for sexism now I suppose.

JW: The lyrics really do sum up how lust can be quite imprisoning.

MJ: Yes. It's about sexual addiction: 'Here they come, the dogs of lust / Out of my mind and into my life'. Sexual fantasy and its manifestation. And you're right, it is imprisoning. It can become incredibly dominating. I suppose that's one of the benefits of growing older; it does become less dominating. I remember a great quote from Kingsley Amis, I think he was in his mid-70s or whatever – and said one of the few benefits of getting older was losing his libido because it was like being chained to a fucking idiot for 60 years!

JW: Aristotle said something similar.

'Slow Emotion Replay' was the third single off *Dusk*. You mentioned Andrew's artwork. I want you to talk about the artwork for the singles, because I really like that artwork. On 'Slow Emotion Replay', the artwork has a football element to it. I remember it having the Three Lions on it.

MJ: That's right – it was actually Bobby Moore's World Cup-winning shirt.

JW: In the song you seem to be saying that there are all these things going on in the world and we're not always going to have the answers. It seems a more relaxed lyric. Was that something that you felt with that track?

MJ: If I'm honest, I probably came across as angry and lacking humour in *Infected* and *Mind Bomb* – which I don't think was true but that's how people may have perceived it. And, looking back – those major life events that we all have to go through change us – whether bereavement, divorce, serious illness, redundancy. We're all destined to navigate these big life events. I think we have to find something positive through these difficulties. And one of the positive things for me was suddenly being very *unsure*. The lyric in that song:

> The more I see the less I know
> About all the things I thought were wrong or right
> And carved in stone

That's how I felt. How I still feel. There was an ego death. It's a very humbling feeling. Suddenly feeling small and awestruck. I read a quote many years ago as a teenager, 'The supreme fruit that can be plucked from the tree of knowledge is the consciousness of our ignorance.' I now know through experience that nothing is truer.

We have a finite, short lifespan, we don't understand anywhere near as much as we think we do. I'm also put in mind of that verse from the Tao Te Ching:* 'He who knows does not speak; He who speaks does not know. To know that you do not know is the best. To pretend to know when you do not know is a disease.' It's enough to make you want to keep your mouth firmly shut!

When we worked together there were some wonderful things Johnny contributed, but possibly my favourite thing was the harmonica in 'Slow Emotion Replay'. It's beautiful and joyous – yet full of yearning and tinged with melancholy – that lovely combination which gives goosebumps.

JW: It's that sweet spot, isn't it?

MJ: Yes, it really does hit the sweet spot. And that song had a resignation, a feeling of just embracing one's ignorance. And when I say 'ignorance', I don't mean that in the pejorative, negative sense but a sense of relief and release in that acknowledgement. That maybe we need to step back and put our trust in life, in the universe.

The sleeve, which was Andrew's suggestion, was obviously a pun on a football match's slow-motion replay. For us personally: we grew up in East London in the sixties, near West Ham, Bobby Moore was our local folk hero and sometimes drank in the Two Puddings, and we watched England winning the World Cup in the swinging sixties. There was our personal connection to all of that; looking back on our own lives and that golden period on a national level too. It just seemed to fit; a nice reference.

Staying with 'Slow Emotion Replay', one of the best videos I was ever involved with – yet another by Tim Pope – was for that song, which we filmed in New York. There's a long version of it

---

* The *Tao Te Ching*, attributed to Laozi, is a Taoist text offering poetic teachings on harmony, humility and living in accordance with 'the Way'.

– about eight minutes. It formed part of our film *From Dusk 'Til Dawn* – a terrific little project that should have been seen more widely – but it got lost, really. It came out on VHS but I don't think it was ever shown on TV.

It was shot between New York, New Orleans and London. Tim set up this sort of magical mystery tour for me and Johnny. I'm not sure if it was one day or two days – but it was this mad shoot where we would climb into the back of this blacked-out van, and have no idea where we were being driven to – or what to expect when we'd arrive! We just had our guitars and our outfits, and we would clamber out of the back of this van at each stop on this mad tour around the city and perform. I think Johnny at one point thought I was in on the joke but I was in the dark as much as he was. Literally. We had to get out of the van wherever we happened to find ourselves and perform the song. We would also talk to random people and have conversations about what was wrong with the world. Sometimes it was in the Meatpacking District, sometimes a brothel, once it was this little bar – Milano's Bar on Houston Street – and you see this conversation with that lovely old man – with his old movie-star face – and he started breaking down and crying after being repeatedly asked what was wrong with the world.

It was filmed by this brilliant cameraman Jamie – a good friend of Tim's who sadly died not long after. I think Jamie filmed a lot of it with his clockwork 16mm Bolex. We also had a wide range of guests appearing with us – some fascinating characters from the New York underworld of that time like orgasm artist Annie Sprinkle, Curtis Sliwa, founder of the Guardian Angels Quentin Crisp, porn star Rick Savage, notorious drug dealer Mickey D, artist Andres Serrano and many others including assorted (back then referred to as) transsexuals, hookers and dealers. My old friend Jim Thirlwell even joined us when we hi-jacked *Taxi Talk*, this bizarre cable TV show dedicated to taxi drivers. There were many other weird and wonderful characters and locations. It was intense for Johnny and me because he was about to leave THE THE – he was having children and concentrating on his new band Electronic. It was an emotional time for us as we both loved that song. That video brings back many memories and summed up the song so well.

It was Tim's suggestion to have all these disparate characters talking about what they thought was wrong with the world – everyone's got a different answer, a unique point of view. You realise we all think we've got some sort of handle on the world's problems whilst in reality we know nothing at the same time.

'Slow Emotion Replay' is one of my favourite singles. I love that song. There's a vibrancy about it, it's an uplifting song that is very questioning whilst I'm also admitting I don't really know what I thought I knew, and just embracing that release.

JW: With that in mind, there's a similar element to the lyrics of 'Lonely Planet', there's an acceptance that some things are just bigger than you are, and sometimes rather than concentrating on the bigger picture, scaling things down to the more personal is important: 'If you can't change the world, change yourself.'

MJ: Yes, but also, the last line twists: 'And if you can't change yourself then change the world.' It throws it back. Again, it's looking back thirty years or so ago, so I can't remember exactly what I was thinking.

'Lonely Planet' is the most ecologically – or environmentally – themed song I've written, that's for sure. The thought of this planet, populated by billions but not really being heard or respected – just used and abused by its human inhabitants. Obviously, things have started to change in recent years with certain agendas being adopted by governments and corporations but even then, one gets the suspicion that many environmental and ecological organisations may have been hijacked by powerful forces – green-washing power-grabs by using ordinary, caring citizens' genuine concerns as cover for a more sinister agenda of control. For instance, instead of tightening laws to protect and promote organic farming and cleaning up water pollution those in power are actually bankrupting small farmers, deregulating GM, grabbing up farmland and privatising water supplies worldwide.

I found out early on – with politics on all levels – the game is rigged. The West is more a collection of pseudo-democracies, corporate oligarchies really, with many politicians in the pocket of powerful establishment interests. Instead of an active citizenry the general public may now be considered a flock, a herd, to be kept in a state of agitated bewilderment, to be fleeced, sheered, taxed – but never allowed to question anything too much. Compared to the old Soviet 'battery-farms' I suppose we live instead on a 'free-range farm'. We're allowed certain freedoms to run around and express ourselves – within limitations of course – because if you wander too far off the farm – shall we say – then you get dealt with. Initially by ridicule, smear, marginalisation and cancellation. And if that doesn't work then maybe by more sinister means.

JW: What do you think you can do about that as a songwriter?

MJ: When I was a teenage songwriter I idolised the likes of John Lennon, Bob Dylan and Bob Marley and really felt popular music could truly change the world, that you could pick up your guitar, write songs, connect with people and really influence things. Maybe in the 1960s this was true for certain artists but the form (protest through electrified music) itself is over fifty years old now and was absorbed by the corporate mainstream decades ago. So, after a while, you realise you're preaching to the converted, to a very, very small choir in the grand scheme of things. Even for musicians who are massively successful commercially, it's still only to a tiny percentage of the overall population. So, if you're a medium-sized band like THE THE you have very little influence. There is a sort of sobering realisation that you're just smashing your head against a brick wall with the idea of trying to change the world. So, where do you go from there? Well, you go deep inside yourself and you try to make the changes there, as that is the one thing that – *maybe* – you can change. Though as everyone knows, it is really hard to even change yourself. Over the years – like many people my age I suppose – I've had various bouts of therapy trying to – but it is hard to change yourself even when you *really* want to change. So, when I hear about people trying to change other people? It's laughable as it takes a Herculean effort just to change yourself.

I do enjoy my own company and I do like myself, but there are certainly things I'd like to change – but it is hard. You can try to adopt the attitude of the Stoics in that the only thing you can really change within yourself is your reaction to the events around you. But even that is difficult.

One of my favourite lines on the album is on 'Lonely Planet':

> All the people I've ever loved
> All the people I have lost
> All the people I'll never know
> All the feelings I've never shown

The sense of fragility, the brevity of our lives, the vastness of the world we find ourselves in – that the world's too big and life's too short – is really about living in the moment. Change what you can change but accept what you cannot. Pretty basic stuff and not that different to the serenity prayer or basic Buddhist or Stoic philosophy.

JW: That's the interesting thing about *Dusk*. For a record which was made in the aftermath of grief, it deals with grief, but it deals with it in a affirmative way. It's quite a therapeutic record, I think.

MJ: I'm glad you feel that because it was very therapeutic making it.

JW: Yes. And I think you've said 'Love Is Stronger Than Death' is a song that a lot of people talk about using to get them through periods of grief; but the whole record is something that goes through the emotions. It goes through the anger and the lust, but then it calms you down.

We've covered all the tracks except 'Helpline Operator', which I think you mentioned earlier. Is there a story to that track?

MJ: During that time – during dark periods before I made that record when I was at a low ebb – I'd spoken to helplines, to strangers on the telephone.

JW: Samaritans types?*

MJ: Not Samaritans but similar and I found it quite intriguing. I found it an interesting process to be able to open up so completely to someone you can't see and don't know. The anonymity without judgement. It provided quite a deep therapeutic avenue. It's a bit of a weird combination but in the song, you can think of the helpline operator as being a cross between a Samaritan and Wolfman Jack. You remember that beautiful scene in the 1973 film *American Graffiti* with the Wolfman? You just see his silhouette in that dimly lit radio station. I loved that atmosphere and that scene particularly – this benevolent figure dispensing positive advice. So, imagine a combination of him with a Samaritan and people phoning in for intense, emotional, sexual advice. I think it's the most cinematic track on the album, very funky, very sensual and very nocturnal. It's an underrated track. It was fun to play that live again on The Comeback Special Tour.

JW: The thing that I like is that you make the records for an audience but you don't strike me as someone that's obsessed with numbers. But *Dusk* was a very commercial record. I think it might have been your most commercially successful record. Three hit singles from it sold very well.

MJ: It missed out on going straight to number one by inches – it was number two instead. It also missed out being nominated – I'm not sure if it was the inaugural Mercury prize or its second year – by inches too, we were told. With better luck it may have been a number one and a Mercury winner. But, to be honest, it has never bothered me too much as I've never been lucky with big chart numbers or hits or winning awards. If you gave me this choice at the start of my career: I could have a short-but-explosive career teeming with number ones and awards; or a career spanning multiple decades but with no number ones or awards – yet

---

* Samaritans is a UK charity which offers support to anyone experiencing emotional distress through its free, anonymous telephone helpline.

songs that continue to be played on radio, TV and films and with a loyal audience that still supports sold-out tours. The choice would be easy.

JW: But the interesting thing with *Dusk* was it sold in big numbers, but it also appeased a lot of people – we've spoken about this a number of times. You've kind of kept critical reaction at arm's length. It seemed to be one of those records that just connected with audiences *and* with critics. I wondered if that was pleasing to you in this instance, given the personal nature of the record and given the events that led to the making of it? Was it pleasing to you that people responded in such a positive way?

MJ: It was pleasing. I mean – to be frank – of course I'd much rather people like my music than dislike it. I do care what people think but not to the degree where it would change how or why I make records. I create music to satisfy myself first.

For *Dusk*, although I had a manager in the US, I was managing myself in the UK and appointed a wonderful PR man in the UK – who's sadly no longer with us – Rob Partridge. Rob was a former *Melody Maker* journalist who also ran the PR department at Island Records. I was his second client after he went independent. Tom Waits was his first. I really liked Rob. He did a terrific job on *Dusk*, giving it to the right journalists – those with open minds. Part of the problem all artists and bands face when they release an album is getting it into the right hands. Whoever you are you're always going to have an equal amount of people who loathe you as much as like you – whilst the majority will be completely indifferent. So, it's a case of trying to get it to the minority that like you or at least are open-minded. Rob managed to do that, so I think *Dusk* got a fair hearing. I think people perceived *Mind Bomb* – maybe they were right, I don't know – as being too preachy and cocky, which I didn't intend, but that's probably how it came over. But *Dusk* was a humble, emotionally open record, and disarming, really.

JW: *Dusk* feels like a warm record.

MJ: There was a lot of warmth during its writing and recording. It was very atmospheric and I was keen to capture that. When people say it feels very 'late-night' – well it was. It was created in the shadows of sodium light and candlelight in a warm, womb-like space. Working closely with a wonderful group of people I loved working with.

JW: The late-night jazz element is reflected in the people that you brought in to work on it. I think it's just such a strong record.

MJ: I suppose *Dusk* is the album I'm most proud of in some ways because of the difficult circumstances under which it was created – there was definitely a form of alchemy at play – turning this awful grief into something beautiful that could help other people in similar circumstances.

CHAPTER SEVEN
Like A Stranger In The Night

Now living in New York, Matt leans in to his love of interpretation with Hanky Panky, *a stripped-back collection of tracks by Hank Williams. There are also a number of remix projects and respect is earned from musicologists and members of the Williams family.*

JW: You mentioned that the band dynamic was not quite as tight during the recording of *Dusk*. At what point did you realise you needed to bring in new collaborators for 1993's Lonely Planet World Tour, which followed *Dusk*'s release? What was the process for doing this? Auditions?

MJ: It all happened naturally and simultaneously as Johnny left to concentrate on Electronic and fatherhood and James signed a solo deal with Polydor. Dave Palmer by this point had moved to New York but when I saw him there – when mastering the album with Howie Weinberg – he was very contrite and asked to hear the finished album [*Dusk*]. As soon as he had heard it he loved it and asked to re-join the band for the tour. As I'd already lost two vital members I thought that bringing back a fully fit and motivated Dave Palmer would at least offset the loss of the other two slightly.

So, I relocated to New York for three months to audition

members and rehearse a new band for the Lonely Planet Tour. I rented an apartment on 12th Street between Second and Third Avenues and DC Collard and Dave Palmer moved in with me. We had a lot of fun. We rented rehearsal rooms at SIR on 25th Street and the three of us started auditioning musicians.

Dave was friendly with Eric Schermerhorn and recommended him as Johnny's replacement on lead guitar. When Eric and I met for the first time we got on well and knew we'd work together at some point. But he was in the middle of a project with Iggy Pop and, quite rightly, didn't want to let him down.

The next suggestions were Marc Ribot – who I admired and met with but who wasn't available – and also Dave Navarro from Jane's Addiction, who had just left his band at that point. My agent Marc Geiger put us in touch but he was already tied up with another project.

Auditions began. We had a few guitarists come in – some quite well known but none who seemed right. We recorded all the auditions onto my little DAT recorder and DC, Dave and I would then carefully analyse the sessions back at the apartment. One of the guitarists we auditioned was a young lad from Atlanta, Georgia – Keith Joyner. But what was strange with Keith was that his body language made it seem he'd rather be anywhere on earth than auditioning for us. He looked awkward to such a degree I'd discounted him in my mind.

But when we listened back to the tapes there was no doubt Keith was head and shoulders above all the other players. He almost seemed embarrassed by his own talent. His shyness and awkwardness during concerts were to become a bit of a bone of contention with me as I would continually nag him to liven up. But, looking back, he had very big shoes to fill. Johnny was naturally at ease with himself and energetic. It transpired Keith was a huge fan of The Smiths so I imagine it was quite nerve-wracking for him as he was only a young lad. But he was a talented guitarist and a person of integrity.

We were also auditioning for bass players too. James was a hard act to follow but after listening to countless auditions we finally found our man in Jared Nickerson. He was a native New

Yorker and more from a jazz-funk background, but was a phenomenal player who could adapt to any style. With his little round glasses and shaved head, he looked like a black Ghandi. Jared was certainly up for fun and he, DC and I seemed to gravitate to each other for various shenanigans.

Lastly, we decided to add a sixth member, a superb harmonica player from Boston showed up, Jim Fitting. Confident, affable and very energetic, he quickly passed his audition with flying colours.

By the end of the Lonely Planet Tour the band included the American drummer Andy Kubiszewski, as Dave Palmer had

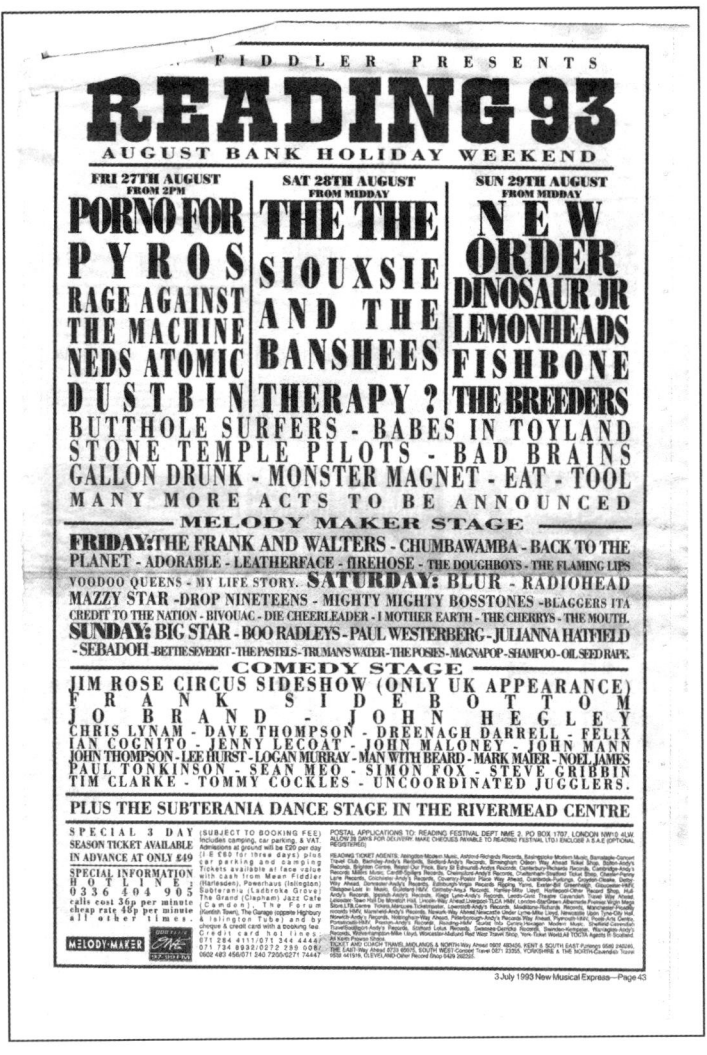

LIKE A STRANGER IN THE NIGHT | 257

suddenly jumped ship to join Rod Stewart halfway through our tour! I was the last to find out – and I was shocked. My manager, Steve Rennie, and I had to threaten to sue Rod Stewart in order to send Dave back and help Andy learn his parts. Obviously, I couldn't compete with what Rod was offering Dave financially and looking back, the decision he made did give him long-term security in that regard. But there are ways of going about such decisions. Anyway, that group was never quite right because it was put together in a rehearsal studio during auditions in New York and never had time to settle and grow. I was under extreme time pressure from the record company with an impending album release and world tour to support it! I had to put a line-up together quickly. They were all good guys though, and I still keep in touch with a lot of them.

JW: What about the *Dis-Infected* EP? The A-side was two versions of older THE THE tracks, re-recorded by the band that had toured *Dusk*.

MJ: That came out after the Lonely Planet World Tour. It was recorded towards the end – we were in London to play Brixton Academy and had a day off so I just said, 'Let's go down to my studio to record a couple of tracks.' The version we did of 'Infected' – retitled 'Dis-Infected' – was the slowed-down version we'd been playing live. With 'This Is The Day' I changed the title to 'That Was The Day'. It was a stripped-down version with DC playing on the original Omnichord I'd written the song on, and featuring Jim Fitting. I thought the two tracks would make a good single but we decided to expand it to an EP. I've always liked EPs – more substantial than a single but not as much commitment as an album. This EP, *Dis-Infected*, was eventually merged with the *Shades Of Blue* EP and issued in the US as an LP called *Solitude* in 1993.

JW: The B-side of *Dis-Infected* was remixes. You had 'Helpline Operator' re-mixed by you and Bruce Lampcov – and your old mate Jim Thirlwell remixing 'Dogs Of Lust'.

MJ: Yes, I liked those remixes. Bruce and I also remixed 'Violence Of Truth'. The sleeve of the EP was funny too. One afternoon I was in Hamburg doing interviews – in a club on the Reeperbahn – it was one of those adult live sex clubs but we got access during the day when it was closed to the public due to my lovely German PR lady – Sonia Bruggeman I believe her name was – always coming up with interesting ideas and locations where we could do interviews. So, we were in there and the off-duty working girls were very funny and just started messing around, putting a wig and lipstick on me and then the photographer started snapping away. I thought the photos were very funny and would make a great sleeve.

JW: Jim Thirlwell is a recurring presence in this book. I really like his remix of 'Dogs Of Lust'. What did you hope he would do with that track?

MJ: I just gave him a free hand. He's one of my oldest, dearest friends and someone I have so much respect for. Definitely one of the most creative and hard-working people I've ever known. I didn't give him any brief, I just gave him the multitracks to play around with. His two remixes of 'Dogs Of Lust', 'Spermicide' and 'Germicide' were released as B-sides on the 12-inch version of that single. I love his use of samples, his sculpting of sounds and the fact you're never quite sure how he creates them.

And the ones I remixed with Bruce we did at Sony's old Whitfield Street studios in Fitzrovia. I wanted to reintroduce elements from the original demos of both 'Helpline Operator' and 'Violence Of Truth'. The piano and organ riffs I recorded when I first wrote the songs got lost when we re-recorded them live with the band.

JW: I've always liked EPs too. People don't seem to do them as much now.

MJ: They were great value when you didn't have much pocket money as a kid weren't they?

JW: Yes. I remember Nick Lowe did one. He was very cheeky; he did one called *Bowi* (1977) that was a bit of a micky take of David Bowie and his album *Low*. It was the first EP to be released on Stiff records. As you mentioned, preceding *Dis-Infected*, there was another EP, *Shades of Blue,* in 1991. This contains a cover version of Fred Neil's 'The Dolphins', probably the song he's best known for.

MJ: No, I'd say he's best known for 'Everybody's Talkin'' as used in John Schlesinger's *Midnight Cowboy* (1969). Don't you think?

JW: Well, this is the thing with Fred Neil. Obviously, he's known for writing songs but he's one of those writers where the versions by other people became better known than his own versions. I think the Tim Buckley version just called 'Dolphins' surpasses his own. The same with Harry Nilsson and 'Everybody's Talkin''. I know that version so well that I think of it as Nilsson. I never think of it as Fred Neil.

MJ: My brother Andrew and I were massive Tim Buckley fans. That's how the cover version of 'Dolphins' came about. Eugene died halfway through the Versus The World Tour and I remember – after the tour restarted in America – sitting at the back of the tour bus when somebody put on an old VHS of *Best Of Old Grey Whistle Test*. On came Tim Buckley performing 'Dolphins'. I hadn't seen it before but it gave me goosebumps and made me cry, because I started associating the words with Eugene. When I got back off tour I wanted to record a cover of it. Andrew and I both ended up loving that song, we listened to it a lot, and he created that lovely piece of artwork for the *Shades of Blue* EP cover, the combination of painting and collage. The song 'Solitude' was also connected to Eugene because I remember one day, down at my mum and dad's house – my dad was a massive Paul Robeson fan – my dad was listening to Paul Robeson's version of 'Solitude' and he just started sobbing – thinking of Eugene. It made me cry too. It's a beautiful song. Duke Ellington, isn't it?

JW: That's right, Ellington and Irving Mills wrote the original.

MJ: I was inspired by that Paul Robeson version as it was a connection with Eugene and with my dad and the deep emotions that had risen to the surface. Very melancholy songs – powerful and moving. That was the inspiration behind the *Shades Of Blue* EP, which, as mentioned earlier, was later merged with the *Disinfected* EP. There was also the live version of 'Another Boy Drowning' on that first EP.

JW: The music, obviously, is the key thing, but you're one of those artists whose record sleeves are incredibly important to your history and your whole aesthetic. The sleeves go in tandem with the music and that's certainly true with the most recent 7-inch singles.

MJ: With the most recent ones Gillian and I have literally just been listening to the respective songs whilst turning pages in Andrew's sketchbooks to find images that resonate. It maintains his presence as a central part of THE THE. I think he would've liked that. They will make a nice set as we plan to release more one-off singles.

JW: You can't beat a 7-inch single. EPs are good, but a 7-inch single…

MJ: 7-inch singles are great.

JW: Playing 7-inch singles, that's my favourite.

MJ: I remember a great session a few years ago when my youngest son George was downstairs in my office with me – I think it was a Saturday afternoon. I got one of my record players out – an old valve Clarke & Smith – and we took turns going through my old singles collection and choosing what to play. All the favourite singles from the seventies that Andrew and I had collected. George absolutely loved it.

JW: Children do like it – my kids used to like playing my 7-inchs. My sister was a big reggae fan and really into Trojan. I remember she had a little Dansette record player and used to put 7-inch singles on. It just sounded like the most exotic stuff. I loved it. I sat there watching them spin round, mesmerised.

MJ: It was exotic, wasn't it? As well as the look of the vinyl and the labels and sleeves, there was the smell of vinyl and of the old audio equipment. Something very comforting about it.

JW: Yes, in cold, grey South London – that's my first memory of hearing music.

MJ: Going slightly off-topic, did you see those Steve McQueen films for BBC One? They were good, weren't they?

JW: Yes. *Small Axe* (2021) was really good.

MJ: The way you were talking about listening to Trojan, ska and reggae just put into my mind the way the party is set up in *Lover's Rock* (2020). I think McQueen recreated that era and the love of records and music so well.

JW: What was so brilliant about the 'Education' episode of *Small Axe* was that it showed that in the seventies – and I had this at school – they didn't know what dyslexia was. They just thought you were thick. They would put you in with people with real behavioural problems, because they didn't know. You can imagine how many young Black kids would've just been assumed to have been stupid. I thought that episode was really moving.

MJ: It was. When he's sat there with his mum and his sister, and she says, 'Okay, now read.' And he couldn't, and they all started crying together, it made me cry. Beautiful.

JW: Back to work! This was also a period of great change in your life. You'd moved to America, and there's a great video for 'That Was The Day' filmed at Alcatraz prison.

MJ: Fiona made that. We were in San Francisco, and that was filmed the day we decided to split up after eleven years together. That night we went out, got very drunk and tearful on champagne. Whilst wandering the backstreets of San Francisco in the early hours we thought it would be a great idea to get 'divorce rings'. Only these would be rings through our navels. So, in for a penny in for a pound, I also asked the young woman at the piercing parlour if she would pierce my scrotum. Which she gladly did. We woke up next morning completely hungover and with only dim recollections of the night before. But my navel piercing had somehow gone wrong and became infected and so I had to go back to the woman to get it re-pierced at a different angle. Ouch!

Anyway, Fiona had her Super 8 camera with her. We were hanging around San Francisco and decided to go to Alcatraz. I'd first visited when I was a teenager and have been a couple of times since. I've always found that place haunting. That day was very poignant. There's also footage of one of my primary schools – the Cangle school in Haverhill, Suffolk. We went back and she filmed me wandering around the old playground. It wasn't a school anymore; it was about to be turned into flats. Plus, there was some footage of when we headlined Reading Festival too. She filmed it and edited it. It was quite a melancholy video.

JW: Are you still in touch at all?

MJ: Yes. We still keep in touch. We see each other occasionally.

JW: That's good. My relationships always end terribly, but I think that's a maturity issue. As you grow older and you get more mature – there's no reason that you can't be friends with someone that you used to be more intimate with.

MJ: I know, and if someone's been a big part of your life it seems a shame to just feed all those shared memories into the shredder.

JW: Okay, so let's have a little bit of *Hanky Panky*. Hank Williams wasn't necessarily your first choice to do an album of material. I think you mentioned people like Howlin' Wolf, John Lee Hooker and Robert Johnson?

MJ: Hank Williams was *always* going to be first and Robert Johnson the second. It was planned as an occasional series. The reason I didn't record *Johnson* was because when I looked into it I discovered there were some odd copyright issues, that Johnson's descendants or family would not have received the royalties or that someone may have assumed control of the copyright but not his family. It's a long time ago and I can't remember the details.

The initial idea was for me to trace various routes of contemporary song writing. Obviously, Hank Williams was very influenced by other singer–songwriters, as was Robert Johnson, but those two – the influence, the magnification and amplification effect they had really changed the course of popular music. Of course, you could go sideways or you could go further back in time, you could go back to medieval days and beyond and over to countries other than America or Britain, but I was simply looking at iconic figures from the recent past who'd had a powerful impact upon my own profession. As I've said a few times, I hate the word 'iconic' as it's over-used but the life of Hank Williams is fascinating. The ups, downs, tragedies and emotional intensity with which he lived. Same with Robert Johnson. They both died young, and were incredibly influential and talented. I found them both charismatic, attractive characters to pay homage to.

A problem was also that Sony didn't really know what to make of it all, because *Dusk* did so well critically and commercially – and I then went into my customary hibernation – so, to come back with an album of Hank Williams covers was a bit of a shock to them. To be fair they did really get behind it, but by this point I was living in America and it did better in the US than the UK. In the States it got very well received, even voted one of the best country albums of the year. Colin Escott – one of his biographers – said they were amongst the best cover versions of Hank Williams' songs he'd ever heard.

JW: Hank's daughter wrote and thanked you, didn't she?

MJ: Yes, she said, 'My daddy would be proud of what you've done with his songs.' Which was nice. So, it got a very positive reaction overall.

For the band that recorded the album, I decided to change things around. I kept Jim Fitting, and obviously DC was a mainstay. I've actually worked with him more than any other musician and he's a good friend. I also used this as an opportunity to finally work with Eric Schermerhorn who, if you remember, I had tried to line up to replace Johnny for the Lonely Planet Tour. We had the wonderful Brian MacLeod on drums, who introduced me to Gail Ann Dorsey on bass. They were a phenomenal rhythm section.

JW: Bowie nicked Gail later on.

MJ: You're right he did! I couldn't blame him. I couldn't blame her!

For the pre-production of *Hanky Panky* we headed down to Mallorca – I often go there with band members prior to tours or albums. This time with DC – who was heavily involved with *Hanky Panky*, working on the arrangements with me. We took my Tascam 688 Midistudio and some instruments and headed to my house in the hills. Eric flew over from the States and it was a very productive time working out arrangements. We tried out so many of Hank's songs; far more than ended up on the album. I took the demo tapes to London for pre-production with Bruce, who was again involved as engineer and co-producer. We recorded and mixed the album in The Garden.

JW: Did you use Pro Tools?

MJ: No. It was recorded on my Akai ADAM system but we did do some chopping up, editing and looping so that part could have been on its precursor system, Sound Tools or in Akai S3200 samplers.

JW: Was this process interesting to work with when it was so new?

MJ: It was – but then again it was really just a continuation of a process I'd been working with for years. Obviously, these days it's very quick and easy, but my mindset was still in the old analogue style of sampling and looping, and these were just digital tools to help us do that much more quickly than we could do in analogue. Particularly on songs like 'Honky Tonkin''. I thought it sounded great. Very slinky and powerful. Bruce did a phenomenal job. But some people can be put off by albums of cover versions – and live albums too really – and can be a bit purist about it: 'We just want a new *studio* album!'

JW: They're not straight cover versions, though are they? They're interpretations rather than note-for-note reproductions. I want to ask why you took that approach and how you chose the songs. I've always been a big Hank Williams fan – there was a melancholia about the way he explored loneliness. People would probably assume you'd choose to cover 'I'm So Lonesome I Could Cry' and 'Jambalaya', but you chose to do some of the more interesting songs rather than the more obvious ones.

MJ: The whole point of doing what was intended to become a series of releases – was to really twist songs around. I don't think there's much point in doing cover versions unless they're going to be radically different, because the originals are usually so wonderful. I wanted to filter his songs through myself. I felt a certain affinity with his words and music. They resonated with me – along with millions of other people, obviously. I wanted to create contemporary interpretations. They're certainly distinct from any other Hank Williams covers I've ever heard. In Mallorca there were lots of songs we demoed that ended up on the cutting room floor. We wanted to see which ones could work in the specific direction we were taking. The most obvious one we left out was 'I'm So Lonesome I Could Cry'. One could look at it from a commercial point of view and wonder, if we'd done a simple cover then maybe it would have been a good thing. But I wasn't thinking commercially. That didn't interest me. Our version of 'I Saw The Light' was so radically different to his. That became the only single.

JW: And it sold well. The single was a Top 40 hit.

MJ: It did well, and the video was very striking.

JW: I re-watched the video just before we started speaking today. It's incredible. You've got eyeliner on – it gave me palpitations watching it.

MJ: The director I decided to work with on that was Sam Bayer. Sam was the hot video director at that time. He was brilliant, a very nice guy and I liked him. Full of energy and ideas. I was originally inspired by those photographs from the top of the Chrysler Building. Was it Berenice Abbott perched on the gargoyles?

JW: It was Margaret Bourke-White.

MJ: Yes, you're right! I've forgotten more than I'll ever know! My favourite buildings in New York are the Empire State Building and the Woolworth Building – but I also love the Chrysler Building. All three, at an early point in their lives, were the tallest buildings in the world. I love them all.

Anyway, when I met with Sam I told him my idea, which was a continuation from the *Infected* videos and some of those stunts – being strapped into chairs on top of boats etc. – but I wanted something even *more* dramatic. And it had to be very 'stars and stripes' American as I was now living in Manhattan and had just made an album about an American icon. So, I met with Sam and said, 'I want you to film me standing on the top of a New York skyscraper singing. I'll let you work out the details, Sam, but that is what I want.' He was very enthusiastic and came back with some fantastic ideas. We had initially talked about filming on the top of the Woolworth Building – which was the tallest building in the world in 1913. Now, remember, this is all pre-9/11 and obviously things changed dramatically after that. But we ended up using the Chrysler Building, though we weren't really supposed to be up there at all.

Sam created three filming 'sets' – or locations. Early in the video we're performing on a lower rooftop which was opposite my loft apartment on Broadway. It was in late January – or maybe early February – and it was bloody cold; freezing in fact. I'm playing a Gretsch White Falcon – another American icon – whilst Eric plays a Gibson Flying V. We tried to get a Nudie-type suit* made for me – similar to what Hank used to wear, but I ended up wearing a custom-made red jacket with a gold sequined back. I wore some eyeliner and put on a cowboy hat. For no specific reason other than for my own amusement, we put DC in a gimp mask for that video. He complained, 'What!? Why me!? You are joking!?' I said, 'DC, you've got to take one for the team.' He's got a twisted sense of the absurd so took it all in good humour – and enjoyed it all a bit too much by the end! It still tickles me that a man in a gimp mask suddenly walks across the frame in a video for a Hank Williams song and nobody knows why!

Sam also knew a helicopter pilot who was one of only a handful who had a license to fly that close to skyscrapers. This guy was in the US military during the Tet Offensive in Vietnam,† if memory serves correctly. On the day we went up the Chrysler Building to film I think it was Super Bowl Sunday.

We all sneakily went up there – the crew trying to hide their equipment in various bags – but there was a security guard on duty when we reached the top. I can't recall how we even got that far to be honest but again, it was a very different world back then. Sam said, 'Look, we've got to keep it quiet.' A couple of us at a time went up there, very discreetly, and said something like, 'We're just on a recce, taking photographs for an advertising agency.' I guess he thought we were just going to photograph from the windows at the top. But it was our lucky day really as he was just sat munching on his bowl of pretzels, slurping on his

---

* Nuta Kotlyarenko (known professionally as Nudie Cohn) designed rhinestone-covered suits, known as 'Nudie Suits'.
† The Tet Offensive (1968) was a major North Vietnamese and Viet Cong attack in South Vietnam that shifted US public opinion.

Pepsi, eyes glued to the Super Bowl and so didn't take much interest in us.

We managed to get to the top. My God it was cold and icy. At one point I nearly climbed out of a window and fell straight to the street. I thought I was going to be jumping down to a short balcony below an open window and hadn't realised it was a sheer drop! So, it was quite dangerous from the off. Now, the funny thing was, we had to get a body double for me. Since I have become a father I've completely lost my nerve for dangerous stunts, but back then I would've happily stood on the gargoyles – and was quite looking forward to that – but the insurance company wouldn't tolerate it. You have to have somebody that is 'qualified'. So, we got a stunt man, an English guy. It's a funny story, because he and I were sat together in a little room just behind one of the gargoyles – you open the window and you climb straight out onto it. We were sat there, dressed in identical outfits, but he was very, very quiet. He looked ashen, absolutely grey. I said, 'Are you alright?' He said, 'I'm just feeling a bit anxious.' I said, 'But you're a stunt man. You must do this stuff all the time.' He said, 'No, I've never done heights. My specialty is fire.' My specialty is fire! He was terrified of heights! Oh my God! So, he was secured with some supporting straps but he was not very happy about it at all.

JW: Did he do it?

MJ: Yes, he did it! He had the invisible support straps attached and he climbed out – right onto the middle of the gargoyle. And it's cold. It's slippery, its icy. The helicopter is circling round closely. And he is shaking with fear. Nowadays, you would do it all with CGI, but this was all for real. Sam Bayer was a terrific director. I love the film stock he used too. It has that gorgeous over-saturated colour. All analogue with no digital trickery at all.

JW: The colours in it are great. You talk about wanting to reference American culture, it's very red and blue – very bright.

MJ: Very much red, white and blue. What Sam also did was he built a second gargoyle on a neighbouring skyscraper. That is when you see me up close on the gargoyle – an identical replica – on top of another skyscraper. You can see the Empire State Building over my shoulder. But it was safer. There was a bit more space around it on this flat roof. In case I slipped, I'd only fall forty feet rather than a thousand. To be honest, it was so cold that I had a little hip flask of tequila to sip now and again to try and keep me warm but I ended up getting quite drunk on top of that gargoyle. A silly thing to do. Anyway, I thought Sam did a fantastic job. It was a superb video. That was the heyday of MTV, wasn't it?

JW: Yes, I think that's where I saw it the first time.

MJ: Do many people still make videos? I suppose they do, but I doubt with that sort of budget.

JW: No, I don't think they have that sort of budget anymore.

MJ: It's one of my favourite videos. Oh, and when they eventually saw the video there was an official complaint from the Chrysler Building. 'Who gave you the permission to do that?!' They swiftly changed their rules and the security guard may have even got fired – which would have been unfortunate. These days there would be no chance. Post-9/11 you wouldn't even get in the door.

JW: You wouldn't be able to fly a helicopter, that's for sure.

MJ: It was a moment in time. I'd moved to New York in August 1994 and that was early '95. All fresh and exciting: new apartment, new relationship and new life. Great memories.

JW: The move to New York: I know that your lyrics around that period were reflecting a kind of dissatisfaction with the UK. What were some of the factors behind the decision to move to the States?

MJ: Several things. One relationship had ended, a new one was beginning. Johanna St Michaels is Swedish and was living in Los Angeles where we met at a party towards the end of The Lonely Planet Tour. Long distance relationships are always difficult and in the first few months we'd meet up in different parts of the world: Stockholm, Mexico City, San Miguel de Allende, Göteborg, New York, London, Mallorca, Los Angeles. It was exciting but ultimately exhausting, both physically and emotionally, so we decided to move to New York together as we both loved that city. I'd been going there since I was 20 and just felt more comfortable in my own skin there whereas in London – or England generally – I was beginning to feel a bit uptight. Maybe the class system had some sort of suffocating effect upon me? I've often felt happier abroad for some reason. Moving to Manhattan was always something I'd planned to do anyway. And Johanna had spent a lot of time there too.

Now, politically, what was going on? Ah, yes, that was before Blair got elected, so Britain was still under the rule of the Conservative Party. It wasn't until 1997 that New Labour were elected – and we all celebrated madly at the time – if we'd only known how Blair would turn out! Thatcher herself said her greatest achievement was 'Tony Blair and New Labour'. Blair himself said, 'I always thought my job was to build on some of the things she had done rather than reverse them.' He was a wolf in sheep's clothing – which is the logo of the Fabian Society* I believe? But that's another story.

The mid-nineties were an exciting time for me. The winters in New York can be brutal but at least the skies are blue much of the time – and the sun shines. Whereas the endless grey drizzle of London was really getting me down. And there's a melancholy and disorientation when coming out of a long-term relationship. Eleven years with Fiona and many intense and wonderful memories. But I already had good friends in New York and moving there I made more. It was an interesting period of my life.

---

* The Fabian Society is a British socialist organisation whose purpose is to advance its principles through gradual efforts in democracies rather than by revolution. Its original coat of arms featured a wolf in sheep's clothing.

JW: I have read that you thought about doing *Hanky Panky* with guest vocalists, and you not necessarily singing all the songs. Is that true?

MJ: Yes, that was true.

JW: Why did that not happen?

MJ: Well, I was always going to sing some, but I had planned to have guest vocalists on most of the songs. My role would be more arranger–producer. Leonard Cohen agreed to do it. Marianne Faithfull too. Possibly Michael Stipe. Plus, there were others I was in the process of contacting. But it all went wrong.

Michael Stipe and I met at the 40 Watt Club in Athens, Georgia. He came to see us play a warm-up show and then stayed behind. We sat in the parking lot afterwards chatting for a while. I mentioned I had an idea for a project. He seemed up for it and I was going to get back in touch with details.

Now, I mentioned this before with regards to Sinéad but I had an American manager based in LA at that time: Steve Rennie. We were chalk and cheese really. Politically I was old-school Labour and he was a Republican. We would continually clash over career tactics. And he would do the most bizarre things without informing me. I'd mentioned to him in passing that I was in the initial stages of a project, and thinking of getting other singers involved. I mentioned a few names of people I was in contact with and the general outline. So, what does he do without telling me? Puts out a press release! Announcing the project with a list of my potential collaborators! You've got to be very discreet, respectful and sensitive about these things. 'Any publicity is good' seemed to be his thinking; it really jarred. I thought, you know what, I'm going to scrap this whole idea. I'm going to sing it all myself. In terms of what other singers I had in mind? There would have been a list of artists to contact. I can't remember off the top of my head as it's now some years ago but possibly Ute Lemper, k.d. lang, Tom Waits – maybe even Sinéad.

Steve and I parted company not long afterwards as he jumped

ship to join Sony as an executive. On a personal level I liked Steve because he always treated people with the same respect if they were a cleaner, a cab driver or a CEO. I think that's a lovely character trait. He was nice to people generally and he was a hard worker and very committed. But we were unsuited to work together and I know I used to drive him mad by refusing lots of promotion opportunities. He said I made his job impossible.

JW: Did you know Tom Waits was going to do an LP of Howlin' Wolf cover versions? He wanted to do an LP called *Waits Does Wolf*, which I think would have been great.

MJ: No, but I like the sound of that.

JW: *Hanky Panky* is a project you've mentioned as being very much a referencing of American culture and American tradition, and that's also reflected in the sleeve. I remember seeing the photograph of Hank Williams with his shirt off and thinking, that would make a fucking great sleeve.

MJ: That was taken when he'd just been released from jail.

JW: He'd been released from jail, yes. He looked consumptive. He looked terrible. But the sleeve to *Hanky Panky* is great. I wonder if you could take us through that. Was it designed by Cally Callomon?

MJ: Yes.

JW: It really fits with the whole aesthetic of the Hank Williams legend.

MJ: Cally actually went on to become my manager for a number of years. This was the first time we'd worked together. He's a very creative, thoughtful man and a lateral thinker. He has an interesting background. He was the art director at Island Records for many years. He'd been an A&R man, as well as a manager for Julian

Cope many years ago. These days he manages the Nick Drake estate as well as managing projects for Bill Drummond.

JW: He had managed Julian Cope – that's right, that's where I knew his name from.

MJ: Cally is an all-rounder – an art director not just a designer. He's created some beautiful sleeves over the years for artists as diverse as PJ Harvey, Max Richter, Tricky and U2.

For *Hanky Panky* we wanted to reference that topless Hank photo. There had to be a hat involved and I had to be bare-chested, of course. I put some black markings under my eyes. I can't remember what the thinking was but it seemed to make the photo more dramatic and twisted.

Cally brought in an excellent photographer he'd been working with – John Sleeman – who used this interesting technique of 'light painting'. He first ensured the room was absolutely pitch black, set a very slow shutter speed and then start slowly 'painting' me in light with a torch. In doing this he created photographic 'paintings' with light and it gave the images an eerie, hyper-real quality. It was all analogue of course although these days I'm sure people can get a similar effect digitally with a Photoshop tool.

JW: It always looked to me like you're in a jail cell with just a single light above you, like a William Eggleston photograph. It's a great sleeve.

MJ: Cally then created fabric stars and stripes to make up the title 'Hanky Panky'. We just made it as American as possible. And it came in some beautiful formats, including a 10-inch double vinyl gatefold.

JW: You have said that Sony were not sure what to do with it.

MJ: To be fair, it was tricky for them. The follow-up to a critically and commercially successful album was a cover album of a long-dead American country singer!

JW: You said Sony were decent.

MJ: Yes, they really were supportive. There was a very expensive video and a lot of lovely formats. Cally really enjoyed himself with those, including beautiful wooden boxes for the CDs branded with the THE THE logo, as well as the beautiful 10-inch double gatefold.

JW: That's what I've got! That 10-inch double gatefold.

MJ: Did I give you one of those?

JW: No, I bought it!

MJ: Oh, you bought it. So, yes, Sony really did get behind it, even though it was a hard one because, again, I wasn't touring. Although we did do a promotional tour across Europe and America performing live on TV shows, we didn't do any live concerts. Also, by this point Gail had been poached by David Bowie. 'Poached' is not the right word of course. It happens all the time. I'd taken Eric away from Iggy, and Bowie took Gail away from me just before we were going to do this tour. That's the way it goes. So, then Brian MacLeod, our drummer, said, 'I know another great bass player you're going to love,' and that was Spencer Campbell, who I *did* love and who then became an integral part of the *NakedSelf* project.

JW: You had put together another great band. Why didn't you tour the album?

MJ: I really don't remember why we didn't perform some concerts promoting *Hanky Panky* – I suppose we'd only learned half a dozen songs from the album to play on TV but it was such a great band that we could – and should – have played a proper concert tour. DC, Eric Schermerhorn, Brian MacLeod, Spencer Campbell and Jim Fitting. What a great band! But it was all just for a promotional TV tour. Thinking back, I've made such a lot of mistakes in my career, and that was yet another one to add to the list. We should've played concerts as that would've given Sony more to build the campaign around.

Anyway, that's where I met Spencer. He and I hit it off immediately. What was interesting about Spencer was that he was an A-list session musician in Nashville and had played with some of the greats, like Johnny Cash and Kenny Rogers. A great all-round musician. He was hardcore and knew Hank's catalogue better than any of us.

JW: It's nice that it was received so well within the country music community and by Hank's family.

MJ: It was fantastic. You never know if you're encroaching on others' territory. But they didn't see it like that. They just saw it as me coming to pay my respects to one of their greatest. I immersed myself in Hank Williams for a year before, listened to pretty much everything he'd recorded and I read multiple biographies; I learned as much as I could.

JW: It was all done from a position of respect, wasn't it?

MJ: Yes, of course, I wouldn't put all that time, energy and effort into a project like that without being respectful. It was a hugely enjoyable experience immersing myself in the life and music of one of the all-time greats.

CHAPTER EIGHT
The Only Thing That Stays The Same Is That Everything Must Change

Inspired by old recording techniques and experimental music, Matt develops a new band and a new sound for (the as yet unreleased) Gun Sluts. Sony express confusion and request a record that is less textured and experimental – and more song based. Influenced by Noam Chomsky and featuring Eric Schermerhorn, NakedSelf *emerges against the backdrop of a new relationship with Swedish filmmaker Johanna St Michaels, the birth of Matt's first son, and the ill health of Matt's mother. There is also a split from Sony.*

JW: Let's talk about *Gun Sluts*. You were living in New York with Johanna and you were writing with Eric Schermerhorn.

MJ: The line-up that recorded *Dusk* was obviously long gone; I'd also recently broken up the one that toured *Dusk* on The Lonely Planet Tour. We'd just released *Hanky Panky* – and been on a European and American promotional tour – but I broke up that line-up too. I then decided to head off in a different direction entirely with a very experimental new album.

DC was involved initially as he was living in Philadelphia at this point and it was easy for him to visit me in Manhattan. Eric had been co-writing as well as recording and performing with

Iggy and suggested he could so the same with me. He played me some ideas which I really liked so he joined this line-up. We spent a lot of time together and became close friends.

JW: I remember your admiration for John Lennon and the Plastic Ono Band. You spoke about the way you appreciated how it was a revolving band of musicians. Was that also something that was influential in terms of how you thought about your band? I know that you were the constant, but the musicians are not just people who come in – they become an integral part. Was the Plastic Ono Band an influence in that sense?

MJ: Yes, but I would point out a contradiction in what you've just said. The Plastic Ono Band *did* inspire me – the idea of a band as more of a conceptual project and less a conventional rock group; even the word *plastic* suggesting flexibility and impermanence – inspired by Ono's Fluxus* background probably. Their project seemed informal and playful and I loved that. But the contradiction is with that certain musicians I've worked with *have* become an integral part of THE THE. So, I suppose I've drifted away from that original concept over the years.

As a young musician I'd read horror stories about bands stuck together because of the money whilst in reality hating each other. I thought I never want to be in that position, forced to work with people I don't like. People evolve at different rates and relationships change over time so I never wanted to feel trapped in a permanent line-up. But it's become more of an 'open situation' – where people I worked with in the past may come back, as they often do, and it remains fluid. Certainly, I thought the Plastic Ono Band idea was ahead of its time; Captain Beefheart and his Magic Band were also a very fluid line-up with musicians coming and going; though I hope I treat my bandmates better than Don Van Vliet allegedly treated his!

Anyway, *Gun Sluts* wasn't – as some have mischievously

---

* Fluxus was an international, interdisciplinary community of artists, composers, designers and poets during the 1960s and 1970s.

suggested – my attempt at a Lou Reed-style *Metal Machine Music*.*
It wasn't that at all. My roots were obviously in the post-punk
movement so that was a side I wanted to revisit. *Burning Blue Soul*
had involved early sampling, looping and sonic experimentation
and *Gun Sluts* was an attempt to get back to that playfulness;
though I wanted to create something aggressive and political as
well as 'experimental', for want of a better word.

JW: This is with Eric and DC?

MJ: Yes. We booked into Sear Sound Studios in New York – Bruce
Lampcov was also with us for a period of that time – but we just
pissed away a lot of money messing around. The idea was to record
with all this beautiful old analogue equipment that Walter Sear†
owned – old valve preamps, vintage microphones and tape
recorders. We loved Walter as he was fascinating and had so many
great anecdotes. But he *really* loved to chat and it got to the stage
we'd arrive each morning to work but would instead be spending
a couple of hours drinking coffee with him whilst he regaled us
with story after story. Before we knew it, it would be lunchtime!

I usually demo quite substantially and work all the parts out
before running up studio bills. I didn't do that this time; I just went
straight into an expensive studio assuming that magic would
somehow just 'happen'. Some good stuff *did* happen and we
created some interesting soundscapes but it all started to get
unwieldy and chaotic. The record company hated what they heard
and it became obvious it was going to become a tricky situation.
They basically said, 'Look, we supported you through the Hank
Williams project even though we didn't understand your logic.
Now this?!' They could see the amount of money I was spending
yet it all seemed to be going nowhere – apart from in circles. But
I was invested in the idea of an aggressive, experimental and
political album.

---

* *Metal Machine Music* (1975) by Lou Reed was initially thought to be released as a joke or a record contract breaker with his label RCA.

† Walter Sear was an American recording engineer, musician, inventor, composer, producer and early collaborator with the electronic music pioneer Robert Moog.

At that time, I was reading a lot of Noam Chomsky* and also other very political books, publications and pamphlets. I was trying to get away from mainstream propaganda outlets – reading a lot about events that were under the radar in terms of the real foreign policy of the West. There was this duality living in America. The manipulation, propaganda and Disneyfication of this TV 'reality' created a cognitive dissonance inside me that jarred against the stuff I was reading and researching. I haven't owned a television in the decades since – I now just use projectors to watch specific films or documentaries as I cannot stand adverts and I find it hard to be in the same room as a television set.

A lot of material was recorded for *Gun Sluts* – and most of it is unreleased – but a couple of pieces did find their way onto *NakedSelf*.

JW: 'Diesel Breeze' for example.

MJ: Yes. 'Diesel Breeze' and 'Boiling Point'. Recently we released – as part of our 'Official Bootleg' series – some very early rough mixes from the sessions. I do want to finish *Gun Sluts* properly but because of the negative reaction I was getting at the time I couldn't see the wood for the trees and it started affecting my confidence in the project. Now, owning my own record label, I can do whatever I want. But back then, I decided to shelve it and refocus on what was to become *NakedSelf*. I did carry over some lyrical ideas – for instance 'Global Eyes' – but I decided to put it in the freezer with a view to reheating it in the future. Maybe it was a bit ahead of its time? Since then artists like Radiohead, Björk and others have taken mainstream audiences on a fascinating creative journey and I do find people generally more open-minded these days.

JW: 'Global Eyes' is obviously a very political song, but it's political in a way that tackles politics from beyond a British perspective. Was that influencing your outlook? Obviously, politics has always

---

* Noam Chomsky is an American philosopher and political commentator, noted for his critique of US foreign policy and media.

been so essential to your songwriting. Did living outside of the UK and living in America open your eyes and your mind to new thinkers? Were you starting to discover new ideas that might have been influencing you in any way?

MJ: Yes, and there was a lot of interesting stuff going on politically – especially regards the globalisation phenomenon. It was around the time of NAFTA (North American Free Trade Agreement),* GATT (General Agreement on Tariffs and Trade)† and the Telecommunications Act of 1996.‡ Add the repeal of the Glass-Steagall Act§ by Clinton in 1999 to that list. Together these deals represented a deregulation and consolidation of power that unleashed the forces of globalisation – basically neo-colonialism – with Washington aggressively expanding its empire.

As mentioned earlier, I was aware of Chomsky but became more interested in his writings. I remember going to see him lecture around that time – my former bass player Jared Nickerson got tickets – we were sat right next to him before he stood up to talk, and that was inspiring.

So, as an outsider – a foreigner – I was often more aware of the shadow side of US foreign policy than a lot of my American friends as a lot of this information seems to get swept under the rug by American corporate media. I would often get into arguments and they'd basically say, 'If you don't like it here, go back to the UK!' Which was fair enough. Nobody likes guests in their own country slagging it off. I understood that. But I have always been at pains to reassure all my American friends that I am *not* anti-American at all. I just don't like the foreign policy of the

---

* NAFTA (North American Free Trade Agreement) – A 1994 trade pact between the US, Canada and Mexico that eliminated most tariffs; critics argue it contributed to wage stagnation and job losses in certain sectors.
† GATT (General Agreement on Tariffs and Trade) – Overhauled under President Bill Clinton; often criticised for undermining domestic industries.
‡ Telecommunications Act of 1996 – US legislation intended to boost competition in telecoms and media, but widely criticised for reducing media diversity and giving a handful of corporations greater control over information.
§ Repeal of the Glass-Steagall Act – The 1999 repeal of key provisions separating commercial and investment banking, widely viewed as having encouraged financial risk-taking in the lead-up to the 2008 financial crisis.

neocons/neolibs. I'd buy boxes of books and pamphlets and pass them out to friends and acquaintances. Most probably ended up in the bin! I'd also dig around independent book shops to find interesting publishers: Seven Stories Press and their Project Censored series of books, Common Courage Press and AK Press.

I'd also tune in to decent local radio stations – WBAI was a great little station back then. Lots of interesting presenters and guests – local, progressive and quite radical. I'd often go to political meetings, talks and seminars too. All very American-focussed really because I felt – as one might feel towards Rome back in the days of the Roman Empire – that Washington and New York were where the power was – the dark heart of the empire, as London was in Victorian times – albeit just as a satellite now. So, I'd be out at a lot of underground gigs, poetry readings, lectures and very much immersed in – I don't like the term 'underground' as I don't think it exists anymore… maybe counterculture? If such a thing even still exists? Maybe it was the fag-end of the counterculture? In recent years the Internet has instantly shone a very bright light on everything. As soon as something happens it's already old news. But my time in New York coincided with the Wild West of the Internet – the golden age for some people, before it became completely mainstream. But unless you knew where to look there was not much beyond 'America Online' and dialling up through a modem was very, very slow and hard to navigate. I barely used the Internet myself in those days.

JW: Did you know many people who were using the Internet back then?

MJ: The first person who told me about the Internet – and this was years before it became mainstream – was my US agent Marc Geiger. He introduced me to his good friend Josh Harris – a digital pioneer who would throw interesting parties at his loft on Broadway and Houston – a few blocks up from my place. It was how I imagined Warhol's gatherings at The Factory must have been a couple of decades previously. He was in the middle of some interesting projects when Marc introduced us – prescient and cautionary experiments about the future of the Internet, privacy and human interaction. Pseudo.com was an early internet television network he founded in 1993 – long before YouTube existed. 'We Live In Public' was his most famous social experiment. After selling Pseudo, he used his fortune to fund this project that tested the human need for privacy and the psychological effects of living under constant surveillance – reality TV shows like *Big Brother* must have been inspired by this. It was a cautionary tale of the Internet devouring our privacy due to people's desire for fame and their willingness to trade privacy for attention. How our data and our lives themselves would eventually become a product.

I used to pass his 'We Live In Public' project every day on my way to and from Harold Dessau Studios – which I'll mention shortly. Josh was years ahead of his time.

JW: How did this feed into *NakedSelf*?

MJ: I've often liked to wander off the beaten track, to read and experience outside the mainstream and bring ideas back. With 'Global Eyes' I intentionally kept the lyrics nursery-rhyme simple: 'Globalise. Mobilise. Hypnotise. Homogenise'. There was a cultural and economic obsession at the time with 'the markets' and 'letting the markets decide'. The lyrics were not only an observation on the burgeoning surveillance state but also how market force had basically become this new dictator – albeit an invisible one – that all governments and media were now prostrate before. Colonialism and unregulated capitalism were rebranded as 'globalisation' and let off the leash to cause havoc internationally. Elements of this mindset could be said to have triggered many of the Forever Wars we've seen launched since.

A couple of decades later, as a direct consequence of this deregulation the West now appears to be ruled by what might be called an oligarchic corporatocracy. BlackRock, Vanguard and State Street collectively manage trillions of dollars of assets – so much that their combined holdings exceed the GDP of many of the world's countries. There was a great quote from the late comedian George Carlin: 'When fascism comes to America, it will not be in brown and black shirts. It will not be with jackboots. It will be Nike sneakers and Smiley shirts.' It's true. Everybody's always looking in the wrong direction. It is more devious than that.

JW: I also think that some of the textures on *Gun Sluts*, by what I've heard from the 'Official Bootleg', remind me of some of the work you've done in the last few years with your soundtracks. Listening to the *Muscle* (2021) soundtrack again and stuff like 'Velvet Muscle Scream' (2020).

MJ: On the *Muscle* soundtrack there's a track called 'Vicious Circus', which consists of heavy, overdriven guitars repeatedly overdubbed to create a wall of sound. That could've come straight out of the *Gun Sluts* sessions. There's a strong connection between it and some of the later soundtrack recordings.

JW: You mentioned your record company was surprised that you were doing this sort of record, but it does go back to how you started with DIY and an interest in experimentation. It seems to be where you've come back to. How many tracks did you play to Sony? And even though they probably knew you were doing something which was experimental, were you surprised by the negative response? Was there any discussion or was it just a no?

MJ: It was just no. They didn't like it at all. At one point the then-UK head of Sony, Rob Stringer, flew over to New York to see me and we hung out for a bit and he just said, 'I can't get my head around this. This is not going to be a record we can do anything with. Could you not just do an album of songs? We need a hit single!' I reminded him I'd never had a 'hit single' in my career! I did take some of his comments on board though, and moved forward with *NakedSelf* instead of *Gun Sluts*. Although the former is a more song-based album, it's obviously still not what might be considered a particularly commercial album.

JW: So, with *Gun Sluts* at that point, you'd have recorded seven or eight tracks?

MJ: More. Maybe thirteen or more. But the vocals weren't finished and it wasn't edited or mixed so it could've even been fifteen pieces of experimental music. Only about a third of all the material ended up on the 'Official Bootleg' rough mix release. The reason we had to put that out is because some thieving scumbag stole a tape, burned it to CD and started selling them on eBay for £100 per CD! Ripping off our audience. So, we released it for one tenth of the price.

JW: With *Gun Sluts*, it sounds like you were mainly recording sounds and textures – but were you writing a lot of lyrics at this time?

MJ: Yeah, I was feeling quite inspired living inside the 'belly of the beast'. When I first moved to the US I quite liked Clinton, but then the horrors were slowly unveiled. My God, it doesn't matter if you have a Democratic or a Republican president, they all do much the same things anyway – especially with foreign policy – because they're all beholden to the same powers. It just reminded me of that insightful Bill Hicks JFK assassination routine. You know the one?*

That deregulation, the Telecommunications Act of 1996 I mentioned earlier, devastated American media plurality because it guaranteed a monopoly by the most powerful. Many wonderful independent radio stations got vacuumed up by the likes of Clear Channel; many local newspapers were swiftly taken over and gutted of their independence. It's no coincidence Murdoch established his FOX News Channel in 1996, the same year Clinton signed the Act, overhauling sixty years of regulation. Now, decades later and as a consequence of these deregulations, billionaire Larry Ellison, 81, is set to become the most powerful media magnate in US history.

As a reaction to this we've had lots of alternative news sites popping up as the Internet has developed, but the authorities are clamping down on those now too. Those that haven't been taken over or infiltrated are branded 'fake news' or 'disinformation' – i.e. anything that contradicts the government is heavily censored or outlawed. It's hard for an alternative information ecosphere to thrive, because it gets stamped down all the time.

So, I was aware of what was going on with the Democrats and the Republicans – as with New Labour and the Tories in Britain – basically different sides of the same entity, two cheeks of the same arse so to speak – just cosmetic differences. And so, with the increasing censorship and surveillance that was becoming apparent

---

* The late American comedian, Bill Hicks, imagines a new president being shown a secret angle of JFK's assassination, making fun of how clandestine players control even those supposedly in charge.

even back then, there were growing concerns about the potential misuse of the powerful new technologies being unveiled.

On the visual front, there were some wonderfully humorous-but-provocative illustrations Andrew had created previously that I was thinking of as a possible cover – masked figures holding machine guns, wearing balaclavas but dressed in flared trousers and platform shoes – 'terrorist chic' you might say. A way of subtly suggesting the fact that many terrorist groups were, in fact, sponsored and trained by the West – operating hand-in-glove with them and used as proxy armies to attack rival countries – or even allied countries. I'd probably been reading up about 'Operation Gladio'* for the first time so it was equal measure fascination and horror. There would be a certain amount of instrumentals and soundscapes but the lyrics would reflect what I was just speaking about.

JW: I know *Gun Sluts* is planned to come out at some point as part of the New York Trilogy series – but will it come out as a standalone release too?

MJ: I'm not sure but I do hope to release it as part of the *New York Trilogy*. I'm trying to license the rights to *NakedSelf* but Universal are not easy to deal with. Though I can't see why they would have any interest in keeping the album as they didn't lift a finger to promote it at the time of release. *NYT* will include *Gun Sluts*, *NakedSelf* and *Karmic Gravity*. A boxset: vinyl, CD and a photographic booklet.

JW: Moving on to *NakedSelf*, how was the writing and working relationship with Eric at this point? Was that something you were comfortable with at the time, or did you have doubts?

MJ: Eric was living in the East Village so he and I spent a lot of

---

* Operation Gladio was a NATO-backed Cold War network in Europe connected to anti-communist operations, but later linked to terrorism and political manipulation.

time together. He'd come over to my loft on many mornings and we'd sit and work for hours. There were different aspects to our writing together. Sometimes Eric might sit and play an idea on an acoustic guitar and I'd say, 'Ooh, I love that bit,' or make suggestions – 'Try a chord inversion here or a substitute there,' whatever. Then I'd take the music and write melodies and lyrics – as with 'Voidy Numbness' and 'December Sunlight'. But with 'The Whisperers' Eric had the chord progression worked out and I then wrote the bass part for Spencer to play. It's one of my favourite tracks on the album. Sometimes we worked like that, but other times I'd already have the chord structure written and Eric might come up with a riff to play over it. Or we might just sit in a room together, plug our guitars in, press record on my 8-track Portastudio and away we'd go. With 'Boiling Point', for instance, that was just me and Eric each with a Boomerang looper, sitting knee to knee and jamming, playing off each other, tape recorder rolling.

He became a very close friend in New York. We had a lot of fun and made each other laugh. I'm very fond of Eric. We want to work together again. He and I went through some big life changes at the same time, moving to New York, having children – he's originally from Massachusetts although he now lives in Los Angeles. We forged a close working relationship.

JW: What about the other members of the new band you were putting together?

MJ: I can't remember what happened with our wonderful drummer on *Hanky Panky*, Brian MacLeod. I assume he must have been unavailable, but around this time I was introduced to a new drummer Earl Harvin by my US agent Marc Geiger. He'd been playing with MC 900 Ft. Jesus and came highly recommended. I met Earl a few times just to get to know him before we played any music together. He was dread-locked in those days – though now sports a similar haircut to me. Age comes for us all! He comes from a jazz background – although very versatile in his style – and is a very thoughtful musician and deep thinker. He's also a gentleman with a taste for the finer things in life – vintage watches, classic cars and a nice glass of red. When I finally got to play with him I was blown away by his feel and finesse, his sensitivity and power. Sometimes on stage when I'm off the mic I like to watch him play as he can be quite mesmerising.

I also wanted to continue working with Spencer Campbell who, as mentioned earlier, joined us for the *Hanky Panky* promotional tour. Spencer is quite a character and put me in mind a bit – looks-wise – of actor Stacy Keach in *Fat City* – especially after he'd had a few shots of Jack Daniel's! He was quite wild and certainly enjoyed a drink. But he was a wonderful all-round musician who could play drums, keyboards – and had a good voice too which blended really well with mine. The other thing is Spencer rarely – if ever – made a mistake.

I'd also invested in a high-end Pro Tools rig and initially installed it in my loft. Back in those days – the mid-nineties – Pro Tools was still fairly embryonic. It was previously called Sound Tools, a 2-track digital editing software system but from the early nineties it expanded into a multitrack system. However, it had a lot of issues and was pretty unreliable back then – the 'bleeding edge of technology' we used to joke. Staff from the company – notably Don Peebles – would often be down at our loft trying to help debug the system and get it back on its feet. Don spent so much time with me and my family he ended up becoming a good friend. I still see him to this day. Anyway, it was complicated because we were using an old 2-inch analogue multitrack at the studio, recording our sessions onto that, transferring into Pro Tools to edit, loop and do unusual things. It just kept crashing.

JW: I wondered: was there a particular reason or impetus behind the decision not to use keyboards for this album? I've read that you wanted to go back to an analogue sound and equipment, but what was the thinking behind getting rid of the keyboards?

MJ: Well, I love DC but I had to take the difficult decision that he wasn't going to be part of the album that was to become *NakedSelf*. He understood my thinking and he took it well. Like I've said, collaborators come and go and come again with THE THE. DC is back working with us now. This decision happened after the *Gun Sluts* sessions at Sear Sound. After those recordings were put in the deep freeze – I suppose what happened was – I was a heavy user of synthesizers and still love them but gradually I was using them less and less on song-based recordings. *Soul Mining* featured quite a lot of them and *Infected* did to a degree. From *Mind Bomb* onwards I started to use more classic, traditional keyboard instruments such as piano, Rhodes, Wurlitzer, Hammond, Mellotron and Clavinet rather than synthesizers. On *Dusk*, again, it was just really acoustic piano, Rhodes and Hammond. Already the electronic synth side had pretty much disappeared. With *Gun Sluts* we did use some synths – including Walter's venerable Moog 3C system – but after those sessions collapsed I had a major rethink. I knew I wanted to create a bold and unusual-sounding album and I wanted to sonically move away from my previous albums. But how to do it? How to create something analogue and organic tonally but also very fresh?

I decided to remove all keyboards but intensively treat the guitars instead. I love playing guitar and Eric is an excellent guitarist. I think our styles merged well. I wanted to manipulate and mangle our guitars so they sounded otherworldly. Eric's a world-class player and easy to work with. He also encouraged me to start using foot pedals again. Nowadays esoteric pedals have become big business – and there are countless new models available – but in the mid-nineties you just had a handful of little, boutique companies – in addition to the big Japanese players – like Boss and Ibanez or Electro Harmonix in the States, even Colorsound in the UK.

I hadn't really used foot pedals since the days of *Burning Blue Soul* and *Soul Mining* as I'd got into more complex digital studio equipment like Eventide.* But Eric turned me back onto funky little guitar pedals. We'd go off together tracking down the most obscure devices – often prototypes – in little backstreet stores around midtown Manhattan. I knew between the pair of us – with

---

* Eventide are manufacturers of world-class, award-winning digital processors for music professionals.

our guitars and pedals – we could create something unusual. Some of the textures we came up with made people wonder, 'What the hell is that?' On 'Diesel Breeze', for instance, where it's all just slowed down, looped, chopped up guitars, it gives the recording an organic but unique quality – you can't quite figure out what is making the sound.

So, I wanted a record that was predominantly analogue – using valve equipment where possible – no synthesisers or keyboards but also no digital reverbs or digital delays. All sense of space and dimension would instead be created by natural room ambience or old tape delays. It was very old-school and we made a concerted effort to head in a particular direction.

JW: Are you always so strict and specific in setting out precise roadmaps for your projects?

MJ: Before a project starts I generally set quite strict parameters. Because there's an ever-increasing number of options and possibilities available to recording musicians in recent years – it's becoming endless, infinite – and, frankly, overwhelming. Personally, I find it stimulating to limit options to force myself to think laterally. Paradoxically, such limitations inspire greater creativity – well, that is my experience. So, that was my thinking back then.

Bruce Lampcov was also key of course. I've been fortunate to work with some brilliant engineers and Bruce is one of the best. I like to co-produce with an excellent engineer as they're such an important part of the process from start to finish. Bruce and I worked really well together over the years and developed a great shorthand. We would know what the other was thinking without much having to be said. I *can* engineer myself but I'm not an excellent engineer and so I like to work with excellent engineers because there are sounds in my head I know I want that I can't get when engineering by myself. Bruce was living in London, so he was flying over to work with us. It ended up being an expensive record because we were in some nice studios and were flying people here, there and everywhere.

JW: I've heard you mention Harold Dessau Studios quite often in previous interviews. It seems that it played an important part in the creation of *NakedSelf*?

MJ: I needed to make things more cost effective so I started thinking about alternative recording studios that would be easier on what was left of the budget – *Gun Sluts* having swallowed more than its fair share! It was Eric who told me about Harold Dessau Studios. He'd heard great things about it, and it was affordable. It soon became an essential ingredient of *NakedSelf*.

The studio was down on Murray Street, a fifteen minute walk from my New York loft, close to City Hall. I loved Dessau. It was owned by Brian Kelly, who I became quite friendly with. The wonderful thing about it was its atmosphere. Technically it wasn't what might be considered a great studio – it wasn't purpose built and it had plenty of issues, but what an amazing atmosphere. It was housed in this dilapidated, light-industrial building previously owned by a metal working company, Harold Dessau Inc. – hence the name. High ceilings, old, creaking wooden floors. Run-down in a characterful way; heavy old red velvet curtains hanging in front of worn window frames. Slow-moving ceiling fans. Brian had created a beautiful space and had some interesting gear: vintage Ampex multitrack machine, old API broadcast desk, some great outboard equipment including old Neves. It was very what you might call 'funky'. But I absolutely loved the place. I've been lucky to have worked in dozens of top studios in various countries across my career, but my three favourite studios of all time would be the original Air Studios above Oxford Circus, The Garden Studio in East London (which I ended up buying) and Harold Dessau Studios in New York.

In fact, I loved Dessau so much I ended up renting a space there for a few years and had this little writing room down the corridor from the main studio. There were quite a few other musicians, writers and producers also in their own little rooms down that corridor, including Lloyd Cole. I used to joke that Dessau was like a mini indie Brill Building.* But it was cheap enough to be

---

* The Brill Building was a legendary New York 'factory' where songwriters created many American songs of the late fifties and sixties.

able to rent the main studio for a long period of time, whereas other places we worked – Sear Sound Studios and also Greene Street Studios where we mixed the album – were more traditional set-ups and therefore more expensive. So, at Dessau we were able to experiment freely and take our time. An interesting aside is that Gillian – who now runs Cinéola for me – actually worked there at the same time. She was very young then – 20 or 21 – and would have been working in an office down a different corridor to the studio, but we never actually met until many years later in London. What a small world!

I'd often be alone in my little room at Dessau chopping things around in Pro Tools, trying ideas out, writing and editing lyrics. I especially used to enjoy being alone down there in the very early hours after a flight back from Europe. I'd often be awake from jetlag at 4 a.m. or 5 a.m. for a few days so I'd head straight down there – picking up coffee and bagels en route from the all-night Korean deli and then be in my little room working away for hours undisturbed. It was a productive period in many ways but also very slow moving as – stupidly – I didn't set myself deadlines and so the writing, recording and editing just drifted onwards with no real end in sight.

JW: You're in a new relationship, you're with Johanna, but the tone of *NakedSelf* is quite dark. Quite claustrophobic lyrically – and claustrophobic sonically as well – with a sense of dread and paranoia. One of the songs is called 'Voidy Numbness'! I was listening to it recently. I think it's right up there with your best work. Was this a contrast with what you were feeling emotionally? Hadn't you also just become a father at this point?

MJ: I'm going to give a lengthy answer to this as there are just so many aspects to my life in New York so forgive my meandering detour.

Yes, I first became a father in 1997. After quite a lengthy, intense and complicated labour, little Jackson was born very early one beautiful May day in a Greenwich Village hospital. One of the happiest days of my life in fact. I was walking on air. Coincidentally,

Eric's first son, Django, was born three months after Jack, so that bonded us even closer. There were a lot of fantastic things going on in my life. We were living in our wonderful loft on Broadway, we had our beautiful little baby boy. Our social life was obviously curtailed by being new parents so we had to find things to do that didn't involve drinking. We were already regulars at Kim's Underground on Bleecker Street – a great video rental store with a huge collection of rare and esoteric VHS tapes. You would have been in heaven in that store! So that kept us entertained. I used to hang around the Village Chess Shop on Thompson Street too and I bought a nice new set. I hadn't played for years but I taught Johanna and she became quite good. We played constantly and as New York has so many outdoor chess boards we'd spend much time outside playing with Jack snoozing beside us in his pram. I remember one summer evening playing chess on the grounds outside City Hall when suddenly the dusk air was lit up all around us by thousands of fireflies. Magic just appearing out of thin air.

We were out and about all the time as New York – especially Manhattan – is such an inviting city, a real walking city. Nothing really seemed that far away and the part of Broadway we lived on was the dividing line between China Town and TriBeCa, yet a stone's throw from Canal Street, SoHo, Little Italy and City Hall. There were lots of interesting characters in our neighbourhood and we'd often see the likes of Willem Defoe or Harvey Keitel wandering around. It was an exciting place to be. There were also many great bars and restaurants locally too but our favourite place always put me in mind of that essay by George Orwell, 'The Moon Under Water' – have you ever read it? In it he described his perfect pub, went into great detail about the staff, drinking vessels, food, furniture and décor. Only at the end do you realise it's a composite of all his favourite pubs and that no such establishment really existed. Well, in New York, I found my equivalent of The Moon Under Water – but unlike Orwell's case mine really *did* exist. It was a little French and Malaysian bistro called the Franklyn Station Café – situated at 222 West Broadway opposite Franklin Station. It was owned by a wonderful couple, Mei Chau and Marc Kaczmarek. The food was outstanding, the staff warm and attentive, the music old-school French, the décor perfect and, situated in a south-facing corner building with huge windows, it was flooded with beautiful light regardless of the season. It was very affordable too. We were there nearly every day. When we weren't eating in we were getting deliveries from there. They absolutely loved Jackson. Sadly, as part of the inexorable gentrification process, the landlord forced them out so he could get higher rents from the rich folk who'd begun colonising that part of the city. I mention all this as I am reminiscing this period of my life for the first time in many years and trying to place the darkness of *NakedSelf* in context.

We also travelled abroad a lot, taking two big European trips annually – between four to six weeks each. We'd pack our suitcases and head over to Sweden to see Johanna's family in Göteborg and Värmland, then down to England to see my family in Suffolk and London. Plus, we'd head across to my house in Mallorca for a while. The order would change but generally a European 'tour' each winter and summer. We were living a good life. Johanna was working hard and studying, taking her degree in photography on her path to becoming a documentarian and I was toiling away trying to write and record.

So, that was a brief outline of some of the positive things going on at the time but – and there is always a 'but' in life isn't there? – there was a deep underlying tension inside me too. My mum had become increasingly unwell during the time I was living in New York. Her illness was a direct result of the deep, unrelenting grief she was experiencing after the death of Eugene. She could not get over his loss. Despite all of us pleading with her not to forget the rest of us, to stay well for our sakes, she lost the will to live. I phoned home a lot, went back to England fairly frequently to see her. But I felt guilty living the good life in Manhattan, knowing my dad and brothers were taking the brunt of it. That was part of the undercurrent, knowing she was dying whilst I was so far away from her and the rest of my family.

I'd speak with her and my dad by phone a few times per week and as well as our lengthy bi-annual visits I'd also head back alone for the odd week a couple of times per year too. My parents visited us a few times in New York as well – the best visit being soon after Jackson was born. Although my mum was quite unwell by this time she was so happy to finally be a grandmother. She adored children and was in her element holding Jackson. I know she was proud of me for fulfilling a personal dream by moving to Manhattan yet of course I felt guilty that I was not seeing as much of her as I should. She never put any pressure on any of her boys – she would always reassure us that all she wanted was for us to be happy, whatever path we chose in life.

I was with my mum at the very end and she died in my arms in the early hours of the morning on one of my trips back to England. One of those life-changing moments which turns you from a boy into a man. It was incredibly intense and profound, on the opposite end of the scale in terms of emotion – though similar in profundity – to when I held my sons in my arms immediately after they were born and they were taking their *first* breaths.

In addition to this feeling of melancholy over my family there was also a weird post-viral fatigue thing lingering in my body. I felt so tired much of the time and it definitely affected my concentration and emotional state. I'd suffer these 'attacks' – terrible periods of extreme low energy that made it feel like I was swimming through treacle – where I could barely string a thought together. I think I mentioned this previously – being hospitalised in the Hospital For Nervous Diseases in Maida Vale towards the end of the making of *Soul Mining*, temporarily losing my sight, my energy and experiencing the strange sensations down my legs and body (see page 199). The symptoms I was experiencing in New York were similar and obviously connected and would flare up periodically – with bouts of extreme fatigue and exhaustion, my mood dragged down as if by an anchor to the sea bed. I was desperate to get to the bottom of it and must have tried every imaginable treatment – special diets, various potions and lotions, forms of emotional therapy, being injected intravenously with high doses of vitamins.

There were a couple of things that did help: a wonderful acupuncturist called Abdi Assadi – introduced by my close friend Justine Chiara. Abdi in turn became a close friend and his powerful treatments helped. Plus, I'd read an interview with Barry Sheene – the late British motorcycle champion – who'd been battling chronic fatigue at some point in his life but found relief through cold-water therapy and ice baths. This was years before Wim Hof became fashionable. I'd been occasionally going to the old Russian Baths on 10th Street since the early eighties but I increased my attendance to several times per week – working out my own hydrotherapy regimes, alternating between sitting in boiling radiant rooms and jumping into freezing plunge pools and ice-cold showers. It really did help.

So, to answer your original question as to the lyrical claustrophobia of *NakedSelf*: no, the album did not reflect the positive things in my life I have mentioned but yes, it mirrored the feelings of melancholy about my family and the deep fatigue gnawing away at me.

What was happening politically in the world was playing heavily upon my mind too. Which is why the album – although there are beautiful elements to it musically – has an underlying dark edge. I suppose songwriting is my therapy and that shadow side must come out. But some people may get the wrong impression that the shadow side represents more of me and my life than it really does. It is only a *part* of my life. With the happier, more fulfilled side, I want to be out and about experiencing it, not sitting in a dark room scribbling away at a desk. Laughing and enjoying myself with people I love and care about. A lot of the time I'm actually pretty happy! Though truth be told I probably should try to learn how to write about that side more and share it.

JW: Lyrically, you tackle the notion of addiction, in all meanings of the word.

MJ: I was trying to write about addiction in some of those lyrics. In 'Salt Water' I meant it metaphorically of course – whatever it is that you are doing to try to quench a 'thirst' that is connected to addiction is, in reality, rotting you from the inside out.

JW: What about 'Shrunken Man'? That is a song which deals, not so much with addiction, but with all the pressures of the world coming down upon your shoulders. Fear for the future, worries about the past. 'Shrunken Man' seems to be where you pour out your worries. Perhaps it crystallises a lot of the things that were affecting you at this time, like the ill health of your mother?

MJ: 'Shrunken Man' is not autobiographical. It was inspired – if that is the right word – by a person I knew who was going through a very hard period at that time, and someone else, independent of that person, who was also going through a very difficult period. I could see their lives and their characters starting to shrivel as a consequence of a lot of negativity and poor life choices.

'Phantom Walls' was about my mother, her illness, and her slowly dying. 'Boiling Point' is one of my favourite tracks on the album. Gritty, urban and written from day-to-day experience, travelling on subways, pushing through crowds, the intense energy absorbed whilst in the underbelly of a massive metropolis, the feeling of being overwhelmed by relentless news, propaganda and stress.

'Swine Fever' was a comment on consumerism. I was always at pains in interviews to stress that I'm not pointing the finger at anyone else. I'm as bad – probably worse – than anyone when it comes to mindless consumerism – endlessly buying things I do not need. That feeling of manipulation, of needs being created and stirred up, of trying to scratch an itch that can never be reached. 'December Sunlight' was also one of my favourites.

JW: That's one of the more upbeat tracks on the album.

MJ: I think of it as a companion piece to 'August & September' from *Mind Bomb*. No accident they both have months of the year as part of their titles. 'Weather Belle' is another I liked. With the instrumentation – the banjo especially – I wanted to go for a sound with a timeless quality, unconnected to what may have been happening musically in the US or the UK.

Bear in mind that I was totally disconnected from Britpop and that entire scene – I was living outside Britain and viewed New

Labour and Britpop through a telescope. *NakedSelf* was about as far away as you could get from all that. I was happy being a foreigner. I like being a foreigner. I like living abroad. Living in England I get so wound up by politics because I care more about it. In America, I cared about foreign policy but domestic politics didn't affect me as much. I felt anonymous, an observer.

I did still miss England a bit though. To feel connected I'd have the *Guardian Weekly* delivered – a smaller version of the paper designed for ex-pats. Plus, I purchased a Drake SW8. This powerful shortwave radio I used to tune into the BBC World Service and various other state broadcasters – Cuban, Chinese, Russian, German. This was effectively pre-Internet and so shortwave radio was my main connection to the 'outside' world. I remember being sat beside it hearing news of New Labour's landslide over the Tories. How we all cheered! A few years before Blair's illegal foreign adventures. I remember hearing the shocking news of Princess Diana's death on my Drake. I used to love listening to English football matches on the shortwave. They just sound more exciting on the radio, don't they? I especially used to enjoy Alan Green's commentary as he had such a passionate voice.

JW: 'Soul Catcher' is about love, but it's also about a fear for the future. Was this song influenced by being a new father? And also by being in a situation where you realised – because of Clinton, because of political situations – that for all the happiness that was in your life, the future for the younger generation was going to be quite difficult?

MJ: 'Soul Catcher' is not about love, but it was influenced by being a new father. Most Saturday mornings when Jack was a little boy I used to take him down to the National Museum of the American Indian – a wonderful place located in the beautiful old US Customs House, not far from Wall Street. He loved it down there and I loved spending time with him there. They had a little side room where they'd show these crude but evocative animated films – parables and mythological tales related to Native American culture. One day we saw an exhibition of soul catchers there.

The soul catcher is a sacred shamanic tool used to heal illness by spiritually retrieving a patient's lost soul and returning it to their body. Whilst not directly causing reincarnation, it upholds the natural cycle of life and death, a cycle which many Native American cultures believe includes the rebirth of the soul. I just loved the phrase and the intense philosophy behind it and it seemed to suit the lyrics I'd written for a new song I was working on about reincarnation and the cycles of life, the choices we make and the questions we ask ourselves: Am I doing everything I should with my life? Am I fulfilling my own expectations? Am I satisfied with my soul's purpose in this life? The last lines are:

> But trapped inside my bones
> Fear, desire and hope are on fire
> And will expand like smoke
> And fall down like rain
> Again, again, again, again, again, again

Essentially, it's about being strapped to the karmic wheel – forever turning. We performed it on the Comeback Special Tour and I was very pleased with that new version.

JW: One other thing it reminds me to ask you is, we spoke earlier on about Wire. One of the tracks on this—

MJ: 'Diesel Breeze'.

JW: Yes. 'Diesel Breeze' obviously makes a reference to Wire.

MJ: Yes, there was a little reference. Funnily enough, I recently did an interview for a Wire documentary. I hadn't listened to Wire for a bit, but I bought another copy of their third album *154* – an expanded edition which included demos and things like that. I listened to it again. I loved that album when it came out and I love it still.

As we spoke about previously I had an association with them as a teenager – they took me under their wing, produced some recordings, we supported them at some of their gigs and we'd hang out with them. I really think they were one of the great British bands of the last forty-odd years. Still underrated. People who know them know how good they are.

In terms of that little reference: 'Diesel Breeze' was actually from the *Gun Sluts* sessions and some of those ideas found their way across to *NakedSelf*. As I was editing it, creating loops from treated guitars, it was starting to give the feeling of a train. So, I tried to write something simple about a suburban train journey through a decaying city – only one verse, and I was trying to think of a line to end it with when 'The Other Window' (Wire, 1979) suddenly came to mind. I always loved those lyrics about a train journey, the line about the horse caught in barbed wire – 'The more it struggled the more it strangled' – and ending the song with the lyric I referenced, 'The other window had a nicer view.' Those words put me in mind a bit of The Velvet Underground's 'The Gift'. Very dark. So, I ended 'Diesel Breeze' with a similar lyric. It was just a little reference to Wire.

JW: It's nice because it goes back to your past. Before we talk about the reception of the record and the release, can we talk about the cover artwork? It's a very striking cover. It reminds me of a William Eggleston photograph. It reflects the content a little bit, the contrast of darkness and light. How did you come to the cover of *NakedSelf*?

MJ: I love Eggleston's work though I don't recall that being a direct influence on the cover. I bought some little vintage Minox* cameras – you know the tiny 8x11mm sub-miniature format used by spies in the Cold War? I bought three of them and spent a lot of time wandering the streets in the early hours and late at night. I loved their limitations. Johanna was obviously heavily into photography too but whereas she was studying it full time in order to take it up professionally I was more of a

---

* The Minox camera was invented by Walter Zapp in 1936 and widely used by intelligence agencies in the USA, UK, Western Europe and most of the Eastern Bloc.

'snap-o-grapher' – a dilettante. I don't take myself too seriously with it although I've used some of my photographs on some Cinéola releases such as *Tony* and *Radio Cinéola: Trilogy*.

We had an inspiring time taking photos, going to lots of exhibitions, galleries and museums. Which reminds me, MOMA used to sell 35mm slides of some of its artwork in their collection. Rather than buy prints to hang on the wall I bought a nice 35mm slide projector instead. During our regular visits to the museum I amassed a nice collection – a hundred or more slides. I'd project them – much larger than life – onto one of the big white walls in our loft. Sitting back with a nice glass of wine we could enjoy Bacon, Magritte, O'Keefe, Hopper, Kandinsky, Grosz, Picasso, Pollock, Rothko, Johns, Kahlo, Matisse, Miró, de Kooning – depending on the mood of the evening. They're all still in a box in storage somewhere. I should retrieve them.

But I'm digressing. Back to the sleeve of *NakedSelf*. At this point I was also working with Cally Callomon – who had taken over from my brother Andrew to work on my sleeves. We didn't fall out over it but Andrew was having trouble sticking to deadlines and decided he didn't need the stress of working on my sleeves. I'd first worked with Cally on *Hanky Panky* and really liked him. I wanted to maintain this new working relationship. He'd sometimes visit New York on other business and we'd hang out. For *NakedSelf* we devised a concept called 'collaborative exposure'. We'd each take a 35mm camera and walk the streets, spending days wandering lower Manhattan, Brooklyn or Coney Island – or taking the ferry to Hoboken, New Jersey. We'd take photos, out of sight of the other, but when our rolls were filled we'd wind them back, swap films with each other and load up again. Off we'd go taking these double exposures but never knowing what we were taking the new photo on top of. Some really evocative – often abstract – images came out of that process. Cally was wonderful to work with. A thoughtful person and a lateral thinker. Some of our photography from those sessions is in the booklet for the deluxe 'hardcover' edition of *NakedSelf*.

In terms of the cover itself? I'd taken a photograph of a bare lightbulb – possibly at Dessau – on my Minox. I liked taking close-up photos of things like half-empty glasses or lightbulbs. I said to Cally, 'I think this should be the album sleeve.' He agreed but said, 'Yes, but the version you've taken is not strong enough.' So, we hired noted photographer Ellis Parrinder to retake. His was definitely better than my version – more dramatic. You're right that it suggests a duality, the low-wattage lightbulb radiating a small glow of light in a very dark space. I felt it was perfectly representative of the music and the lyrics.

JW: There was an issue with *Gun Sluts* and it has remained unreleased. How did the release of *NakedSelf* materialise? Was it something that Sony were going to do at one point? I think I remember they spoke about a worry that there weren't singles on it, which, you've said to me before was odd because you were never really a singles artist. You were more of an album artist. How did *NakedSelf* finally emerge?

MJ: Well, as mentioned earlier, Sony UK was run by Rob Stringer – who's now chairman/CEO of Sony Music globally I believe. He's even been made a CBE. His big brother, Sir Howard Stringer, was in overall charge of the company back then – all a bit of a family affair. I liked Rob but he didn't like the direction I was going in. It was a tricky situation because I was coming towards the end of my contract and *NakedSelf* would be my final album for Sony unless we agreed a new deal. One of my bugbears was that my deal was so old and the royalties so poor. So, we were discussing extending my contract. I felt I deserved X amount of percentages and advances. Not greedy – just what I considered fair and proper after eighteen years at the label. But they weren't convinced about the commercial viability of my new direction. Bearing in mind at this time Napster* was emerging too, with illegal downloading starting to spread like a virus. All the major labels were in a state of panic and confusion. They saw physical

---

* Napster was a controversial American proprietary peer-to-peer (P2P) file sharing application primarily associated with unauthorised digital file distribution.

sales collapsing and they started prioritising big-hitting pop acts rather than bothering with slow-burning album artists like me.

I think there was only one person left at Sony who really had any faith in me. That was Dave Gottlieb in the New York office who had been my product manager since *Mind Bomb* and who had become a good friend and is someone I still meet with regularly. A person of great integrity. But in all honesty the direction I was taking musically probably would have suited the late seventies – not really the late nineties. After taking on board some of the criticisms from Sony over *Gun Sluts* I had started work on *NakedSelf*. Towards the end of recording we started contract re-negotiations – oh, I also had new management by this point: Roger Cramer who was based in New York. Steve Rennie having decided to jump ship and join Sony as an executive a couple of years earlier. Roger was a lawyer by training and a gentleman – probably too nice to be a manager in some ways – or even a lawyer for that matter! So, we were negotiating with Sony but they told us they couldn't see much commercial potential in this album and couldn't offer the kind of deal we wanted. An impasse was reached. They wouldn't release and promote the new album without guarantees I would stay – but I wouldn't stay unless they offered me a deal I felt was commensurate with the value of THE THE. So, it was mutually – and amicably – agreed I could leave. I'd officially reached the end of my contract.

At the time I would've been quite happy to stay with Sony if they'd offered a decent deal. I liked the people and didn't really want to leave. But at the same time when I handed *NakedSelf* in to Sony it was met with *three months* of silence. Three months! There was no acknowledgement. They wouldn't return our phone calls. In the end I was so irked that I managed to get hold of Rob's home phone number, rung him up very early – woke him when he was still in bed – and basically asked, 'What the hell is going on?!' The reply I got was, 'Oh, we've got too much respect for you to tell you we didn't like the album!'

JW: Did you buy that?

MJ: Well, he *was* being honest about not liking the album but if he'd respected me he wouldn't have kept us waiting three months to hear this verdict.

Around this time Polly Anthony – who Sony had recently appointed President of Epic Records in America after throwing Englishman Richard Griffiths overboard – requested a meeting. I suggested we meet at the Ear Inn (my favourite NYC bar). So, she was driven downtown to see me. She came into the bar with my old friend from Sony Dave Gottlieb – her Lincoln Town Car and driver sat waiting outside. I liked her. She was a character and straight talking – a heavy smoker who enjoyed a drink. We started chatting about my new album when – out of the blue – she offered me a job as an A&R man! I didn't know whether to take it as a compliment that she respected my taste or as an insult that she didn't like my new album. I declined – obviously.

JW: You'd sold a lot of records for them. *Infected* was in the charts for about thirty weeks.

MJ: Yes. I was their longest-signed UK artist at the time I believe. Which reminds me, for some reason, shortly before leaving the label I was invited to the Grammy's in Los Angeles. I can't remember why – it certainly wasn't because I'd received a nomination. When there I was introduced to various members of the company hierarchy but most memorably someone wanted me to meet Bruce Springsteen as at that time he was the company's longest-signed *American* singer–songwriter whilst I was their longest-signed *British* singer–songwriter. The Boss was very gracious and we shook hands and had a chat about this and that. Though I was familiar with 'Born In The USA', I'm not sure he was familiar with 'This is the 51st state of the USA', the refrain from 'Heartland'!

The break with Sony was a bit disorientating and I had mixed feelings. It was the end of a relationship and I was sad but also excited I was finally free to negotiate with other labels. We immediately received offers from other majors proffering the terms Sony refused to give. We also received a strong offer from Trent Reznor's label, Nothing Records, which was part of Interscope, itself part of Universal. They came in with an offer of a decent advance and royalties but – most important of all – they were very passionate about the new album. So, we went with them. Which was unfortunate looking back as it ended in complete disaster! Trent was wrestling with problems of his own but the entire conglomerate was going through a tumultuous period of change – mergers, takeovers and 'streamlining'. What was originally MCA had been bought by Edgar Bronfman Jr, who was heir to the Seagram's fortune. He changed the name to Universal and then bought the large Dutch multinational PolyGram and absorbed that into Universal. Then it ended up being bought by the French water company Vivendi. It was a chaotic time and the people you were dealing with one week were thrown overboard the next. You just never knew who you were supposed to talk to and morale was on the floor. So, *NakedSelf* slipped through the cracks and just disappeared as there was no one left at Universal who had any interest in promoting it. Paradoxically it got the best reviews of my career at the time. There's a moral in there somewhere.

JW: We spoke about you wanting to release *NakedSelf* on vinyl at some point because it does really stand up. Were you making new discoveries of things that you were listening to and places you were going in New York?

MJ: Lots of music, lots of gigs but also cinema, political meetings and poetry readings. It's all nearly thirty years ago so it's hard to remember details but we were out all the time. So many incredible places on our doorstep – venues like Knitting Factory, Tonic, CBGB & 313 Gallery, Continental, Mercury Lounge, Sin-e, Bowery Ballroom, Luna Lounge, Arlene's Grocery. Or we'd be at the Angelika or Film Forum cinemas a couple of nights per week – or occasionally head up to the Ziegfeld Theatre, which was massive and stunning. Sometimes we'd go to jazz venues like Arthur's Tavern, Sweet Basil or Village Vanguard or just hang out in bars like Max Fish, Mars Bar, Ear Inn or the Aztec Bar. There are far too many to name individually. It is a *very* easy city in which to blow all your money – which I kind of did looking back.

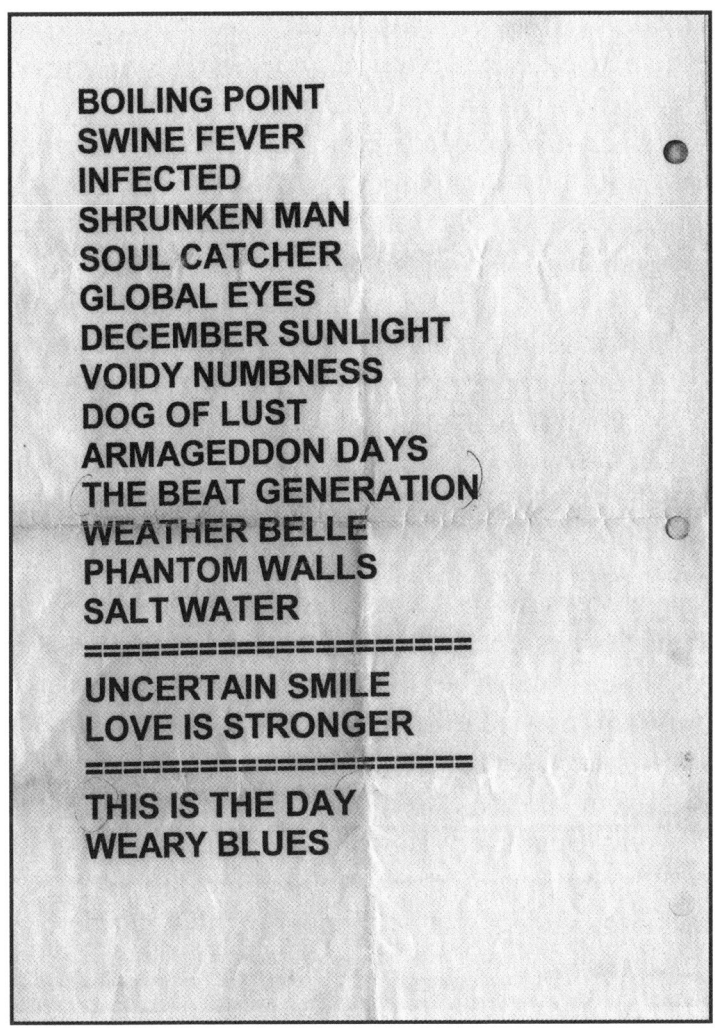

JW: Just to clarify, you decided to go on a world tour to promote *NakedSelf*. Was it the same band that played on the album?

MJ: For the Naked World Tour, it was the same four-piece that played on the album: Eric Schermerhorn, Spencer Campbell, Earl Harvin and myself. A really powerful band. Great guys, great musicians. We couldn't have worked any harder but we were fighting a losing battle. It was like being sent to the front line without ammunition. I decided to extend the tour out of my own pocket and I lost a lot of money I couldn't afford to lose. I just wanted to give the album a chance.

JW: It must have taken a physical and mental toll. You've made a record which as you said is getting some of the best reviews of your career, because sometimes critics have been slow to appreciate your work, but here you've got a record which is getting very, very good reviews. It's the first of your records at that point not to be pressed on vinyl, which might be linked to the fact that at that time CDs were so big. You've got a great band, you're touring, but you're having to pay for it out of your own pocket because you're not being supported by your label. That obviously takes a toll on you financially. But what was this doing to you? Was it making you unwell? The lack of promotion, the lack of help from the label, the lack of support, and the fact that you're having to dig deep into your own pocket?

MJ: In many ways this is a single person's profession. The effects upon family life can be harsh. People don't realise what they're getting themselves into when they become involved with a musician. Most musicians are egotistical and selfish – including myself. You have to be to an extent to be any good. But you feel torn. You're married to your career yet you have important responsibilities in the real world. I put every ounce of my energy and intensity into writing and recording *NakedSelf* and then into touring it.

Sometimes on stage I'd feel almost slightly outside of myself and my mind might drift off. Sometimes when confidence is low you can't help wondering, 'Have I lost it?' or 'Am I any good?' or 'Was I ever any good?' There can be a random existential crisis – often triggered by fatigue or negative news. Sometimes, halfway through a set I'd wonder why these songs just don't express the way I really feel. Other times I'd wonder how I wrote something that so perfectly captures my inner life and it's as if time slows and I'm sitting inside each word, steering it towards the perfect nuance and shade of meaning. The trick is to try to cover up when you're feeling a bit lost or spaced-out on stage. Sometimes you've got to act and just grind it out. Much of it could be down to biorhythms

I suppose. Of course, you have to hide these doubts from the outside world – even from your band mates. You just can't let your mind go to these places. It is to risk complete defeat of the mind, and you may as well pack up, go home and go back to bed.

I've always been fascinated by people who have the integrity to just turn their backs on what they love – or what they are good at – if it no longer feels right, a romanticism exemplified in the book and film from the early sixties *The Loneliness of the Long Distance Runner*. I've also long been fascinated by sportsmen who went on too long, who couldn't accept time overtaking their bodies. When do you know if you're over the hill? The title 'Twilight Of A Champion' was inspired by an article about this. Once you are deemed to be out of fashion, the oxygen of publicity starts to get shut off and there's not much you can do. You start to feel yourself and your career banished to the margins; you can't even get on the radio or television as easily anymore. Confidence ebbs away. I'd always told myself *I'd* know when to quit. You wouldn't find *me* overstaying my welcome. Going beyond *my* sell-by date. I now realise you never *know* when your sell-by date is.

I was still writing about political issues and existential affairs of the heart and soul – as if anybody still cared. Less and less people seemed to. An inquisitive population doesn't seem to fit with what's required in our modern world – society and popular culture being increasingly atomised and consciences bought off with cheap consumables or distracted by infotainment. So, there has been this gradual but steady shift as we've been morphed from citizens into consumers. The idea of principles in this industry is deemed naive and foolish I suppose, but then again you have to try and have a bit of dignity about your career, but I'm digressing…

JW: So, were there some particularly low points on the Naked Tour?

MJ: Roskilde… oh Roskilde.* We had played a fantastic show to a packed audience but didn't know until we got off stage what

---

* On 30 June 2000, nine people died in a crowd rush during Pearl Jam's set at the Roskilde Festival in Denmark.

had happened on a neighbouring stage just before we came on. Nine young people had been crushed to death at the Pearl Jam concert that happened just before ours. We all felt sick. I just kept thinking about the families too – the knocking on doors in the dead of night as the police carried out their gruesome rounds. I didn't realise people had died at Glastonbury that year as well. For all those poor souls as for the rest of us it just goes to show you never know what's lying in wait around the next corner.

At times like that on tour you couldn't help your mind wandering down philosophical cul-de-sacs, keeping you awake. It's eerie if you wander the tour bus in the middle of the night. It's a docile trust we place in the bus driver's hands as the vehicle hurtles along highways, city to city, coast to coast in the dead of night. Here lay the band and crew, almost in a state of suspended animation, in their little pods, drifting off to the land of nod – a bit like being in a submarine or spaceship. Hour after hour, day after day, week after week, month after month we're together. You have to learn how to compromise as there are little skirmishes between people on odd occasions and the humour can get a little rough round the edges sometimes.

But it is so important to stay focussed on the road – trying to stay insulated from negativity from the outside – or the inside. The slightest thing used to trigger me sometimes. Incompetence and bad news from the record company. Or a random conversation. A look from a girl. Sometimes, rather than numb myself with a drink or zone out with a film, I'd allow myself to just slip into this feeling, this painful void I write about in so many of my songs. A void I've tried to fill in the past with alcohol, sex, work, consumerism – in fact any distraction. It's something I've carried inside all of my life. It serves as the hotbed for my creativity. I cannot really run away from this aching void. In the past, even unrequited sexual feelings served as fuel for the creative furnace, but I'm too old and tired to bother writing about that anymore and I realised that no thing – and no one – could ever fill this part of me except an inner peace and connection with God – or whatever you want to call it – our higher self? – in a word, Grace. So, I would sometimes lay down, close my eyes and try not to run away from this feeling but slowly melt into it, allow it to gently run over me and then through me and then slowly reveal itself. Only then would I start to realise how tired I really was. How tired of running away from my own pain. That was a sentiment I tried to convey in the lyrics to 'Phantom Walls', though it was written about my mother's struggle with emotional pain.

JW: And what sort of spirits were the band in on the Naked Tour?

MJ: The spirit within the band was strong and we had great people on our crew. I loved hanging out with them, loved being onstage with them. We had a lot of fun and laughter on that tour. And, being a new father, it was great during breaks in the tour coming home and seeing Johanna and Jackson – we'd take little trips away in between legs of the tour.

Later on, Sony did admit they'd made a mistake and wished they *had* put the album out. I wished they'd put it out too! Ironically, all across the world on that tour there were more people from Sony coming to watch us play than from Universal! All telling us they were disappointed the company had not released the album. *NakedSelf* always felt a bit like a lost child – orphaned off to the wrong label.

JW: I know on your recent tours: The Comeback Special and Ensouled, you said you felt satisfied – even energised. What was the general feeling at the conclusion of *this* tour?

MJ: After the Naked Tour finally finished – and it was a long tour of fourteen months on and off – I felt exhausted and deflated. But I finally had a chance to sit down and survey the wreckage that was now my career.

I'd already left Sony, I was now trying to leave Universal, I'd lost a fortune on tour, was about to fire my manager and my publishing company Sony/ATV also decided not to renew my deal – which was another financial blow. The sky was now darkening, shadows on the horizon moving closer, a time of reckoning was on the way.

I was obviously extremely unhappy about the situation with *NakedSelf* so I met with John Malm – the manager of Nine Inch Nails who ran Nothing Records for Trent. I just said, 'Tear up the contract. I'm really unhappy and I'm never going make another record.' He agreed. It saved them money not having to pay for another album so I'm sure they were relieved too. In exchange for releasing me early Malm insisted I sign some sort of NDA as they were scared I might badmouth them publicly by revealing too many details. Fine, I signed it. Of course, I kept my word. I'm not a bitchy person and wasn't planning on saying negative things about Trent anyway as the chaos unleashed by the series of mega-mergers around Universal wasn't his fault. I just wanted out. As soon as possible.

JW: I wondered if you could say a little bit more about another unreleased album of yours, *Karmic Gravity*? For a lot of people there will be an awareness of it, but that's a grey area in your discography. You recorded the album around 2000?

MJ: *Karmic Gravity* was post *NakedSelf*. I worked on it prior to signing the Universal deal and going on tour but also after leaving Universal too – and just before leaving New York to go and live in Göteborg. I had most of the lyrics finished and had even finished some vocals. The project has now had a lengthy gestation period – distilled by time.

Karmic Gravity in a way is more commercial than *NakedSelf*. It contains some beautiful songs, very haunting and melodic but with a stripped-down toughness that I love. I listened to these recordings recently and actually think it's a stronger record than *NakedSelf*. I'm looking forward to finally finishing it. I spoke with Eric Schermerhorn about it a few months ago, we discussed it during a phone call that lasted about four hours. We're both keen. He may even pop over to London to record some overdubs with me.

JW: Was it just you and Eric?

MJ: Myself and Eric, but also Spencer and Earl on some tracks plus some other drummers on a couple of tracks too: Brian MacLeod on one and Frank Ferrer – now with Guns N' Roses – on another. Bruce engineered some tracks, and in-house Dessau engineers Dave Lee and Roger Scheepers worked with us when Bruce was back in the UK.

Some songs might be just a baritone guitar and my voice, or even just a banjo and voice. It's in a similar vein sonically and instrumentation-wise to *NakedSelf* in that there are no keyboards or digital reverbs – and it fits very comfortably with both *Gun Sluts* and *NakedSelf*.

When listening recently I thought, 'My God, why didn't I finish this?!' Of course, I know why I didn't: I was so exhausted and became so disillusioned with the industry and my confidence was just so low that I wanted out of my own career. Everything was a mess and I was feeling quite beaten up. The Pro Tools multitracks for *Karmic Gravity* had been backed up on an old format called Jaz Drives. But – as with many digital technologies – they are not so reliable over time and quite a few of these drives started misbehaving and I couldn't get all the information off. I had to send them off to various data retrieval companies and managed to get about 90 per cent back in the end – plus I have rough mixes of most of the material to refer back to. But it was a strange project really as it was recorded in fits and starts and was dependent on whoever happened to be in New York at the time, plus my mind was a bit disorientated as I just wasn't sure who I might release it through.

JW: I think it's something to look forward to – being able hear it. The record industry and the infrastructure have changed so much but with Cinéola you are captain of your own ship so can put stuff out that excites you without having to worry what the vice president of the label might think. You can just go with your instinct. That must be quite empowering.

MJ: It's thrilling. We have so many interesting projects on the go. Not only music but also films, books and merchandise that I find exciting too. Knowing that I'm controlling – with my small, trusted team – the whole process. Being able to release vinyl, CDs, films and books in a high-quality format. Big inspirations have been the Folio Society and the Criterion Collection. Obviously, the former is books and the latter films, but Cinéola was conceived along those lines. Beautiful high-end editions that are not subject to the strict budgetary controls of a major conglomerate which tends to prefer releasing things as cheaply as possible no matter how much time and care was spent creating it.

When CDs were introduced everyone was cheated by the record companies. The general public suddenly had to pay twice the price of vinyl for a CD album yet artist royalties were simultaneously cut in half. Because – the record companies claimed – it was a 'trial period' for CDs. This went on for years! The packaging also shrank dramatically, of course – cheap, flimsy and less interesting. Downloads are better for the environment I suppose but we don't really own them and I think humans in general are naturally quite tactile creatures who like holding things and feeling weight and texture. I'm quite old-school I suppose and still wedded to the concept of the album as a format. Part of the joy of having my own little record company is that I can approve decisions about high-quality packaging.

JW: Do you know Fitzcarraldo Editions?

MJ: No.

JW: They're books. And they're beautifully done. They are editions you want to own because they're such gorgeous artefacts. You can see how much effort they put into what they do. They published *Pretentiousness and Why It Matters* by Dan Fox (2016).

CHAPTER NINE
The Lust For Unsung Dreams

Influenced by sonic experimentation and an early love of cinema, Matt begins to work on a series of soundtrack compositions, most prominently for his talented filmmaking younger brother, Gerard. Tony, Hyena, Muscle and Odyssey become signature THE THE records. Matt discusses his soundtrack work with Nick McKay in the 'Kino' edition of The Modernist.

JW: You were interviewed by Jane Giles for her documentary *Scala!!!* (2023). It was rough as hell as a venue, but I loved it.

MJ: Yes. I didn't actually go to the King's Cross Scala, I used to go to the original Scala on Tottenham Street. This would be early days of THE THE and around the time of *Burning Blue Soul*. London was an entirely different place in those days and not a late-night city. It was hard to get a drink after hours unless you were a member of a private club or found an illegal drinking den – of which there were a few. There were also some Spanish bars on Hanway Street – between Oxford Street and Tottenham Court Road – that stayed open quite late but regular pubs closed around 10:30 p.m. or 11 p.m. at the latest in those days because of the UK's licensing laws at the time. But the Scala was one of those few places – with its all-nighters – you could enjoy some after-hours action. To stay awake all night, speed in the form of sulphate was the drug of choice when you were broke and on the dole.* But God, it was disgusting stuff!

JW: It could make you feel terrible, but it would keep you up.

MJ: Yep, you'd take a toothbrush and toothpaste for the morning but some sulphate to stay awake to watch the films – and the gigs too. Final Solution promoted some concerts at the original Scala. I remember seeing 23 Skidoo amongst others.

JW: I was going there at 15 or 16 – probably too young to be honest.

MJ: How old are you now?

JW: I'm 52.

MJ: Still a kid! That's why you didn't go to the Tottenham Street one. If I was in my teens in 1979 you would've been...

JW: 10 years old. The thing with the Scala was that it was where you could go to see sex on screen. You'd watch these films by great auteurs but also exploitation stuff. I liked feeling part of it; it was my education and where I learned about cinema. I was never interested in mainstream cinema, like the Star Wars series. I saw John Waters movies and *Taxi Driver* (1976) at the Scala and all that sort of stuff. You'd come out of seeing a film like *Taxi Driver* and King's Cross was like Times Square. You could come out and you would think you were in *Taxi Driver* because you would just see reprobates and prostitutes and drunks.

MJ: Yes, even high-profile characters would sometimes get arrested for curb-crawling there. What a different world going back just a few decades – obviously pre-mobile, pre-Internet, when there was

---

* The dole is a British informal term for government unemployment benefits paid to people who are out of work and seeking a job.

such a thing as a cultural underground, slowly spreading through word of mouth. These days it's impossible to keep anything quiet even if you want to. News spreads worldwide like wildfire within seconds. Previously art, music, film and books were all allowed to develop over time at a slower pace of exposure.

JW: There was something nice about waiting to see a film on a cinema screen. Now, if I was to mention a film within seconds we could probably find it online and watch it. I used to like having to seek out a venue playing it and go to watch it. For me that was all part of the process. 'I've always wanted to see Jacques Tourneur's *Cat People* (1942), the original. Oh great, it's at the Scala next week.' You'd go to it. Culture wasn't at your fingertips. You had to seek it out. I quite liked that. I think it made you work a bit harder.

MJ: Yes, there's definitely something more satisfying in having to seek things out rather than being spoon-fed. It's why people are naturally drawn to esoteric things, whether hard-to-find objects or works of art with rarity value.

I remember you and I once had a conversation about watches. I've never owned a Rolex but it's the best to invest in because of the way they manipulate the market, ensuring demand outstrips supply, prices going up and always a willing market eager to buy if you need a quick sale at a good price – it is almost like buying gold. There is something about human nature that makes us desirous of things others don't have, whether a watch, car, relationship, item of clothing, an album or book, or having access to culture or information that the majority are unaware of. Membership to private clubs feed that need too.

JW: To seek out obscure or imported books I remember going to the Compendium Bookshop in Camden Town in the eighties and nineties. It was an incredible place to seek out books to expand your horizons in an intellectual sense. The same with records. A record would come out and you'd read about it in *NME* or wherever, and you wouldn't be able to just order it. You'd have to seek out a shop that would have it. That would invariably be Rough Trade on Talbot Road. You'd go there and you'd have to ask for it. I've got records from the 1980s that have got a sticker on it with my name. You'd have to reserve it, otherwise it would be gone. I've got about five records with 'Jason Wood' written on them by Geoff Travis because he was working in the shop. I love all that. There was something about having to find it and having to go there and work for it. I think that's coming back a little bit.

MJ: Do you think?

JW: I think people are interested in artefacts. People certainly like buying vinyl records again. I think there is a general sense that people are recognising that it's nice to have something in your hand. I've never liked downloading music. I like to read the sleeve notes and I think there is a return to that.

Let's talk about cinema. You have obviously drawn inspiration from it and forged part of your career from it. What was your first interaction with the medium? I understand there was also a cinema in Stratford that your dad used to take you to. Was he a film fan?

MJ: Yes, he was – all the family were film fans. On Stratford Broadway was the Rex, an old art deco cinema which closed in 1975. It was a few hundred yards down the road from the pub. Our dad would take us or sometimes go by himself during the pub's afternoon closing hours.

JW: What sort of films did he watch?

MJ: I vividly remember him coming back one afternoon saying he couldn't stop laughing in the cinema whilst watching *It's a Mad, Mad, Mad, Mad World* (1963). But he loved all sorts of films.

JW: What about other family members?

MJ: Our Uncle Allan was a film extra and famously was a triffid in *The Day of the Triffids* (1963), which we loved as kids. He was in many other films and on occasion we'd visit a film set where he was working.

My cousin Peter Ferdinando is also in films but on a far higher level than our uncle ever was. He's made a huge number of films, many in leading roles with leading directors. I think Peter's a brilliant actor, incredibly versatile and driven. He's a heavyweight in my opinion as I know how hard he works behind the scenes and what an intense character he is but he remains underrated at the moment. His older sister Emma was a child star and acted on TV and on stage.

Film has always been a huge part of my immediate and extended family. My earliest memory of going to the cinema – I should say 'the pictures' really because that's what we used to call it – is being taken to see *Mary Poppins* (1964) with Andrew by Nanny Ginny – our dad's mum, as well as being taken by our dad to the old Rex cinema. But my most vivid memories are of going to the Saturday morning children's film club with Andrew at the Odeon in Forest Gate. Children's film clubs were a nice way of introducing kids to cinema and probably also giving parents a few hours respite! It closed as a cinema in the mid-nineteen-seventies to become a snooker hall. Subsequently that closed in the mid-nineteen-nineties and since the early noughties it's been a mosque and Muslim cultural centre. The building looks pretty run down these days.

But I can still smell those Saturday morning cinema screenings, a fragrant blend of popcorn, sweets, coffee and disinfectant, mingling with the smells still lingering from the previous night's screening – cigarettes, perfume and cologne. The sound in those old cinemas was distinct too – a certain tone, timbre, a muted reverb hard to describe in words though I can still hear in my mind – what I'd call an 'acousti-memory'. A combination of the old-fashioned sound system and being housed in a huge old art deco building – its particular reverb muffled by the carpeting and décor. Upon entry into the children's film club – as part of the ticket price – you'd be handed an orange drink and a Jamboree Bag. For people who don't know, it was a small paper bag with a few sweets, cheap little plastic toy and a joke on a scrap of paper – like in a Christmas cracker. There would then be a cartoon and a short a B-movie, then the main feature, which might be an Abbott & Costello, Laurel & Hardy or Flash Gordon film. And you'd get those adverts for local businesses. It was very busy. Packed with kids.

Compared to the small screens of multiplexes and art house cinemas of today there was a grandeur about those old buildings and a sense of occasion – hungover from the glory days of motion pictures – and that atmosphere had as big an effect upon me as the films themselves. The overall experience was magical and dream-like and created a lifelong love of cinema.

Films that stayed with me from childhood – a combination of those we saw at the cinema and the re-runs we'd watch on TV – include: *Zulu* (1964), *Lawrence of Arabia* (1962), *2001: A Space Odyssey* (1968), *King Kong* (1933), *Angels with Dirty Faces* (1938), *101 Dalmatians* (1961), *Reach for Glory* (1962), *Billy Liar* (1963), *Forbidden Planet* (1956), *Ice Cold in Alex* (1958), *Spartacus* (1960), *Them* (1954), *The Incredible Shrinking Man* (1957) and *The Day of the Triffids* (1963). I used to love Laurel and Hardy's films too – still do.

When it came to the crossover between film and music I don't think there was one particular moment, rather just a familiarisation with theme tunes of favourite programmes such as *The Avengers* (Laurie Johnson), *The Saint* (Edwin Astley), *The Prisoner* and *Doctor Who* (Ron Grainer), *Thunderbirds* (Barry Gray), *The Adventures of Robinson Crusoe* (Robert Mellin and Gian-Piero Reverberi), *Batman* (Neal Hefti), *Lost in Space* (John Williams) and *The Persuaders!* (John Barry) to name a handful. There were so many good composers working in film and television back then who really understood melody, harmony, tension and arrangement. Far superior to the theme tunes created for TV today.

It was a golden age for British television in so many ways. There were powerful current affairs and investigative documentary programmes broadcast on many weekday evenings – even *they* featured beautiful music. I loved the harmonica version of Tony Hatch's *Man Alive* theme and Granada TV's *World in Action* theme featured this haunting Hammond organ piece by Mick Weaver and Shawn Phillips.

And – slightly digressing – it wasn't just the music; some of the writing and direction was so impressive too. There was an explosion of creativity in the post-war years, with increased social mobility and a new media form, meaning more risks were taken. If you think of the talent involved in TV drama back then: there were programmes like *Play for Today* (1970–84) featuring the writers Dennis Potter, Alan Bennett, David Hare, Alan Bleasdale and Ian McEwan; and directors Ken Loach, Alan Clarke, Stephen Frears and Mike Leigh. *Armchair Theatre* (1956–74) featured the work of Harold Pinter and John Osborne; and people such as Jack Rosenthal, Ray Galton and Alan Simpson regularly wrote for the small screen. Television is impoverished in 2025 by comparison.

But back on track with the music – as luck would have it my job at De Wolfe on Wardour Street as a 15-year-old meant I gained some rare insight into the world of film and TV soundtracks. When I started transferring tapes in their 'Transfer Bay' I'd recognise lots of music from my childhood and youth. Soho was then at the heart of the UK film industry and De Wolfe's huge catalogue was a rich resource for British productions through the sixties, seventies and eighties.

They had an impressive stable of composers who were accomplished and incredibly prolific: Johnny Hawksworth, Reg Tilsley, Roger Webb, Simon Park, Ivor Slaney, Keith Papworth, Jan Stoeckart and many others. They'd often work under pseudonyms too for some reason. Most of their work wasn't composed for specific films or programmes but was library music, used incidentally and in the background. It was designed to be functional and often anonymous so film credits back then rarely listed the composers or the specific tracks used. But their music was in a lot of films I knew: *Performance* (1970), *The Texas Chain Saw Massacre* (1974), *Death Wish* (1974), *Monty Python and the Holy Grail* (1975), *The Man Who Fell to Earth* (1976), *Suspiria* (1977), *Dawn of the Dead* (1978), *Scum* (1979), various Hammer horror films and many others. It was also on TV: *Vision On* – the famous gallery track, *The Avengers* (1961–1969), *Doctor Who* (1960s era) and countless others.

But it wasn't only the theme tunes or incidental music that affected me – sound design did too. At the time I didn't understand who – or what – the BBC's Radiophonic Workshop* was but it definitely impacted me – and no doubt countless other children in Britain in the sixties and seventies. In later years I was intrigued to discover the roles played by various women inside this experimental sound department hidden away inside the corporate BBC: Daphne Oram, Delia Derbyshire and Maddalena Fagandini were so creative and years ahead of their time. It's heartening these women have finally gained some recognition.

Nick McKay: As music took more of a hold in your life did your interest in film continue and run parallel, feeding into the music at any point?

MJ: It's hard to say if any specific film inspired my own music but in general culture works by osmosis – the more we're exposed to it the more its various forms will find a way of expressing themselves through us.

As I left school so young a large part of my education naturally came through my exposure to culture whether books, music or

---

* The BBC Radiophonic Workshop was an innovative sound design and electronic music unit that pioneered experimental audio techniques for radio, television and film.

cinema. Having watched thousands of films since childhood the ones I found most inspirational tended to be from directors we think of as auteurs – individuals with a singular vision conveying their distinct version of reality: Hitchcock, Orson Welles, Kubrick, Tarkovsky, Melville, Lynch, Schrader, Lumet, Fellini, Truffaut, Bergman, Coppola, Cassavetes, Leone, Kurosawa, Scorsese, Wilder, Herzog, Wenders – there have been so many. Actually, thinking about those names now it is totally male dominated isn't it? I can't think of any great female film directors from the sixties or seventies off the top of my head. There must have been some – more likely from Europe than the UK or US I suppose. In later years the balance has been redressed a bit with the recognition of directors like Sofia Coppola, Lynne Ramsay, Joanna Hogg, Andrea Arnold, Jane Campion, Claire Denis and others who have been making brilliant films.

I've actually seen far more films than concerts over the years and the soundtracks have played an important part of my favourite ones. Music is such a powerful accompaniment to life's emotional journeys. Consider how many times you might read a favourite book – or even watch a favourite film – compared to how many times you listen to a favourite piece of music. There is no comparison and music's power does intensify with repetition. It has this special power to embed itself where our deepest emotions hide. With standalone songs we add our own mental imagery without being influenced by the visuals of a film or advert; but having said that, there's no doubt when powerful music combines with powerful imagery – as with a great film – it takes the experience to a different level and enters the world of dreams.

I've tried to make my albums a 'cinematic' experience insomuch as I try to write vivid lyrics and often juxtapose acoustic instruments: accordions, marimbas, flugelhorn, cellos, harmonicas or congas for instance with esoteric pieces of electronic equipment. The goal being to try and draw listeners into a dream world

NM: What for you represents some of the most successful moments of music working with film? Which film composers inspire you?

MJ: Many of my favourite soundtrack composers struck up long-term relationships with film directors and over the course of those collaborations established unique musical languages specific to those directors. In fact, it's impossible to imagine many of these films with alternative soundtracks. Think of Bernard Herrmann with Alfred Hitchcock and the score for *Vertigo* (1958), which I consider one of the greatest of all time – full of yearning and mystery; or the long-lasting collaboration between Nino Rota and Federico Fellini – *La Dolce Vita* (1960) being my favourite of their collaborations. Or Ennio Morricone with Sergio Leone – I loved the simple harmonica theme in *Once Upon a Time in The West* (1968) that suggested the complex backstory to Charles Bronson's character, also in *Once Upon a Time in America* (1984) Morricone's use of a pan flute in selected scenes was so simple yet powerful. Eduard Artemyev's collaborations with Andrei Tarkovsky were incredibly evocative – his work on *Solaris* (1972) is my second-favourite electronic score; my favourite being Bebe and Louis Barron's pioneering soundscapes for *Forbidden Planet* (1956). Zbigniew Preisner with Krzysztof Kieślowski and the sparse gravitas of his scores for *Dekalog* (1989) beautifully matching the pathos of the Polish director. Popol Vuh's score was haunting in Werner Herzog's *Aguirre, the Wrath of God* (1972).

I should mention some of the wonderfully evocative scores from directors creating their own soundtracks too: John Carpenter and the deceptively simple, pulsating scores he created on his Prophet-5 and other synthesisers. Vincent Gallo's lo-fi tape recorder musings for *Buffalo '66* (1998). David Lynch was a pioneer of sound design with his subtle but highly unsettling background drones and rumbles. Talking of sound effects and music I was also a huge fan of Coppola's *The Conversation* (1974) and not just David Shire's beautiful, haunting score but also its ground-breaking sound design from Walter Murch.

There are just so many films that are impossible for me to think of without the soundtrack and composer immediately coming to mind. Roy Budd's brilliant score for *Get Carter* (1971) remains one of my favourites; Neil Hefti's uplifting yet melancholic scores for both *Duel at Diablo* (1966) and *The Odd Couple* (1968); John Barry's score for Cy Endfield's *Zulu* (1964), which my brothers and I loved as kids – so full of foreboding, tension and release; *Diva* (1981) and Vladimir Cosma; *Betty Blue* (1986) and Gabriel Yared. Henry Mancini's score for Orson Welles's *Touch of Evil* (1958) is a masterclass in how a composer can perfectly capture the mood the director is striving for. You can almost taste the sweat and sleaze dripping from the score of this noir classic. One of the greatest uses of pre-existing music was Kubrick's placement of Johann Strauss's 'The Blue Danube' in *2001: A Space Odyssey*, when splicing from the 'Dawn of Man' sequence to the spaceship slowly spinning through space.

But it's not just about the past. I'm continually blown away by the quality of soundtracks and sound design of new films and always find myself checking the credits. There have been so many brilliant director–composer partnerships in recent years: Jonathan Glazer and Mica Levi, Paul Thomas Anderson and Jonny Greenwood, Darren Aronofsky and Clint Mansell, Denis Villeneuve and Jóhann Jóhannsson, Christopher Nolan and Hans Zimmer, Bong Joon Ho and Jung Jae-il, Claire Denis and Tindersticks, Trent Reznor and Atticus Ross with David Fincher. There's a long and growing list.

NM: How has the process of working with your brother Gerard evolved over time?

MJ: Well, Gerard and I started collaborating almost twenty-five years ago with his first short film *Lone Man* (2002). For that he just used some pre-existing music of mine from a rare, non-commercial album called *Film Music Volume 1: Silent Tongue*. It featured forty-six pieces of instrumental music and was something my former manager, Cally and I put together as a means of drumming up interest for THE THE to be considered for soundtrack work. Ironically, the first person to show any interest was my own brother! He also used some music from that album for his second short film, *Mug* (2004), but the first time I composed specifically for one of his films was his third short, *Tony* (2005). Obviously, when this developed into a feature-length film the process became more involved.

Over the years we've settled on a fairly consistent system. Firstly, he'll send me the script, then he'll create a compilation of various pieces of third-party music he feels conveys the general atmosphere he has in mind. He'll also create a visual mood board – something he shares with his cinematographer and producer but will also send to me.

Armed with these elements I'll plan which instruments and equipment I feel will help create the right tonal colours and timbres. With each soundtrack I try to have a limited tonal palette. I have a lot of equipment – a lot more than I need – so it's important to create parameters. Over the years I've worked on very large multi-track format projects but my preferred format – especially for soundtrack work – is sixteen tracks. It just forces me to make decisions as I go along rather than filling up dozens upon dozens of tracks and putting off decision-making until the mixing stage.

For instance, with *Muscle* (2019), I used just a Mellotron, a Minimoog, an electric guitar and selection of guitar foot pedals, and then a machine called a Repeater, a four-channel looping device I've owned for over twenty years. I also used a drum machine and an Omnichord – a machine I bought back in 1981 and used to write 'This Is The Day' and 'Perfect'. I used looping and over-dubbing within the loops to build up textures. I don't like things getting too fussy or busy. I'm very much of the 'less is more' school of thought and by having fewer instruments in a mix they all have more space to breathe and – of course – it leaves space for the images too.

Gerard has a clear idea of what he likes and there's a large overlap in our tastes regards film, music, books and humour – just as there was with our older brother Andrew. We have a shorthand and I find it easy to collaborate with him – and I think vice versa.

I start to create ideas in my studio from having read the script and seen the mood board. Once he starts filming he'll then start to send me scenes, sometimes with temporary music attached and sometimes no music attached so it's a blank canvas. After I've composed a significant amount of music Gerard will visit my studio and we'll then start flying-in different pieces of music to various scenes and play around to see what resonates and is worth pursuing and which ideas can be cast aside. It's generally a smooth process and something we both enjoy.

Now, bear in mind I'm working with very small budgets on these soundtracks. These are not big-budget films so I have to cut my cloth accordingly. I cannot record in huge studios and bring in orchestras, choirs, arrangers and session musicians. Sometimes I might feel a little envious of the contemporary composers I mentioned earlier and the huge budgets they often get to play around with, but in all honesty, I don't mind as I enjoy the creative challenge of a cottage industry approach – plus it means I have more control.

NM: Were there key themes in *Muscle* that unlocked the creative journey for you in creating the soundtrack? Do you reference other films when working with Gerard in terms of reference points?

MJ: We often discuss other films as shared reference points. There's the obvious nod to *The Servant* (1963) with *Muscle* – Gerard and I are both big fans of Joseph Losey. Also, the subtle references to elements of Donald Cammell and Nicolas Roeg's *Performance* (1970) and *Get Carter* (1971) by Mike Hodges too. *Muscle* was also inspired by the British kitchen-sink dramas of the 1960s with its northern setting and black-and-white cinematography.

Also, I thought *Muscle*'s subject matter of confused masculinity was particularly pertinent given the extreme political correctness of our times. Gerard is not afraid to swim against the tide even though he could very easily have been misinterpreted by less open-minded critics. The fact he chose to film *Muscle* in black and white and use actors who he believed were the best for their respective roles, rather than trying to get bigger box office names attached to the film, also showed a lot of confidence and self-belief. But it is a very tough industry if you don't play the game and so sticking forcefully to your guns does not come without financial risks and penalties. Perhaps that's a reason why Gerard is currently considered one of the most underrated British directors. Despite his loyal following and his films consistently picking up great reviews he still seems overlooked by the industry in general. Maybe it's just because his films are too dark and uncompromising – a film critic suggested he's like a fusion between Abel Ferrara and Mike Leigh when the pair were at the top of their game. As a director he has this wonderful talent for extracting career-best performances from his actors: Peter Ferdinando's roles in *Tony* and *Hyena*, Cavan Clerkin and Craig Fairbrass in *Muscle* and now Polly Maberly in *Odyssey*. So many powerful performances. As the composer I get to watch the scenes countless times whilst trying out musical ideas and I really notice the emotional range and subtlety of these actors and what an amazing job Gerard does in coaching and coaxing great performances from them.

NM: The first release from *Muscle* was the single for Record Store Day, 'I Want 2 B U'.

MJ: Yes. I'd finished the score but something was nagging at me – that it wasn't quite complete. I think a score should have a lead song and one afternoon I glimpsed the Omnichord on a shelf gathering dust – having not used it for years. So, I started playing around with some ideas and came up with the chord sequence that became 'I Want 2 B U'. It has a distinct strumming harp accompaniment that relates it to 'This Is The Day'. As a song it came together quickly though we were working to a very strict deadline. One stressful morning, I was due to start mixing it with Matt Lawrence at a studio in Borough, but I was desperately trying to finish off the vocals at my place whilst an Uber was waiting outside to take me there! We pulled it off with seconds to spare. I'm very happy with the work Matt does for the 5:1 mixes on my soundtracks. He's wonderful to work with and not a Grammy Award-winning engineer for nothing.

After we'd finished both the film and soundtrack mixes I then had the thought of bringing in another Grammy award-winner to mix the 7-inch single version. Craig Silvey had been a partner at the studio I owned – The Garden – for a few years. He'd borrowed a grand piano from me when we closed it down – in fact it was the same Yamaha C3 on which Jools Holland played the solo for

'Uncertain Smile' – so he owed me a mix or two as a favour. I was delighted with his mix.

The B-side to the single is 'Velvet Muscle Scream', a track used in one of the party scenes. For that I wanted something more contemporary so I created the rhythm by layering and filtering various loops, added a simple, low-frequency bass line that just repeats trance-like, and lastly created these ethereal lines from the Mellotron that give it the slightly warped atmosphere. I think it fits the scene well – hypnotic, druggy and sleazy.

NM: The soundtrack obviously exists in its own right but how well do you think it served the film?

MJ: Very well. I especially like the scene towards the end where the protagonist – Simon (Cavan Clerkin) – is going on a job for Terry (Craig Fairbrass). He's driving through the rain and the dark and the penny slowly starts to drop that something is very wrong. I like the tension in that scene and the segment of music is quite long and involved but I was happy with the way it evolved and kept ratcheting up the stress.

NM: Was there ever the temptation or the opportunity to do soundtrack work in America?

MJ: I've worked in Hollywood but to be honest I didn't enjoy the process so much. The budgets and fees are much higher – of course – but there's more interference and it can easily become 'creativity by committee' – too many people sticking their oar in and trying to justify their jobs. It didn't suit my personality. I've been approached by agents to represent me over there but I wasn't really interested and I've turned down a fair amount of offers. My dealings with Hollywood are mainly related to syncs these days – that is, using my pre-existing music in films. And that is something I do like.

Over the years my songs have been used in many films by a diverse range of directors – from cult films like Muscha's *Decoder* (1984) using *'Three Orange Kisses From Kazan'*; to Greg

Araki's use of 'Love Is Stronger Than Death' in *Nowhere* (1997). Fatih Akın even quoted some of my lyrics in *Head-On* (2004). And there are the bigger-budget films like Francis Ford Coppola's *Megalopolis* (2024) and his use of 'Lonely Planet'. 'This Is The Day' gets a huge amount of use too, from smaller films like Nora Fingscheidt's *The Outrun* (2024) to blockbusters like James Gunn's *Guardians of the Galaxy Vol. 3* (2023).

But working on scores? Although the budgets and fees are much smaller with independents and documentaries it does mean I have more creative control and retain my rights. At this stage of my career I can pick and choose who I work with – and I just want to have fun and collaborate with people I enjoy spending time with. That's always been more important to me than money.

NM: And is the approach different when you are composing for a documentary film as opposed to a fictional one? Your work for Swedish documentarian, Johanna St Michaels, includes *Best Wishes, Bernard* (2004), *Snap Shots from Reality* (2005), *Going Live* (2009), *Travriket* (2007), *About Dina* (2010), *Penthouse North* (2013), *The Inertia Variations* (2017) and *Fabiana* (2023).

MJ: Some of the work I've done for Johanna also includes exhibitions and documentary work for other directors includes *Moonbug* (2010) for Nichola Bruce, and *Je t'aime Infinement* (2010) and *End of Season* (2014) for Nikolaj B. Larsen (2010).

It was interesting how the creative collaboration started with my former partner, Johanna, because ironically, she was the second person to show any interest in *Film Music Volume 1: Silent Tongue*. She used some pieces for an early exhibition and as she started doing more projects – both exhibitions and documentaries. It evolved from there and I became increasingly involved, creating new music as new projects developed. A couple of these early films involved people wanting Johanna to document their deaths – one of whom was a personal friend of ours. They were very intense projects but Johanna is the least squeamish person I've ever met. Probably something to do with her dad being a doctor and her hanging around hospitals from a very young age – as opposed to my childhood of hanging around pubs from a young age!

Obviously, we'd been in a long-term relationship for ten years and so know each other very well. I'd watched over the years as Johanna worked extremely hard studying and then putting into practice all she learned. But the work wasn't just confined to the creative side. Raising the funding for these projects is also a full-time job and projects were often touch and go until the last minute.

Penthouse North was probably the hardest project I've worked on for her as she wanted a jazz-orientated score for this film, which was set in uptown Manhattan. I'm obviously not a jazz musician, so this took me out of my comfort zone – not a bad thing but I felt I was often going against my musical instincts. We were both happy with the end result, even though the documentary is full of pathos and deals with a difficult subject.

I was also happy with the soundtrack for *The Inertia Variations* (2017). I used a powerful synthesizer I'd recently purchased – a John Bowen Solaris – for parts of it. Through this beautiful instrument I was able to channel my inner Bebe and Louis Barron! This was a more experimental score than some of the others I've done for Johanna and the tone of the Solaris helped create an eerie undercurrent throughout. The soundtrack was released as a triple album on vinyl and CD and the volume that contains the electronic elements of the score is *Midnight To Midnight*. Although it is sonically uncompromising it is very emotional too – at least to me.

Johanna and I have worked together a lot over the years and we also have our own shorthand way of working – different to how Gerard and I work – but effective for us. The budgets are also small with these documentaries so I have to keep things simple and use lateral thinking. Johanna is incredibly hard working and driven and always has multiple projects on the go. I've not been able to work on all of them as in recent years I've often been tied up on other projects or on tour but I will do some more with her.

NM: Are there plans to release all your soundtrack work? Obviously, some have been released already as standalone issues.

MJ: I've released most of the work I've done with Gerard and we are planning a volume or two that features some of the scores for Johanna's documentaries – tentatively titled *Oden*. This will bring together much of the work I've done for her to date, including short films, feature-length documentaries and exhibitions.

The work I did with Nikolaj B. Larsen's documentaries will likely form another volume. I am playing around with the title for those, but quite like *Helios*.

Jason Wood: *Odyssey* marks the latest of your soundtrack collaborations with Gerard. Can you talk a little about how the relationship has evolved over time? Are there similar processes for each project?

MJ: We follow a similar pattern that's worked in the past – albeit streamlined and faster than when we first started. I use a small team on the audio side: Mark Allaway, in-house engineer at Studio Cinéola; Matt Lawrence for 5:1 mixing; and Finnbar Eiles for stereo mixing.

JW: It feels as if a film by Gerard wouldn't be complete without a THE THE score. However, his film *Odyssey* (2025) also corresponded with an intense period for you with the Ensouled Tour and *Ensoulment* (2024), an entirely new album of THE THE material. How did you find time to balance the two projects? I imagine there is a sense of creative fulfilment but also a sense of an accentuated commitment given your kinship.

MJ: It was difficult. I was due to start intensive rehearsals for the world tour literally the day after I was expected to deliver the soundtrack. Deadlines were very strict and set in stone for both the soundtrack and the world tour so – as you can imagine – there were a lot of very late nights involved. Normally I wouldn't take on two such big projects with such a tight overlap but I love working with Gerard and really wanted to be a part of his new film.

JW: The film contains a number of themes that recur throughout Gerard's filmography: toxic misogyny, a changing London, the undercurrent of violence, drugs and especially pronounced here, the evils of capitalism. Are you find it easy to fit your music to these themes?

MJ: There is a certain amount of overlap with songs I've written over the years – particularly the changing face of London, addiction, drugs and the dark side of capitalism. Although it has become fashionable for the media these days to talk about toxic masculinity or toxic misogyny, there are also toxic femininity and toxic misanthropy. The world is far more complex and nuanced than it being either men who are toxic or women who are emotionally balanced.

JW: I think *Odyssey* may be your most varied soundtrack to date. There are snatches of minimal electronic, funk, disco and even in one sequence a form of motorik. Was it liberating to be able to work across such a broad spectrum?

MJ: I never feel constrained by styles. It is whatever works for a film – or an album for that matter. I've always enjoyed a bit of krautrock and the early electronic music that was part of the roots of THE THE. I have a large collection of esoteric equipment and working on soundtracks gives me a chance to play around with these instruments, synthesizers and outboard processors other than the guitars and traditional keyboards I use when composing and recording for my own song-based albums.

JW: There are two tracks which feature a female vocalist. Who is the vocalist?

MJ: The female vocalist on *Odyssey* is Gillian Glover. She provided backing vocals on *Ensoulment* as well as performing the beautiful version of 'Phantom Walls' in Spanish for *The Inertia Variations: Trilogy* project. She's an excellent singer – very versatile and fast in the studio. I thought she'd be perfect for this. 'Unrequited' is a duet, but she sings the lead vocal on 'Live & Let Live', the first time someone other than me has sung sole lead vocals on a THE THE song. We released both of those tracks as a double A-side 7-inch single when *Odyssey* was released in cinemas.

JW: Are there any elements of the score that particularly stand out for you?

MJ: Perversely, I really like the impact of the *almost* silent score in parts of the nightclub scene where I removed all of the music apart from just occasional, short bursts of eerie sound to accentuate the slowly pulsating strobe lights inside the club.

JW: You also appear in a short scene, one of Gerard's signature nightclub sequences. Is this the beginning of your acting career?

MJ: Gerard does love to include slightly surreal club/party scenes in his films and *Odyssey* was no exception. We had a lot of fun filming that day as lots of Gerard's mates were there plus my eldest son and some of my mates too. It was hilarious! It's certainly not the beginning of my acting career, though it could be the end of it!

Funnily enough, I had small cameos in a couple of recent Star Wars films – I even had a speaking role in the last one but it was cut in the final edit. I met JJ Abrams after he contacted me and asked to meet as he'd long enjoyed my albums. What was interesting is that he was more excited to talk about musical instruments and recording equipment than films! He's a complete gear-head so we often have long chats about the latest synthesisers etc. Anyway, he was in London making a Star Wars film and he invited me to appear in a small cameo role. I spent a few days at Pinewood Studios and what impressed me was how – despite the tremendous pressure he must have been under, responsible for such a massive budget on such a high-profile film – he was so relaxed. I also noticed how he treated all crew and staff with equal politeness and consideration regardless of whether they were a producer, cinematographer, make-up artist, gaffer, driver or part of the catering team. A notable human quality I thought.

As is customary with these epic films they always shoot far more material than they'll ever need and most of my scene – including a bit with Chewbacca – was cut. But I went back to appear in a second Star Wars film after JJ offered me a small speaking role. I spent another few days at Pinewood and even had my own trailer and make-up artist. I was meticulously dressed up as an Imperial Officer and had a small part opposite Adam Driver. My role consisted of me saying something like, 'Supreme commander! We have secured the perimeter!' What made it quite stressful was that my cameo came at the very end of a long sequence lasting a couple of minutes. So, if I screwed up the whole thing had to be shot again. JJ is a gentleman on set and very encouraging but an additional problem was that we were filming outside on a freezing cold day in January and my face was frozen! I could barely move my lips so the words were coming out as, 'Supweem cmmmder! We 'ave secquooood the pewimmmter!' Obviously, my part was cut. And that was the end of any speaking roles in my acting career!

CHAPTER TEN

You Would Think, By Now, That People Would Know Better Than To Ask Me What I Have Been Doing With My Time

Matt returns to Europe, withdraws from music, lives out of a suitcase as a flâneur before becoming a conservationist opposing the destruction of London. He discovers the poetry of John Tottenham which then leads to The Inertia Variations, *an ambitious international multi-media project and radio broadcast. The death of Matt's older brother, Andrew, inspires a return to songwriting with 'We Can't Stop What's Coming'.*

JW: How much material were you writing in NYC after the *NakedSelf* album?

MJ: Quite a lot. I'd been working on *Karmic Gravity* both before and after the world tour. Towards the end of our time living in Manhattan I spent some time in upstate New York to write. Sam Kirby, an agent friend, gave me use of her small weather-boarded house on the outskirts of Woodstock. I'd been fascinated by that part of New York state for years – more for its association with Bob Dylan and The Band than the eponymous music festival. She only used it at weekends and let me have a set of keys to go up during the week. I loved the countryside and would take long walks in the woods during the day and sit beside a small log fire at night to work on my trusty 8-track recorder. Johanna and Jackson came to visit a few times and we seriously considered moving to Woodstock for a year or two whilst renting out our loft in Manhattan instead of heading back to Europe. I wrote and demoed 'Pillar Box Red', 'Deep Down Truth' and 'Slow Rider' up there.

JW: And how was your relationship with the record labels?

MJ: As I've mentioned, shortly after the Naked Tour I wriggled out of my contract with Universal. Rob Stringer then suggested I re-sign for Sony as I think the company had some regrets over the *NakedSelf* situation. But it was a very weird period for the music industry in general by this point – things were starting to shift dramatically in terms of priorities. The major labels – in panic mode – handed over much of their catalogues to new entities such as iTunes for pennies on the pound as they were so terrified of the prospect of losing everything for nothing to the likes of Napster.

JW: You had new material. How did you set about recording it?

MJ: Back in London I went into the recording studio with producers Clive Langer and Alan Winstanley to record what I thought were a couple of strong songs, 'Pillar Box Red' and 'Deep Down Truth'. I enjoyed working with Langer and Winstanley who I'd long been aware of and admired. I flew Eric Schermerhorn, Earl Harvin and Spencer Campbell to London and even had my old friend, the late Angela McCluskey, guest on vocals. I was happy with the results and we arranged for Tim Pope to make a video for 'Pillar Box Red'.

Despite these fresh songs – along with a new version of 'December Sunlight' featuring a duet with Liz Horsman – being released as part of my new compilation album, *45 RPM (the singles of THE THE)*, things didn't really work out after going back to Sony and we decided not to proceed with a new studio album. The industry was changing so fast and the order of the day seemed to be quick-fix hit singles rather than slow-burning album artists like myself. By this point I was feeling like a man out of time and I decided I'd had enough of the industry. I was feeling deeply tired and losing the joy of creating music. I thought I'd never want to sign another record contract again.

At the invitation of David Bowie I performed at 2002's Meltdown Festival at the Royal Festival Hall. I collaborated with my old friend JG Thirlwell to create an experimental, electronic set but soon afterwards decided to put all my instruments and equipment into deep storage – and all career-related projects into the deep freezer. Over the next seven years I didn't even pick up a guitar or sit at a keyboard once! It is astonishing now – when I think back on it – as I love my instruments.

JW: That is a surprisingly long time. And were you still happy being based in New York?

MJ: We'd intended to leave New York temporarily to move to Sweden and then come back. In fact, our return plane tickets were actually for 10 September – the day before 9/11 – but we received an offer on our loft for a year's rental in advance and so we decided to stay longer in Göteborg and – after 9/11 – it became a permanent move.

But over the next year or two Johanna's and my relationship gradually broke down. I then became a bit of a nomad for a few years, living between Sweden, Spain and London – also popping back to New York periodically. It was a very strange and difficult period – living out of suitcases and traveling a lot. I very rarely slept in the same bed more than three nights in a row. In fact, I'm quite like that to this day. I still move around a lot.

During this time, I decided to place myself into a kind of 'solitary confinement' at my cottage in Mallorca for a while as I needed to try and clear my head and resolve the issues I was dealing with. Apart from a weekly telephone call to speak with Johanna and Jackson I didn't speak to anyone at all for almost seven weeks. It was a very intense period. I didn't drink alcohol or caffeine; I did a lot of meditating, walking and thinking; and it ended up being an incredibly emotional experience. I ended up crying a lot for my mum as I'd been holding so much grief in. I was also crying for Jackson as Johanna and I were separating and I was concerned about the impact this would all have on him – both now and in the future.

JW: And did time alone in your house provide any answers?

MJ: Strange things happened on this trip. I witnessed the most powerful full moons I'd ever seen. And for the first time at the house bats visited me. This had never happened before but they would come down the chimney and just fly around my head whilst I was sitting there meditating. It was hard to get them out as it was impossible to catch them! They're so fast, with such an erratic flight path, and their sonar helped them evade the net I was trying to throw over them. I looked up the symbolic meaning of bats and found different interpretations depending on the culture. To some they symbolise death and rebirth, the Native Americans observed them to be a highly social creature and considered them a symbol of communication. In European cultures, they've long been associated with witchcraft, black magic and darkness. In China many legends associate them with good fortune. Most seem to agree that a bat arriving in your life signifies change.

So, the notion of ego death and allowing myself to accept my fears and embrace change then became uppermost in my thoughts. My mind wandered back to my experience off the coast of Kenya when I went scuba diving before I'd even learned to swim and I remembered the sense of calm that took over when things started to go wrong and I allowed part of me – beyond my own ego – to just take control. Thoughts started to coalesce in my mind that I might now prefer 'no profile' to 'low profile'. I then stepped back and – for want of a better description – started played truant from my own career. In a way, that's when life started to get interesting: embracing this ego death. Also, there was a part of me that felt there was just too much music everywhere and do I really need to be adding to this overwhelming din?

JW: Although your music career was in stasis you weren't totally indolent. Did you miss writing, recording and thinking about sound? Or had sound ceased to be a source of pleasure for you?

MJ: Between the end of 2002 and 2009 I was in a state of deep inertia regarding my music career, but I was also very busy doing other things during this period; travelling, journalling, photography and reading copious amounts on geo-politics and more esoteric matters. I had been involved in music since the age of 11 and since that time it had completely dominated my thoughts and my life. But due to a combination of factors mentioned before my appetite for it had dwindled and I would rather not do anything musical at all than do it half-heartedly.

This period could be looked upon as my 'lost years' but that doesn't tell the full story. There was a part of me that was willingly embracing this 'ego death' and in many ways it was a time of huge personal development for me. It is the ego that causes so much individual suffering and so many ills within society. It's the ego that is the cause of so much constricting fear that dominates the lives of many. Unconditional love is expansive and leads us in the direct opposite. I was also curious to see where this life without music might lead me as I was increasingly uncomfortable with the modern western narrative that unless you are visibly 'doing stuff' – and continually bragging about it – it is as if you simply don't exist.

My belief is also that music is powerful and sacred – across cultures and centuries it's been central to ritual and ceremony. Long before it was used as entertainment it was considered a spiritual technology – a way to summon emotion, invoke the divine and connect communities. Ancient Greece spoke of 'music of the spheres'; Gregorian chants in medieval cathedrals were designed to lift spirits towards heaven; in Sufi practice, rhythmic chanting and whirling are forms of prayer through sound. Indigenous cultures worldwide use chanting and drumming to connect with ancestors or the spirit world.

Yet in the 21st century everywhere you go, in shops, taxis, restaurants, bars, television – even just walking down the street – there is this incessant four-on-the-floor beat around 124 bpm with a caterwauling auto-tuned voice on top! Our aural nerve endings are being desensitised as music is stripped of its sacred charge. It is like being force-fed food you don't like when you're not even hungry! And now we have music created by AI algorithms to contend with too. It drives me round the twist.

Back in the early nineties – to protect my ears and emotions from being continually hijacked – I purchased a wonderful little book called *Muzak-free London: A Guide to Eating, Drinking and Shopping in Peace* by Philip Kogan (1991). It listed all the capital's bars and restaurants which did *not* play music. One of my favourites of recent years is Sweetings in the City of London. Opened in 1830, it's like a time capsule – no music, just the sounds of people talking, laughing and crockery and cutlery in use. My dad, Uncle Kenny and their friends used to frequent it in the sixties. These days it is owned by my friends Sue & Rick.

JW: Did you disengage from music entirely? Even for your own pleasure?

MJ: During this period, I don't think I went to a single concert. I played very little music at home, apart from, on occasion, Gregorian chants or esoteric pieces from Tony Scott (Jazz musician-turned-global wanderer), maybe some Schubert or Bach or Arvo Pärt. I was actually very busy in many ways but it's just that I was not doing what everyone else *wanted* me to do. I was coming under pressure from friends, family, my financial and legal advisors – as well as my audience – to get back to music. But I just didn't feel like doing what everyone else wanted me to do. It didn't feel right. I had my reasons.

JW: Did anything replace music as a creative passion?

MJ: I met Helen Edwards at a party via our mutual friend, the wonderful Ian Tregoning. We got along extremely well, laughed a lot and started seeing more of each other and began a relationship. I don't think Helen even knew I was a musician for a few years. Actually, she still might not know! We started travelling – a lot – heading off to Istanbul, Budapest, Lisbon, Florence, Barcelona, Prague, Venice, New York, Croatia, Morocco. In 2006 Helen suggested I come along to Paris Photo, the massive annual photography fair she'd been visiting every year for her work. I absolutely loved it and found the same thrill of excitement I once got from going to concerts. I discovered lots of new photographers but my favourite was someone from the past, the late Saul Leiter, whose work had been re-published that year. We visited Paris Photo for about six years straight and our trips were made more enjoyable by my old friends from New York, the photographer Alvin Booth and his wife Nike Lanning. We'd be taken to the most wonderful bistros by day and brasseries by night and go to numerous parties associated with Paris Photo. I was much preferring being amongst the photographic crowd than the music crowd.

We used to take photos everywhere we went. Helen has an MA in Fine Art and Photography and it's long been one of her passions too. She was very encouraging towards me taking photos and we spent lots of time travelling, around the coastal areas of England as well as countless trips abroad. Just walking for hours, investigating and taking photos. I found it a great creative outlet with none of the pressures and stresses that had come to taint my enjoyment of making music. I took tens of thousands of photos over this period. I'm friends with a few world-class photographers so I really don't take myself too seriously in this regard.

JW: Your creativity began to find a way to the surface again…

MJ: Creativity seems to find a way out even if you suppress it. As mentioned previously I'd bought a few Minox spy cameras when living in New York. As the film format was so small they were like still versions of Super 8 and taking photos with these cameras was like using a tiny time machine as they made present-day scenes look decades old.

During this time Helen curated a few art shows with many of the artists she represented through the art publishing company she owns and I showed some work in a couple of them. One was a video installation of 'Fone Films' I'd been making. They were really video postcards I filmed on my old Nokia phone and sent to Helen when I was abroad and they were pretty funny. I edited a lot of them together and created an electronic mosaic displayed on a couple of video screens – 'A Life In The Day' the piece was called. And for her next exhibition, The One Ton Show, which featured many other artists, I created a photomontage based upon the poem 'London' by William Blake. Andrew also exhibited at this event.

In England my main base was at my dad's house in Suffolk. Not only was I flying back to Sweden a lot to spend time with Jackson – courtesy of Ryanair – but I was also staying in cheap hotels in London, making trips back to New York to see my friends as well as escaping to Mallorca via easyJet. I travelled very light with just a backpack. Helen jokingly referred to it as my 'parachute'. It certainly seemed as if I was parachuting into one situation before quickly escaping to another. I was on and off planes like other people were on and off buses. It was an absolutely mad period of my life and whilst I was having an exciting time, ultimately it was exhausting. I felt like a man on the run – trying to escape from my own life.

JW: And having, in effect, put your life on hold, how did you begin to try and make sense of your situation? I also wonder about your belongings. You love your vintage musical equipment but also have an eye for fine objects.

MJ: I'd previously placed most of my belongings and equipment inside storage containers on a farm on the Suffolk/Essex border. Three old shipping containers each filled with past lives – one with stuff from New York, another filled with my old London life, and a third teeming with career-related stuff – flight cases of musical equipment and instruments, old promotional material and merchandise. I became friendly with the family who owned the farm and, as I loved the peaceful atmosphere there, decided to rent a small cottage from them between 2006 and 2007 as a way of creating a pause in my insane schedule and getting some headspace.

It would also give me the time to begin the onerous task of sorting through these past lives. Over the twelve months I was there I went through piles and piles of old personal paperwork and career-related detritus and made regular bonfires of them. Helen and Jackson would both come and visit and life seemed to slow down nicely for a while. I'd take long country walks and regularly cycle around local villages to pick up fresh bread, cheese and wine on an old bicycle Cally had kindly bought for me – a 1937 Humber 'Gentleman's Sports Roadster', complete with front basket.

I remember one morning I awoke to find the room – and my bed – covered with dead hornets! I hadn't been stung in the night and all seemed eerily quiet and strange. As with the bats in Mallorca a couple of years previously I was curious to find out what this could mean. In some African traditions, the wasp is a symbol of evolution with control over our life circumstances. Some Native American tribal myths point to the wasp as a symbol of order, organisation and productivity. Ancient European legend recognises that the wasp plays a big part in pollination and is symbolic of fertility and sexuality. Dreams about hornets and wasps can portend of a positive ending to a project and can foretell of improved luck and prosperity. Maybe things were looking up?

One valuable lesson I learned from having my stuff in storage was the meaning of 'entropy'. I had assumed that after a few years I would simply retrieve my belongings from storage and that they would look as they had always looked, and I would pick up where I had left off. Not so fast. Years later I was distressed to find that strings had rusted to the necks of guitars; in some instances necks of valuable guitars were warped out of shape; rare synthesisers and outboard equipment were rusted up and unusable. I then had to spend thousands of pounds bringing much of this sentimental gear back into a usable state, and had to throw away a lot of other stuff. All this expense was on top of the thousands I'd spent on storing it. An expensive lesson learned was to just get rid of 'stuff'.

JW: What precipitated a reconnection with London? And what form did this connection now take?

MJ: I was spending a lot of time with my dad. His house in Suffolk was now my main base in the UK – primarily my old bedroom there! Another example of ego death really after the beautiful loft I'd owned in Manhattan. But I was grateful to be spending so much time with him as I loved my dad and still felt guilty about living in America whilst my mum was slowly dying.

But I did eventually move back to East London in 2007 and couldn't help myself getting involved in local politics, like conservation and fighting the overdevelopment and destruction of parts of East London. I got very heavily involved in that for about seven years of my life. Through this period of 'doing nothing' I was also a founder member of various campaign groups: Save Shoreditch, OPEN Shoreditch, East End Preservation Society and the East End Trades Guild as well as co-chair of the Shoreditch Community Association and sitting in on endless committee meetings. I was going to the local Town Hall to give 'speeches'. One could consider it all displacement activity on a grand scale I suppose. Anything

to avoid getting down to the *real* work of writing songs. I met so many lovely, civic-minded people who really cared about their neighbourhoods – many of whom have remained friends.

I had many bruising encounters – metaphorical bare-knuckle battles – with venal property developers and it took me a while to adjust to the reality that many of these people take as great a delight in demolishing old buildings as I do in writing new songs. You may occasionally bloody their noses but it's impossible to win because they have the council on their side – the game is rigged. The decisions are already made in private meetings, behind closed doors, before the charade of the public consultation.

I ended up going to so many planning committee meetings at the local town hall, with neighbours and members of the local community; we'd fully done our homework and received solid advice from rights of light specialists, local surveyors, planning advisors – even some ex Council members helping us. We would make impassioned speeches – but yet somehow, in these Planning Committee meetings, the councillors would just fully ignore everything the local community had laid before them and vote for the property developers, often being swayed by the Chairperson, which seemed unethical to me. It happened time after time after time. You might have an occasional dissenting voice amongst the councillors in a meeting but never enough to sway the matter. There would also be the odd condition or two attached to an approved application – but just a token gesture and never enough to affect anything. On many occasions the Chairperson of the planning committee would even be openly hostile to local community members, whilst on the other hand these council planning officers could barely hide their cosiness with the property developers and their planning agents. In fact, the latter were often former Council planning officers themselves. You'd often spy them all huddling together in little side rooms. Unfortunately, the part of London I live in seems to have become infected with spivs, chancers and opportunists.

A perfect storm of low interest rates, cheap, low-skilled immigrant labour, deregulated planning laws, the neutering of planning watch dogs such as English Heritage and the unfettered avarice of developers triggered an orgy of greed in London. It has been like watching snakes devouring their own tails. Large buildings that were erected as recently as the late 1990s or early 2000s were now being demolished to make way for even larger soul-crushing, spirit-numbing office blocks and luxury penthouse apartments – which are usually then bought by foreign investors and left empty rather than used by local communities. It seems like nothing is allowed to grow old anymore. It's like an architectural version of *Logan's Run*! In every direction you look the cranes are moving on the skyline. London Town is falling down around our ears but not enough people care to actually help stop it.

After watching this process endlessly repeat, you're thinking, 'What is *really* going on here?' The only way to make sense of it – the missing part of the equation if you will – is that 'envelopes' were being passed around and that the people involved in the planning decisions were simply being bought off, one way or the other. Although It's more on the surface in certain other countries – parts of Latin America for instance – England is equally corrupt. But it's the pretence that it's *not* that I find galling.

So, it was a demoralising time – spending years trying to preserve historic parts of London. There were similar groups across the city that we would sometimes team up with too, trying to protect our respective neighbourhoods, ordinary people who really cared about local history and who wanted to preserve in order to pass on to their children and grandchildren – to everybody's children and grandchildren. These links with the past, particularly the working-class links – which nobody seems to care about but which are vitally important – are the lifeblood of any city. I suppose, if we were able to go back in time, one hundred years, two hundred years or longer, people may have felt the same way and hated many of the new buildings going up in their time that we now look back upon with such affection. London – like all cities – and life itself, is constantly changing, continually renewing.

I ended up serving a seven-year tour of duty with local politics and local campaigning – handing out leaflets in the street; attending countless meetings with campaign groups, planning committees and licensing committees; being interviewed in local newspapers;

helping design slogans and logos; speaking to countless local residents to try and get them involved. It becomes all-consuming and, like pretty much everyone else who gets involved, you end up getting sucked deeper and deeper into it because you feel so outraged at the corruption and incompetence of local government and the sheer unfairness of it all. But it can end up bleeding you white. A big part of the problem is that most people don't care about old buildings being demolished or children's play areas being removed.

JW: You mentioned photography as a creative outlet. What else did you do, conservationism aside, to maintain a toe in the world of 'making'?

MJ: My dad had always been a voracious reader and he'd always written too – short stories primarily but in more recent years he'd become an inveterate writer of 'Letters to the Editor' to both *The Independent* and *The Guardian* newspapers. He'd never had a book published though so I thought it would make a nice 80th birthday present to publish a book about our family's time at the Two Puddings that he'd been writing on and off for years. There were quite a few things he'd written that I had to remove though, for legal reasons and not wishing to get certain people into trouble with the authorities! It took me a year to properly edit and I then set up my own little publishing company, 51st State Press.

In 2012 I published *Tales From The Two Puddings.* It seemed fitting to publish it the year the Olympic Games came to Stratford as I knew I could generate a bit of interest. It picked up great reviews, we got some great publicity – I even got my dad onto BBC Radio 4's daytime *Midweek* programme during Christmas week. I arranged an event at the Bishopsgate Institute and for Robert Elms to interview him on stage. We got a double-page spread in *Time Out* and I managed to get him on BBC's *Newsnight.* Sadly, he couldn't get there from Suffolk in time, so I went on in his place. The book did well and went on to sell around 15,000 copies and is still selling. I became an editor, publisher and promoter through 51st State Press and I was as proud of that project as any album release. It was wonderful to creatively collaborate with my dad as well as with Andrew and Gerard.

JW: I sense that things were beginning to accumulate for you again.

MJ: 2012 was turning out to be one of the most intense years of my life. Apart from all the work I just outlined on *Tales From The Two Puddings*, my partner Helen gave birth to our son, George, at the Royal London in Whitechapel. What was another one of the happiest days of my life was quickly turned upside down when Andrew was shockingly diagnosed with a brain tumor just weeks after suffering some severe headaches. It quickly became one of the lowest points in my life. It was so sad as all of the family had been so happy and excited to welcome little George.

In addition, I was releasing the soundtrack to *Moonbug* – a 2010 documentary about the meetings between the Apollo astronauts and my old friend photographer Steve Pyke – but my manager at that time, Cally, had personal problems of his own and was unable to help with this release. So, I made the tough decision to relieve him of his duties and started managing myself again. A few months later the wonderful Lee Kavanagh quit her job as my assistant as she was offered full-time work close to her home, which was a long train journey from where my office is. It was a blow as Lee is one of the kindest people I know and like family to me. She was always such a huge support.

JW: So, this was a period, albeit manager-less, of return?

MJ: Managing myself again, I set about rebuilding my career from the ground up and to become *properly* independent – far more so than I was back in the early eighties when signed to independent labels like 4AD and Some Bizzare. The big nagging question for me was how to make myself completely financially independent of the music industry? I was being offered plenty of recording contracts but they involved handing over copyright. I was damned if I was going to make that mistake again. I knew there must be a better way forward.

It was a case of building a team bit by bit. I received a recommendation for a potential replacement for my long-time assistant Lee from an artist friend, Lucinda Rogers. Gillian Glover turned out to be perfect for the job and what was strange was that there were so many coincidences. She had been living in New York at a similar time to me and, as mentioned, also spent time working at Dessau Studios at the same time I was there – though we'd never actually met then. She'd also spent time living in Göteborg during a similar time to me too, and we'd never met there either. Gillian has been crucial in helping make my new infrastructure work (that being my own Cinéola label, production company and offices). She's such a talented all-rounder and so pro-active that her role has grown and grown. She's also a musician and has now sung on many THE THE recordings. Coincidentally, she'd even recorded at The Garden Studio, during which time she met Mark Allaway...

Mark is another essential member of the team and is the manager/in-house engineer for Studio Cinéola. I've known him a long time as he worked in The Garden Studio for many years. He is exceptionally hard-working and conscientious. For artwork design we have Martin Lewis. PR has been handled by Steve Phillips (press) and Joe Mallott (radio). I still have my old friend and long-time accountant in place, Ronnie Harris. John Kennedy's nephew, Kieran Jay at Harbottle & Lewis, takes care of legal matters and there are many other good people on the team.

JW: *The Inertia Variations* documented the Radio Cinéola project, which seems increasingly important in a current climate in which the media seems dictated to by mainstream and right-wing propaganda. Despite your own tendency, as you say in the film to 'simply do nothing', did you feel a personal responsibility to present an alternative and to challenge notions concerning local, national and international ideas about politics and democracy?

MJ: It began as a simple idea but grew into a multi-media project – a term I'm not that fond of – and eventually involved a documentary film, two live radio shows (twelve hours and three hours long), a triple album boxset and two art exhibitions (in Edinburgh and Göteborg). It was the most ambitious project I've been involved with since *Infected* and was orchestrated with Johanna's company in Sweden and through my UK companies – Lazarus and Cinéola – so on a much smaller budget than with CBS/Sony.

The genesis was the collection of poems – *The Inertia Variations* – by John Tottenham. But I'll need to rewind a bit to convey the circumstances and why these poems were so pertinent to me. They arrived at a very low point in my life.

JW: And why was this a difficult moment for you personally?

MJ: Well, Johanna and I sold our loft in New York in 2003 to buy a nice apartment in Göteborg – but I wasn't living in it because we'd separated a year or so after moving to Sweden in 2001. After the chaos of the previous couple of years I was in a lot of debt and under a lot of stress. This entire period was discombobulating and I'd lost a lot of money on the Naked Tour, I'd left my recording and publishing deals, fired my manager, left my relationship and – trying to stem the financial haemorrhaging – had partially moved back to my old bedroom at my dad's house in Suffolk. I felt humiliated but what could I do apart from embrace it, try to be philosophical and look at the positives? I loved my dad so it was good to be spending more time with him, but I didn't have easy access to a personal studio anymore. The Garden Studio was now managed for me by MiloCo and was constantly fully booked. My confidence was ebbing away and I felt myself slipping into a deep rut – emotionally, financially and creatively. I felt very dispirited with the music industry and I didn't know how to get back into it – or more pertinently, if I even *wanted* to get back into it.

My debts were now so large that the paltry income I received from The Garden and other rentals wasn't making a dent. Plus, whatever money came in I'd just carelessly spend on travelling. So, although ostensibly living at my dad's house, I continued to visit friends and family in the same places I always had – especially to Sweden to spend time with Jackson. When in the UK, most weekends I'd head into London on a Friday evening for some escapism and debauchery – travelling back to Suffolk with a Monday morning hangover. This went on for a few years. But running away from yourself is like running away from your own legs isn't? I was out and about, here, there and everywhere meeting lots of new people and having fun – or so I thought – but deep down I was floundering. I was lost. Night after night, getting pissed, talking shit. Speaking about what I was *going* to do instead of actually doing it. I had now fully embraced life as a flâneur and a contradictory combination of wanderlust and inertia seemed to have finally put paid to me. Maybe they aren't strictly contradictory, but rather complementary opposites. Wanderlust being an impulse that pushes against inertia. Without inertia, wanderlust would have no resistance to give it meaning; without wanderlust, inertia would just be stasis without tension.

JW: How did you pull yourself out of life as a flâneur?

MJ: One night someone said something that hit me hard – in fact I wrote it down and can still remember it. At the time I was having what I'd call an intense platonic affair with a German actress – we were not actually romantically or sexually involved but we were inseparable as friends for about six months during this period. One evening as I was getting drunk and being my usual evasive self about my creative life – i.e. talking about projects that never seemed to go anywhere – she just looked me in the eye and said, 'You have to make up your mind if you want to fool about flying here, there and everywhere seeing friends or if you really have the urge to create. It's not where you *are* that's important but what you're *doing!*' It was like a slap in the face – a bucket of iced water tipped over my head. But it's what friends should do for each other – call each other out. It served as a wake-up call. Months had turned into years and I had forgotten who I was.

One day shortly after this – whilst sitting in the front room at my dad's house idly surfing the Internet – I received an email from Jim Thirlwell. This would have been around 2006 I think. Jim was also someone who was continually nagging me to get back to creativity – always pulling me up, telling me off – like a close friend should. He'd sent me John Tottenham's collection of poems – *The Inertia Variations* – and advised me to read them. He said they reminded him of me. When reading them they also reminded *me* of me! The life I had somehow collapsed into – procrastination and idleness.

I read them all in one sitting– something like 100 verses – and I was laughing and crying. They resonated so deeply that I knew I wanted to do something with them, though I wasn't sure what. Jim and I have known each other pretty much since we were teenagers and he and Tottenham have known each other for a similar length of time. Tottenham and I had never met but Jim put me in touch with him. I told John how much I loved his poetry and asked if he would be okay with me doing something with them. He was very generous, told me to go ahead and do what I wanted – even giving permission for me to re-edit the running order for my version. I didn't change any words – of course – just the order, with the intent of doing a spoken word project. I then divided them into seven chapters of seven verses – cutting down to forty-nine poems. I narrated them at the little studio I'd set up in my bedroom at my dad's house and created sound effects and musical interludes to bring them to life. I then booked myself into The Garden Studio with engineer Pete Hoffman to mix them. I wasn't quite sure at this point how I would release them.

JW: Did you also begin to think about a more permanent mooring now that something had ignited your creative spark again?

MJ: Well, yes, I had the desire to stop moving about here there and everywhere. But I couldn't work out how to do it initially as life was so complicated and I had so much debt. My former partner, Fiona, highly recommended a life coach she'd been seeing. In the past I might have scoffed at such a thing but this lovely lady, Sara Longmuir, was incredibly helpful and over the course of several weeks we sat and plotted a route back into London and into my life and career again. Part of the plan was to close down The Garden. It was a tough decision as it was one of my favourite studios – and a favourite of many other artists too – but I had to rejuggle my finances and make investments elsewhere.

I also went on an intensive course of therapy, which involved group therapy and dealing with the Quadrinity: physical, emotional, intellectual and spiritual. A close friend had been on this particular course and having seen the dramatic impact it had on them I decided to follow. It had a profound impact and from there things really started to shift for me.

Johanna then heard *The Inertia Variations* – though we'd separated we remained close friends – and the idea for an exhibition or documentary film about the poem came from her. It took many years though. We had interest from various Swedish art institutions and film companies but the project kept evolving and shifting. Johanna went on a filmmakers' workshop in Croatia and the feedback she received was that it was a good idea but for it to properly work as a documentary there had to be an element of tension. Matt Johnson loafing around, pontificating about losing his mojo and living the life of a flâneur wasn't really going to cut it. So, she came back with the idea of tying it into the British General Election of 2015. That's how many years had already elapsed in the lifetime of this project! Inevitably, many other things were going on in my life at the same time – like my involvement with conservation in East London and working on my Dad's book – quite a chaotic few years in many ways. Most of what I have said in the last couple of hours still feels quite muddled to me in terms of chronology!

JW: Were others involved in planting the seed of the project as an idea?

MJ: Well, a quick diversion: I can't recall the exact timeline but it was around 2009 that the idea of Radio Cinéola was hatched. The initial concept came from my manager at the time, Cally – a lovely fellow – but unfortunately for him, he was managing me during the most unproductive period of my entire career. There were a few unfinished pieces of music and sections of songs I was working on but I just couldn't seem to drag them over the finish line. He phoned one sunny day – whilst he was driving around the countryside in one of his open-top vintage cars – and suggested I put together a 'radio broadcast' – really a podcast – containing these various pieces of unfinished music as a way of finally getting my creative juices flowing. I thought it was a great idea so immediately ran with it.

I've been a fan of shortwave radio from childhood to the present day so I wanted it to sound like the signal was bouncing off the ionosphere as if travelling from the other side of the world. I worked out a way of processing it through my old analogue equipment to give the desired effect. Then what to name it? I liked the name Cinéola and had already decided to use that for my soundtrack projects. It put me in mind of the old Moviola machines I used to see as a teenager when working at De Wolfe – dropping tapes off at smoke-filled editing suites around Soho. So, I decided to incorporate that as part of the name for the broadcast. Then, of course, all good shortwave stations must have a call sign, so I took the guitar melody from my song 'Shrunken Man' and reworked it as a simple Cold War-era theme. I also wanted one of those cheesy seventies-style radio idents, so I recorded some harmonies

singing 'Radio Cinéola'. To kick it off we decided to create one 'broadcast' per month across 2010. I loved recording them and they ended up featuring not only the obscure pieces of unreleased music but also interviews with friends and collaborators.

Fast forward a few years: Johanna approached me with the idea of us doing a live Radio Cinéola broadcast on Election Day 2015 – then just a few months away. The broadcast would also involve Tottenham's poetry and live music – including a brand-new song written and performed by me! My initial reaction was one of horror: 'Absolutely *not*! I can't do *that*!' I was extremely resistant but Johanna kept on haranguing me and eventually persuaded me that doing it all live – on election day – was the essential ingredient to give the project the required tension.

JW: And how did you begin actually realising the project?

MJ: Working with my old friend Kerry Sewell – an interior and architectural designer I've worked with for years at my building in London – we created a set that looked like a Cold War-era radio station – even choosing the appropriate shade of grey for the acousti-board panels and hanging my old Gent's clock on the wall to perfect the atmosphere. We ended up doing two internationally live-streamed broadcasts from Cinéola HQ – twelve hours and three hours – but in the documentary they are combined to appear as one.

Hosting these broadcasts was very exciting – conducting interviews and taking calls from all over the world whilst live on air made me feel so alive and energised. The twelve-hour broadcast focused on the recital of the poetry and on local and global politics, whilst the later three-hour broadcast was purely music-based. I interviewed a number of people via Skype in the days leading up to the first transmission, people like William Engdahl, one of my favourite geopolitical analysts; Abdi Assadi, a spiritual healer and my friend from New York; David Edwards from Media Lens; Neil Clark from the *Daily Express*, *Russia Today* and various other outlets; Zoe Hepden, professor of philosophy; Neil Sanders, a mind-control expert; Thierry Somers, writer and designer; and

Marian St Laurent, semiotics expert. We had a lot of interesting guests and drop-ins on the day including local activists and friends, such artists Brad Lochore, Lucinda Rogers, Tim Pope, Zeke Manyika and many others, including my brother Gerard and cousin Peter. We broadcast live for twelve hours on Election Day with the intention of speaking about the things that were not being spoken about in corporate media.

JW: What sort of things did you feel were not being spoken about?

MJ: Even then, you could sense an impending authoritarian drift. This was all pre-Brexit, pre-Trump of course, but there was a sense we were drifting into a dark, new world and I wanted to reach out to like-minded people. We use the term 'mainstream' or 'corporate' news these days but in reality, most of it is pure propaganda, either 'extreme centre', faux-left or ultra-right. There is so much polarisation now – obviously exacerbated by social media – with most people seeming to just follow outlets that reinforce their own prejudices rather than seeking a balanced view. I am guilty of this myself. Since that broadcast, freedom of thought, speech and expression has been clamped down upon ever more severely under various guises such as 'Online Safety'.

Anyway, as the project was continuing to grow, a few months later we decided to add the second broadcast to the plan. This time with the musical element. Johanna had by then persuaded me to write and perform a new song. I hadn't sung since 2002 at this point. In fact, in the documentary I think I even described myself as a conservationist rather than a singer–songwriter because for seven years that is what I had done.

JW: And what sort of place were you in personally as the project evolved?

MJ: *The Inertia Variations* was filmed over a few years and during this time Andrew became very ill. As mentioned previously, his diagnosis of cancer was within just a couple of weeks of my youngest son George being born. I was devastated and completely thrown off balance. He died before the project was completed. I'd been trying to write a new song for the live music broadcast – about London and its destruction. That song was actually 'Some Days I Drink My Coffee By The Grave Of William Blake' and although I had the first verse and chorus I just couldn't seem to finish it. When Andrew died I felt compelled to write a song about him instead. I'd written 'Love Is Stronger Than Death' for Eugene; 'Phantom Walls' for our mother – so I felt driven to write a song for Andrew. Musically, 'We Can't Stop What's Coming' was based around this simple electric piano motif that I'd been playing with for some time. It just seemed to suit the mood of the moment.

JW: As we have discussed throughout you have experienced an undue amount of tragedy. What effect does this have on your psyche?

MJ: My family aren't the only ones who have had to deal with such tragedy. It is happening to some family, somewhere, every moment of every day. I've had various bouts of therapy over the years to try and soften the edges. I'm not a religious person and even the term 'spiritual' I find corny and trite, but I have always had strong, inherent beliefs about the human soul and spirit. I've had many strange experiences in my life. I don't believe in projecting beliefs and value systems onto other people but this interest in the metaphysical has helped me. The therapy I've had also helped me deal with the impact and after-effect of bereavements. It's important to work out if you are mentally and emotionally strong or just numb and compartmentalising in order to cope.

JW: Did it not eventually take a toll on you?

MJ: A couple of years later I went a bit off the rails. I wondered if this was a result of suppressing my grief so I decided to go back into therapy, partly to explore the cumulative effect of all these bereavements. I'm quite a strong person but it is hard to go through it all again. Of course, the older you get the more you have to lose. All of our lives are lives of loss really, aren't they? Over time we lose the places we know, the people we love; we eventually lose our own health. At the end of all this loss we have to consider what is left. What is our true essence? I don't believe we are born into this world as just a blank slate. I believe we are each born with certain attributes. And we each leave with certain things – an essence inherent in our soul but altered by the experiences of the life just lived. In some ways I think these bereavements have made me a kinder person. On some deep level, you have to decide: do you let the experiences of life destroy you or make you stronger?

JW: You have had a creative relationship with both Gerard and Andrew. Can you talk about Andrew's role in the visual evolution of THE THE?

MJ: I can't overstate Andrew's importance on the creative life of me and my other brothers when we were growing up. If Andrew recommended something, I knew I'd like it – and vice versa. Funnily enough, I'm currently reading a book Andrew bought me, *The Smoking Diaries* by playwright Simon Gray. Certain sections have been making me laugh out loud just as I know it must have done with Andrew. My brothers and I have all shared a similar sense of humour, from Laurel & Hardy, Tommy Cooper, Tony Hancock and Fawlty Towers, to George Carlin and *Curb Your Enthusiasm*, to more recent British comedians like Marc Wootton and shows like *The Office*. We had a very creative childhood, drawing, dressing up, creating our own little radio shows on tape recorders and building our own little fantasy worlds. It was a fertile, vivid and happy childhood – but yes, there was some darkness too and we had plenty of ups and downs and punch-ups. But we were confidants and collaborators. I loved working with Andrew. He was the single biggest inspiration on my creativity. In *The Inertia Variations* documentary we see a lot of his artwork. Our new releases feature artwork by him, including the reissue of *See Without Being Seen*, all the recent 7-inch singles and *Ensoulment*. We've been digitising all of the drawings in his sketchbooks – and he was also a very good writer – so I'd like to publish books of both at some point.

JW: What was the process of writing 'We Can't Stop What's Coming'? It is about the passing of Andrew but also more generally about the cycles of life and the inevitability of death. How did it feel to be writing music again that was less about ambience and textures than the instrumental soundtracks you had been working on? The lyrics also contain a lot of imagery about nature. Was this inspired by the fact that Andrew loved nature?

MJ: Andrew was very close to nature. He loved animals and they seemed to love him. Birds would come near him and sit on his hand. Even bees would. Crows also played a big part in his life towards the end. He started seeing crows everywhere and – even before he was diagnosed with terminal cancer – became convinced they were a harbinger of doom for him. Look at the illustration used for 'We Can't Stop What's Coming', which we found in one of Andrew's sketchbooks – this was drawn before his diagnosis, and features this deathlike figure on a penny-farthing. He started drawing more and more crows, so this had to be part of the lyric: 'An owl by night, a mourning crow'. The sense of acceptance, inevitability and the cycles of life are expressed in the line, 'The

bonfire is burning, the birds returning' and in the lines, 'We can't hate the river for flowing, can't blame the wild wind blowing'. It's a hopeful song. The relationship between our true selves and nature is so much more profound than the egocentric viewpoint that we experience it through much of the time. There is an inherent intelligence behind the cycles of life. Ultimately, all is well. It was important there was optimism in this song.

JW: After all the instrumental soundtrack material, you came back to being a lyricist with 'We Can't Stop What's Coming' and later 'I Want 2 B U'. How were you finding that process – I imagine coming up with a melody is one thing but lyrics? Has that been harder to get back into?

MJ: Yes, in some ways. 'We Can't Stop What's Coming' took a lot of work. I like to weigh the meaning of the words I use very carefully and to shape the lines to ensure they correctly fit the melody. No one is more critical of my lyrics than I am. I've got hundreds of pages of lyrical ideas. I'm always, continually, daily, writing things down.

JW: Do you write in a notebook?

MJ: I used to write on small, pocket-sized notebooks or on small credit-card-sized slips of white card I kept in my wallet. But these days – for convenience – on my phone and then transfer onto my laptop.

JW: I've gone back to notebooks.

MJ: Have you?

JW: There's something lovely about them.

MJ: I agree. There is. I have a stack of fresh Moleskines in my desk drawer as well as a few boxes of Black Wing pencils ready for sharpening. Like you, I'm a big fan of analogue. I've got hundreds of pages of lyrics, printed up and in folders. I've just got to roll up my sleeves and start editing. They wouldn't make much sense to anyone else though as they are what I call 'seed lyrics', just row upon row of unconnected lines that have been jotted down and collected over the years and that need to be added to other lines to make sense.

There are several different methods of writing songs for me. My preferred route – or most heavily worn path – is with guitar in hand or sat at a piano. I'll start by working out chord sequences. Just playing around until a sequence resonates with the mood I'm feeling. From that, melodies come quite simply to me. I'll do what I call a 'scat vocal' – just singing melodic ideas without words and capture it into a voice recorder. I'll then look through my lists of titles or lyrics trying to find ideas or sentiments that fit the mood. If a title comes first it may suggest a theme and guide me to the right lyrics. I then go through notepads and folders trying to find some 'seeds' in that theme. Then, using those 'seeds' as starting points, fresh lyrics gradually fill the page until hopefully serendipity – or perhaps synchronicity – intervene and all sorts of magical ideas appear in my mind to connect everything. Once written out, I'll play around with the tense, alternatively setting it in the past, present or future – but also playing around with point of view from first, second to third person. I'll go through the lyrics from each and every angle playing with these devices to find the best vehicle for what I'm trying to say.

Now, what I've just explained is only one way, another way is starting with a rhythm or groove. I love creating rhythms with drum machines, samplers or loops. Grooving around on my electronic machines, creating repetitive patterns building on top of each other – then creating melodies on top of that. I also love writing bass parts. I used to play bass in a punk band when I was a teenager and that is a fundamental part of song-writing for me.

Another way is starting with the lyrics alone – no music at all initially – that may be more Dylanesque I suppose? I will write out the words completely and just see where they would like to lead me musically. That would be a piece like 'Down By The Frozen River'. Lyrics first, music later.

JW: If we look back at the lyrics you've written, there are recurring themes there and also in our conversations. Politics, the dichotomy between lust and love. We spoke about 'We Can't Stop What's Coming'. I think that's such a beautiful song, because of the intensity of it and the subject matter. It is difficult to listen to the lyrics because I know the story – but there's somehow a sense of acceptance, and a kind of peace with it, which I think might have been missing from some of your writing in your 20s and your 30s.

MJ: I could not have written the songs I'm now writing when I was in my twenties, which is probably due to having experienced bereavement too often for my age. Unfortunately, in my life – as in many peoples' lives – that natural sequence was disrupted. We are helpless in the endless torrent of events we call life and our options are to try and fight the inevitable or to exist with it in a more philosophical or stoic state of mind.

JW: That's quite Dylanesque.

MJ: Well, what can we do but accept what comes our way?

JW: I'd like you to talk through the Radio Cinéola Band that you put together for *The Inertia Variations* and 'We can't Stop What's Coming'. You told bassist James Eller that you wanted it to be like a jazz trio. What was your thinking and how involved were you with Eller choosing musicians Chris Whitten and Iain Berryman?

MJ: Due to the size of the space we would be playing in at the Election Day live recording I wanted it to feel intimate and low-level. It also needed to fit the fifties-style set. I work on intuition and instinct much of the time and James was the first person I called. I was feeling quite insecure about getting involved in music again and performing and I needed someone I could really trust. No one other than James could have played this role at that time. I love James. He's not only very talented but also very kind, calm, experienced and has a great sense of humour. We are on a similar page politically so he was the perfect person to collaborate with. We started to discuss who else we needed to get involved and he suggested Chris Whitten – a great drummer who's played with the likes of Dire Straits and Paul McCartney. Chris had given up drumming for years and had been living in Australia as a grape farmer. So, this was a bit of a comeback for him too. Somebody else suggested Ian Berryman for keyboards. He was very mellow and fitted in well with the gentle, warm atmosphere. I appointed James as Musical Director as I was too busy with other elements of the project and he then rehearsed the band and worked out the arrangements of the other songs that would be played during the broadcast.

We thought about who we'd like to sing when it came to interpreting the songs and Thomas Feiner was someone who'd become a good friend from my times in Göteborg. He had already recorded a beautiful, slow version of 'This Is The Day', so it made sense for him to perform this. The wonderful Swedish singer Meja Kullersten – who I'd actually met whilst I was living in Mallorca – wanted to sing 'Slow Emotion Replay'. Liz Horsman was someone else I wanted involved. I'd sung a duet with her on 'December Sunlight' a few years earlier so it made sense for her to sing that again – by herself this time. Colin Lloyd Tucker, my old mate from De Wolfe days wanted to perform 'Bugle Boy'. We also had Tom Bright, who I met when he was a waiter in a local restaurant I frequented. He was so affable and friendly to everyone he was serving. I liked him. He didn't know who I was but he mentioned he was a singer–songwriter so I got him involved. He's a talented lad. He chose 'Love Is Stronger Than Death'.

JW: It's a very emotional moment in the film when you perform 'We Can't Stop What's Coming'. People on the day commented that until the very last moment it looked unlikely that you would perform. At this point you get the sense that there is a 'lightning in the bottle' element of *The Inertia Variations* as it captures your rediscovery of performing.

MJ: I hadn't sung live for something like thirteen years. It was a very powerful and moving moment for me. As I was about to perform – with cameras in my face and the fact it was being broadcast live across the world – what crossed my mind was, 'Don't fuck up!' I was very worried I'd forget the first line and have to start all over again. There was a lot of pressure and I wanted to do justice to the song and to the event. I didn't want to let myself or Andrew down. It was a very cathartic moment. That was also the moment that led to the next world tour. I knew then that I was ready to come back.

JW: I believe the performance of 'We Can't Stop What's Coming' that you recorded on the day of the broadcast was the one you released on 7-inch vinyl for 2017's Record Store Day. It sold out immediately.

MJ: After I made the decision to release it as a single I asked Meja Kullersten to record some backing vocals and Zeke Manyika to play tambourine on it. Then Johnny Marr happened to drop round my place one afternoon for a catch up and I played him a rough mix. Whilst listening he picked up one of my guitars and started playing along with it – something quite beautiful – and said 'I'm just saying...'. He overdubbed his parts back at his studio and sent me the files. His soulful guitar really finished it off. Mark Allaway had engineered the recording on the day of the broadcast and Finnbar Eiles then mixed it at my place. The Record Store Day release went really well and was one of the biggest sellers of that year's event.

JW: And was the eureka moment you had when you first performed the song multiplied by the fact the single sold so well?

MJ: It was. But just the pure joy of making music again – after so many years in the wilderness – flooded back. I've previously moaned about my frustrations with the industry, feeling trapped in bad deals, poor royalties, losing copyrights in perpetuity etc. but to discover a pathway into the future I had to go back into the past – and back to my post-punk roots.

I've worked full time in the music industry since I was 15 and over the years I've learned from many brilliant people. So, I knew what I needed to do. Yes, I didn't have the financial power of a major corporation behind me anymore but instead this was a journey back to rediscovering the innocent excitement and joy in music. When I was a kid in my first band, Road Star, I'd record our rehearsals and gigs on my little Amerex cassette recorder and I'd sit in my bedroom and design the covers of the cassettes and fantasise they were on my own little record company. It was something I'd always wanted to do.

JW: Are you more contented and less restless now than when you were previously hyper-creative in the past?

MJ: It's funny really. At the height of my commercial success in the eighties – with albums like *Infected* – I was always dissatisfied. Something always felt lacking. But I've since learned to enjoy the journey as much as the destination. There is a phrase I use when I'm really enjoying moments with friends or family: 'Well, if this isn't nice, I don't know what is.' It's something I heard Kurt Vonnegut Jr. say in an interview. It was something his dad used to say to him and his family. It is about acknowledging the good moments in our lives, otherwise you will experience nothing but dissatisfaction.

We all moan about things when they're not to our liking but it is so important to acknowledge things when they *are* to our liking. In a word – gratitude. I used to keep journals, which I've now destroyed, as I only used to write in them when I was pissed off about something or someone. They were quite negative and really didn't represent who I was at all or what I really felt about the people I was venting about. What is the point in even writing that stuff or in keeping it? Or if you do write it then just burn it as soon as you've got the negative thoughts out of your system and onto paper.

During the strange period of descent my career went through in the noughties I just looked on impassively as I slipped from low profile to no profile. My career just got further and further away in the rearview mirror. I suppose I'm what might be called an autodidact but I'm also a bit of a dilettante in that I tend to easily flit from one obsession to another. I devour all knowledge and information I can find about a particular hobby or interest for a while before moving on to another obsession. At the moment that obsession has come round once again to music.

JW: The denouement of this project was *The Inertia Variations* documentary directed by Johanna St Michaels. It operates on a wider scale as a film about grief, friendship and the creative process and it was well received at Edinburgh International Film Festival (EIFF) where in his programme notes Niall Grieg Fulton wrote:

> Captured at a pivotal point in his creative life, *The Inertia Variations* is an endearingly candid picture of this extraordinary British artist, and with the enigmatic Johnson valiantly exposing his heart on his sleeve, St Michaels has turned his hesitation at the artistic crossroads into a compelling work of conceptual art in its own right. One other thing is certain: whether it's as cool ringmaster of Radio Cinéola or as the mighty THE THE, Johnson's own art is clearly now more resonant than ever, and judging by the state of the current political landscape, his return to the fray could not be more timely.

That's quite the recommendation.

After EIFF the film also enjoyed sell-out cinema screenings across the UK, Europe and US. You attended many of these and saw first-hand the level of appreciation for the band. You had only announced a few tour dates then…

MJ: *The Inertia Variations* was incredibly important. Johanna and I have known each other intimately for many years – obviously, we have a son together – and I think this helped with the film because I trusted her. I enjoy working with her. And we're still close friends. In fact, my partner Helen and I have just been on holiday with Johanna and her husband Jacob. As a filmmaker she is very discrete, but she knows what she wants. I didn't interfere in the film – actually there was only one moment I wasn't comfortable with and Johanna took it out. Johanna is also very strong-minded. Which is probably why we split up. Two Leos. She's a photographer and often acts as her own cinematographer and does so in a way that is non-intrusive. She really encouraged me to perform the song in the film when I was dragging my feet. Andrew dying was the catalyst that finally compelled me to start writing and singing again. The process of making the film was enjoyable and I liked the idea of it bringing together a different type of band: a filmmaker, a poet, lighting designer, architect, political writers and traditional musicians too. It was a real collaboration across disciplines. I found it thrilling. It was also nice to step back a little and not be in control of everything. I can be a bit of a control freak.

The Inertia Variations incorporated a number of projects I was struggling to bring to fruition and really helped to bring my career back to life. Its importance in my career cannot be overstated and without it there would have been no Comeback Special Tour. The defining moment of the documentary was certainly the live performance at the end. I clearly remember standing there after I'd finished singing and thinking, 'I'm back!'

CHAPTER ELEVEN
The Bonfire Is Burning, The Birds Returning

Much to the surprise of his agent, Matt accepts an offer for THE THE to perform live again for the first time in sixteen years. He puts together the band for the Elvis Presley-referencing The Comeback Special World Tour. Matt's beloved father Eddie passes away suddenly but Matt decides to continue with his obligations. A live album and concert film directed by Tim Pope are released in 2021.

JW: Did performing 'We Can't Stop What's Coming' lead to a swell of creative momentum?

MJ: For many years, I'd been turning down all offers to perform live. Actually, for many years I'd been turning down pretty much everything connected to my music career. But after the positive feelings that flowed from *The Inertia Variations* and 'We Can't Stop What's Coming', I decided to start saying 'Yes'.

My agent of many years has been Paul Boswell at Free Trade Agency. I've known him since I was 21. He was actually my agent between the ages of 21 and 29 when I didn't tour or even play live at all – apart from the Marquee residency. Over the years, when I appointed different managers they all had their favourite agents they would insist on working with so when I did start finally touring I'd already left Boswell. Many years later, after the Naked Tour I went back to him. He helped facilitate our appearance at Bowie's Meltdown Festival in 2002 but of course straight after that I disappeared and it looked like I would never play live again! He just didn't seem to have much luck with me. Despite all this we kept in touch and he was very patient. Each year we'd have our annual luncheon and he'd broach the subject of me touring again, suggesting there was a lot of interest out there. Each year I would demur. But then, with Andrew's death and the realisation – as if I really needed reminding – that we each have a finite amount of time, it crystallised in my mind that I don't want any regrets. So, over luncheon, a few weeks after 'We Can't Stop What's Coming' was released Boswell informed me he'd received a big offer from Heartland Festival in Denmark for THE THE to headline. Even the name seemed right and with Andrew's death making me want to start saying 'Yes' to things I just said, 'Let's do it' and we shook hands on it. I think he was a bit shocked.

JW: Had you thought yet about what the new line-up might look like?

MJ: Well, as we'd recently worked together with the Radio Cinéola Band the first musician I approached was James. Then Earl as he and I had been speaking about working together again for years. They both said yes straight away. Then there was some serendipitous synchronicity... or maybe synchronised serendipity! I spoke with Johnny and, although he wasn't available – he was in preparation for his own tour – he strongly recommended Barrie Cadogan, who records and performs as Little Barrie. Johnny sent him round to my place and we instantly hit it off. He fitted perfectly with the ideas I had for the tour. I then started to ponder the keyboard position – various people put names forward – but something told me not to rush. Then, out of the blue, I received an email from DC. We hadn't spoken for a few years at this point. I knew he was living in Chicago but I actually thought he'd retired. He told me THE THE was in his blood, that he still had his British passport, that he'd pay for his own flight to London and that he was ready to go. I couldn't have been happier.

JW: What were the key criteria for selecting the musicians and for the rehearsal process?

MJ: The musicians I had for the Naked Tour were living all over the world and I knew I couldn't afford to fly them all over and pay for hotels. It had to be London-based and DC told me he could stay with his sister in East London. I made an exception for Earl though, who is Berlin-based these days.

With the rehearsals I wanted to continue where I left off with

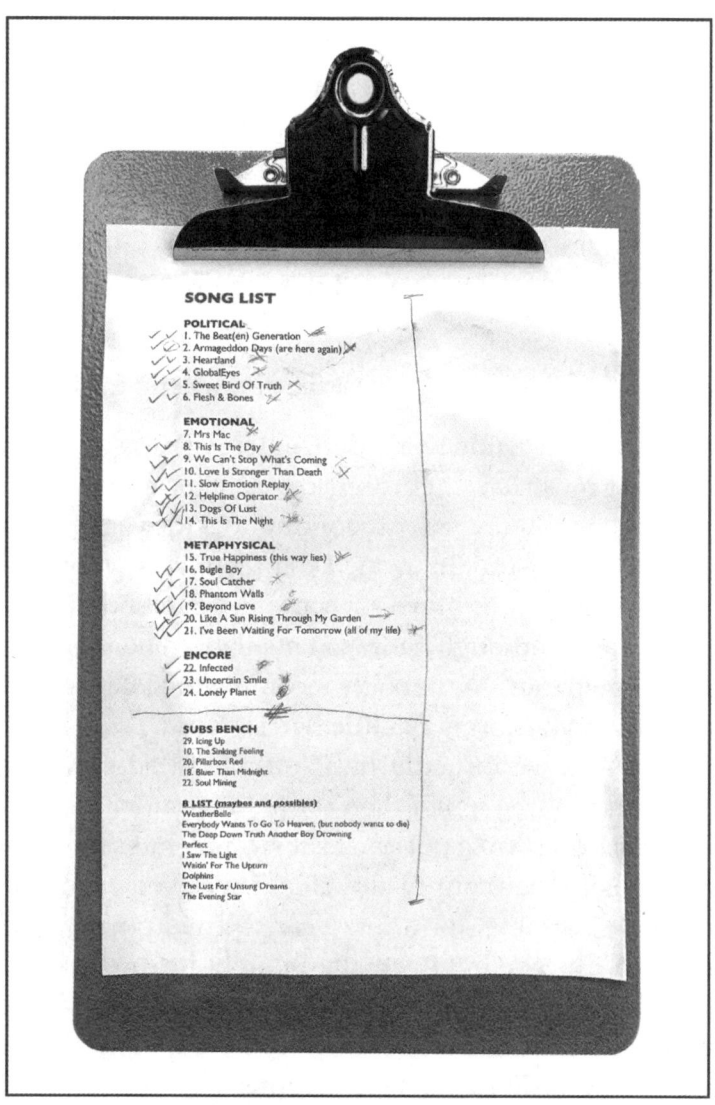

the broadcast. I wanted it to feel intimate. So, at my place I set up some old wooden folding chairs in a tight circle with just a small drum riser. I told the band I wanted it to feel personal, low level with small amps, minimal equipment and for us to be physically close to each other. We started with just James and Barrie for the first few weeks, running through my entire catalogue of songs, trying ideas out as we worked out which ones would most suit the new aesthetic. After several weeks DC joined us and then finally Earl joined, starting off on a little practice kit. Then we went into rehearsals at The Joint in Kings Cross. I like to over-rehearse and then dial it back from there.

JW: Did it all work out as planned?

MJ: I have to say The Comeback Special was probably my favourite tour ever. Maybe because I honestly didn't think I would ever play live again. I was just so happy to be back playing music with my good friends. Every moment on that tour was intensified by a gratitude that I was able to get back to doing what I loved doing – and that there was still an audience out there supporting us. I've never been one to suffer from stage fright or nerves, but even though I had not been on tour since 2000 there were no nerves at all. Whether walking on stage at the Royal Albert Hall or the Sydney Opera House – or anywhere else – it was like walking into a living room for me. It all felt so comfortable. I think this was partly due to having gone through such horrors in recent years with family members dying – such massive but awful things in comparison to standing on a stage in front of five or ten thousand people, doing what you love doing, in front of friends, family and people who are on your side. What is there to possibly feel nervous about?

I also knew I had an amazing band. We'd all worked so hard in rehearsals and they are such great players and good human beings. I loved being with them. There was a great spirit. Technical issues can always arise; a piece of equipment can malfunction or one of us might occasionally make a mistake but we were so well rehearsed we could easily cover for each other. The confidence flowed from that.

JW: And fans of THE THE also had access to you and your music for the first time in a while.

MJ: I have a lot of respect for the audience and this is why, for the live performances as well as the recordings, I always work so hard. I hope it's an honest, non-exploitative relationship. Of course, an audience often wants more than you are able to give – another record, another tour, another this, another that. Or a selfie – which I do not like giving as I loathe them – though I'm always happy to sign an autograph. Also, we're often asked why we haven't played a specific country or city. But it is not up to the band. We can only go to cities where the promoters invite us. We can't just randomly show up. There are so many places all over the world I'd love to visit and perform in but we have to receive financially viable offers otherwise it quickly turns into a loss-making venture. I've been there in the past and have no intention going back to losing fortunes on tour.

When we announced The Comeback Special Tour I genuinely didn't know what the reaction was going to be. Or even if people would want to come. That 'ego death' I spoke about previously had certainly worked its magic on me. I was in a zen-like state of mind with zero expectations. In any event, the Royal Albert Hall concert sold out in seven minutes. Then the next London show sold out in minutes and then the next one too. Boswell was far more confident than me. I kept saying, 'Let's not add any more and overplay our hand', but I trusted him and took his advice.

JW: You played three quite different London venues: Troxy in Stepney, the Royal Albert Hall and Brixton Academy.

MJ: Ideally, we'd have played three nights at the Royal Albert Hall as we had on the Versus The World Tour in 1990 but it was only available for a single night. I like playing there. It's prestigious, with a sense of occasion – much like it may feel for a tennis player at Wimbledon. We chose the Troxy because it was 'home turf'. My parents were born about five minutes from there and my Uncle Peter and Aunt Kay owned the pub that used to be next door, the

Brewery Tap. I've always liked the Brixton Academy for other reasons. Gritty, down and dirty. A number of elements go to make a great concert: one's personal performance, the band's performance, the sound on stage, the sound front of house, the lighting and of course – possibly the most important – a receptive, responsive audience. So, there are all these variables and very rarely do you get a clean sweep.

We came off stage after the gig at Brixton quite down on ourselves. We were underpowered on stage – which was my fault as I'd insisted upon small amps for intimacy. But the Academy is quite a cavernous venue so we were hearing more of ourselves echoing off the back wall from the PA than from our amps on stage! It was very disorientating. So, when we played the Troxy the following night we were very fired up to put things right and I think we put on one of the best performances of the tour. Zeke Manyika even came on at the end to sing 'Lonely Planet'. And being local I had a lot of family there. It was magical.

JW: Can you elaborate on the tour title: The Comeback Special?

MJ: It was tongue-in-cheek, of course, and named after Elvis Presley's '68 Comeback Special* where he wore black leathers and rolled back the years. But I did also feel that I shouldn't hide from the fact that it was a big comeback for me. I felt it was important to embrace that. I deal with pressure well, so I thought let's put even more pressure on it. It's got to be a great tour. But it was also supposed to be playful.

JW: Then, amidst all this joy disaster suddenly struck when your father Eddie passed away. This loss must have hit particularly hard. You put out a statement to fans that you would not be cancelling shows, partly down to the financial responsibility that you shouldered for the tour.

---

* *Signer Presents... Elvis* was a concert television special, marking Presley's return to live performance after seven years. It's commonly referred to as the '68 Comeback Special.

MJ: I had nobody – and nowhere – to fall back on. No record company for tour support. It's not cheap setting up a tour. And we'd already had advances from some of the festivals to enable me to pay for all the rehearsals etc. I've had various managers throughout my career but I'm now managing myself – and very happy doing so – but it does bring a lot more responsibility. Having learned from past mistakes when I was very young I have long had good legal representation and accountants. However, the main reason I wanted to carry on the tour is because it is what my dad would have wanted.

My dad and I often had deep, intense conversations. We would talk about everything – apart from sex and drugs. The drugs bit I kept quiet about. Talking about sex for someone of his generation wasn't really done. But we could talk about politics, relationships, emotions, football, films, books, music, family gossip. One day I was at his house in Suffolk and he was feeling a bit down. He'd been suffering from heart failure and had some respiratory issues – but he was still incredibly sharp mentally and very well informed. He was still driving and shopping and coming up to London to watch films and going on marches when he could. He was an active, independent man. So, this day we were sitting in the front room and chatting about this and that when I asked him how he felt about death. I asked him if he was frightened. He replied that he wasn't frightened for himself but that he thought about Gerard and me and his grandchildren. He said in the event that anything happened to him that he wanted Gerard and me to promise we would carry on with our careers. He made light of it but I think he knew on some level he had very limited time left. He'd seen what we'd gone through as a family after Eugene died – my career had never really recovered, despite putting out a few more albums, and it had a horrendous impact on our mum, and on Andrew and Gerard. But my dad made me promise that Gerard and I would carry on and not let it derail our lives and careers again. He was very explicit that this was what he wanted.

So, the tour started, we played some warm-ups in Barrie's hometown of Nottingham, then flew to Denmark to perform at Heartland Festival. The morning after – at Stockholm airport – I was checking my phone messages whilst waiting at the baggage carousel. There was a voicemail from West Suffolk Hospital asking me to call them about my father. I didn't even know he was in hospital but it transpired he'd gone in for a precautionary check-up. I knew it must be bad as hospitals don't call out of the blue unless it's serious. So, I called the hospital but couldn't get through. I tried Gerard but couldn't get through to him either. I tried the hospital again and this time got through. They told me the awful news. It was a hammer blow. Luckily, the band and Gillian were with me and stood around and held me. I could not have been with better people.

Our dad had suffered some terrible blows in his life. But at this moment in his life he would have been relatively content. By that I mean Gerard and his partner Polly had recently had beautiful twin daughters and Gerard had also got the funding to make his new feature film *Muscle*. I was about to finally go back on tour again – and my dad loved my boys, his two grandsons. Maybe it's my imagination but I feel on some level he thought that it was now okay to let go? Having been through absolute horror with the death of our mum and Andrew I did not want to see him subjected to a similar long and lingering demise. He was a proud and intelligent man and I think he went out of this world the way he would have wanted to go: still full of curiosity and mischief.

I was already scheduled to meet up with my son Jackson later in the day – he was studying in Stockholm – but I asked him to meet me immediately at my hotel. He arrived and knew straight away from my voice and demeanour what had happened. I phoned my dad's sister, my Aunt Doreen, who I'm very close to, and we cried and talked about my dad. It was great having Jackson around. He was due to take photographs of the concert anyway, but I really needed his emotional support. Someone who loved my dad as much as I did and who understood what I was feeling. But it was all so surreal. I'm on that stage trying to remember lyrics but all I could think about was my dad. I had to be professional though and that involves the necessity of being able to mentally compartmentalise and just do your job. In a couple of days we were due to play the Royal Albert Hall. My dad had been organising the guest list for my extended family and he would have been in one of the boxes with my immediate family looking down at the stage. I have to say the audience that night was incredible. I really felt their love, warmth and support. They helped get me get through it.

JW: You've always been a very visual artist. We've touched upon the sleeves with Andrew and the collaborations with Tim Pope. A lot of thought goes into the visual element of the live presentation: on The Comeback Special you worked with lighting and production designer Kate Wilkins and audio-visual collage artist Vicki Bennett (AKA People Like Us) who created the kaleidoscopic video installation for the tour.

MJ: Kate is an old friend. I've known her since 1993 and the Lonely Planet Tour. She designed the Naked Tour visuals as well as our Meltdown concert and was also involved in the two exhibitions for *The Inertia Variations*. She's worked on some huge projects, including the lighting for the opening of the Tate Modern. She's a very creative, positive person and we share similar sensibilities so I put her in charge of the overall look of the stage production for the tour.

I also wanted some large film projections. As this tour was not promoting a new album but was a retrospective I wanted images from my past to the present day. I got to know Vicki through Jim Thirlwell. Her and her partner Peter have since become good friends. Vicki's work is incredible, these intense kaleidoscopic mash-ups. She's an extremely hard worker, very creative and very driven. She's also very funny and a lot of fun to work with, very open-minded and experimental. I gave her a lot of old material to play around with: videos, Super 8 films and photographs etc. but we couldn't sync the visuals to our live performance each night because we don't play to a click track.* As a consequence, images would appear at slightly different times in the songs for each concert. It felt less mechanical that way – more like a living,

---

* A click track is an audio cue which provides a consistent tempo sometimes used by musicians during recording or performances.

organic experience. This was especially true of the Royal Albert Hall concert. I couldn't see it at the time as obviously I am facing the audience, but I'm told that images of my parents came up at some very prescient moments. It wasn't intentional. It just happened. And was magical.

JW: And (and this may be crass) did managing everything yourself ensure that the tour was financially rewarding?

MJ: I'd lost a lot of money on my first three tours, and it really put me on the back foot and into some financial difficulties for a time. Everyone on those tours – and I mean *everyone* – would get paid except for me. I was at the very back of the queue and not only did I *not* get paid but I also lost hundreds of thousands of pounds into the bargain. A lot of incompetence on the management level – put it that way. With this tour Boswell assured me I would *not* lose money. We had decent guarantees and I appointed an uber-efficient tour manager in Levi Tecofsky, who also does an incredible job mixing the front of house sound. He runs a very tight ship and cracks the whip on the rest of the crew – a bit too sadistically at times apparently! But he helped keep the costs under very strict control to ensure a smooth-running tour with no repeats of the financial debacles on earlier tours.

JW: We've spoken about The Comeback Special as a tour, but can we talk about the two elements that have come out of that: the film and the record? We'll start with the film. How did the notion of documenting The Comeback Special concert and working again with Tim Pope arise? Was it something that you discussed, or was it something that he suggested to you?

MJ: So much work went into this tour – it being my first in sixteen years – that I wanted to document it. We had a lot of photographs taken in rehearsals – some by the brilliant John Claridge for instance. We had many photos taken at the concerts themselves too. We'd also decided to record *all* the British shows. So, I involved engineers Mark Allaway from Studio Cinéola and Finnbar Eiles, who I've worked with for many years on Cinéola soundtrack releases. We hired a recording rig and took it with us for the UK tour. So, I wanted at least an audio document but then Tim and I began discussions on making another concert film.

My relationship with Tim has lasted over forty years, back to the mid-eighties. Tim, his wife Victoria and their lovely children are family really. I've always enjoyed working with him. He knows how to get the best out of those he works with. He also has a very clear vision of what he wants. I like working with such people because *you* know that *they* know what they're doing so you can relax in their company.

Our main problem was that we had trouble raising the finance for the film, which was a completely separate entity to the tour. While the tour's finances were working well, thanks to Boswell, we were still trying to find production partners for the film at the eleventh hour but, despite some interest here and there, no one came forward. So, I had to put my hand in my own pocket and fork out tens of thousands to pay for both the recording and the filming. I just thought I had to take this chance. Either we lose this opportunity – and I thought it was a great band and production – or I pay for it. What I didn't realise, of course, was that the emotional drama would be intensified multiple times by my dad dying a couple of days before we were due to appear. Although we recorded all the UK concerts, the Royal Albert Hall was the only one I wanted to film, because it has a certain gravitas.

JW: It's also got a connection with the band as well, because you've played there before on previous tours.

MJ: This was our fourth time performing there and would be our second concert to be filmed there – nearly thirty years apart. I think *The Comeback Special* is a better film with a stronger performance but *THE THE Versus The World* was a good live film in its own right too.

JW: The high ceilings lend themselves to filming. The thing I liked about the film is that it actually feels very intimate. There are not that many shots of the audience; it's mainly on the band. You could, if you weren't there, think that you were playing quite an intimate venue. I think that's because of the way you've rehearsed the band. They're on it and in the pocket. The way Tim films it is very compact. It's only when the cameras pull back later on that you see the size of the audience.

MJ: At the very start you get a few shots from behind Earl, looking outwards, but it's quite dark, so you don't get a sense of the space.

I'm obviously very comfortable working with Tim and his crew. We've worked together so much and I trust him. We have similar aesthetics. We discuss things extensively beforehand and we're pretty much always on the same page.

JW: You've got a good sense of cinema as well, haven't you?

MJ: I hope so. What was interesting this time compared to the first live film was how technology has evolved. In 1990 for *Versus*

The World we had to increase the ambient lighting levels on stage because of the camera technology – it didn't respond sensitively in low-light situations. But with the latest technology we were able to keep the lighting levels as they normally were, so it's more dramatic with a cinematic feel and you get the sense of Kate Wilkins' lighting design, which errs more on the side of theatre.

Tim chooses good people to work with and drills them clearly about what we're going for. He's a bit of a Sergeant Major when he's working. Leading up to the concert was quite intense, my first appearance on a London stage for sixteen years, exacerbated by knowing it was all being recorded. Then – with my dad suddenly dying days before – and having all those cameras on me? There was a *lot* of pressure. But on the night itself, the band and I were barely aware of the cameras. The operators were very discreet around the stage although they did manage to get in close – so you really see the relationship between the musicians – we were very unselfconscious and didn't really notice them at all, which is a testament to Tim.

JW: That's even more impressive, isn't it? Because the film crew have to be really on it.

MJ: To be honest, it was one of our first concerts on that tour and we performed better and better as the tour progressed but listening and watching it back I still think it was a great concert as there was a huge amount of emotional intensity involved from every aspect. You can't fake that.

What was impressive for me – listening back whilst mixing – was how few mistakes there were. I don't think DC made any; James and Barrie made some – as did Earl. I probably made the most. But we didn't change anything. Finnbar and Mark were responsible for recording the concert and mixing the album version, which was done at Studio Cinéola over quite a few months. There are actually three different mixes of the concert: the main, stereo album mix just mentioned – which is the vinyl, CD and streaming version; the 5.1 mix by Matt Lawrence – who also did the television stereo mix.

JW: When the film was coming together, how involved were you in the editing process? Was Tim showing you shots, saying, 'I'm thinking of including this sequence; I'm not sure about that one?'

MJ: He was.

JW: That must have been very collaborative.

MJ: Yes, but Tim and Leigh Brooks – his editor – did the donkey work. They went through all the footage and would send me rough edit ideas to watch and approve. Most of the time I'd be really happy, though there would be times I'd think, 'Ooh, that's a terrible shot', or see something else that didn't work so they would change it for me. Leigh did a great job as well as Tim.

JW: The concert is very well-drilled. There are not a lot of theatrics to it, and I mean that as a compliment. There are no fireworks going off. You play as a band, a really tight band – there isn't a sense that there are egos involved. It's a working band, playing.

MJ: I told Tim I wanted the band members' personalities to come through. It's not all just about me. Yes, I'm the founder and sole permanent member but it is collaborative – they are a great band and they contribute a lot.

JW: There's a nice moment when DC plays the piano solo to 'Uncertain Smile'. He does it, and then you give him the opportunity to have a bit of a wig out. He seems to really enjoy that, when he puts his head on the piano. I imagine for him having to reproduce that solo must have been a tall order.

MJ: There's always this lovely interplay between DC and Earl as they take the song down and bring it back up again. I think that's what works well about this film – there is an intimacy between the band members, and for the viewers it's like being a ghost on the stage, invisibly walking amongst the musicians.

JW: I think, again, that comes from the fact Tim films quite close-up, without getting the sense of this big space, and it feels like a really intimate concert.

I love the way a THE THE concert naturally goes through the history of the band and references different parts of your career. I like the way you introduced a part of *The Inertia Variations* documentary by saying, 'When people ask what I've been doing with my time…' before going into 'We Can't Stop What's Coming'. That was a lovely moment. And a screening of that film was how we met.

MJ: *The Inertia Variations* is the perfect companion to *The Comeback Special*. Johanna persuading me to write a song and me resisting – it became the catalyst. Andrew's death led to 'We Can't Stop What's Coming', through Johanna pushing and encouraging me. The ending of *The Inertia Variations* and finally performing again for the first time in many, many years, led naturally to *The Comeback Special*, particularly as my dad features in the first film. These two films will make a great double-bill at some point.

JW: During the filmed concert, there's also footage on the screen of other members of your family who are no longer with us. I think that also gives it intimacy. I also noticed that in the film you're not a detatched performer – you're very much there to play the songs for an audience.

MJ: We cut out a lot of my interactions with the audience on the live album and film soundtrack mixes as you don't really want all that chat.

JW: When I went to the concert at the Royal Albert Hall, I don't remember a lot of chatting. I think you may have found it hard coming on stage to explain what had happened to your dad. Sometimes you go to concerts and it's the singer just playing along with the audience and getting them to do choruses. There wasn't really any of that, and I liked that. It felt like a grown-up approach. But you're saying you did cut out—

MJ: There was actually quite a bit of chatting but we cut it out to make it leaner. I think what's nice about this band – and the songs and the overall production – is that it has a certain weight and gravitas without even trying because it's now over four decades of songs that so many of our audience know intimately and have grown up with. We've been around a long time and don't have to pretend or distract or indulge in theatrics.

JW: I liked that. I think without theatrics it gives the music a potency. I also like the leanness of it, the professionalism of it. When we were talking about the *Mind Bomb* press shots we were laughing at the fact that everyone was dressed in white T-shirts and jeans. In this, there is a different aesthetic: black, understated clothing.

MJ: Well, just as Manchester United play in red, white and black, every THE THE touring band has always performed in all black. You can look back at all of the photos of all the world tours we've done and the band are always in black. It's our home strip, so to speak, and keeps things instantly identifiable and simple.

JW: You can't go wrong in black.

MJ: Once you've performed in all black… you'll never go back! It does look timeless and if it's good enough for Johnny Cash… Actually, in the very early days in the late seventies we used to wear khaki-coloured military outfits. And once we even wore all white on stage. It was at the end of the Naked Tour at our concert at the Royal Festival Hall in London. I just thought it might make a nice change to perform in our 'away' strip. So, we performed in all-white.

JW: How did you find the premiere of the film at the Troxy because that would've been the first time you'd seen it on a big screen with an audience.

MJ: That was a brilliant night. The Troxy was originally an old art deco cinema – but of course it's not a cinema anymore it's a music venue and the audio for the film soundtrack just played through their regular PA system. We had a great turn-out and there was a phenomenal reaction. I especially enjoyed it as that was a big year birthday-wise for me.

It was memorable watching it with the band as they'd never seen it before. I think initially – as is human nature – they were all checking on themselves – how do I sound? Did I make any mistakes? How do I look? They are normally highly critical but they were all blown away by it and loved it. We stayed up until 11 a.m. the next morning partying. The whole night was fantastic. Maybe added to by the relief – after all the lockdowns and paranoia – of being back in the 'land of the living'. Tim and I both received great feedback. Like a lot of these things, you never know what to expect – you try your hardest, you do your best and you hope people are going to like it, but you never know.

JW: At the Troxy screening there was someone who put their hand up and asked a question. She was sat in front of me – she was 19 or 20, and she'd just gotten into your music, and of course she wouldn't have seen you live before. She was seeing you live for the first time on the screen. Are you hoping that it's going to attract both the people that know the live experience, and also attract people who may not have seen THE THE? Because you're a great live band.

MJ: I'd hope that would be the case because you always want to attract new generations of listeners. Hopefully this film will help.

JW: Did you look at other concert films that seemed to capture the spirit of a live performance? Something like Prince's *Purple Rain* (1984) isn't a concert film, but it's got concert footage in it, and really, to be honest, the only good thing about *Purple Rain* is the footage of him live. Were there other films that you thought, yes, this is an element that I'd like to try and replicate?

MJ: No, is the short answer.

JW: A very short answer!

MJ: A rude answer! Although, I do recall back in the late eighties, just before the Versus The World Tour, I'd purchased a VHS of *The Doors: Live at the Hollywood Bowl*. What I loved about it – and it stuck in my mind – was although they were on a big stage they were all quite close together physically. And there were no theatricals or bullshit rock show lighting effects – just four guys performing. It was brilliant.

For this tour I wanted us to be sonically stripped-down and as physically close together as we could reasonably get, playing through small 15-watt amps, no samplers, sequencers or auto-cues. Just old-school without being overly stylised. When we started rehearsing – as I mentioned before – we sat close together in a circle on some old wooden fold-up chairs at my place, almost knee to knee. Gradually, as we worked things out we sat back a bit and brought the amplifiers in but I wanted to try and maintain that aesthetic, that closeness.

JW: How difficult was it going through the mixing and editing process – songs were in and then they were out; other songs were out, then they were in? What was the method by which you whittled down not only what you would perform in the concerts, but what would make its way into the film and to the live record?

MJ: They *all* made their way into the record and film. It is the whole concert. I spoke about this at length with Max Vaccaro – who heads our partner label earMUSIC – and I took his advice. He said that if we had taken anything out, people would've complained. And I think he was right.

In terms of what songs made it into the setlist itself, certain ones like 'GIANT', 'Good Morning Beautiful' and 'The Mercy Beat' we just couldn't do with this particular concept – being so stripped down and simplified. Next tour I'd like to do at least some of them.

JW: Can you talk more about the live record you released of the tour? As with Tim Pope's movie, were there specific influences or reference points?

MJ: I tried not to be influenced by other live records, although there are some truly great ones out there. When growing up Andrew was a huge fan of *Slade Alive!* He used to play that all the time. It's a great live album and I remember tracks like 'Darling Be Home Soon' and 'Born To Be Wild' and Noddy Holder's powerful voice and their ecstatic audience. But we're not Slade and I wasn't specifically thinking of anyone else during the making of *The Comeback Special*.

JW: The reason I ask is that for some bands a live album can feel like a contractual obligation. A bit like a Greatest Hits compilation. But for other artists a live album is an artistic statement in its own right. I am thinking of Tom Waits and *Glitter and Doom* (2009), Talking Heads and *Stop Making Sense* (1984), James Brown's *Live at the Apollo* (1963) to name but three. I imagine that you see the album as an artistic statement in its own right.

MJ: Most definitely. It's actually our first officially released live album – something I should have done many years ago. Bizarrely, we released a full-length *film* of the Versus The World Tour but with no actual album release to accompany it. I cannot remember what my thinking was behind that decision but it was pretty stupid of me to say the least.

JW: Just to be clear, the album replicates the film in terms of including the same songs, although there is some chat with the audience in the album version that isn't in the film version and vice versa.

MJ: It's not *exactly* the same but pretty much the same. For instance, speaking about my dad. That was at the beginning of the film to provide context but I didn't include on the album. With a record, people are just going to skip over the talking. They don't want that much talking. We just left in some little bits here and there for atmosphere.

JW: Have you left between-song applause? Because some live albums take that out, and I don't think it feels like a live album if you do that.

MJ: Why would you not leave in the sound of the audience on a live album? They are an essential part of the concert. With our recording you really do get a sense of where you are as we placed microphones in the audience.

JW: That's something you're very hands-on about, isn't it? The mixing.

MJ: I don't do the mixing myself. I've got excellent engineers who I let get on with it but, of course, I oversee it. Finnbar Eiles did a terrific job. As did Mark Allaway. Before we started mixing we listened to a few live albums that had been recorded at the Albert Hall. We were surprised how bad some of them were – quite mushy sound-wise. *The Comeback Special* record almost sounds studio-quality, I think.

JW: You want clarity, don't you?

MJ: Yes. We had good feeds from each of the musicians. Obviously having great musicians helps, because they've got great tone coming out of their hands, instruments and amplifiers to start with. Also, mixing at Studio Cinéola we were able to do it over several months – not continuously but working on it a few days solidly, going away for a few weeks, then coming back to repeat the cycle. It was a luxury. Years ago, in a commercial studio, I'd have to get it mixed within a week or so and that would be that; if we made mistakes we often couldn't remedy them. So, with this, we chipped away gradually, to sculpt the sound so it feels studio quality but of course, it is very much live. You can hear the interaction between the instruments and the audience. I'm very happy with it.

When I was putting together the set list for this tour I wasn't thinking about a possible live album. But if you put together a strong enough show then the live album will take care of itself. There were certain songs we knew could not be dropped: 'This Is The Day', 'Uncertain Smile' and 'Heartland', for instance, are bedrocks of my catalogue. We tried a huge number of songs during rehearsals but some just didn't feel right for this particular line-up. We did tweak the setlist for the American leg of the tour though, by replacing 'Phantom Walls' with 'I Saw The Light'. As a tour progresses you know from the feedback of the audience when you need to add some pace or when to allow a lull. 'Phantom Walls' remains one of my favourites of the live recordings, but it's so quiet and contemplative and whilst playing it live I'd sometimes hear people in the audience talking. It's such a sensitive song for me and it felt like it was being disrespected by certain members of the audience so I took it out of the firing line.

What I did not want to do on The Comeback Special Tour was to just repeat the existing album recordings. Rather, we deconstructed the songs, stripped them down to their essence on just an acoustic guitar and rebuilt them. I didn't want the tour to sound like some eighties revival band – forever trapped in aspic. They had to feel contemporary and fresh. I need to feel excited as a performer otherwise it's all just going through the motions. You're then cheating yourself as well as the audience. However, there was one song I wanted to be very similar to its album version – that was 'Uncertain Smile'. DC asked me if he could just do his own thing on the keyboard but I had to say, 'No. I'm sorry but you need you to learn it note for note.' His face dropped a bit but the audience know that solo so intimately. Credit to DC as he learned it perfectly after practising and practising. It was ironic really as Jools Holland had originally improvised it.

JW: I love what Pete Paphides noticed about your relationship with DC, who wrote the foreword to *The Comeback Special*:

> Fifty-eight minutes into THE THE's Royal Albert Hall show in 2018, Matt Johnson takes a moment to wander among

his bandmates as they negotiate the instrumental break of 'This Is The Day'. As his keyboard player DC Collard takes his solo, Matt gazes on at him. The song is soaked into their bones. Its memory lives in the muscles of every musician on stage. So, all things considered, it can look after itself for a few seconds. And although there's no exchange of words, the expression directed by Matt at his old friend is freighted with over three decades of shared experiences and also perhaps the relief and delight that comes from realising that this still feels good. That when you combine the right songs with the right musicians and an audience that never forgot, it's like coming home.

JW: Though the concert at the Royal Albert Hall took place in 2018, the filmed and recorded release of *The Comeback Special* did not come out until 2021. Was there a sense that, due to the delays caused by the COVID-19 lockdowns, it changed the way you approached the mix and edit?

MJ: Definitely. We just chipped away at it over an extended period. It made for a stronger album. The film itself was edited by Tim and Leigh and they did a very thorough job. Although, as I said, we couldn't find partners to help fund the filming – which was financed by Cinéola in the end – we did end up signing a partnership agreement with earMUSIC to release it.

JW: Where are they based?

MJ: Hamburg, Germany. We signed a partnership deal, licensing *The Comeback Special* and the next studio album. We're really enjoying working with them. A great team of people.

JW: What was it that made you go with them? I imagine you had quite a lot of others interested.

MJ: Well, there is an interesting story. It was all down to Max Vaccaro the general manager at earMUSIC. Max is Italian but has lived in Germany for years. He's a lovely man and is a genuine fan and collector of music. You remember those old-school record company heads from years ago? Before accountants and lawyers took over the industry? I have many good friends who are accountants and lawyers so obviously nothing against them or their professions but they shouldn't be running record companies. Years ago, you actually used to have people who *listened* to music and would get behind projects on a hunch or gut instinct because they *loved* music. He's one of those.

JW: Was he a THE THE fan?

MJ: Yes. Max actually approached me many years ago about working together. But I wasn't sure at the time as I was not sure what I wanted to do or how I wanted to do it. Even though I was completely out of the game back then – and was at quite a low ebb – he was very keen. He'd personally collected my records for years and really wanted us to work together. Fast forward a few years: we announced The Comeback Special and concerts started selling out everywhere in minutes – then out of nowhere I had representatives from every major label in the UK contacting me about signing a deal – even representatives from many of the larger indie labels too.

JW: That must have been quite nice.

MJ: It was *very* nice. I met up with a few of them but then I reflected, who do I really want to work with – a person who has been showing genuine interest in me even when I was at a really low ebb, or people who are only showing interest when I'm at a bit of a high point? Another contributing factor was when Gillian introduced me to her dad Roger – some of whose songs I covered in Road Star – and over luncheon he told me that Max and earMUSIC have been the best record company that Deep Purple has ever had, which was good enough recommendation for me. I really like Max and know I made the right decision to work with him and his team. So far, we've all been delighted with how our partnership is developing.

JW: You've also managed to retain your rights.

MJ: These days I will only do licensing deals. All my new copyrights – recording and publishing – are owned by Cinéola and Lazarus respectively. I've been trying to right the wrongs of earlier career mistakes and am working hard to regain ownership of my old copyrights too. I've been successful with a few so far and I'm still chipping away at the rest.

My team in London maintains the Cinéola identity within the partnership deal. We have full creative control and earMUSIC are absolutely fine with that. It's a really good collaboration.

JW: Let's talk about the sleeve. I was there when you were looking at images for the sleeve, and you've chosen such an iconic image. I know you were very particular about getting the colour right. You've really got an eye for detail. You follow things through properly. It's a great sleeve.

MJ: It was taken by the photographer Steve Collins. He's been very helpful and generous in sharing images with us. He sent some through and as soon as I saw that particular photo I knew it was the front cover. Everything about it was perfect, including my Gretsch Country Club guitar and little Vox AC15 amp. It just looked like a classic album sleeve and perfectly reflected the mood of the concerts. We then took the image to our designer, Martin Lewis. As usual he made some great suggestions including different versions highlighting elements within the composition. So, all the different formats contained a slight variation, with most of the image in black and white with just the microphone stand, or the guitar in colour etc. We had the triple-vinyl, luxury CD book, standard CD, Blu-ray, DVD and a beautiful coffee table book and box set.

CHAPTER TWELVE

Brain Fevered, Body Limp, In Altered States The Truth Is Glimpsed

COVID-19 brings more reflection and Matt is able to indulge his love of London as quiet returns to its streets. However, a medical emergency brings a brush with the Grim Reaper. Matt's natural tendency to question authority also sees trial by social media. Freedom of speech is rebranded as hate speech and intolerance as fascism starts to rise again in the west.

JW: You had a period of illness. Things got very serious I understand.

MJ: It came amidst one of the strangest years of my life – and I've had a few strange years. Then again, 2020 was one of the strangest years of most peoples' lives. We saw the lockdowns appear on the horizon – then they happened. We then witnessed panic-buying sprees of pasta, paracetamol and toilet rolls. A very strange atmosphere swiftly swept across the country – across the world – and it brought out both the best and the worst in people.

Helen, George and I decided to stay in London rather than head for the hills. It was the right decision because London suddenly became *our* city again. It was deserted. It felt like being in a sci-fi disaster film from the 1970s – or inside a very strange dream. I actually spent more time outside than I had done in ages.

Matt & Johanna St Michaels in Mallorca, 1995.

ack and his dad in Mallorca, 2002. Photo by Johanna St Michaels.

Helen Edwards & Matt in Mallorca, 2007. Photo by Justine Chiara.

George and his dad in Mallorca, 2023. Photo by Helen Edwards.

Radio Cinéola cityscape graphic designed by Thomas Feiner.

Radio Cinéola broadcast, 2015, with Daniel Moyler, Johanna St Michaels, Matt and Pam Esterson.

Portrait of Matt's younger brother, Gerard, by Conor Masterson.

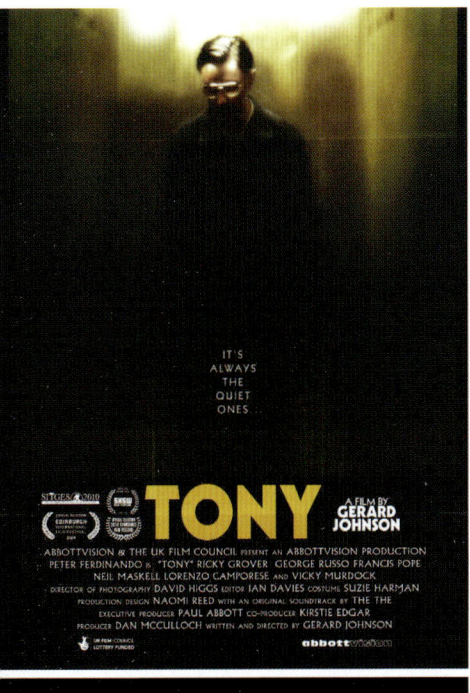

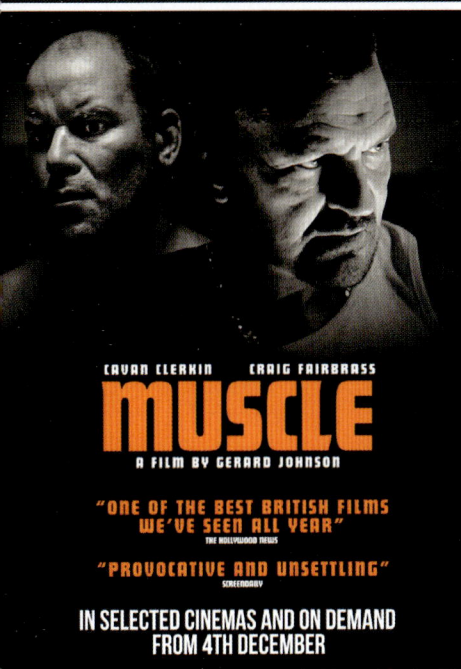

Posters for feature films directed by Gerard Johnson. *Tony* & *Odyssey* posters designed by Gary Dalton.

Tim Pope and Matt promoting *The Comeback Special* film in Suffolk, 2021. Photo by Gillian Glover.

Jools Holland and Matt in London, 2025. Photo by Gillian Glover.

Random assorted reprobates, including Jim Thirlwell, Johnny Marr, Peter Ferdinando, Tim Pope, Ian Tregoning, Vicki Bennett, Jason Wood, Zeke Manyika, Mark Allaway, Paul Boswell, Gillian Glover, Justine Chiara, Colin Lloyd Tucker, Nick Freeston and Paul Webb.

THE THE's traditional pre-concert team talk and huddle during the Ensouled Tour, 2025. James Eller, Earl Harvin, Barrie Cadogan, DC Collard, Matt. Photo by Julian Hayr.

Performing at Heartland Festival in Denmark, 2025. Photo by Julian Hayr.

Lots of long walks and cycle rides. The weather during that first lockdown was sensational. Clear blue skies, no planes or trains, just quiet, empty streets. It was wonderful.

JW: Against an awful backdrop of suffering it was a period perhaps unlike any other.

MJ: It was. But about six weeks into the first lockdown I woke up with a bit of a sore throat. I was generally feeling a bit rough and achy and also a bit anxious. I took echinacea, garlic, ginseng, ginger, lemon and honey etc. all the normal stuff I'd do. This was on a Thursday morning. By Friday the pain hadn't gone away. By Saturday it was worse. It was mainly around my ear at this point, but only on one side. I took ibuprofen and paracetamol alternatively, used a hot water bottle on it but nothing helped.

On the Saturday evening I did something I'm convinced led to the crisis – though doctors said otherwise. I have a powerful muscle massager called a Hyper-volt, which is designed for athletes to use on aching muscles after training hard – not really for lazy musicians! But I used it on my neck area because nothing else was helping. This did seem to relieve the pain a bit at the time, but I woke Sunday morning feeling much worse. The pain was now radiating intensely around my whole throat and neck. I spoke to Helen and we decided to call 111.* I was prescribed penicillin over the phone. As the day wore on I felt worse and worse. We called 111 again and they advised me to go straight to A&E. As we seemed to be approaching the peak of this pandemic I really didn't want to go to hospital if I could help it. Helen, George and I went but after allowing me through the doors they turned my family away. Then began two weeks of horror.

The hospital I first went to, Homerton in Hackney, did an MRI scan and blood tests but by 11 p.m. told me it was very serious and they didn't have the facilities to deal with it. So, they sent me by ambulance to the Royal London Hospital in Whitechapel. I arrived into a really strange atmosphere. It was actually quite

---

* 111 is a free-to-call, non-emergency medical helpline operating in the UK.

deserted and in semi-darkness, everyone was masked and in a very subdued mood. An ear, nose and throat specialist saw me and I had to undergo a highly unpleasant procedure where a small camera was forced down my nose and into my throat. He was able to detect a pharyngeal abscess. He said I'd need an operation but I was reluctant and informed him that I was a singer and didn't want one. I was then placed in a cold, dark ward alone. When I tried to speak my voice sounded like Donald Duck on helium. It would have been funny if it wasn't so frightening. I then began to fear I was going to need a tracheotomy or similar as the abscess was expanding – up against my windpipe and vocal chords – and my neck was swelling.

The next morning, I was placed on an antibiotic drip and given codeine for the pain. Within a couple of days – and after having another MRI scan – they noted the infection was subsiding. They took me off the drip and put me on oral antibiotics, with the inference that I'd be allowed home the next day. I was feeling a little better and much cheered. This was Wednesday.

But that night was one of the worst of my life. The oral antibiotics were obviously not powerful enough and the infection absolutely roared back. As the night wore on my neck swelled to twice its normal size, my face was bright red and it felt like a small python was wrapped around my windpipe and tightening its grip. I was really struggling. I called the nurse but in the hierarchy of a hospital they can't do that much without the permission of the doctors. The nurse was very worried and tried repeatedly to contact a doctor all through the early hours of the night – to no avail. I obviously needed more than just painkillers but there were no doctors around to help! I was really starting to feel my own mortality. I've had friends and family go into hospital and die unexpectedly so I started to wonder whether my time had come.

JW: I hadn't realised at the time that it was that serious. Certainly not that it was life threatening.

MJ: But then something strange happened. I actually started to drift into an extremely calm zen-like state. Something deep inside told me I had plenty more life left in the tank and to be positive. I made it through that night in extreme discomfort and in the morning explained the situation to the junior doctors doing their rounds. I was still adamant I didn't want an operation though as I was so paranoid about losing my voice – just get me back on that drip! I was informed that I was in fact now booked in for an emergency operation later that day. They did also put me back on the antibiotic drip in the meantime.

The main surgeon was an impressive man. He gathered with his team around my bed – who all obviously had deep respect for him as they were hanging on his every word. He spoke in a quiet but very solemn manner and explained again the need to operate. When I protested, that I was a singer and frightened of losing my voice, he simply said, 'This is no longer about tone of voice – this is now a matter of life or death.' It chilled my bones. Without an operation immediately, it was made quite clear that I may find myself in a situation where I have thirty minutes to live and a medical team just wouldn't be able to get to me in time. Having just gone through the previous night's torture when the nurse spent hours trying to find a doctor without success I quickly agreed to the operation. Yes, I was worried my career as a singer would be over – but some things are more important than a career.

JW: It must have been a terrifying and sobering experience.

MJ: The operation lasted over three hours. When I came around I felt like I was in a military field hospital. I've been very high on drugs in the past but this was off the scale intense. I was completely out of my head, with various tubes up my nose and in my arms – and a catheter – and I couldn't move a muscle. I was in the intensive care/recovery ward. To deal with COVID-19 patients – who were in a separate, quarantined floor of the hospital – they'd drafted in nurses from across the NHS to work on other floors, so you had dental nurses and orthopaedic nurses helping out.

The noise in the room was an absolute cacophony, everyone wired up to noisy machines, lots of shouting and screaming. It was bedlam. Directly opposite were police with radios blaring, surrounding a man who'd been stabbed. There was another man opposite who was about to have his leg amputated, shrieking with pain. On the bed to my left was someone speaking through an interpreter. Chaos. I was in that ward for three days yet I never saw the same staff member twice. People would do their shift and then disappear off somewhere else. I couldn't eat through my mouth because of the huge, gaping wound in my throat, so I had a feeding tube stuffed down my nose. It was a very disturbing experience.

After a few days I was wheeled off to another ward, still off

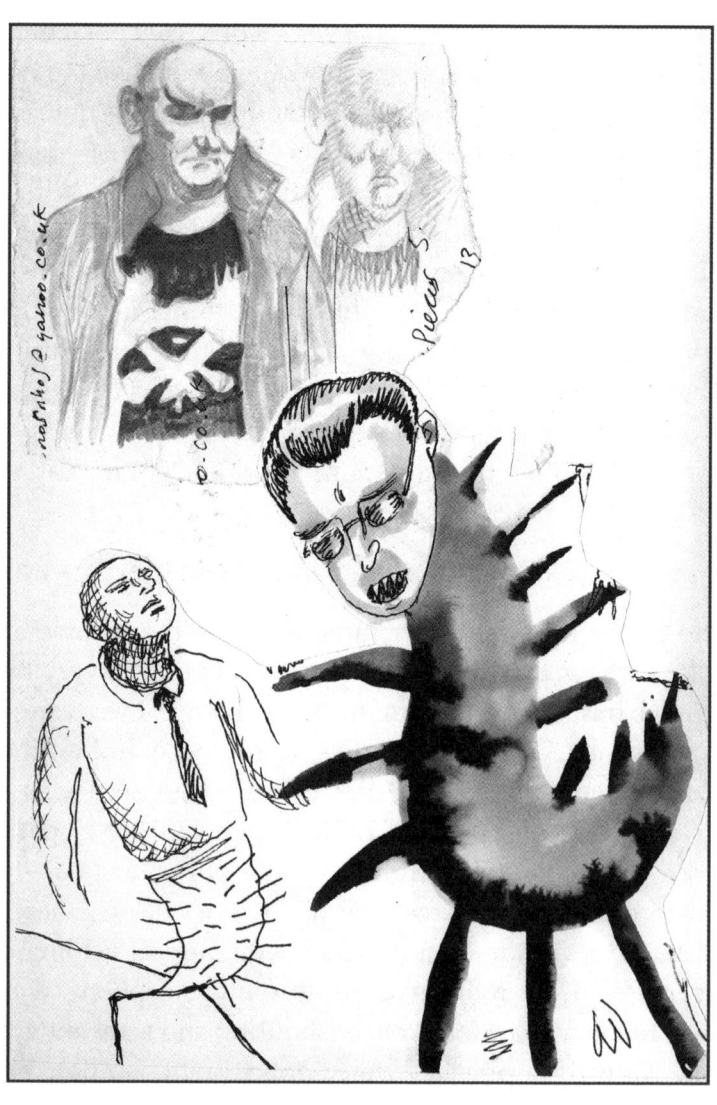

my head on morphine and disorientated. All staff were masked and seemed distant and emotionless. The new ward I was placed in was the trauma ward. It was dark and cold. I was alone. I could hear staff talking outside but I struggled to understand what they were saying – it transpired they were speaking Bulgarian! I remembered accounts I'd read about the experiences of people who had temporarily died but their ego had refused to accept death. This seemed to chime with my disorientation and the distant behaviour of all these staff, and the fact I couldn't see any family or friends. I was starting to feel like Bruce Willis' character in *The Sixth Sense*! For a few moments I actually thought I'd died and was in a waiting room between this world and the next.

In the middle of the night they wheeled me into yet another room on this ward. When I woke up in hazy, semi-darkness I saw a giant pelican making sudden movements across the ward. I tried not to freak out. It turned out to be a chap named Aboul doing his morning exercises, dressed in white robes and hopping about the ward in a crouched position. He'd gone in to have brain surgery. He was very friendly but extremely intense. He just wouldn't stop talking. All I wanted was to be left alone with my own thoughts so I'd draw the curtains around my bed and write in my notebook. That was actually when I started to write the words to what would become 'Linoleum Smooth To The Stockinged Foot'.

JW: Were you completely alone at this time? Or were you able to keep loved ones informed? Visitors must have been kept to a minimum.

MJ: Visitors? No one was allowed to visit me. But by this point I had a small WhatsApp group with Helen, Gerard and Jackson and I was texting them my daily experiences. This contact helped keep me sane as they were trying to motivate me from a distance. Adrian Whiteson – my long-term doctor – was also phoning on a daily basis to give me pep talks. Gillian was also texting daily, trying to keep my spirits up and distract me with positive work-related news to keep me looking forwards.

JW: When did it become clear that you were no longer at risk of death?

MJ: After that successful operation. They had to leave my wound open so all the poison could seep out. I had to sleep propped up, virtually upright, which was starting to give me terrible pain in my ribs. I was also developing a cough and of course every time I did cough nurses would quickly rush over to test me in case I had COVID.

Several days later they were able to take one drain out of the wound, leaving just two, but they said I'd have to remain in hospital for at least another week. As the days wore on I asked to come off the morphine because it was making me very uncomfortable and spaced-out. Everything seemed drenched in crimson and I started feeling paranoid. Unusual for me because I normally enjoy drugs but I was having the most bizarre daydreams – hallucinations really – that involved Joseph Merrick the Elephant Man, Bach's Toccata and Fugue in D minor running through my head, and visions of things that may – or may not – have happened in the former hospital on this site in Whitechapel in Victorian London.

JW: What else can you recall of this period or is it mostly a haze?

MJ: I was on several antibiotics at this point and the combination gave everything a highly unpleasant metallic taste and smell. I couldn't stand being fed through the nose anymore so I asked to have solid food. They used to bring me what looked like baby food and I'd try to eat it but all I could taste were the chemicals. It used to make me heave. So, I had to go back on the feeding tube. But it was vile slop if it went in via the mouth *or* the nose. Another example of private companies earning God knows how many millions of pounds of tax-payers money for doing a terrible job. They should put Jamie Oliver* in charge of deciding who gets

---

* Chef Jamie Oliver launched a campaign to help improve school meals and raise awareness of child nutrition, prompting government investment (Institute for Social and Economic Research, 2009; *The Guardian*, 2010).

the lucrative catering contracts for the NHS. As Hippocrates said, 'Let food be thy medicine and medicine be thy food.'

As I started to improve I spoke to a few more patients in the ward, including a lovely man named Muhammad who was in there for a serious spinal operation and could barely move. We struck up a nice rapport and would humorously complain to each other about Aboul's constant chatter.

JW: What else did you witness in terms of medical emergencies? It wasn't all COVID-related.

MJ: Being in a trauma ward you'd see people being wheeled in who were in a terrible state, particularly as the hospital was also the base for the London Air Ambulance Service. I'd often hear the low, pulsating vibration of the helicopter descending onto the roof a couple of floors above and knew some poor soul had suffered terrible, probably life-altering injuries. This helped put my own situation in perspective. I found it all a deeply emotional experience. In the early hours one night I heard a young boy being brought in – he must have been around 16 or 17 – who had been involved in a terrible accident. I think it may have involved a stolen car or something as the police were at the hospital discussing with the nurses.

The curtains were around my bed so I couldn't see but I overheard an awful phone call. A specially-trained councillor – a woman with a gentle Irish voice – speaking to the mother of this very seriously injured boy. His injuries were so bad it seemed he'd never walk again – assuming he'd even survive. I started to sob listening to this because it reminded me of when the police came to the house of my parents to inform them Eugene had died. I remember the effect upon my poor parents. I was sobbing for the poor mother at the other end of this shocking phone call, being talked through the horrors of her son's situation by this councillor with the most kind, loving voice. I found it so upsetting and disturbing yet also felt my heart open up with waves of intense empathy. I couldn't stop crying.

JW: When did you start to feel that you were on the mend?

MJ: A few days after the operation I was able to walk around. Wearing a gown and surgical stockings – a drip on a small trolley attached to my arm – I would go shuffling around the linoleum-lined corridors during the day and late at night. I instinctively knew I had to drink lots of water and keep my lymphatic system moving to flush the poisons from my body. I was up on the eighth floor and during my regular walks through the corridors I'd peer out the windows, down at the trees and birds, and feel this overwhelming, visceral yearning for nature. I was desperate to breathe fresh air again. The air in the wards was so heavily filtered, sterile and dead. I felt suffocated.

I was desperate to go home. After a few more days they agreed to let me leave but – as anyone who has been in hospital will know – the administration moves slowly and I was trapped for a while longer. Eventually I said my goodbyes to the other patients on my ward and to the wonderful NHS staff who had so kindly cared for me – and without whom I would not be here to tell this tale. I clearly remember wanting that moment – when I finally walked out of those hospital doors – to always stay with me. To remember that feeling of breathing fresh air, the sunshine on my face, the sight of my family again. I felt so weak though, as if I were a 90-year-old man. The doctors advised it would be at least a month before I could really do anything. And that I must not even *attempt* to sing for at least six months. I was finally back with Helen and George, slowly enjoying proper food again, but I clearly recall not wanting to forget that yearning for nature – for trees, plants, animals, water, air – that I had felt so keenly from deep within my soul.

JW: That must have been a relief.

MJ: It was. This experience felt like a shot across the bow. A reminder of the fragility of life. I'm very lucky it wasn't worse. As unpleasant as it was, it was nothing compared to what I've witnessed some family members and close friends endure.

JW: How did you make use of your time immediately after release?

MJ: We were renting an apartment in the Barbican at that time and during the recovery period over the next few months I'd go for these lovely walks with George, then 8 years old. The two of us walking slowly, hand in hand, through the private gardens there. We would sit together for hours, feeding the fish, ducks, moorhens and pigeons. It was a wonderful feeling to be close to water, trees and animals, in the fresh air with my beautiful little boy. I developed an almost-childlike appreciation not only of nature but also family and friends. I never want to lose that feeling – they are the most important things in life.

My main anxiety was how it would affect my voice. I took the doctor's advice very seriously and did not sing for over six months. Funny enough the first time I sang was at Tim and Victoria Pope's New Year's Eve karaoke party where I sang 'Suspicious Minds'. God, it felt great! The timbre and tone of my voice sounded the same as it ever did. I was so lucky to have had a very good surgeon. The wound took several weeks to close though. It's known as healing by granulation – when a wound is so big you have to allow it to heal from the inside out rather than try and stitch it up. It was quite disturbing looking in the mirror to see this huge hole in my throat looking back at me!

Several things helped keep me going when in hospital: seeing my family and friends again and also the prospect of purchasing a Condor bicycle – it's vital to think of positive things in the future when going through something daunting in the present. A few years earlier I'd been at a local street market when a young man offered me an obviously freshly stolen Condor racing bike. It was gleaming beautifully in its gun-metal grey livery and was offered for a very low price. But I just couldn't do it. I was thinking of the poor sod who'd just found out it was stolen. Anyway, I'd always wanted one so as soon as I was out of the hospital I shuffled down to their show rooms in Holborn and spoke with a lovely man there called Julian – who put me in mind of you, funnily enough! He helped me design my own Condor – though I wanted a tourer not a racer. It took several months to arrive and then I was out on this bike endlessly – countless nights throughout the rest of the lockdowns. It was pure joy, cycling around a completely deserted Parliament Square, Soho, Buckingham Palace, Bank of England. It was a dream world.

JW: That sounds wonderful! To what extent do you think these experiences impacted your creative process – which was beginning to stir?

MJ: In terms of how it affected what I wrote about? Those sensations, that yearning – when you feel you are perhaps on your death bed – does have a magical effect upon your priorities. From this experience, I think there may be a subtlety added to my writing and performances.

JW: You had also started to publicly express concerns about the way the government and media were handling the pandemic.

MJ: Look, I don't want to trigger readers as I'm aware how sensitive many still are about the subject we're about to discuss and that they may just shut down and switch off. But I do feel it's worth talking about.

There is an old quote from the Scottish writer Charles Mackay* that perfectly summed up this period: 'Men, it has been well said, think in herds; it will be seen that they go mad in herds, while they only recover their senses slowly, and one by one.' 2020 was like being trapped in an episode of *The Prisoner*,† where questioning authority was the ultimate crime.

The pandemic was the most divisive period in living memory and nobody wants to go through that again. Families and friendships were torn apart as the public were subjected to a relentless onslaught of behavioural science-fuelled propaganda and 'nudging'.

---

* Charles Mackay was a Scottish journalist, poet and social commentator. The line appears in his 1841 work *Extraordinary Popular Delusions and the Madness of Crowds*, in which he analysed historical episodes of mass hysteria.

† *The Prisoner* was a surreal British TV series in which Patrick McGoohan's ex-agent is held in a strange village where people are stripped of their identities.

SPI-B* encouraged fear-based emotional cues to boost compliance – an approach later described by some as ethically questionable – and this contributed to feelings of pressure and mistrust among parts of the public, who felt they were being steered and manipulated rather than informed. A recent investigation by the *Telegraph* alleges that England's Chief Medical Officer side-lined the government's ethics advisory group, MEAG, after it raised concerns about COVID policies.†

It was disturbing to watch how anxiety, repetition, and peer pressure could so easily sweep entire communities into a single mindset. Dissenting voices became rare, and independent thought disappeared almost overnight – it was a masterclass in behavioural science techniques. Anyone who dared ask even the most innocuous questions was publicly jeered or shamed and met with hostility, ridicule, and pejorative labels. It was an episode of mass hysteria.

JW: And trusted and supposedly partisan media outlets were worthy of circumspection?

MJ: I remember a revealing exchange in a famous interview between Noam Chomsky and BBC journalist Andrew Marr back in 1996. Marr was defending himself by exclaiming, 'How can you know I'm self-censoring?' Chomsky replied, 'I'm not saying you *are* self-censoring. I'm sure you believe everything you say. But what I'm saying is, if you believed something different, you wouldn't be sitting where you're sitting.' It summed up corporate media more succinctly than anything I'd seen before or since and certainly coloured the way I viewed the media's handling of the crisis.

The atmosphere became increasingly strange, with many contradictions. One red flag arose – not immediately, but a few months after the mRNA COVID19 vaccines were rolled out under

---

* SPI-B is the behavioural-science subgroup of SAGE, which advised the UK government on public communication and behavioural responses during the pandemic, reportedly advising that 'the perceived level of personal threat needs to be increased ... using hardhitting emotional messaging'. (SPIB, 22 Mar 2020).
† *Telegraph*, 6 Dec 2025; MEAG remit and membership: GOV.UK; MEAG referenced in UK Covid-19 Inquiry documents (INQ000474302).

Emergency Use Authorisation – when mainstream media began assuring the public that the vaccines were 'safe for pregnant women.' * This followed the UK JCVI's April 2021 guidance, which advised that pregnant women could be offered vaccination. Prior to COVID19, vaccine development typically took 5-10 years or more, including early research, phased clinical trials, and long-term follow-up. No mRNA COVID19 vaccine had undergone such multi-year trials, and long-term pregnancy-specific safety data did not exist. Without that data, how could anyone – or any organisation – know the impact on pregnant women and their unborn children? It seemed a strange claim to make so authoritatively. Instead of adjusting the narrative to fit the facts, were the facts now being reshaped to fit the narrative?

JW: You remained a critic of the willingness to take government directives at face value.

MJ: Yes. Many questions – harshly ridiculed at the time – later turned out to be grounded in reality. Officials *did* eventually acknowledge that protection waned quickly and that vaccinated people could still catch *and* transmit the virus. Even the promise of 'just two doses' for protection quietly morphed into an endless cycle of boosters. Fears of side-effects that were initially dismissed – myocarditis† in young men, and the AstraZeneca-related clotting disorder‡ – *were* also eventually acknowledged. Fears raised about the prospect of a Digital ID control grid being assembled were – at the time – brushed aside as the paranoid ramblings of

---

* UK guidance in April 2021 allowed COVID19 vaccination for pregnant women; major media, including the BBC and *The Guardian*, reported the vaccines as safe (JCVI, 2021; PHE, 2021; BBC, 2021; *The Guardian*, 2021).

† Public health agencies, including the UK's Medicines and Healthcare products Regulatory Agency (MHRA) and the US Centers for Disease Control and Prevention (CDC) in the US confirmed that mRNA vaccines have been linked to myocarditis, most often in young males.

‡ The MHRA (Medicines and Healthcare products Regulatory Agency) and the European Medicines Agency (EMA) formally acknowledged that the AstraZeneca (ChAdOx1 nCoV-19) vaccine can cause a rare but serious clotting condition known as Vaccine-induced Immune Thrombotic Thrombocytopenia (VITT) or Thrombosis with Thrombocytopenia Syndrome (TTS).

'tin-foil-hat'-wearing cranks. Yet many governments *are* now swiftly unveiling Digital ID systems as part of their official policy agenda – at great expense and against massive public opposition I might add. With hindsight, many of the voices labelled 'irrational' were simply asking questions that would later be accepted as level-headed.

JW: Do you think there was a profit motive behind this?

MJ: Big Pharma's interest in public health appears about as sincere as an arms dealer's interest in world peace. And, you only need to think back a few years to understand why a sizable minority remain sceptical of the claims of the authorities too. In the UK, regulators – including the MHRA and its predecessors – have often faced criticism for offering confident reassurances long before the full dangers were understood. Thalidomide, contaminated blood, sodium valproate, pesticides, PFAS, endocrine disruptors: these are grim, persistent examples that many people point to. Across the Atlantic, the FDA has been equally scrutinised over tobacco, DDT, asbestos, OxyContin and the opioid crisis, SSRIs and adolescent suicidality, and Vioxx. To many observers, the pattern is clear: reassurance comes early, but accountability only after the damage is done – if at all.

Yet there is a sizeable percentage who are *still* reluctant to disbelieve anything the authorities tell them despite what official disclosures have since revealed, e.g. the numerous instances where senior politicians or advisers, including Prime Minister Boris Johnson, did not comply with the authoritarian restrictions they were imposing on everyone else. In one particularly draconian edict, members of the public were barred from even comforting dying relatives in hospital. Meanwhile, government gatherings – including drinks parties and discos – were reportedly taking place in breach of those rules.* I'm surprised there has not been more public outrage.

---

* "Partygate" refers to lockdown-breaking gatherings in Downing Street during 2020–2021. Sue Gray's official report (May 2022) found repeated breaches of COVID rules, a permissive culture of drinking, and serious failures of leadership by senior officials. The police issued 126 fines, including to the Prime Minister.

Even many 'fact-checking' sites that claimed impartiality were revealed to be funded by foundations with a stake in maintaining certain viewpoints.* Over time, the whole situation began to feel less like a public health response and more like a mass psychological experiment – Hegelian dialectics at work, keeping the population confused, distracted, and compliant.

JW: At the same time, there was a united front globally amongst the political class…

MJ: Yes, all of a sudden, we had world leader after world leader suddenly repeating the same, odd mantra: 'Build Back Better', 'Build Back Better'. Biden, Johnson, Macron, Merkel, Trudeau and others just kept repeating 'Build Back Better'. It was like *The Stepford Wives* – as if they were all suddenly activated on cue – and reading a pre-prepared script. Many were from the World Economic Forum's 'Young Global Leaders' programme mentioned

---

* Fact-checking sites such as PolitiFact (funded by the Poynter Institute and Knight Foundation), Snopes (venture and private backing) and FactCheck.org (Annenberg Public Policy Center) have funding sources which some observers argue could influence perspective.

previously. Actually, talking of the WEF we also had its chairman Klaus Schwab – like a Bond villain straight out of Central Casting – aggressively promoting his book *COVID-19: The Great Reset* (2020) that was suspiciously published almost as soon as the crisis started.

There were so many other odd things – so many red flags fluttering. I don't want to go into it here but I just found it all quite bizarre even though the majority of people I spoke with didn't seem to notice or care. But, like that old Magic Eye* optical illusion trick, when at first you can't see it – you can't see it – you can't see it – but aah! Once you *can* see it, you can't *un-see* it!

JW: I think part of the problem is that people may take the bare essence of something that's said, but don't necessarily look at the detail. It's like when a newspaper prints a headline and that's what sticks – not the retraction that may follow. Quite often there's a deeper thought process when you're talking about something, but people don't see that. They just see the headline; they see the bit they want to fixate on. That then becomes the stick that they use to beat you with. They don't want a dialogue; they want a battle. It's a very dangerous situation we find ourselves in. A very strange climate socially and politically post-COVID-19. Both the US and UK political leaders seem to be inept and fascistic. As someone who has always been a political observer what do you make of it?

MJ: Without wishing to sound alarmist, the path the West has begun stumbling down reminds me, in some ways, of Germany in the early 1930s. Of course, that didn't *start* with concentration camps – it started with general intolerance, censorship of speech, books, art, theatre, and other cultural expressions.

A similar phenomenon seems to be unfolding today across large parts of the West, albeit more slowly and subtly. We see growing intolerance toward those holding views contradicting the

---

* Magic Eye images are autostereograms – 2D patterns designed so that by slightly diverging or crossing your eyes, the brain perceives a hidden 3D image.

government, and increasing deployment of technology to monitor citizens extremely closely. Tools such as facial recognition cameras, spyware in electronic devices inside homes and 'backdoors' in smartphones allowing authorities to track movements, communications, and digital activity with unprecedented reach. A digital panopticon. The Stasi's wet dream!

While often justified in the name of security, critics are warning this widespread surveillance is normalising intrusion into our private lives and eroding fundamental civil liberties. Growing concerns are just met with that old 'nothing to hide, nothing to fear' excuse. But what about our right to privacy? Having curtains on our bedroom windows doesn't mean we're trying to hide something it just means we want some privacy.

Social media and tech companies – under pressure from governments – are increasingly banning, or shadow-banning, opposing points of view. In Britain, the crackdowns we've been seeing on protests, the censorship of dissenting views, and signs of judicial overreach are, to many, hallmarks of a government losing legitimacy. Ministers claim they are trying to *protect* the public – these measures look like efforts to *control* the public. And now jury trials may be scaled back.* Juries are one of the last ways ordinary people can hold power to account. Concentrating more authority in the hands of judges might seem efficient, but history shows it rarely leads to greater freedom. It's far easier to corrupt one judge than twelve citizens – and that alone should worry us. It does seem Orwellian and illustrates how authoritarianism often begins.

JW: And how would you broadly define your political position?

MJ: Nothing very radical, I'm afraid. Broadly speaking, I'm a peace-loving, free-thinking moderate with old-fashioned principles: fairness, transparency, equality of opportunity, accessible

---

* The Court Reform / Crown Court Bench Division proposals (2025) would curtail the right to jury trial in England and Wales, shifting many criminal cases from citizen juries to judge-only verdicts, including for lesser offences. (UK Ministry of Justice proposals, Nov–Dec 2025).

healthcare and education for all – though the caveat is what sort of education, I suppose. The kind I believe in would prioritise creativity and encourage free thinkers, rather than trying to hammer round pegs into square holes. I support a fair, proportionate tax system that favours small businesses over multinational corporations, and public ownership of utilities and transport networks so profits are reinvested rather than handed over to private shareholders. I'd like to see genuine media plurality and would prefer a system of proportional representation to first-past-the-post (FPTP). Decentralisation. I don't trust governments with huge majorities – they often push through policies that weren't even in their election manifestos.

The political lobbying system needs complete reform and the revolving door between Westminster and big business fully investigated. Immigration should be managed properly so people can actually integrate rather than end up ghettoised. But if we really want immigration under control, we should start by stopping the wars that turn people into refugees in the first place. We can't keep bombing countries back to the Stone Age and then complain when their people flee. Oh, and I also believe in diplomacy over military action and that sovereign nations should be free to pursue independent foreign policies reflecting the interests of their populations.

JW: And your circle of friends?

MJ: I have friends from across the political spectrum: conservatives to socialists. A number voted for Brexit, for instance. We had debates and disagreements but I didn't fall out with any of them. I didn't agree with their decision but I respected it. I *love* Europe and I miss the freedom of movement citizens of the UK used to enjoy across the continent, though I do agree that the EU Commission itself is becoming increasingly unhinged, war-mongering and unaccountable in recent years and is starting to act more like the Soviet Politburo! I think there should have been a third choice on the ballot: 'Remain and Reform' and that the populations of Europe should have been given the power to directly influence the appointment of those in charge of the EU – and given the power to remove them when their policies cause harm.

The truth is, most of us have far more in common with each other than we don't. I have friends across faiths and philosophies: Muslim, Jewish, Christian, Hindu, Buddhist, Agnostic and Atheist and I find it depressing and dispiriting watching divisions and hatreds being whipped up and imposed upon us. As I've gotten older I just try to look for the qualities that unite rather than divide. Hopefully we all become more open-minded and empathetic after the experiences life throws at us and as a result try to see all sides of arguments. I'm strongly opposed to the bullying digital-lynch-mob mentality of the expanding cancel culture.

JW: When you were questioning politics in prior decades you were praised for it. What changed?

MJ: Much has changed. Maybe I'm an old-fashioned idealist but I've always believed opposing ideas and disagreements in a democracy should be hammered out on the anvil of public debate rather than driven underground – which can lead to all sorts of extremist groupings amongst disgruntled segments of the populace. But, without genuine media plurality and a healthy exchange of information and ideas, how can a democracy properly function – let alone thrive?

Free speech seems to be being rebranded as 'hate speech,' and 'mind traps' are being set for the populace everywhere. Show sympathy for Palestinian women and children slaughtered in Gaza, and you may be branded an anti-Semite; support women's rights to private spaces and you could be shouted down as a transphobe; question the motives of unaccountable oligarchs, and you are a conspiracy theorist; criticise NATO expansion or its Forever Wars, and you are likely to be labelled a Kremlin apologist; raise questions during the pandemic, and you'd be dismissed as an 'anti-vaxxer'. Another trick is simply to condemn people whose views you disagree with as 'extreme left' or 'alt-right,' or to apply any number of other pejorative labels. I suppose one can discern an evil form of genius in how these 'mind traps' have been set up and how the lexicon of public discourse has been weaponised and the populace set against each other. But it is all just divide and rule and control at the end of the day.

JW: And, of course, technology has evolved.

MJ: Agencies such as the 77th Brigade* – and many similar units abroad – have access to powerful technology which they use to conduct online surveillance and psychological operations, often using social media and other digital platforms to influence public discourse and perceptions and to even destroy reputations. Many feel this is creating a chilling effect upon our democracy, making individuals feel isolated or intimidated, and leading them to self-censor rather than risk stress or professional consequences.

JW: Social media does seem to have bred a witch hunt mentality. Do you feel that this cancel culture has radically affected or re-conditioned us as human beings?

MJ: The fear of ridicule runs deep in our society and you can observe this behaviour from primary school – the desire to belong and not feel like an outsider. Countless young people all wanting to dress the same, listen to the same music, hold the same opinions. Social engineering is relatively easy because of this herd instinct – which helps explain why fashions spread like wildfire amongst the young.

If you can make people believe that *everyone else* agrees with something, most will follow along. Through the power of peer pressure and groupthink people start doubting their own judgment and often conform to avoid social isolation or ridicule or just to gain acceptance – even when they may *know* something is wrong.

---

* The 77th Brigade is a British Army unit, created in 2015, specialising in information operations, psychological influence, and strategic use of social media – officially aimed at overseas audiences. Its role in monitoring online narratives during the pandemic has raised concerns about how clearly those boundaries are kept.

Many are anxious to stand alone as this fear of ridicule runs very deep. Playwright Eugène Ionesco* was quoted as saying, 'The supreme trick of mass insanity is that it persuades you that the only abnormal person is the one who *refuses* to join in the madness of others.'

Most of us just want an easy life, to blend into the crowd, and are terrified of being singled out and ridiculed. But that fear then leads to something far more dangerous: self-censorship. And self-censorship is the most effective form of societal control and a serious danger to any democracy.

I can understand why people do self-censor and keep their heads down, because certain subjects – it's been made very clear – are now no-go zones. If you question the narrative pushed 24/7 by corporate or state propaganda outlets you may end up ridiculed, shamed, smeared, de-platformed, sanctioned and marginalised – with your career and life in tatters. If you dare to carry on after that? Ask Julian Assange.

I really feel sorry for the younger generations coming through. They've already lost freedoms and liberties they didn't even know they had. You and I grew up in those still-golden, post-war decades of the sixties and seventies, going into the eighties, and had a freedom that we didn't really appreciate, because it was like air, it was all around us. I wouldn't want to be 17 now.

One must always reserve the right to change one's mind in a changing world. Yet a cultural bias has emerged that mischievously conflates healthy scepticism with irrationality. Were governments more enlightened and less secretive and manipulative toward their citizens, then delusional conspiracy theories would simply evaporate. Perhaps the true conspiracy theorists are not those who *scrutinise* power, but those who *accept* its narratives without question.

---

* Eugène Ionesco (1909–1994), Romanian-French playwright and leading figure of the Theatre of the Absurd. The above quoted line echoes the central theme of his play *Rhinoceros*: how collective hysteria can redefine the lone dissenter as the abnormal one.

CHAPTER THIRTEEN
The Future Is Closer Than We Think

The first studio album of new songs in a quarter century, Ensoulment *(2024) is released. Cementing a collaboration between Cinéola and earMUSIC,* Ensoulment *enjoys some of the best reviews of Matt's career and continues the strong aesthetic style of THE THE records with striking artwork from the late Andrew Johnson, AKA Andy Dog.*

JW: *Ensoulment* is a significant event, because it's twelve new songs with multiple musicians. Why did the time feel right for this record? Was the success of The Comeback Special Tour an impetus? Did it give you your mojo back?

MJ: For many years – right up to *The Inertia Variations* – I would start songs but struggle to finish them. There's a song on *Ensoulment* I consider one of my strongest lyrically – it was the first I finished for the album and I consider it an equivalent of, say, 'Heartland' or 'Love Is Stronger Than Death'. That song is 'Some Days I Drink My Coffee By The Grave Of William Blake'.

In *The Inertia Variations* documentary, I mentioned a song about London I was struggling to finish, and it was that song. I had the first verse and chorus for a long time but I just didn't know where to take the song. I'd often pick up the guitar, go over the chords for the verse and chorus but would always hit a dead-end for some reason.

The song is partially about the destruction of London through property development, corruption, social engineering and the subsequent loss of identity – as well as the opaque shenanigans of those ruling Britain.

I felt my 'mojo' returning during the live performance of 'We Can't Stop What's Coming' at the end of *The Inertia Variations*, which in turn led to The Comeback Special Tour, which then led to *Ensoulment*. It infused me with a fresh energy and changed my state of mind. The power of music in action I suppose.

For many years I've carried this quote in my notebooks – often attributed to Goethe but it's from *The Scottish Himalayan Expedition*, by William Hutchison Murray (1951):

> Until one is committed, there is hesitancy, the chance to draw back, always ineffectiveness. Concerning all acts of initiative and creation, there is one elementary truth, the ignorance of which kills countless ideas and splendid plans: that the moment one definitely commits oneself, then Providence moves too.
>
> All sorts of things occur to help one that would never otherwise have occurred. A whole stream of events issues from the decision, raising in one's favour all manner of unforeseen incidents, meetings and material assistance which no man could have dreamed would have come his way. I have learned a deep respect for one of Goethe's couplets:
>
> Whatever you can do or dream you can, begin it.
> Boldness has genius, power and magic in it. Begin it now!

I have experienced over the years the magic that follows from making decisions with boldness. Suddenly, everything fell into place.

JW: It felt like a very cohesive band unit on the album. You began by disclosing that 'Some Days I Drink My Coffee By The Grave

Of William Blake' was an older title. Were there other songs on *Ensoulment* you'd had in your mind for a while?

MJ: There were two or three unfinished songs that had been knocking around – 'A Rainy Day In May' was another. Again, I had the first verse and chorus – in fact the chorus is hummed, a non-verbal chorus, which I'd not done before. 'I Want To Wake Up With You' was something I'd started to write in Sweden a few years before. Again, just the first verse and chorus. I just couldn't seem to finish any of these songs. Not sure why. I'd had the title 'Kissing The Ring of POTUS' for quite some time but that song hadn't even been started yet. 'Zen & The Art Of Dating' was also a title I'd had for some time. The lyrics to 'Linoleum Smooth To The Stockinged Foot' came to me when I was in hospital, on morphine, whilst recovering from my operation. It's partly about that and the hallucinogenic state of mind I was in but also musings about the nascent biosecurity state.

JW: Were you surprised that the songs eventually came together in a relatively short period of time?

MJ: If not for COVID intervening *Ensoulment* would have happened much sooner – probably two years after The Comeback Special Tour. That was the plan anyway, to record and release an album fairly quickly. But – as with many people after COVID and the lockdowns – a sense of drift set in. Many became confused about life and lost momentum. I did too. I was very focused after the tour but suddenly being hospitalised – and all the surreal stuff the world was going through – really knocked me off track for a while. But then the power of the deadline came to my rescue.

My agent Boswell and I sat down for another luncheon to discuss the new offers we'd been receiving for another tour. But I didn't want to do another 'Comeback Special'-style tour – just playing old material. So, I backward-planned the writing, recording, mixing, mastering and promotion. I considered the new album could be ready for release in autumn 2024. We set the tour dates around that timeline and a sense of urgency was injected into the proceedings.

Now, I've often got a huge amount of material in various stages of completion and in various formats. Obviously, I write both music *and* words so I started listening to recordings and reading through notebooks, finding the snatches of music and lines of lyrics that felt right.

JW: Who else were you collaborating with on the writing?

MJ: DC occasionally e-mails ideas over – which sometimes I like and sometimes I don't – it all depends on what resonates. There was a very old idea of his I asked him to resurrect. This originated from around the *Gun Sluts* period when we'd recorded some sessions at Walter Sear's old studio in New York. There was this beautiful little jazz motif DC had played that had stuck in my mind for all the years since. So, we found some different parts to add to that and the song became 'Down By The Frozen River'. The lyrics were from a poem I'd written many years before about my truancy at school.

The music for 'Kissing The Ring Of POTUS' came about after DC emailed an idea. I liked the verse chords but didn't like the chorus chords. When he was in the UK he came to my studio and I had him try out other ideas – experimenting with different keys, chord sequences, inversions and substitutes until it felt just right. I love working with DC. He has such a lovely temperament as well as being a brilliant musician.

I also asked Barrie if he fancied doing some co-writing and he came over to my place for a few afternoons. It was a simple process. He sat with his old Gibson and played me a few half-finished ideas he had. Ideas that he liked but that didn't fit into plans for his Little Barrie project. The process was very much: 'Mmm, don't like that one… not sure about this one… play me something else.' He started playing the chords to what would become 'Cognitive Dissident' and I immediately went, 'Oooh! I like that!' He then set about trying other parts that might fit and we created the basic structure of the song and recorded it into my little Tascam

Pocketstudio. I would endlessly listen to it whilst working on vocal melodies and lyrics, working out where it needed more or less bars or repetitions or deletions. Barrie came over again and we worked on the structure until it was tight. I didn't actually finish the lyrics to that song until after we'd recorded the music with the band.

The other song I co-wrote with Barrie is 'I Hope You Remember (the things I can't forget)'. He was sat in front of me and said, 'Okay, here's a weird one: I've been playing this for a while now but it just doesn't suit any of my other projects.' But as soon as he started playing it – I thought it had a little bit of a Django Reinhardt vibe to it – I said, 'Oh, I like that! Yes please!' Again, we recorded it onto my little Tascam and I listened to it on repeat whilst writing the lyrics. In the next session we adjusted the structure to fit the lyrics.

By this time, I'd already started demoing the other songs I was writing on my trusty little Tascam. I'd written the chord structures and the backing tracks: bass and drums. Then I brought the musicians in individually to finesse their respective parts. I remember a particularly productive day with James at my studio, going over the parts I'd initially written for him; but then, with his beautiful playing improving them and making the parts his own. I repeated a similar process with Barrie and DC. I really enjoy working with band members one-on-one as part of the pre-rehearsal/pre-recording process. I like to refine the parts to ensure the different elements of a song are simple and without unnecessary embellishments. Earl is based in Berlin though so I didn't really have the chance to work with him in the same way prior to our rehearsals.

Then we started the pre-recording rehearsals – a week at mine – and, as usual, we sat close together in a circle on my old wooden fold-up chairs and got the band dynamics going again. But – unlike *The Comeback Special* – we now had my old co-producer and engineer Warne Livesey back in the fold as part of our team.

JW: Having worked with Warne on *Infected* and *Mind Bomb* was there a sense of security and of him providing a safety net?

MJ: Yes, there was in a way. There was a lot of pressure with it being my first song-based album in a quarter century, and I wanted a combination of old and new collaborators. Warne has lived in Canada for many years but we'd stayed in touch. When we last met up a few years ago – on one of his trips back to England – we had discussed working together again. Unfortunately, since then, Warne had suffered some terrible bereavements himself. His beloved wife Barbara lost a long battle with cancer. In fact, he lost his dad, wife and a close friend all in a very short period of time and it absolutely hammered him.

Warne is a thoughtful, sensitive person and quite prone to introspection so it really hit him hard. When I saw him the year before we started the album he was really down and I thought working together would help him focus. And it did help to energise him. Obviously, the main reason for my working with Warne is not out of sympathy but because he is excellent at his job.

It was the right move to bring him in, especially in terms of me knowing there's someone I can trust on the other side of the glass taking care of things. Warne did exactly what I wanted him to do. I'm delighted with the job he did. Putting this team together for *Ensoulment* I knew very much in my mind what I wanted and expected from everyone. I'm a control freak I suppose and I do like to have the final say but I'm always open to input and if someone on the team has got a better idea than mine then I will go with it. I just want the best for the record. There was no clinging onto ideas that didn't work.

JW: Where did you decide to record the new album?

MJ: After the intensive week-long rehearsals at my studio we went to Real World Studios. It's owned by Peter Gabriel and situated just outside Bath. It's one of the best studios I've worked in – and I've worked in lots of great studios in my career. There were a few other studios we'd considered – RAK in London, for example, which is also wonderful, but the problem is, the schlep – getting there and back each morning and night – was that the best use of our time? Warne suggested Real World, even though he'd not worked there.

JW: You can live there as well?

MJ: Yes, it's residential, in a beautiful location, very well-maintained and with lovely staff. I don't know Peter Gabriel – having only met him once when I was a teenager – but I imagine he's a nice guy as there's such a warm feeling amongst his staff – many who've been at the studio a long time.

We were only there six days, but it was extremely productive. Up at 8 a.m., cold shower, breakfast and in the studio and working hard by 10 a.m. on the dot – and we'd put in a solid twelve-hour shift. We might have one glass of wine each and listen to a bit of music for an hour, but we'd all be in bed by 11:30 p.m. We were extremely disciplined and there was a nice vibe amongst everybody.

After six days at Real World Warne came back to my studio with me to start editing the sessions and preparing for overdubs whilst the band went their separate ways home. After we'd chosen the best takes Barrie popped in to fix a guitar part or two and DC overdubbed some glockenspiel. I'd only sung guides at Real World so Warne prepared some rough mixes for me to work to. He then went home to Canada for a while.

I prefer to be alone and engineer myself when recording vocals. I need to feel un-self-conscious when doing my voice exercises and freely experimenting. I sometimes like to sing at strange hours too – maybe get up very early to obtain a certain tone of voice or sing very late into the night. Whilst Warne was back in Canada I recorded the lead vocals and also replaced most of my guitar parts. We had Mark Allaway engineering musical overdubs such as fiddle.

Warne came back after a month or so to work on the mix and we started by comping my vocal takes. I only keep the best five takes to edit between. I know some singers who record dozens upon dozens of takes and keep them all to edit between. That's ridiculous, you're just making work for yourself. Best to just make decisions as you go.

JW: Were there any musicians in addition to the main band line-up you wanted to get involved?

MJ: With Warne now back, all the backing vocals were also recorded at Studio Cinéola, between Barrie and Gillian. I'd also wanted my old friends Zeke Manyika and Colin Lloyd Tucker to sing backing vocals with the other two as all four have wonderful, distinct voices and I knew they'd blend together incredibly well, but sadly both of them fell ill at the same time.

I also invited legendary horn player Terry Edwards to get involved. I've known Terry socially a long time and we've often said we should do something. He's a fantastic player and is very fast and responsive. Then there was the brilliant fiddle-player, Sonya Cullingford, a friend of a friend who I'd seen play live a couple of times, and who I really like – both as a person and a player. She's also a very good singer and an all-round talent. Sonya was easy to work with and gave the recordings exactly what we needed.

Lastly, we brought in Danny Cummings, who'd played percussion on *Mind Bomb* – he's still one of the UK's best percussionists. The core of the band is small and tight but the additional musicians and singers added some beautiful colouring – brass, fiddle, backing vocals and percussion – in just the right places to make the album feel a bit more widescreen.

JW: I think that there are certain things that people expect you to write about. And *Ensoulment* delivers on that front.

MJ: Well, love and sex, God and religion, war and politics are in every album – we also drop in a bit of fear and loathing here and there.

JW: And I think also loss.

MJ: That would come under life and death.

JW: I meant a sense of personal loss. I think with this record there's a sense of dissatisfaction with how the world is going and of how Britain has gone. When I listened to this record for the first time in your studio I felt it had the perfect balance between the sonic experimentation of the early work and the concision of a 'pop' record. I don't think any song is over four minutes.

MJ: Nina Simone once said, 'An artist's duty… is to reflect the times. I think that is true of painters, sculptors, poets, musicians.' And that is what I've always tried to do. Just as *Infected* reflected the 1980s, for instance, I think *Ensoulment* reflects its time too. I also tried to keep all of the songs concise.

JW: It's punchy, which makes it feel accessible.

MJ: I wanted to synthesise different elements and bring them together. The last decade and a half creating film soundtracks has been very useful, being back in the studio, experimenting with new equipment, new techniques, developing sounds. Slowly bringing my confidence back. If something sounds good, it *is* good.

I now try not to overthink. I make notes before I start writing a project – a general map of where I want to go. I wanted the songs on this album to be simple and succinct – around four minutes in length with strong choruses and strong melodies.

I knew I wanted to use the same band as *The Comeback Special*. And I knew I wanted the album to feel hopeful. Every song has a little 'uptick' at the end – a light at the end of the proverbial tunnel. Even 'Linoleum Smooth' finishes with 'Beneath the light that casts no shadow / The path is forked, but the gate still narrow'. Obvious biblical references. That there will come a judgement upon the dark forces orchestrating negative world events. But every song is positive in its own way and I wanted that to come across in the music as well as the lyrics. I think the album deals with pertinent and current topics head-on, but ultimately it is positive. It's very important for me, in such strange times, to be positive.

JW: It gives comfort and security.

MJ: Absolutely. I think it's a warm-sounding record. A positive record. Tough in the right places and doesn't shy away from difficult subjects.

JW: Being the first record of its kind for a quarter of a century you could have indulged yourself, but I think you've shown great discipline.

MJ: *Ensoulment* is the most focused and disciplined record I've made. The process of writing it was a happy one. I inherited an old writing bureau, which belonged to my dad. His dad – my Grandad Charlie – bought it for him when he came out of the army as a young man after national service – to encourage my dad to follow his passion and write. From when I was a little boy – at every place we ever lived – this lovely old, oak bureau would be sat – benignly – in a corner. It travelled with us whenever we moved home and although all the other pieces of furniture would be replaced over the years this one obviously held great sentimental value within the family and remained with us. Its last home – before it ended up with me – was in Andrew's bedroom. It was a bit bashed up and sorry for itself by that point; one of the glass panes had broken and the drawers didn't fit snugly.

Anyway, after Andrew and my dad had died I couldn't bear parting with it. It's such a big part of my childhood. I had it restored, the broken glass replaced, a carpenter fixed the drawers and a French polisher returned the wood to its original lustre. And there was something Gerard said to me, 'When you write lyrics, you should only sit *there* and do it. Make it a creative-only space.' He'd read something David Lynch once said about having a creative space you go to, where you only do one thing – and that is *all* that you do there. So, I don't sit at that bureau to graze the

Internet – I sit there purely when I want to write creatively. And it has become quite sacred to me.

There was also a lovely set of encyclopaedias Grandad Charlie bought for our family, when my dad was a young father and we were little boys. And they used to be sat on the shelves behind the glass-panelled doors of the bureau. Grandad Charlie died when I was about 7 years old, but he was the patriarch of the family. A very powerful presence. All those books stayed in our family – now very old and beaten up of course – but I have now put them back on the shelves of the bureau where they belong – alongside my own reference books, dictionaries, thesauruses, etc. Every time I sit there, it is just to write creatively. Writing the lyrics to *Ensoulment* I'd often get up at 5 a.m. and light some Tibetan incense, make a small pot of white peony tea in my small iron Japanese teapot. Johnny Marr had recommended that particular tea to me as it really charges you up. I'll then sit and write lyrics in four- or five-hour sessions each morning. Personally, I really like rituals, routines and regimes. There's something about starting the day with intent that helps magic flow.

JW: White peony tea is the new cocaine.

MJ: It certainly is. I'll have my little Gibson L-00 acoustic and Tascam Pocketstudio on the side and just sit and write and focus. Writing words, recording chord sequences, playing them on repeat, going over certain sections again and again and again – trying to find the right melodies and rhythms for the words. I was very disciplined writing this album but it was so enjoyable – I was absolutely loving it. Just remembering, this is who I really am, this is what I love to do.

There are periods many of us experience at certain points, when we're doing a job we love, and we're in a great mood and we may just slip into a meditative state, one of unaffected, blissful happiness. I wanted that positivity, how I felt, to somehow bleed into the album. It's an album that deals with tough subject matter, but ultimately, it was created from a very positive place.

JW: You are someone who is very much immersed in the world and in culture. You read a lot, you enjoy cinema, you're engaged in cultural activities. With this record, were there any influences that you drew upon from any other discipline, whether it was music or literature?

MJ: Not from the arts so much, more geopolitics and reading. That's what I spend much of my spare time doing, reading independent journalists, scouring the news – and alternative sources of news – to try and see behind the headlines. I do watch a lot of films and listen to a lot of music. But for the personal subjects, from drawing from life experience.

JW: Does the fact that the making of *Ensoulment* has been so positive for you set a direction for the future? There'll be people reading this book that will have heard and loved record and so will want more records. THE THE is no longer in the past, but now also in the present.

MJ: I'm feeling as inspired as I've ever felt so I hope so; though you never know what life is suddenly going to throw at you to upset even the best laid plans. And the industry I'm involved in has changed so much, of course. Things have been economically unstable. Touring post-Brexit and post-COVID has been difficult for many. Overhead costs have doubled or tripled and bands can't just put prices up to match. Because of streaming we all know physical sales are way down. Vinyl is doing okay, but it's a very small, niche market. Re-numeration isn't what it should be with the streaming platforms. Musicians have not been properly cared for – which is no great surprise based on the history of the recording industry I suppose. But all that aside, I feel excited and happy.

This will hopefully be the first of a few book projects. Plus, the partnership deal we have in place with earMUSIC is working well. The last few years I've tried to build the foundation of a solid, independent business after one too many bruising encounters with big corporations. I've worked very hard to achieve creative freedom and independence, to be able to work on projects that excite me with people I like – like yourself.

JW: The records you make are personal to you but it's also clear that you want people to enjoy them.

MJ: Absolutely. I have to satisfy myself first though, of course. I like to feel goosebumps when writing music and words. I sometimes cry when writing songs, sometimes dance around the room, sometimes laugh.

When we spoke about *Dusk* it reminded me that 'Love Is Stronger Than Death' is a song people play at funerals whilst 'This Is The Day' is often played at weddings. As a songwriter what greater accolade and reward can you receive than people inviting your songs into their lives to celebrate – or commemorate – significant moments in their lives? A songwriter can't wish for anything more than to become a part of the soundtrack of the lives of others. I love the fact that songs go out into the world and forge their own relationships with people and their lives.

JW: I think it's important to note that the first time I sat down with you and you played me *Ensoulment* was in Studio Cinéola. I had a sense of anticipation but when 'Cognitive Dissident' kicked in I couldn't believe how good it was. Genuinely. I think people were really, really surprised by this record. And I say that as someone who's quite jaded. It was beyond what I was expecting and I think others felt the same.

MJ: That's nice to know. I hope they did. It was a team effort. Everyone did what I hoped they would do. I often use football analogies and it's the job of the manager to bring in different players for different positions and different tactics. For the different projects I work on I think about what I want to do and where I want to get to. Everybody performed their jobs perfectly: the band, the session musicians, Warne and Mark and Gillian at my studio and office. A real team effort.

JW: Can I also ask about the 7-inch singles you released before embarking on *Ensoulment*? 'We Can't Stop What's Coming', 'I Want 2 B U' – which is from *Muscle* – and '$1 One Vote!'

MJ: They form part of a larger singles collection I've been working on periodically. I used to love it – years ago – when bands would release one-off singles that were not part of an album but just singles for their own sake. So, these are all very different musically but the one connection they have is that they all feature sleeves with illustrations taken from Andrew's sketchbooks. He left behind a lot of work and I feel a responsibility to look after it and help get it seen.

I also plan to publish a beautiful coffee table book of his artwork – something I promised him before he died. He was also a very good writer so I'd like to publish some of that work too. I just want to keep his work alive. Knowing Andrew, I think he'd be pleased his work is still featured on THE THE's covers. It's important to me and important to my family.

JW: I think Andrew's work is so connected with THE THE. When people buy a record, they expect his artwork.

MJ: Yes, they do. None of those singles are part of an album but I intend to continue releasing one-off singles and eventually put them together as a boxset or something. What's enjoyable is that, instrumentation wise, they're all so different from each other so it enables me to just do whatever I want with each of them without the baggage of an associated album.

I wrote and recorded 'I Want 2 B U' on my original Omnichord. '$1 One Vote!' was previously known as 'Justice 4 Jesus' and was part of *Karmic Gravity* – the unfinished follow-up album to *NakedSelf*. It was recorded in New York with Bruce Lampcov engineering, Eric Schermerhorn on guitar, Earl Harvin on drums, and myself on guitar and vocals. For this updated version, I tweaked the lyrics and added Barrie and Gillian on backing vocals. It's a simple commentary on the farce that now passes for democracy in the West – rotten to the core with lobbying interests.

JW: Can you explain the title of the new record, *Ensoulment*?

MJ: I wanted to do a similar thing that Neil Young did with *Harvest* and *Harvest Moon* and use a title that connected with earlier work. *Burning Blue Soul* and *Soul Mining* obviously have 'soul' in the title but I also preferred a single-word title, as with *Infected* and *Dusk*.

Ensoulment is the moment that – supposedly – the soul enters the human body. Of course, people from different religious and philosophical backgrounds have different views on this – whether it's at conception, some point *after* conception or even if we have a soul at all!

In this day and age, we're also living with nascent AI technology, which is starting to infiltrate and impact more lives. it's going to cost a lot of jobs and radically change the world we live in. But judging humanity on its current trajectory it will likely find most use in military, surveillance and control purposes.

And at this moment in time, a question many are asking: what does it really mean to be human? What distinguishes us from this artificial life form that's becoming increasingly powerful and prevalent? A recent survey found that the majority of people could no longer tell the difference between humans and AI when communicating online. This number will only increase. Perhaps it will turn out to be more ethical than us? Make a better job of running the world than the mess we've made? It *could* become the greatest thing to ever happen to humanity if it ends up in benign hands. Although I worry that it does seem to be inheriting similar biases and prejudices as humans as it learns from our online behaviours.

JW: Let's go through the album song by song.

MJ: I usually don't like spoon-feeding the meaning of my songs as I think it preferable everyone brings their own imaginations and interpretations, which are often far more interesting than mine! But many of the lyrics are quite self-explanatory.

I wanted to sum up contemporary British society in the first two words of the new album: 'Servile, surveilled'. 'Cognitive Dissident' is a commentary on a reality in which surveillance and censorship are normalised, truth distorted and societal norms inverted. An unseen force which compels individuals to conform to a manipulated narrative or face the consequences, which is where we seem to be living right now.

JW: There's an Orwellian element to it as well, isn't there? You mentioned 'wrongthink', which I think is *1984*.

MJ: It is *1984*. Winston Churchill once said, 'The empires of the future are the empires of the mind' and it certainly seems our minds have become the latest battleground. We often hear a form of bragging by the political class about so-called 'British values', but what *are* those values if not freedom of speech and expression, rather than Soviet-style suppression?

JW: New Hate Crime Laws have been introduced in Scotland.*

MJ: Yes, well this is where it's going, isn't it? But where do we draw the line? Is it about intent or about perception? Should musicians, artists and writers start suing critics over bad reviews because our feelings are hurt and we consider it 'hate speech'?

We seem to be living in this hall of mirrors with a quicksand floor, where war is peace, lies are truth, up is down. Over recent years I've become more of a political atheist, observing from the side-lines what increasingly seems a bizarre reality show. I'm not so interested in left or right anymore, just right and wrong.

JW: You mentioned that 'Some Days I Drink My Coffee By The Grave Of William Blake' was a song you'd had in mind for some time. It also speaks to your work as a conservationist and your interest in a rapidly changing London.

---

* The Hate Crime and Public Order (Scotland) Act 2021 – implemented in 2024 – is controversial because it expands 'stirring up hatred' offences, sparking concerns that vague definitions and broad reporting could undermine free speech.

MJ: It's a simple reflection about loss of belonging in a changing city, and also a commentary on the deceptive façade of freedom in a country under threat from increasingly oppressive laws. Blake was a dissenter, and his radical critiques of authority and organised religion unsettled the establishment. When he died, he was buried in a common grave in Bunhill Fields (Islington), a nonconformist burial ground. The establishment had dealt with him by largely ignoring or dismissing him during his lifetime, but ironically, he's now celebrated as one of England's greatest poets and painters – in an age that is cracking down on freedom of expression. Praising dead rebels while silencing living ones is one of the oldest and most revealing tricks of the cultural establishment.

JW: Jah Wobble is a big William Blake fan.

MJ: Is he?

JW: He made an album, *The Inspiration of William Blake* (1996). It's brilliant.

MJ: There are actually two graves. There's the tombstone, upon which is written, 'Nearby lie the remains of William Blake'. And then there is another grave. That spot was found by Carol and Luis Garrido who spent a decade and a half searching through old maps and the history of Bunhill Fields. They located the exact position he was buried. I actually drink my coffee by both of them. Well, it's really a decaf flat white with oat milk these days but that would have made the title far too long! In my early 20s I lived with Fiona in her flat in Braithwaite House, which is directly opposite the cemetery and looks down upon Bunhill Fields. Funnily enough, it ties into my childhood in a way as I believe it's where one of the Kray twins was arrested. They had bought a flat for their mum there. I've known that graveyard for many years. It's very tranquil. George's primary school was also close

by. It can be quite haunting and melancholy, especially in certain seasons when there aren't many people around.

JW: You play on words: 'Green and pleasant land' becomes 'Greedy—'

MJ: '—Unpleasant land.' Yeah. Our popular culture, our media, our quality of political leadership. It's not in a healthy state. The entire country feels façaded doesn't it? Like one of those film sets with the buildings propped up but nothing behind.

JW: I also feel that the song is a kind of eulogy for a London which is gone. As a Londoner and someone who still lives in London—

MJ: —I'm a Zone One person and I don't like wandering out of Zone One. My favourite parts of London are the oldest parts – EC1, EC2, WC1, SE1, W1, E1. The old London with its historic buildings, narrow streets and alleyways – at least what is left of them – that is my neighbourhood. I consider the rest of London to be suburban to be honest. Like when I lived in New York. For me it was Manhattan or nothing. I like being in the centre of things. Or, alternatively, in the middle of the countryside. Just not the suburbs.

As I've mentioned, during my 'lost years' I became heavily involved in local residents' associations, conservation groups and local politics. I met some wonderful people during that time – some of whom have become good friends – but ultimately it ended up a waste of time and energy as we were unable to achieve very much. The property developers are just too cosy with the local planning departments and the whole game is rigged against local communities.

I remember – as kids – our dad taking us on drives around London, through the City and the old East End, pointing out the places where buildings he knew and loved used to be. It wasn't so much the damage from the Luftwaffe he was referring to, but the damage done by rampant property developers. I remember looking up at these awful sixties and seventies monolithic blocks that had replaced beautiful old buildings and wondering, 'Why isn't anybody protecting the city?' And then many years later – whilst trying to protect old buildings myself – I saw at close quarters the mechanics of the planning process and slowly realised the level of corruption ordinary people are up against. I'd naively clung to a belief that we lived in a democracy and that the general public could participate in this democracy at a local level. But sadly, it is not really the case.

JW: I noticed that on your film shelf you've got *The London Nobody Knows*, the 1968 documentary by Norman Cohen based on the book by Geoffrey S. Fletcher.

MJ: Yes! In the film James Mason goes to Mark's Deli, which I mentioned previously that we used to go to as kids in 'Petticoat Lane Market', which is actually on two streets: Middlesex Street and Wentworth Street. On Sundays we'd have family trips there to buy beigels, smoked salmon and potato latkes. Notice I pronounced it 'beigels' [pronounced bigels], not 'bagels' [pronounced baygels]. And in the film, James Mason says, 'Mark's

Deli has been here a hundred years. No doubt it will be here for another hundred years to come.' But it wasn't. It was gone within twenty years, sadly. But it's a wonderful film. So evocative of the old London I distinctly remember from my childhood. For you and me, growing up in that old London was a magical time. But, I suppose, for a kid growing up here now, this will be *their* magical time and they will look back and complain about all the things being lost to London in forty years.

Of course, there have also been many improvements in the city over recent years, particularly when it comes to food – you can eat from around the world. Public transport has been invested in and expanded too. Culturally London remains a world hub. But I do think we've lost a lot – characterful buildings, shops, venues, cafés, pubs and the places people congregate around have changed dramatically. Personally, I like cities that are on a human scale, but when you have these entire city blocks – like the American system really – where they will demolish twenty distinctive, higgledy-piggledy buildings from different eras, just to be replaced by some vast piece of monolithic slab architecture, I find it incredibly soulless and dispiriting.

JW: I think it is affecting all British cities, actually. Manchester is the same.

MJ: Yes, I noticed. It's astonishing the changes up there.

JW: Tell me about 'Zen & The Art Of Dating'.

MJ: I wrote the music to this when on a family holiday in Portugal. I'll often take my little travel guitar on trips. It portrays the modern-day struggle of seeking connection and love through the lens of online dating. Highlighting the paradox of yearning for a deeper intimacy whilst navigating a landscape of superficial encounters and fleeting connections. Ultimately it suggests genuine love may only come when one actively stops searching for it, which is the zen part of the title. Obviously, it's a pun on *Zen &*

the Art of Motorcycle Maintenance by Robert M. Pirsig (1974) – which was itself a pun on an earlier book Eugen Herrigel's *Zen in the Art of Archery* (1953) which a young lady gave to me upon our first meeting many years ago.

JW: But the song does also talk about how, as a civilisation, everything we do is now mediated by technology. I mean, the line 'Swipe to the left, swipe to the right' describes how people connect with each other.

MJ: It is potentially dangerous. Not so much for us – we're getting old – but for younger generations. They will know nothing else. There used to be a stigma attached to online dating but now it's normalised. I remember when mobile phones first came out in the eighties – great big clunky things – and when you saw someone with one you'd think, "What a buffoon!' And for quite a while, that stigma persisted and mobile phones were considered 'uncool'. I didn't have one myself till I came back from New York in 2001. I was a late adopter. But gradually everything becomes normalised. People will be accepting – even insisting upon – injectable technologies before we know it.

JW: 'Zen & The Art Of Dating' offers both a male and a female perspective.

MJ: It starts from the female perspective. I'd originally written four or five verses but it was just getting too long so I condensed to three verses: female, male and then an overview. The male perspective made me laugh out loud as I was writing it, because crisps are such a British quirk aren't they? 'At the bar, eating crisps and thinking.' And that typical, selfish male thing – he didn't want her but he didn't want anyone else to have her, and suddenly, she's not as upset as she should be – in his mind – and so he starts becoming very insecure. There's a lot of humour in it – black humour. But again, like most of the songs on *Ensoulment*, there is a positive line at the end:

> Though it's a cliché, maybe it's true?
> That only when you stop searching for love
> Will love come searching for you

As humans we always seem to be searching for 'another' to save us, to make us feel complete. But the most attractive people – those who naturally attract other people, and attract love – are those who are the most complete inside, who already possess inner peace and happiness and are not looking for someone else to complete them. So, just unplug from this system. Be yourself. Live your life fully and happily and things – including love – will naturally gravitate towards you.

JW: Let's talk about 'Kissing The Ring Of POTUS'.

MJ: People assumed it was about Trump, but it's really about the coup that nobody noticed – the neoconservative/neoliberal shift that has occurred over the past few decades. Trump is a symptom of a diseased system. Some think he's playing 5D chess whilst others think he appears to be suffering from some sort of narcissistic personality disorder. His predecessor, Joe Biden, often struggled to finish a sentence or walk in a straight line – observations reported by White House insiders and widely discussed in the media. It reminded me of the Charlton Heston film *El Cid* (1961), about a Spanish knight whose cadaver was strapped to a horse to lead his army into battle. Biden appeared far too ill to be running the United States, and controversy has since erupted over the excessive use of the 'autopen' during his administration. So, who was really behind all that?

The pro-war and pro-privatisation forces that have infiltrated many major political parties in the West have performed a magic trick, presenting themselves as 'moderates' in the centre of the political spectrum while, in reality, acting as extremists.

Yes, there are cosmetic differences for domestic audiences but ultimately, when it comes to foreign policy, Forever Wars, the privatisation and asset-stripping of public property and transfer of wealth from the public to the private sector, the major political parties in the West appear remarkably similar.

And we all know how tightly mainstream media is now controlled. For instance, in the UK, we have *The Guardian* – which was a powerful newspaper – quite radical in terms of standing up to power. Actually, that reminds me of a quote I always found irritating: 'speak truth to power.' Those in power already *know* the truth about their policies; it should be 'speak truth to the powerless' in order to motivate the majority to act. But anyway, like many newspapers in the Internet era, their circulation has been falling, and since launching their online edition, they realised a lot of their advertising income was coming from America. In my view, their editorial line shifted to reflect that.

Do you remember, back in 2013 – when Alan Rusbridger was editor – officials from GCHQ raided *The Guardian's* offices and made a public show of smashing up some of their computers and hard drives?* It was a public pantomime, but also a shot across the bow. In my view, they were effectively neutered after that. Kathy Viner took over from Rusbridger a couple of years later, and it has been relatively risk-averse ever since. Many of their old-school investigative journalists were thrown overboard, and it has become more like BBC News, which itself had been similarly constrained, of course, after it bravely confronted the Blair government over the 'sexed up' intelligence used to justify the illegal invasion of Iraq and which prompted a bitter public row between the broadcaster and Downing Street.†

I grew up as a little boy under the Harold Wilson Labour government of the 1960s and 1970s, and I remember my dad talking fondly about the achievements of the post-war Attlee government. But by the 21st century, the political parties that were meant to represent working people and provide hope for an enlightened, fair, and peaceful future had been infiltrated and were

---

* On 20 July 2013, agents from Government Communications Headquarters publicly supervised the destruction of hard drives containing Edward Snowden's leaked documents at *The Guardian*'s London offices, an event widely reported in the media.
† In 2003, the BBC challenged the Blair government over its 'Dodgy Dossier' on Iraq's alleged WMDs, exposing that intelligence had been exaggerated to justify the war.

rotting from the inside out. We saw it with the Clintons and their coterie with the Democrats in the US, and Blair and New Labour in the UK. Right-wing ideologues had taken over left-of-centre parties. What was it Lenin said? 'The best way to control the opposition is to lead it ourselves.' So, in my opinion, that's what we've ended up with – a 'Uni-Party' system.

In the lyrics to *POTUS*, I used a quote from Hillary Clinton who, following the brutal murder of Gaddafi – reportedly subjected to a violent and degrading death – cackled with delight on TV: 'We came, we saw, he died!' I referenced Mike Pompeo – former Director of the CIA and US Secretary of State who publicly and proudly exclaimed – in an interview while describing his time in the CIA – words such as 'We cheated, we stole, we lied'. I also referenced the powerful Nobel Lecture Harold Pinter gave in 2005 (*Art, Truth and Politics*) and his excoriating attack upon Washington's vicious foreign policy over the decades: 'Even when it was happening, it wasn't happening'. The song is about the immoral actions of empire and its mafia-like use of deceit, coercion, and violence to maintain power at any cost. The lyrics question whether its downfall will be inevitable, due to spiritual decay as well as moral and financial bankruptcy.

JW: You talk about the 'hidden hand' as well.

MJ: Proxy wars – which is what we've seen in Ukraine and elsewhere. We see the effects of the 'hidden hand' everywhere – and over the years these regime-change operations are 're-branded' and go by names such as 'Arab Spring' or 'Color Revolution' but they all seem to use the same playbook with NGOs, three-letter agencies and other shadowy forces in the background stirring grievances up amongst the local populace for the benefit of western institutions. They could all really be considered wars of liberation I suppose – liberating countries from their own resources!

JW: We spoke about the positivity on the album. I think this is the one track where there isn't room for that.

MJ: I don't agree. I think it does end on a positive note:

> So, is this how the Empire dies?
> Its constitution withered on the vine
> Propped up by the dollar and the drone
> Slumped upon a degenerating throne

I think we may be witnessing the death throes of empire. Who knows how long it will take but it is happening. All empires die and something new takes its place.

JW: Do you think?

MJ: It can't carry on the way it's going.

JW: Let's move on to the next song: 'Life After Life'.

MJ: Okay. 'Life After Life' explores the cyclical nature of existence, suggesting life transcends death and that human experience partly involves remembering forgotten truths and navigating the paradoxes of physical reality. It emphasises the importance of introspection and self-awareness in understanding the true nature of our existence. The opening line—

JW: 'No one lives forever / No one dies for long'.

MJ: I had quite a disturbing drug experience a few months after *The Comeback Special*. A friend recommended a particular brand of CBD for stress. As you probably know, CBD is not one of the psychoactive ingredients in cannabis, it's the one that's calming – supposedly. My friend told me about a place in Amsterdam that sold an especially pure and effective version. So, I duly ordered the oil and a couple of bottles arrived in the post – nicely wrapped in silver foil. 'I'll put them in the drawer and try later,' I thought. I then headed off to Super Booth – the big synthesizer fair in Berlin – for a few days. I picked something up – probably flu – and was in bed for about five days after I got home as I felt really, really rough. I was very tired but also restless. I just wanted to sleep.

So, one night, I took a dropper-full of the CBD oil – which is the amount I'd normally take with a CBD oil. I went to sleep at 11.30 p.m. but woke up at midnight feeling *extremely* spaced-out – and not in a good way! I tried to get back to sleep but woke up again at 1 a.m. and didn't know where I was. By 2 a.m. I didn't know *who* I was! I was so completely off my head. It was incredibly unpleasant, especially as I was feeling dreadful with the flu anyway. By 3 a.m. I was crawling up the stairs in my underpants pleading with Helen to call an ambulance! It was a bloody nightmare. She had to spend hours holding my hand. I was high for forty-eight hours. It took about a month to fully get over that episode! Afterwards, I contacted my friend and said, 'What the hell was in that stuff?' She said, 'Well, you knew it was THC.' I said, 'No, I didn't. I thought it was CBD!' She asked, 'How much did you take?' I replied, 'A dropper-full.' She said, 'Fuck! You're only supposed to take a *single* drop. It's extremely pure and very strong!' I'd taken twenty times that amount. Twenty times!

But anyway, the point of the story is that when I was in that state, I felt like I was clinging on to my sanity. I thought I was going to do a Syd Barrett or Roky Erickson. And how do you know if you've gone mad? Do mad people know they've gone mad? It was a waking nightmare and I was clinging on by my mental fingertips. But there was a lyric that kept going round in my head for what seemed like hours – round and round – 'Nobody lives forever / Nobody dies for long'. I thought, I've got to write this down. I've got to do something with that line.

JW: 'Listening to the growing of the grass / Watching time-lapsed clouds pass'.

MJ: That's the hallucinogenic element.

JW: But it's also linked to the natural world. Something you reference in 'We Can't Stop What's Coming'.

MJ: Absolutely. There are several reasons it's become increasingly important to me. For instance, take the experience I had in hospital

– that birthed 'Linoleum Smooth' – when I was in a hermetically sealed environment with filtered air, on very strong antibiotics that affected the taste and smell of everything. I was just craving nature so intensely. I'd never experienced anything quite like it. I realised that in this increasingly technological age – where we're encouraged to become less and less connected with our natural surroundings – how important it is that not only do we *stay* connected but that we actually start to *increase* our connection.

JW: There are other overtures to nature in this album.

MJ: 'I Want To Wake Up With You' also contains references to nature. But also reminisces about past love. I tried to evoke longing, nostalgia and reflections upon the passage of time and the transient nature of relationships and the bittersweet realisation that fulfilment often comes with a loss. It's not about one person. It is really a composite. In the second verse I tried to write about that moment – some of us experience once and some of us multiple times – or those initial moments of intimacy between two people where you're both uncertain if something will happen – that magical moment you both *know* intimacy is about to happen… when the walls between two people start to dissolve and emotional and physical intimacy begins… a combination of euphoria, bliss and a deep connectedness.

JW: It's also melancholic with that kind of sweetness to the mixture of nostalgia, sadness and euphoria. 'Through the leaves / Silver birch and copper beech'.

MJ: There's a reason I chose those particular trees. The copper beech was my mum's favourite. She loved them and I think of her whenever I see one of those beautiful trees – especially in autumnal sunlight. I love silver birch trees too, with the distinctive markings on their trunks that – in a wood full of them – almost look like many eyes watching. I love the gentle rustling sound their small leaves make in the wind too. Silver Birch was also the name my favourite spirit guide went by. The books of

Silver Birch helped me through the loss of Eugene. They were published originally in the 1930s and were recommended by a medium during my bereavement. They provided a deep source of comfort.

JW: The line, 'Summer never really ends'—

MJ: —'It just moves elsewhere'. Again, trying to reflect the cyclical nature of love and life. Apart from the unconditional love we feel for children, parents and family members, the love we feel for others can be transient and wax and wane and sometimes disappear altogether – but that is not a negative way of looking at love it's just that it – like summer – is always happening *somewhere*. It may have moved on from one person in our life but will come back round again, even if it is shining upon someone new.

JW: Let's talk about the track 'Down By The Frozen River'.

MJ: This is based on the poem I mentioned I wrote many years ago (see page 35). It's about my experiences as a chronic truant during my school days. The words highlight themes of rebellion and disillusionment with working class education but ultimately celebrate a divergence from the conventional path and towards one of personal independence.

JW: You said earlier that you hated school.

MJ: Well, I made good friends at school and I had a good social life, so it was okay from that point of view. I was never bullied or anything like that. But I cannot remember a single teacher who ever took an interest in me personally. I left school at 15 and it was all a deeply unfulfilling experience.

JW: As far as truanting, you mentioned you would sometimes go further afield to escape school.

MJ: Yes, we'd get buses to other towns. There was more fun in Romford than in Brentwood and Chelmsford as I remember. As a teenager I was a late developer and smaller than my mates, some of whom could just about get away with looking 18 in dim lighting. I remember once going into a pub my mates told me was a soft touch for youngsters to buy booze – I was only about 14 or 15 – so, they'd all bought their pints and encouraged me to go up to the bar and buy one too. So, up I went and said, 'I'll have a pint of lager please, mate,' thinking I was pulling it off. But the governor replied in a loud voice, 'I think you mean a pint of lemonade, don't you, Sunny Jim?' He told me off. I went bright red in the face and sloped back to the table with a pint of lemonade with a straw in it. We would sometimes go to an old playground and just sit on the swings for hours. If one of our friends' parents were out at work, we might go to their house to raid their drinks cabinet.

Unfortunately, some of the teachers sometimes drank in my parents' pub. When you're a kid, you just don't think logically or long term or about the implications of getting caught. But I remember my mum coming up one night and saying, 'Right, I want a word with you!' I said, 'What? What?!' feigning innocence. She said, 'Some of your teachers have just been in and asked me, me, "How's Matthew? I hope he's feeling better." I said, "What do you mean?" And they said, "Well, he's not been to school for the last three weeks!" What have you been up to?!'

JW: There's also a very pertinent comment in 'Down By The Frozen River' about what's expected of you if you're not academic or brilliant at sport. Which is to say there are *no* expectations. 'Facing a future to which my kind is consigned.'

MJ: The system just grinds and churns through the motions, pushing endless little bodies through the sausage factory.

JW: But the final line, 'I escaped with an empty head but an open mind'. Now, that stood you in good stead.

MJ: It did. That line had been knocking around for ages. I have my 'seed lyric' notepads and folders with hundreds and hundreds of lines I've collected over the years – they could be a stray thought, overheard conversation, a newspaper headline, a snippet of dialogue from a film – from anywhere really. That line I jotted down following a conversation many years ago with Roland Gift from The Fine Young Cannibals. We were sociable acquaintances, didn't know each other that well, but might have a drink and a chat if we bumped into each other. He was asking me about my childhood and I said, 'Yeah, I left school at 15 – empty-headed!' and he instantly replied, 'But open-minded.' And I thought, that is a great way of looking at it, so I squirrelled it away and eventually – decades later – it found its home.

So, the lyrics of this song started life as a poem. I've changed them a bit, improved and honed them, but essentially, I wrote most of those words years ago. But then I lost them! They were on a typewritten piece of paper not a computer file. I often thought, 'I wish I could find that bloody piece of paper' because the poem was about a crucial part of my life and my disillusionment and frustration with school but more generally how working-class boys and girls are treated by the education system. It's been a real bone of contention for me. School can be very wounding for so many young people because it screws your confidence up. You can feel like a real failure – for life – and you haven't done anything wrong. You just haven't fitted in. You're a round peg that cannot be hammered into a square hole. Also, people just grow at different rates and so many don't know what their passions are – or even develop a thirst for knowledge – until later on in life. So, I'm really glad I found that piece of paper. I went through many boxes and files until, 'Yes! I've found it!'

JW: It is delivered as a spoken word rather than sung. Tell me about the music component for this piece.

MJ: Finding those words coincided with music I was working on with DC – as mentioned previously, this beautiful jazz motif from an idea he'd brought to me decades ago. It was very fitting that an old piece of music from him and some old words from me found a home together in this new creation.

I envisioned these words being delivered as spoken word having enjoyed reciting *The Inertia Variations*. I also felt that gave us the license to be more experimental musically. It all fell into place beautifully, especially when we played it live in the studio. I thought it needed a bit more colour than just the band though, so this was one of the tracks we had Terry Edwards play horns on and I was delighted with his contribution. And Gillian sang beautiful, haunting backing vocals that provide a sense of relief from the tension of the verses.

Then there is DC's fantastic piano solo. Similar to the solo he played on 'This Is The Night' in some ways – which I've always loved. They both have that Germany 'between the wars' feeling – you can imagine him playing in some dark, candlelit underground bar in old Berlin. DC excels at that. Barrie then had the idea of playing these aggressive chord stabs throughout the solo, which really heighten the tension.

JW: I think life is different now. If you weren't academic you were diagnosed as thick. Advancements into dyslexia and ADHD have changed that. Back then, you were just stupid, and so discarded.

MJ: I know a lot of dyslexic people, many very bright over-over-achievers funnily enough, maybe even driven on by the troubles they experienced at school. But being told, 'You're useless!' has done terrible damage to so many young people, who then never fulfil their potential. The reason I am discussing my truancy so publicly is not to encourage kids to follow my path. I actually think they *should* study hard at school and learn self-discipline and make the most of their educational opportunities. The reason I mention it is to encourage them to follow their dreams and that if someone tries to destroy their dreams to hang on to their self-belief come what may. Who knows what potentially wonderful writers, artists, philosophers – politicians even – were ruined by school before they could even get started in life?

JW: What about 'Risin' Above The Need'?

MJ: It's about the struggle with addiction and pursuit of gratification; though ultimately, it's about embracing the journey towards self-discovery and transcending material desire.

JW: 'We can live our lives under false pretences / We can deny reality, but not its consequences'.

MJ: I'm pleased with the lyrics with this one: 'Stripped of my addictions and deceit / I'm feeling somewhat incomplete.' Over periods of time I've suffered from destructive, addictive patterns of behaviour.

JW: And how do you cope with your addictions now?

MJ: By giving in to them!

JW: I don't think you do.

MJ: Over the years this addictive personality has seeped out in various ways and has attached itself to so many different things – if I manage to pull it away from sex and drugs it might then attach itself to other obsessions, like collecting books, films or vinyl or other material objects. It could be chess I obsess over or politics or Super 8 cameras, shortwave radios, sub-miniature cameras, bicycles, classic cars, pens, pencils or watches. I can become very obsessed and investigate things thoroughly and exhaustively before getting bored and moving on. Quite obviously, there is a deep hole inside that I feel the need to fill. I'm improving over time but I cannot deny I have an obsessive nature. I suppose I have some OCD tendencies – and no doubt many other things that haven't been 'diagnosed'. Then again, if you hold anyone up against the light you will see they are quite odd. Certainly, most people I know are. But this partly explains how I can be so focused on songwriting and recording when the mood takes me – where I can listen to something so intensively and intricately, again and again and again whilst working out minute details in my mind.

I'm still chipping away at my issues, still trying to become a nicer, kinder and more balanced person. The pertinent line – which is, again, trying to embed a positive message within each song – 'All good things will come through the door / To those who do not even want them anymore' is similar to the final verse in 'Zen & The Art Of Dating' in some ways. It's about taking ourselves out of a permanent state of wanting, desiring and craving – for things we don't *really* want or need – by somehow letting go of this permanent, grasping state of the ego – and the insecurities and endless craving for things outside ourselves. It's a bit like being in water and you're fighting and struggling – you may drown. But if you can just learn to relax, lie on your back, breathe and naturally float on the surface, you would be fine. It is all about letting go and trusting.

I'm pleased with the guitar work on this track. The interplay between myself and Barrie – particularly Barrie's beautiful arpeggios when we move into the last chorus – I think are stunning. I remember when he first played his part – it gave me goosebumps. When we are rehearsing in a circle at my studio on our little wooden chairs, I'm always sat with Barrie to my left. Watching him coming up with things, I'm often exclaiming, 'Barrie! That's it!' because sometimes he'll play so many wonderful ideas he may even go straight past the one that's perfect so I try to stay alert to what he's doing. What comes out of his fingers is beautiful. He has such a natural, fluid, soulful style.

JW: I think *Ensoulment* really shows Barrie off. The guitar motif on 'Cognitive Dissident' is so memorable.

MJ: I agree and generally the tastefulness of his parts – for instance, on 'I Want To Wake Up With You' – is just gorgeous. In 'Kissing The Ring Of POTUS', the verse parts, underplayed, understated – are beautiful; you just can't get enough. No overplaying, no showing off. Simple, tasty tones. He knows his instruments and his amplifiers intimately. I could pick up Barrie's guitar and plug into his amp and *try* to play similar but, of course, I couldn't do it and I wouldn't sound anything like Barrie. It's in Barrie's fingers. That's the thing. People obsess over vintage guitars and amplifiers or esoteric foot pedals but ultimately the real magic is in the player's fingers. I've been blessed to have three world-class guitarists in my band – Johnny Marr, Eric Schermerhorn and Barrie Cadogan. All three are world class in my view.

JW: It does feel like a continuation of the relationship with Johnny.

MJ: Johnny is a smart, thoughtful person and knew Barrie was the perfect person for us at that point in time. Me and the rest of the fellas in the band have all been delighted with him. He has an old guitarists' soul and it's as if he stepped, fully formed, out of the 1970s and into the 21st century.

JW: When you first played me the record two tracks immediately stood out, 'Cognitive Dissident' and 'Linoleum Smooth To The Stockinged Foot'. The latter was written after your brush with the Grim Reaper.

MJ: The title for this song was inspired by when I was in the hospital, literally walking around the corridors, attached to a drip on a trolley, wearing those stockings they give you, and the little robe which ties up at the back.

JW: Humiliating, so everyone can see.

MJ: Yes, everyone can see. I wonder who came up with that design? It's quite kinky. I was exhausted after the operation but my survival instincts kicked in, so I was drinking lots of water, keeping my body moving whenever possible So, I'd be shuffling around the corridors whenever I could – during the day and during the night, when it was dark and atmospheric – nodding to any nurses or doctors I'd come across as I was doing my rounds.

Funnily enough, the hospital I was in – the Royal London in Whitechapel – was where my youngest son George was born. I was very spaced-out on morphine but part of me was always thinking, 'You've got to fight this thing.' So, I'd get up at every opportunity and shuffle about the corridors. Linoleum is such a fifties and sixties thing, isn't it? 'Lino.' So, 'Linoleum Smooth' and 'stockinged feet' just came into my mind.

Over the previous few years we've been hearing more and more about the gradual, corporate takeover of our medical system and the potential dangers of merging it with the security apparatus to create a bio-security state – with the potential roll-out of digital IDs, medical passports etc.

In the UK, there's a deeply embedded love for – and trust in – the NHS. But what many don't realise is how it's been quietly privatised over the years. From clinical services and IT systems to hospital cleaning and catering contracts, more and more NHS functions are now run by private companies, often owned by financial institutions or foreign corporations. While the public still sees it as a cherished, publicly-owned institution, the reality is a creeping infiltration – a stealthy takeover by the private sector that is eating the NHS from within. When you look closer, the nation's image of its NHS is largely a façade.

Anyway, I was in a disturbed state of mind due to the drugs and the extreme weirdness of the situation – both inside and outside the hospital walls – and my imagination just started to run riot so I was scribbling away in my notebook to stay sane.

JW: 'And endlessly nudged to scrub their hands / To bang their pots and beat their pans'.

MJ: 'Nudge units' usually work in the background for the government and the public may not be aware of them at first, but the lack of government transparency can really start to erode trust, especially when people find out after the fact they're being 'nudged' and 'steered' without realising it. They may then resist or rebel. Is it really democratic to treat the citizenry like infants? To manipulate their behaviour on sensitive issues like health, freedom or compliance?

And then you had this… clapping. Everyone encouraged to stand in the streets once per week, to bang their saucepans and clap their hands for the NHS – like performing seals. Meanwhile, the wonderful staff themselves were over-worked and underpaid, as members of the government syphoned off millions – and potentially billions – to enrich their cronies with kickbacks and fraudulent procurement deals.*

The whole thing seemed farcical and aroused suspicions in my mind from the outset. But, of course, if you dared poke your head above the parapet to question the madness that was unfolding all around us you were instantly shrieked at and abused. I was quite disappointed by the amount of people I know who consider themselves alternative thinkers – many tattooed, pierced and seemingly

---

* Transparency International UK, *Behind the Masks: Corruption Red Flags in COVID-19 Public Procurement*, 2024. The report analysed over 5,000 UK public-sector contracts and identified 135 'high-risk' contracts worth £15.3 billion, flagged for issues including lack of competition, political connections, and unproven suppliers.

rebellious in spirit – who, as soon as the government ordered them to fall into line did so instantly and without question. As citizens we must *always* question those in positions of power and authority. The government are supposedly the servants of the people *not* the other way round!

Once control systems like Digital ID are finally established, I guarantee they will then start marketing 'smart tattoos' that contain all of our data – this technology has already been developed. It will initially be aimed at the gullible as the next must-have trendy accessory to make their lives easier – sometimes, the younger generations remind me of the Eloi in HG Wells' *The Time Machine* – but eventually of course it will become required in order to access healthcare, travel and banking. It does put one in mind of the *Book of Revelation* 13:16–17:

> It also forced all people, both great and small, rich and poor, free and slave, to receive a mark on their right hands, or on their foreheads, so that they could not buy or sell unless they had the mark, which is the name of the beast, or the number of its name.

JW: 'Linoleum Smooth' has something of the experimental nature of your very early recordings. Not just *Burning Blue Soul* – where you were interested in shortwave radio signals and audio dissonance – but also in some of the early recordings you reissued under Cinéola.

MJ: Well, the rest of the band aren't on this particular track. We had eleven tracks from the Real World studios sessions but I wanted twelve. I also knew I had the lyrics to 'Linoleum Smooth' and that these had to be on the album as it was still fairly topical. Warne had gone back to Canada by this point and everyone else had left. I thought, I fancy doing something a bit more electronic and experimental so I asked Mark Allaway to fire up the studio. I quickly worked out the chords on guitar, plugged in a drum machine, programmed a straight kick drum part but put it through a delay to create a syncopated, swinging beat. I recorded a simple bass line on my Hofner and then had Gillian sing wordless harmonies on the instrumental 'choruses' and played around with them to make them more ethereal by reversing, delaying and filtering. I wanted Sonya Cullingford to play fiddle on this as I knew she'd be perfect for it. I also wanted Terry Edwards to play horns on it.

What we did with Sonya – and she'd never worked like this before – was to manipulate the effects – distortion, tremolo, wah-wah, reversed, pitch-shifted delays – whilst she was playing, so she was reacting in real time to what I was doing on the floor with my various foot pedals. We then got her to do three or four passes – all without hearing what she'd done before – with me manipulating as she played. I then did the same with Terry a few days later – but I didn't want him to hear what Sonya had done. I thought, let's just do it all blind. After they had finished and left we listened back to the various takes in different combinations – trying to find those 'happy accidents' – the beautiful sonic and harmonic collisions that were happening all over the place.

JW: It reminds me of PiL's 'Flowers of Romance'.

MJ: Ah, that was Keith Levene, wasn't it? I like to leave everything open to experimentation, like playing in a big sonic sand pit, 'OK, what happens if we do *this*? What happens if we do *that*? If those two things collide here, how would *that* sound?' Much is accidental, of course, and you just don't know what's going to happen – but the key is recognising when it works and then swiftly acting upon it.

JW: I think the reason I like that track so much is that it feels like a thread connecting all your work.
So, 'Where Do We Go When We Die?'

MJ: Existential questions about life and death. Reflections on the passage of time – the inevitability of loss – the enduring cycles of renewal. A gentle contemplation upon the mysteries of existence beyond our physical realm.

JW: It fits into that cycle of songs – 'We Can't Stop What's Coming' for Andrew; 'Love Is Stronger Than Death' for Eugene; 'Phantom Walls' for your mother; and now 'Where Do We Go When We Die?' for your father?

MJ: Yes, I wrote this for my dad – I think he would have liked this song and felt quite moved by it.

JW: Was it a difficult one to write?

MJ: It was and it wasn't. Funnily enough, I'd had the title and some of the melodic ideas knocking around for a long time, waiting for a home. And obviously the event of my dad dying brought it sharply into focus. I cried when I was writing it; I found it very emotional.

JW: Was it cathartic as well?

MJ: Yes. It was positive – loving, warm and a gift to my dad really. He was a lovely father to us – as our mum was a mother. I was blessed to have lovely parents who really loved their children. It was a gift from me and an acknowledgement of what my dad gave me.

JW: It deconstructs masculinity as well. 'You're on my mind all the time / Weak men lie, strong men cry'. It's not seen to be done, is it, to cry?

MJ: No, but things have been changing. Particularly compared to thirty, forty, fifty years ago, where it wasn't seen to be done. And seeing my dad break down after losing Eugene.

My parents went through terrible bereavements. Their business suffered after Eugene died and they lost the house he and my mum loved. My dad went through so much loss – he lost both his parents at a young age, lost his wife, lost two children, lost his business, he had triple heart-bypass surgery. He went through so much emotional pain and hardship but he never became bitter – he instead grew kinder, warmer and bigger. His soul grew. He was incredible to our mum when she was ill. It really brought home what the marriage vow 'in sickness and in health' really means. A strong man is not afraid to express his emotions or even show his weakness.

JW: There's the lyric:

> To the sound of raindrops
> To the ticking of the clock
> We packed your clothes and your books
> And took them to the charity shop

That's not something you might normally hear in a song, but that is the reality of what happens, isn't it?

MJ: It is. Funnily enough, Gerard and I had been down at our dad's old house, finally preparing to sell it, taking some of his books to the charity shop – we'd already done the clothes. The next day, Gerard asked to hear the album. We listened to it together and it made him very emotional. This song brought him to tears, and he simply said, 'That's just what we've been doing.' It is what we do when someone dies. It is what someone will do after we die. It is part of the process – both banal and profound in the same moment.

JW: The final line, 'The sun may fall, but the moon will rise' has the positivity you have been talking about.

MJ: Absolutely, about rebirth – from this life and into the next. It is ultimately an optimistic song about love transcending death and the spirit rising.

JW: 'I Hope You Remember (the things I can't forget)' – you quite like a bracket!

MJ: I do. It must be the lingering influence of Hank Williams! This lyric contemplates the encroaching influence of technology on human experience – the erosion of privacy and authenticity – and its effect upon memory. And, as I mentioned previously, in this age of nascent AI we seem to be redefining what makes us human. This is a question that's going to be pondered again and again in the coming years and decades as AI becomes increasingly powerful and prevalent. Many will start to wonder what on earth they've been born for. They're going to still have to consume – food and other products – so therefore, how are they going to afford it if many of the jobs have disappeared? I suppose they can be put on some sort of 'universal basic income' so they can enjoy their 'leisure time' – sitting around watching Netflix and ordering Deliveroo maybe?

Ironically, it didn't take long for the sci-fi fantasy world of robot workers freeing humans to create art to be overtaken by the reality – instead of robots flipping burgers, we have AI writing the stories, making the music and painting the pictures whilst the humans flip the burgers! Or maybe the inscriptions on the Georgia Guidestones* were a prophesy and the population of the planet will be reduced to half a billion?

As you know, I don't have a television, I can't watch adverts. Even travelling on the Underground or walking the streets our minds are bombarded. I don't know how they measured this, but back in the 1970s, it was reported the average person saw 500–1,600 adverts per day. By 2024 the average person was apparently bombarded with 6,000–10,000 adverts daily!† What is the effect of all this manipulation, this mind pollution. You can't breathe. You can't think. But at some moment, surely, there's got to be a breaking point where people wake up and realise there is more to humanity and existence than being passive receptacles for propaganda and advertising. As Krishnamurti‡ once observed, 'It is no measure of health to be well-adjusted to a profoundly sick society.'

---

* The Georgia Guidestones were a mysterious monument in Georgia, USA inscribed with ten cryptic guidelines for humanity in multiple languages, often interpreted as advocating a new world order and were destroyed by an explosion in 2022.
† A trend confirmed by Media Dynamics, Inc., DoubleVerify and Dentsu.
‡ Jiddu Krishnamurti was an Indian philosopher who rejected all religious, political and ideological authority whilst teaching about freedom, awareness and the transformation of the mind.

JW: The reason I feel a connection with this song and with 'Sometimes I Drink My Coffee'... is because of a sense of looking back.

> The fireplace glow, the coal tar soap
> The Sunday roast, the tobacco smoke
> The Jamboree bags, the penny chews
> All now disappearing from view

MJ: There's a bit of a John Betjeman influence in this lyric, a subtle nod to his autobiography *Summoned by Bells* (1960) in the lines you just quoted. When we were kids our dad used to tell us stories about his being a little boy in East London during the Blitz and – as he was telling us these stories, in my mind they were all in black and white, the effect of old films and television on the mind of a little boy, I suppose. The past was in black and white. But obviously, to him, his memories were in vivid colour – filmed in Kodachrome. And I've realised, when I'm talking to my own kids about my childhood, it seems so ancient, so long ago, a fading world of Tizer, Sherbet Fountains, Whizzer & Chips and Jamboree bags.

When we would visit my mum's parents, Grandad Joe and Nanny Sue, the centrepiece of the front room was the fireplace. The television back then was just a little box in the corner that would be brought out for certain occasions. We'd all sit round the fire, with cups of tea, sandwiches, cakes and biscuits. The adults would be telling stories and it was great for us kids as they were such great storytellers. Nowadays, television, films and social media do the storytelling for us. Back then, people seemed to have better memories. And I remember, as a little boy, sitting there, watching the flames in the coal fire with their endless patterns and shapes, cigarette smoke drifting around the room – and the smell of my nan's perfume. Certain scents and sounds trigger memories; as Proust sensed, smell, like music, is a portal through time, reaching memory before thought via molecules or waves.

JW: When I smell Brylcreem I think of my dad.

MJ: It's so powerful isn't it? It just transports you. My nan's perfume, my dad's aftershave, the smell of the flickering coal-fire and then the autumnal light and lengthening of the shadows. It all stirs up a yearning and a melancholy.

JW: 'Our lives will teem with love and regret / I hope you remember the things I can't forget'.

MJ:

> More than just the molecules that animate our flesh
> We are eternal beings, sempiternally blessed
> Free as the day we die, pure as we are born
> Our souls remain deathless, no need to mourn

Now what could possibly be more positive than that!?

JW: We come to the final track, 'A Rainy Day In May'. There is a kind of tradition in film and music of this kind of chance encounter. *Brief Encounter* is a good example. This song captures that experience very well, an 'if only' moment.

MJ: I wanted to capture the fleeting-but-transformative power of a chance encounter, symbolised by a rainy day in May. It ignites a sense of connection – and a longing – leaving this very slim possibility of an alternative future life.

JW: Was this documenting an actual moment?

MJ: It's a composite. Like many people, I've had many of those little moments. As one gets older it's possible to draw from a lifetime of experience and all the moments you collect along the way. I wanted this song to be less wordy than the others. The choruses are instrumental, which is unusual for me – although I also did that on 'Linoleum Smooth'.

You suddenly have this momentary connection. You're never going to see each other again. It's just a tiny moment – a flicker of recognition. I think when we're younger – or when I was younger – it would make me melancholy as I'd want to hang onto and own something that was completely elusive and transitory and which disintegrated as soon as I tried to close my hands around it. But with age and experience you get to appreciate it for what it is – one of those beautiful, fleeting moments in life. Rather than trying to hold water in your hands you just let it run through your fingers. Or like a cool breeze on a hot day and that transitory, beautiful, pleasurable sensation you don't need to own or possess – just experience.

Growing up one of my favourite songs was '(Sittin' On) The Dock Of The Bay' by Otis Redding and Steve Cropper. I wanted 'A Rainy Day In May' to have a similar simplicity. This is another track that was marked down as a potential single. Prior to the album release, we asked sixteen trusted friends and colleagues to listen to the album and vote on 3 potential singles. Every song on the album got at least one vote. This one got a few – including from me – but I decided not to at the end. I find it philosophically uplifting because it's accepting the transitory nature of our lives. Everything about life is transitory.

JW: It's very clear how much effort you put into everything – the songwriting, choice of the musicians and your collaborators in general. I have compiled two records with Bob Stanley for Ace Records, *Café Exil: New Adventures in European Music 1972–1980* and *Fantastic Voyage: New Sounds for the European canon 1977–1981*. Bob is the founder of Saint Etienne and working with him I really got an insight into the importance of track order.

MJ: It's a very different world now, because we know music will mainly be heard on Spotify, Tidal, Apple Music, Amazon and other streaming services. However, *Ensoulment* is a double-vinyl album and I'm still old school.

I knew very early on I wanted to start with 'Cognitive Dissident' because it's such a bold, strong and aggressive track to kick off with after a twenty-five-year absence. And it's not that dissimilar to some of the things on *NakedSelf*. It's got balls.

JW: It knocks you off your feet.

MJ: The songs on the album are such a contrast, I wanted it to feel like a journey so the listener has a sense of moving and going somewhere. I also wanted there to be very few gaps, so they often segue, as with *Burning Blue Soul*. Lastly, I wanted the songs to be three to four minutes in length and concise: punch, punch, punch.

I always knew I wanted to end with 'A Rainy Day In May'. The perfect closing track. Warne and I went through every permutation in the studio late one night. 'What about this? What about that? How about this instead?' To be honest, it started to dictate and choose itself pretty quickly. Apart from tempo and mood there's also the 'relative minor' technique where you listen to how one key fits the previous key and subsequent key. Some songs fit and some songs don't.

JW: Having sat with this record what are your reflections after a relatively short distance?

MJ: I'm proud of it. To have come back with a record as strong as anything I've ever done – and after twenty-five-years... I'm very pleased on a personal level for having the discipline to do it and for bringing the right people in and seeing it through. I always used to enjoy that time between finishing an album and its release. It's like a little golden period where you're still full of positivity and expectations, where it has neither been damned by the faint praise of critics nor excitedly embraced by the audience, nor perhaps ignored entirely. It's still my little baby. Yes, it's nice to get good reviews and acknowledgement, but the most important thing is *always* the audience. They are the ones who spend their hard-earned money on it and who – hopefully – in twenty-years' time may still be playing it and keeping it alive. I have a sense of pride in a job well done as a craftsman on the one hand, and as an artist on the other. Once it's out in the world, it has to fend for itself. There's nothing more you can do.

JW: I like the fact that you obviously take pleasure thinking about your audience.

MJ: There is a word that used to make my skin crawl at record company meetings when they talked about the audience: 'consumers'. I hate that word. This idea that 'consumers' are just one big blob sitting there with their mouths open waiting to be exploited. I don't like the word 'fan' either as I also find that demeaning. I just always refer to the 'audience' as it's made up of countless thousands of individuals who all have different lives, different emotions and different feelings that sometimes happen to converge around certain cultural moments, whether it's films, books, music or politics.

Do you know the word 'sonder'? It was coined by John Koenig as part of his book project, *The Dictionary of Obscure Sorrows* (2021). Sonder is the realisation that every other individual is living a life as full and real as one's own, in which *they* are the central character and *you* have only a bit part or an insignificant role in their lives. It is very important to remind ourselves of this. That we are *not* the central character in the lives of others. So with every record I release, every concert I play, I just do the best I possibly can. It's the old working-class ethic I suppose.

JW: And was there a commercial imperative with this album?

MJ: Not really. It's not like the eighties where I spent hundreds of thousands of pounds per album. My costs are now intentionally kept low, just so the albums can be commercially successful at a fairly low threshold, because I'm thinking longer term. As long as they pay for themselves and don't lose money everyone's happy and we can move on to the next one.

JW: What about the visual aesthetic of *Ensoulment*?

MJ: It was important – as mentioned earlier – to continue to use Andrew's artwork. I would never use another artist. If there were going to be sleeves that didn't feature his artwork it would be photographs, as with *The Comeback Special* and – in the past – *Hanky Panky* and *Mind Bomb*. Luckily Andrew left a large archive of previously unseen work. There are over a hundred sketchbooks containing some wonderful images. There are also digital archives and hi-res work as well as paintings that haven't been scanned yet. There's enough material to last for the number of records I'm likely to make. I'm pleased about that and I think Andrew would have been pleased too. There were a few beautiful colour images I'd put to one side that I felt could potentially be used for *Ensoulment*. But I didn't make the decision until it was recorded... because you never know. The image we've used is simple and powerful and the expression on the face inscrutable.

JW: It's like a wood cut.

MJ: Yes, a wood cut or African mask. People have also remarked that it resembles a 1984 Big Brother-style poster. There's certainly something slightly authoritarian about it, which fits in with a lot of the themes. I kept a print of this image on my writing bureau whilst finishing the lyrics. I was often looking at it and wondering, 'Does it feel right?' It did feel right.

For the sleeve of the 'Cognitive Dissident' single we used this evocative, slightly sinister drawing of a figure with a pointed hat, cyclops-type eye and two faces either side of his head. In 2023 with the Mickey Mouse-esque sleeve used for '$1 One Vote!' we'd been worried we might have issues with Disney, so we had this sleeve lined up as an alternative. But luckily the Mickey Mouse copyright had just expired. When it came time to think of a sleeve for 'Cognitive Dissident', my son George pointed out, 'Dad, what about that one you showed me before?'

The drawing we used for the 'Linoleum Smooth' single release was another image from one of Andrew's sketchbooks. I liked the snakes; the association with the World Health Organization is an interesting one as sometimes the Rod of Asclepius (the ancient symbol for medicine featuring a snake coiled round a staff, used in the WHO logo) is confused with Caduceus (two serpents entwined round a staff topped with wings, symbolising commerce,

negotiation and trickery). So, that seemed appropriate. And then the mask put me in mind of one of those early, sinister plague costumes.

For the album booklet we also used photographs by Gerald Jenkins, who's done some fascinating work over the years. What we went for – between Andrew's drawings and Gerald's photography – has a slightly hallucinogenic feel. I didn't want photographs that were too straight, because the album is so varied and was written under slightly hallucinogenic circumstances. So, the combination of Andrew's artwork and the unusual photographs with the lyrics make the overall listening experience more vivid. It's a double-album – the vinyl at least – so we created a lovely booklet with each song's lyrics illustrated by either one of Andrew's drawings or Gerald's photographs.

CHAPTER FOURTEEN

Every Step Of The Climb Led You To This Place And Time

THE THE take to the road (and the skies) for the globe-spanning Ensouled World Tour. The set is performed in two halves: the album in its entirety and a second set of beloved THE THE classics. The tour is a success and witnesses Matt's transformation from the laziest man in showbusiness to the busiest.

JW: The world tour was titled Ensouled not *Ensoulment*?

MJ: All the tours have had different names to the albums they're supporting: Versus The World for *Mind Bomb*, Lonely Planet for *Dusk* etc. For the tour artwork we worked closely with Martin Lewis, our long-term designer. He's worked with us on most of the Cinéola soundtrack releases, many one-off singles as well as larger projects such as *The Radio Cinéola: Trilogy* and *The Comeback Special* and also the book *Tales From The Two Puddings*.

    We love Martin as he is highly professional but very easy going. For the tour artwork we chose the same colour palette as the album sleeve, and an image with a globe that evokes the old 1960s TWA* logo. Martin then suggested the passport stamps to consolidate

---

* Trans World Airlines.

the international feel. We'd also decided to connect the tour artwork to the album sleeve with the red eye. So, they are connected even though they are separate entities.

JW: Last night you played me the B-sides to the singles. Let's talk about those.

MJ: 'Mycelium Muse' is the B-side to 'Linoleum Smooth'. Mycelium is the vegetative body of fungi sometimes referred to as the Internet of the plant world. It links plant roots across forests, grasslands and even gardens. Plants can send chemical signals through the fungal network for example, warning their neighbours of insect attacks. It seems to connect everything biological under the soil. I find that quite fascinating though I'm not sure how much of this information is relevant to our readers as, to be honest, I was just looking for a rhyme for 'Linoleum Smooth' when I chose that title for an extreme remix! It's the same performances from Sonya and Terry – and my guitar and keyboards – but I've radically treated and remixed them.

JW: It almost acts like a mirror.

MJ: Exactly. The other B-side I played you used 'Zen & The Art of Dating' as a starting point. I took my guitar from this track and created another rhyming title, 'When Is The Heart of Waiting'. Though I've changed it so much you wouldn't recognise it. I retained one of my guitar parts – which was quite low in the mix for 'Zen' and I then built around that. I also brought my Prophet synthesiser out, which I used on the *Odyssey* soundtrack too. It's just me playing guitar with the main pulse from the Prophet – plus I did some low humming. B-sides, for me, are always good fun. Vinyl 7-inch singles are a niche product now but I still enjoy the B-side as a time to play and experiment. That's what they're there for.

JW: And the B-side for the third single?

MJ: The B-side to the third single, 'Some Days I Drink My Coffee By The Grave Of William Blake' is 'Frozen Clouds'.

JW: Let's talk more about the Ensouled Tour. Initial dates sold out immediately. Were you expecting that after the success of The Comeback Special?

MJ: I was quietly confident but a lot has changed and you just never know. Post-Brexit and post-COVID-19, the live music scene had been severely dented. Costs shot through the roof because a lot of companies went out of business during the pandemic and those that remained felt they could ramp up their prices due to demand. It has made it more complicated for bands. Another unexpected consequence of so many simultaneously postponed tours was that they all resumed their schedules at the same time as soon as they were able – and the touring circuits and markets were saturated. By the time of the Ensouled Tour, audience numbers had thankfully started to pick up but I never take anything for granted. I don't like to feel over-confident or under-confident, but just stay focused, work as hard as we can and hope we don't get any nasty surprises – because you just never know.

JW: What was your approach to the Ensouled Tour? Did it differ from The Comeback Special Tour?

MJ: The process was the same in that we started at my studio – just James, Barrie and myself on acoustic guitars, working out which songs could work in the new format. Then we brought in DC and finally Earl.

The plan with the Ensouled Tour was always to play two sets: *Ensoulment* in its entirety and *Retrospect* – selections from the back catalogue. Certain songs we had to play and then there are other well-known songs we didn't play last time we decided to bring back. 'GIANT', for instance, plus a few others that got requested such as 'The Whisperers'.

There was also an issue of musician availability as my band members have other projects. Earl is also a member of Tindersticks, for instance, and they had an album out the same time to which Earl was committed to tour and promote. He's an honourable man who fulfils his commitments. He could only do the early part of the tour in 2024 – although he came back for the 2025 leg of the tour. Dave Palmer and I have repaired our friendship in recent years and he sat in on rehearsals for a couple of weeks to help us out until Chris Whitten stepped up and stood in for Earl. Chris is a phenomenal drummer who's played at the very highest level – including for Paul McCartney – so we were very lucky to have him. Audience members may also remember seeing Chris in the Radio Cinéola Band in *The Inertia Variations* documentary.

JW: What did you do to get in shape? Physically and after the operation, in terms of your voice?

MJ: My voice is fine. It didn't change after my throat operation, thank God. When preparing for a tour – and on the road – I do quite a specific voice exercise routine. I start that as we approach the rehearsal period. In terms of physical exercise, when I'm at home I'll do a twenty-minute yoga, sit-up and push-up routine and then another twenty minutes on the rebounder. An ice-cold shower afterwards. I keep up the same routine – minus the rebounder – when on the road. I meditate too.

But it can be a strange life on tour. Trying to maintain a calm centre in the midst of constant change. Those daily ups and downs. You can have a sold-out show one night, a half-empty hall the next. And different beds every night. Countless new people encountered, most of whom you'll never see or speak to again. Different problems. Good news one day, bad the next. Oh, and food. When you're very hungry and in the middle of a highway to nowhere you'll be surprised at what you'll end up eating. So, there are rituals, routines, habits and neuroses a musician builds up over years of touring. Obviously, I can only speak for myself but these will be small things from the way you pack your suitcase – and what you put in your suitcase – to your morning routine to pre-show rituals.

For me it has always been the same. From Versus The World through Lonely Planet, the Naked Tour and up to the present day. Eat three hours before the show. A swim and sauna in the hotel – if they have them. Twenty minutes' meditation. Dose myself up with herbal energy elixirs and exercise for thirty minutes, voice exercises for another thirty minutes. Hot bath, cold shower and then some Olbas oil rubbed into my chest and throat to clear the airways. And drink plenty of water too!

Some of my bandmates over the years have preferred hanging around the venue from sound check onwards but I like to arrive literally a minute or two before we go on stage as it is more intense that way and I feel more of a high. Unless there's very good reason for hanging out afterwards, I prefer to leave the venue minutes after leaving the stage. I suppose I'm lucky as unlike some people I've never suffered stage fright. In fact, the bigger the concert the more nerveless I become. Maybe because I've been playing gigs since I was a 12-year-old kid I feel comfortable on stage. Also, no alcohol allowed for me – either when rehearsing or on tour.

JW: You don't find it that hard to stop drinking alcohol though, do you?

MJ: No, in the past I've stopped many times. I can drink heavily for months and then, luckily, I can just stop. I've quit a few times – for three months, six months, a year, eighteen months. The longest I've quit is seven years. It's important for me to regularly test my will power. As you get older you have to do all this stuff. But being disciplined for touring is just respecting your bandmates, the crew and the audience.

Touring is expensive, ticket prices are expensive. People pay hard-earned money to come and support you and they deserve the best you can do. Of course, they may end up not liking the show, for one reason or another, but it won't be because we haven't tried our hardest and done our best. Sometimes circumstances are beyond our control – it might be an odd venue with strange acoustics, technical problems with equipment, a band member feeling poorly. But we have great professionals in the band and the crew, and everyone tries their hardest.

JW: Are there particular songs from *Ensoulment* that you especially enjoyed playing live?

MJ: 'Cognitive Dissident', because that was our opening song not only for the album but for the entire tour.

JW: Were there any that presented more of a challenge?

MJ: 'Linoleum Smooth' because none of the band played on the recording. It was just me, Sonya, Terry, Gillian and Danny. But we worked that out in rehearsals and Barrie used a bow on his electric guitar to recreate Sonya's fiddle parts. I thought it sounded amazing.

'GIANT' presented a minor challenge – on the last tour we didn't use sequencers or samplers so we brought some along for this tour, and DC did an excellent job programming. In fact, during rehearsals we even got Zeke Manyika down and we all sung the chants at the end multiple times to recreate as closely as possible the original record, and DC then loaded them in as samples.

JW: How about the visuals for the tour?

MJ: It's tricky. I wish we had a bigger visual budget but because of the massive increase in the costs of touring it was limited. But THE THE have never been a stadium band: we're a medium-sized band who play small arenas and large theatres. We have to cut our cloth accordingly. Production designer Kate Wilkins worked wonders again and I was really happy with her designs. She's not a typical rock/pop music lighting designer, and that's why I like working with her. She's a lateral thinker. She brings a lot of interesting ideas, which we'll develop together.

JW: What were the circumstances that led to the revisiting and re-recording of 'Slow Emotion Replayed'? It must have been a part of the rehearsal process for the Ensouled World Tour. Why focus on this song and what did you want the new version to have that the original version on *Dusk* didn't? I recall David Bowie re-recording 'Cat People' because he felt that it needed 'more balls'…

MJ: There's an interesting story behind that. During the initial tour rehearsals, the way we were playing 'Slow Emotion Replay' was starting to irritate me. It just felt too straight and ploddy and I was about to throw it overboard when we decided to give it one last chance. No drums, stripped down to DC playing the chords on the Omnichord, with Barrie playing Johnny's harmonica part on guitar; James playing bass and me just singing and not playing guitar. The first time we played it through like that it made me incredibly emotional. I felt goosebumps on my arms and tears in my eyes. I loved it. So, we obviously played it on the tour like that and I decided at tour's end I'd like to release it as a single, titled 'Slow Emotion Replayed'. Similar in some ways to the re-working we'd done of 'This Is The Day' all those years ago.

JW: Can you take me through the recording process and the personnel? I imagine you recorded in Studio Cinéola.

MJ: Yes, we recorded and mixed at Studio Cinéola with Mark Allaway engineering. I played the Omnichord, as DC was back in Chicago. Barrie came over to play guitar and perform backing vocals with Gillian, and James added the bass.

JW: You have a penchant for re-interpreting old material. Lydon was once going to do a record of new versions of PiL songs – I personally don't think he can improve them. What is the beauty of re-visiting the songs and would you ever consider a whole new album of re-interpretations?

MJ: I do tend to play around with the back catalogue when playing live. Sometimes I'll keep an arrangement faithful to the original but often I like to stretch the songs out a bit – like doing cover versions of my material in a way as I feel it also maintains excitement by creatively reinterpreting rather than just duplicating exactly what's gone before.

An entire album of re-interpretations is something I have considered. Funnily enough when Cally was managing me we started a project called *Interpretations* but it was other artists' interpretations of my songs. On Volume One we had three different versions of my song 'Shrunken Man' from *NakedSelf* by JG Thirlwell, John Parish and DAAU respectively. We had some artists lined up to do the second volume but we then fell out with Universal and the project was aborted.

JW: I love the title of the B-side, 'Crow Commotion Displayed'. Can you tell me about both the title and the track? I recall that your brother liked crows.

MJ: Andrew was fascinated by crows and drew them often. We included some of his illustrations of them on the back cover. Musically, it is a radical remix of 'Slow Emotion Replayed'. You can hear elements that have been slowed, reversed and chopped about. It's a great dance track I think.

JW: You are on a burst of creativity at the moment. How do you balance writing new material with maintaining and re-performing the extensive catalogue of songs you have written? You'll soon be having to do four-hour Springsteen-style concerts…

MJ: Personally, I don't like concerts being too long – either when I'm in the audience or on stage. I think all cultural forms, whether a book, film, album, concert or whatever, have an optimum length. For a concert I think about two hours is the max. So, no, you won't be seeing me doing Springsteen-length shows.

JW: Can you tell me about the sleeve of 'Slow Emotion Replayed'? It's another unpublished work by Andrew. Cumulatively, the recent singles from when you began recording again serve as a lovely tribute to his work.

MJ: Yes, it uses some more unpublished work from Andrew's sketchbooks. 'Slow Emotion Replayed' uses a collage of some doodles and illustrations he did of me.

The collection of one-off singles we've been building up will at some point be released as an album in its own right. We also released a double A-side 'Unrequited' and 'Live & Let Live', both taken from Gerard's most recent film, *Odyssey* (2025).

JW: We first met and started talking during the release of *The Inertia Variations* in 2017. That was a period of reflection for you in which major THE THE activity was very much on hold. As I just said, your creativity and output has really burst alive again. You mentioned in a recent interview in *The Guardian*, 'I've gone from the laziest man in music to the hardest-working.'* Does it feel good to be this active again?

MJ: It simply feels like I've gone back to being myself again. I was always very energetic and ambitious and I absolutely love my job, every aspect of it, whether writing by myself or in the studio or on stage with others. Or working on artwork, books, films. I'm very lucky because I live and breathe my job. I had to take time away from who I am in order to rediscover who I am. I just didn't think there would be almost twenty-five years between albums of songs! What should really have been my peak years as a songwriter have all been lost. Who knows how many songs I could have written in a quarter century or how good I might have become if I had worked harder? I like my sporting metaphors so – assuming the career of a songwriter is more marathon than sprint – I suppose I'm now about ten laps behind my contemporaries. I'll just have to put my thinking cap on, dig deep and find a way to catch up.

---

* '"Fame is like inhaling a toxic substance": THE THE's Matt Johnson on pop, politics and his death-defying return', Dave Simpson, *The Guardian*, 9 August 2024.

JW: Your future plans are such that we have joked about this book project never ending but sadly it has to. I know we have the soundtrack to *Odyssey* but to conclude, what else is on the horizon? I know you are busy writing at the moment. What are the imminent projects you are working on and how do you see your future in terms of musical activity?

MJ: We have multiple projects in various stages of completion. We're always very busy at Cinéola HQ, always on the back foot with our backs to the wall! So, in addition to the releases of the *Odyssey* soundtrack and its singles, *The Inertia Variations* was finally released on Blu-ray/DVD.

We're also preparing the release of *Ensouled: Live At The Sydney Opera House*, a film, book and album in the same format as *The Comeback Special: Live At The Royal Albert Hall*.

We also have *Cinéolascape,* a collaboration with our good friend Kevin Foakes (AKA DJ Food) wherein he's remixed the Cinéola catalogue into an album-length sonic journey. This was a project Kev started when he was special guest for our UK concerts on The Comeback Special Tour.

We have just started *Esoteric Vaudeville* (companion to the *Official Bootleg* series), a small imprint of Cinéola where I get to indulge my love for musique concrète and elektronische musik and play around with pieces of esoteric equipment from my collection I don't get to use on regular THE THE albums. These recordings are abstract and non-commercial and only warrant a low-key release. But it's something that is important to me. Going back to my roots in some ways. There are also some more book projects planned as soon as we have this one published.

JW: Having looked back through our interviews for this book, you strike me as being someone who's in a good place mentally, physically and spiritually. There's perhaps a sense that – whereas before, you were tackling big subjects, you were ambitious (I don't want to use the phrase 'angry young man') – now you seem a lot more relaxed. Does that give you more levity to write about things that you might not have written about before? I don't get the sense that you're constrained by anything.

MJ: I do feel in a good place. Pretty relaxed. I think a lot of it is down to life experience. I've gone through too many 'walk through the fire to get to the light'-type experiences – and I really don't want any more. I want to write songs that are uplifting and positive – albeit still searching and questioning. There's so much darkness in the world at the moment.

JW: Does it feel freeing, in a way, to be back in this groove of writing more?

MJ: Yes.

JW: I get the sense now that, rather than thinking, 'I *should* write a song,' it is now, 'I *want* to write a song.'

MJ: I care less about what others think than when I was younger. I think that's just being happier inside and realising that it doesn't really matter what others think but it's how we think and feel about *ourselves* that ultimately counts. Trying to be a decent, kinder person to others – not always succeeding of course.

JW: It's nice to know that possibilities are infinite and that you are feeling so positive. You've never come across to me as a bitter person.

MJ: Why would I be bitter? I've had a great life and career. I come from a very close family, I've been blessed with lots of wonderful, long-term friendships, been lucky in my personal relationships, travelled the world doing what I love doing. I'm very lucky and very grateful. I've obviously had – as most of us do at some point – hardships and bereavements and countless things have gone wrong in my life and career but to be fair a lot of it was my own doing. There's a phrase I've often used: 'I've made all the wrong career moves for all the right reasons'. Turning down things that would've guaranteed more success, sales and profile; but I just didn't want to do certain things. It also brings a certain inner confidence being your own person – following your own path.

There were quite a few years after leaving Sony and Universal where I did have a very fallow period and didn't do much creatively but instead, indulged in my love of flâneuring across multiple countries. Sex, drugs and rock'n'roll – only not much rock'n'roll!

But in recent years, I've turned down all sorts of offers from big companies and instead set up my own company and work with people I love working with – and now have so much creative freedom. I really don't think I would have had the confidence to do all that if I hadn't been a self-taught and self-sufficient individual.

As I've said in the past, I'm a songwriter and producer rather than a musician. But I play to write. I love instruments and playing but I *really* love overseeing the entire creative process of making records, books, soundtracks etc. I love being involved in every aspect of my career – managing myself, producing, artwork, putting teams of people together – I love it all. I think that those early difficulties – rejections and ups and downs of a career – can really toughen you up and make you as a person, can't they?

JW: 'All the wrong career moves for all the right reasons.' I think that's important. I mean, at the end of the day anyone with any sort of conscience has to look themselves in the mirror. I think if you make so many decisions that might be good financially or whatever, but you don't feel good about them, there's going to come a time when you're not going to want to look at yourself in the mirror at all. I think what happens when success spoils some people is that they no longer do things for the joy of doing them. Each time you chip away at yourself with those decisions it leaves less of the original you.

MJ: But it is complex and comes to down to the individual and to personal circumstances and ambitions – and at a certain moment in time. There is no wrong or right way and we shouldn't judge.

To quote another of my lyrics, 'What will I regret the most / The things I do, or the things I don't?'

I suppose one might lead a life of regret, of thinking, oh my God, if I'd only done this, this, *this*! There are people that make decisions that I wouldn't have made, for personal financial gain, and they're probably quite happy with the decisions they've made. There are others who made opposite decisions – also that I may not have made – but who are equally happy.

JW: You're still making the records, still in charge of your career. You are self-sufficient. I think for anybody that's the dream, isn't it?

MJ: It is. Although, of course, sales generally for recording artists these days are a fraction of what they were thirty years ago. Artists make most of their money from live performance now. It's the complete reverse of what it used to be. But having said that, I wouldn't go back. I'm much happier than I was then. There's a real sense of being in control of one's own destiny, and the day-to-day pleasure of collaborating with people you like and get along with.

JW: I like your enthusiasm. It always feels like you're enjoying what you're doing.

MJ: I *do* enjoy what I'm doing. I *love* it. I value my freedom and I've been trying my hardest in recent years to become free of all debt: financial, spiritual and emotional. I do not want to owe or be owed. I do not want to lead or be led.

You *also* enjoy what you're doing too, don't you?

JW: I enjoy doing this.

MJ: Okay, so as we enter the final pages of our book I would like to leave things on a philosophical note about time and the human spirit.

All this thinking about the past whilst we've been working

on this book has given me a kind of vertigo – realising just how far and fast technology has evolved just within my lifetime. Our perception of time seems quite elastic doesn't it? It speeds up as we age. To a 2-year-old, one year is fifty percent of their life and goes by so slowly. To an eighty-year-old, it's 1.25 percent of their life and just whizzes past their eyes. Time – and our health – are the most valuable resources we have. How do we make the most of time? Is it through professional achievement or emotional development? What really constitutes a well-balanced life? And as technological development now seems to be rapidly outpacing spiritual development, how can we possibly keep up with it?

I remember my parents talking about their childhoods: transistor radios, electric kettles, ballpoint pens, vinyl records, nylon clothing, electric typewriters, fridge-freezers or jet aeroplanes were not even invented. Yet now, in my adult life, we have artificial intelligence, genetic engineering, humanoid robots, nanotechnology, facial recognition, 3D printing and space travel.

Where will humanity be in fifty years' time? Is it really so far-fetched to imagine scientists will by then have created organic, self-replicating, artificially-intelligent humanoids? And is it too far-fetched to imagine that we ourselves might be a form of artificial intelligence? Self-replicating robots created by a race perhaps only a hundred years more advanced than us? Many of the world's great religions and philosophical belief systems refer to a 'creator' or divine clockmaker. Perhaps God is simply an eccentric scientist a couple of hundred years ahead of us.

There are also theories and beliefs suggesting that what we perceive as solid matter is, in reality, only an illusion – that we are living in a holographic universe, where time and space are constructs. People often look back condescendingly at those who thought the world was flat, but perhaps in a few years' time people will look back and laugh at *us* for thinking the world was solid. 'They thought space-time and matter were fundamental – adorable!' 'They didn't realise consciousness was non-local.' 'They still thought of reality as 'stuff' instead of patterns of information or energy.'

For most of human history, people *did* think the Earth was flat; then round, but fixed at the centre; then round and orbiting the Sun; then merely a speck in a vast universe. Every time, the old 'common sense' view seemed obvious… until it didn't. What's happening now at the cutting edge of quantum mechanics and quantum field theory seems to be leading us in that same direction. Esoteric traditions have been saying this for a long time, of course. In Hinduism, māyā teaches that the material world is merely an illusion or veil. In Gnosticism, this realm is a copy or simulation of a deeper truth. Modern physics and ancient mysticism are beginning to align.

Robert Monroe,* a pioneer of out-of-body experience (OBE) research through his Monroe Institute, coined the term 'loosh' to describe the energy generated by humans through strong emotions and feelings – fear, love or pain. According to him, beings or systems collect 'loosh' for sustenance, much as humans harvest crops for food – perhaps even feeding on human suffering. For a

---

* Robert Monroe was an American researcher and founder of the Monroe Institute, was a pioneer in the study of out-of-body experiences and consciousness exploration. He developed techniques for inducing OBEs and published his findings in books such as *Journeys Out of the Body* (1971).

time, the CIA was involved with the Monroe Institute and its experiments into OBE and remote viewing, but who knows what conclusions were ultimately drawn? And would they really tell the general public anyway?

Sometimes I play little mind experiments. I imagine myself in distant eras – medieval streets thick with smoke and noise, the pyramids standing silent in the heat, or an ornate Victorian gin palace glowing with gaslight and teeming with voices. From those perspectives, I try to picture what the 21st century might have looked like.

At other times, I look far forward instead: abandoned satellites drifting through space, cities reclaimed by nature and patrolled by rusting machines, or humans thriving underground beneath artificial suns. Maybe the future is a utopia where knowledge flows directly into the mind. From each imagined vantage point, I wonder what traces of us might remain – what faint evidence would reveal who we were. Everything around us feels solid, yet almost all of it is temporary.

I also sometimes imagine a perspective far above the world, looking down – witnessing the brutal wars and devastating poverty, yet also marvelling at humanity's astonishing discoveries, inventions, and works of art.

I imagine time-lapse images of our lonely planet endlessly turning: day into night, summer into winter, peace into war and back again – civilisations rising and falling, strong people creating good times, good times breeding weakness, weakness bringing hardship, and hardship forging strength once more. These cycles repeating.

And then there's the question of personal death. Total annihilation of consciousness? Heaven, nirvana, limbo? Perhaps our fragile bodies are just avatars – projections of higher selves entering a world that is merely a dim shadow of a greater reality, to experience consequence, joy, suffering, and growth. Maybe we are here to learn, to refine our souls, to understand.

In truth, it is all probably an unreachable stretch trying to understand things far beyond our capacity – like trying to explain a refrigerator to a goldfish.

But to end our book on a positive note – despite the authoritarian gloom gathering on the horizon – I believe most people are fundamentally kind. And what gives me hope is that the human spirit cannot be extinguished by the generations-old forces determined to keep our world shrouded in darkness – and that, just as plants yearn for sunlight and water, humans yearn for truth and beauty. That was true in the distant past, and I believe it will always be the case.

Every day, good souls are born and bring light into our world. And for that, I have hope.

ACKNOWLEDGEMENTS

Matt Johnson:

I'd like to thank Jason for his friendship and for suggesting this book in the first place.

Gratitude for the support of my family, relatives and friends especially my sons Jackson and George, brother Gerard, my partner Helen Edwards and also Johanna St Michaels and Fiona Skinner.

Also, a very big thank you to Gillian Glover at Cinéola for her eagle-eyed surveying of this text and unwavering commitment to this project.

Thanks also to the fine team at Omnibus including David Stock, Claire Browne, Millen Brown-Ewens, Neal Price and especially former editor David Barraclough who originally suggested a partnership between Cinéola and Omnibus.

And, finally, all others who contributed to the creation and promotion of this book including: J.J. Abrams, Samira Ahmed, Mark Allaway, Jonathan Barnbrook (for allowing use of his Save Shoreditch logo), Justine Chiara, Mark Curtis, Rob Delaney, David Edwards, Alex Fordham at Authority Communications, Photographer Christie Goodwin, Tony Hawk, Jools Holland, Kieran Jay, Martin Lewis, Joe Mallott at Mallott Media, Johnny Marr, Nick McKay, Steve Phillips at Carry On Press, Tim Pope, Trent Reznor, Marc Riley, Jim Thirlwell, Cheryl Waters, Transcription Divas, Louder Than Words (for their early support), Brigette Bard (who kindly and unexpectedly arranged access to my old bedroom at The Kings Head, Ongar) and to Nicky Beaumont for her superlative breakfast and hospitality in Manchester.

Jason Wood:

I start by thanking Matt for his time, company, insights, music and ultimately, his friendship.

I also express my eternal gratitude to all of the Cinéola crew but especially to Gillian Glover who has gone above and beyond in providing materials, access and encouragement.

My deepest appreciation to Nick McKay who provided music, enthusiasm, intel and the interview material in this book relating to Matt's soundtrack compositions. Thanks to Eddy Rhead and Jack Hale at *The Modernist* for allowing me to reprint Nick's interview from the 'Kino' edition of their magazine.

I add to the roll call Gerard Johnson, Michael Leake, Ben Lewis, Marc Riley, Guy Smith, Bob Stanley and Becky Thomas.

Omnibus have been incredibly understanding and supportive as the project came together. A shout out to David Stock and a fulsome round of applause also to David Barraclough.

FILMOGRAPHY AND DISCOGRAPHY

Filmography

Infected: The Movie (1987)
THE THE Versus The World: Live At The Royal Albert Hall (1991)
From Dusk 'Til Dawn (1993)
The Inertia Variations (2017)
The Comeback Special: Live At The Royal Albert Hall (2021)
Ensouled: Live At The Sydney Opera House (2026)

Album Discography

See Without Being Seen (1978/2020) Cinéola
Spirits (1979) (unreleased)
Burning Blue Soul (1981) 4AD
The Pornography of Despair (1982) (unreleased)
Soul Mining (1983) Some Bizzare/Epic
Infected (1986) Some Bizzare/Epic
Mind Bomb (1989) Epic/Sony
Dusk (1992) Epic/Sony
Solitude (1994) Epic/Sony
Hanky Panky (1994) Epic/Sony
Gun Sluts (1997) (unreleased)
NakedSelf (1999) Nothing/Universal
Karmic Gravity (2000) (unreleased)
45 RPM (The Singles Of THE THE) (2002) Epic/Sony

Tony: A Soundtrack by THE THE (2010) Cinéola
Moonbug: A Soundtrack by THE THE (2012) Cinéola
Hyena: A Soundtrack by THE THE (2015) Cinéola
Radio Cinéola: Trilogy (2017) Cinéola
See Without Being Seen (2019) Cinéola
Official Bootleg series (2020) Cinéola
Muscle: A Soundtrack by THE THE (2020) Cinéola
The Comeback Special: Live At The Royal Albert Hall (2021) Cinéola/earMUSIC
Ensoulment (2024) Cinéola/earMUSIC
Odyssey: A Soundtrack by THE THE (2025) Cinéola/earMUSIC
Esoteric Vaudeville series (2026) Cinéola
Ensouled: Live At The Sydney Opera House (2026) Cinéola/earMUSIC

Singles Discography

'Controversial Subject'/'Black And White' (1980) 4AD
'Cold Spell Ahead' (1981) Some Bizzare
'Uncertain Smile' (1982) Some Bizzare/Epic
'Perfect' (1983) Some Bizzare/Epic
'This Is The Day' (1983) Some Bizzare/Epic
'Sweet Bird Of Truth' (1986) Some Bizzare Epic
'Heartland' (1986) Some Bizzare/Epic
'Infected' (1986) Some Bizzare Epic
'Slow Train To Dawn' (1987) Some Bizzare/Epic
'The Beat(en) Generation' (1989) Epic/Sony
'Gravitate To Me' (1989) Epic/Sony
'Armageddon Days Are Here (again)' (1989) Epic/Sony
'Jealous Of Youth' (1990) Epic/Sony
'Shades Of Blue' (EP) (1991) Epic/Sony
'Dogs Of Lust' (1993) Epic/Sony
'Slow Emotion Replay' (1993) Epic/Sony
'Love Is Stronger Than Death' (1993) Epic/Sony
'Disinfected' (EP) (1994) Epic/Sony
'I Saw The Light' (1995) Epic/Sony
'Gunsluts' (2000) Lazarus

'Shrunken Man' (2000) Nothing/Universal
'Pillar Box Red' (2002) Epic/Sony
'Mrs Mac' (2007/2023) Lazarus
'We Can't Stop What's Coming' (2017) Cinéola
'I Want 2 B U' (2020) Cinéola
'$1 One Vote!' (2023) Cinéola/earMUSIC
'Cognitive Dissident' (2024) Cinéola/earMUSIC
'Linoleum Smooth To The Stockinged Foot' (2024) Cinéola/earMUSIC
'Some Days I Drink My Coffee By The Grave of William Blake' (2024)
Cinéola/earMUSIC
'Risin' Above The Need'/'Where Do We Go When Die?' (2025) Cinéola/earMUSIC
'Slow Emotion Replayed' (2025) Cinéola/earMUSIC
'Unrequited'/'Live & Let Live' (2025) Cinéola/earMUSIC

BIBLIOGRAPHY

Bohn, Chris, 'The Definitive Article', *NME*, 9 October 1982

Bonner, Michael, 'I was hallucinating giant spiders!' Matt Johnson interview, *Uncut*, 21 July 2016

Butt, Gavin, Eshun, Kodwo and Fisher, Mark (editors), *Post-Punk Then and Now*, Repeater, 2016

Dessau, Bruce, 'THE THE's Thatcher Years', *The Guardian*, 12 May 1989

Fraser, Neil, *Long Shadows, High Hopes: The Life and Times of Matt Johnson & THE THE*, Omnibus Press, 2018

McKay, Nick, 'Less Is More: Scoring *Muscle*', *The Modernist Magazine #37: Kino*, December 2020, edited by Jason Wood

Powell, Russell, 'Matt Johnson: "A Master of All Trades"', *Time Out*, December 1983

Reynolds, Simon, *Rip It Up and Start Again: Postpunk 1978–1984*, Faber & Faber, 2005

Reynolds, Simon, *Totally Wired: Postpunk Interviews and Overview*, Faber & Faber, 2009

Savage, Jon, *England's Dreaming*, Faber & Faber, 2016 edition

Snow, Mat, 'THE THE: *Dusk*', *Q*, February 1993

Somers, Thierry, 'Matt Johnson The 200% Interview', 1 May 2007 reproduced from thethe.com

Sullivan, Jim, 'THE THE's True Self Founder Matt Johnson Continues To Break New Ground', *The Boston Globe*, 28 April 2000

Taylor, Neil, *Document and Eyewitness: An Intimate History of Rough Trade*, Orion Books, 2010
Watson, Don, 'Soul Mining', *NME*, 22 October 1983
Wilde, Jon, 'THE THE: Lip Tripping', *Volume*, 1993
Wood, Jason, *Green on Green*, Faber, forthcoming
Young, Jon, 'THE THE's Normal Guy', *Cream*, October 1984

PERMISSIONS

'Maybe I'm A Loner'
Words & Music by Matt Johnson
© Copyright 1975 Lazarus Limited.
All Rights Reserved. International Copyright Secured.

'Perspective And Distortion'
Words & Music by Matt Johnson
© Copyright 1979 Lazarus Limited.
All Rights Reserved. International Copyright Secured.

'Time (again) For The Golden Sunset'
Words & Music by Matt Johnson
© Copyright 1981 Lazarus Limited / Universal Music.
All Rights Reserved. International Copyright Secured.

'(Like A) Sun Rising Through My Garden' Words & Music by Matt Johnson
© Copyright 1981 Lazarus Limited / Universal Music.
All Rights Reserved. International Copyright Secured.

'Another Boy Drowning'
Words & Music by Matt Johnson
© Copyright 1981 Lazarus Limited / Universal Music.
All Rights Reserved. International Copyright Secured.

'Bugle Boy'
Words & Music by Matt Johnson
© Copyright 1981 Lazarus Limited / Universal Music.
All Rights Reserved. International Copyright Secured.

'Angels Of Deception'
Words & Music by Matt Johnson
© Copyright 1986 Lazarus Limited / Universal Music.
All Rights Reserved. International Copyright Secured.

'Slow Train To Dawn'
Words & Music by Matt Johnson
© Copyright 1986 Lazarus Limited / Universal Music.
All Rights Reserved. International Copyright Secured.

'Sweet Bird Of Truth'
Words & Music by Matt Johnson
© Copyright 1986 Lazarus Limited / Universal Music.
All Rights Reserved. International Copyright Secured.

'Twilight Of A Champion'
Words & Music by Matt Johnson
© Copyright 1986 Lazarus Limited / Universal Music.
All Rights Reserved. International Copyright Secured.

'The Mercy Beat'
Words & Music by Matt Johnson
© Copyright 1986 Lazarus Limited / Universal Music.
All Rights Reserved. International Copyright Secured.

'Good Morning Beautiful'
Words & Music by Matt Johnson
© Copyright 1989 Lazarus Limited.
All Rights Reserved. International Copyright Secured.

'Beyond Love'
Words & Music by Matt Johnson
© Copyright 1989 Lazarus Limited.
All Rights Reserved. International Copyright Secured.

'True Happiness (this way lies)'
Words & Music by Matt Johnson
© Copyright 1992 Lazarus Limited.
All Rights Reserved. International Copyright Secured.

'Dogs Of Lust'
Words & Music by Matt Johnson
© Copyright 1992 Lazarus Limited.
All Rights Reserved. International Copyright Secured.

'Slow Emotion Replay'
Words & Music by Matt Johnson
© Copyright 1992 Lazarus Limited.
All Rights Reserved. International Copyright Secured.

'Lonely Planet'
Words & Music by Matt Johnson
© Copyright 1992 Lazarus Limited.
All Rights Reserved. International Copyright Secured.

'Soul Catcher'
Words & Music by Matt Johnson
© Copyright 2000 Lazarus Limited.
All Rights Reserved. International Copyright Secured.

'The Other Window'
Words by Bruce Gilbert Music by Graham Lewis
© Copyright 1979 Carlin Music Corp/Round Hill Music.
All Rights Reserved. International Copyright Secured.

'Diesel Breeze'
Words by Matt Johnson
Music by Matt Johnson and Eric Schermerhorn
© Copyright 2000 Lazarus Limited and Rocket Seed Music.
All Rights Reserved. International Copyright Secured.

'We Can't Stop What's Coming'
Words & Music by Matt Johnson
© Copyright 2017 Lazarus Limited / Kobalt Music.
All Rights Reserved. International Copyright Secured.

'Zen & The Art Of Dating'
Words & Music by Matt Johnson
© Copyright 2024 Lazarus Limited / Kobalt Music.
All Rights Reserved. International Copyright Secured.

'Kissing The Ring Of POTUS'
Words by Matt Johnson
Music by DC Collard
© Copyright 2024 Lazarus Limited / Black Dream Music / Kobalt Music.
All Rights Reserved. International Copyright Secured.

'Life After Life'
Words & Music by Matt Johnson
© Copyright 2024 Lazarus Limited / Kobalt Music.
All Rights Reserved. International Copyright Secured.

'I Want To Wake Up With You'
Words & Music by Matt Johnson
© Copyright 2024 Lazarus Limited / Kobalt Music.
All Rights Reserved. International Copyright Secured.

'Down By The Frozen River'
Words by Matt Johnson
Music by DC Collard
© Copyright 2024 Lazarus Limited / Black Dream Music / Kobalt Music.
All Rights Reserved. International Copyright Secured.

'Risin' Above The Need'
Words & Music by Matt Johnson
© Copyright 2024 Lazarus Limited / Kobalt Music.
All Rights Reserved. International Copyright Secured.

'Cognitive Dissident'
Words by Matt Johnson
Music by Barrie Cadogan
© Copyright 2024 Lazarus Limited / Kobalt Music and Bucks Music Group.
All Rights Reserved. International Copyright Secured.

'Linoleum Smooth To The Stockinged Foot'
Words & Music by Matt Johnson
© Copyright 2024 Lazarus Limited / Kobalt Music.
All Rights Reserved. International Copyright Secured.

'Where Do We Go When We Die?'
Words & Music by Matt Johnson
© Copyright 2024 Lazarus Limited / Kobalt Music.
All Rights Reserved. International Copyright Secured.

'I Hope You Remember (the things I can't forget)'
Words by Matt Johnson
Music by Barrie Cadogan
© Copyright 2024 Lazarus Limited / Kobalt Music and Bucks Music Group.
All Rights Reserved. International Copyright Secured.

Image Credits

Page 18   An example of Uncle Kenny's promotional concert posters
Page 39   Matt's handwritten lyrics from his first band Road Star
Page 70   Typewritten lyrics for 'Perspective And Distortion' from the unreleased *Spirits* album
Page 75   Rejection letter from Ralph Records
Page 113   Early THE THE typeface and logo development by Fiona Skinner
Page 132   Early illustration of Matt by Andrew (AKA Andy Dog)
Page 147   *Infected*-era bull skull illustration by Andrew
Page 188   *Infected – The Movie* sales poster
Page 209   Sheet music for 'Good Morning Beautiful'
Page 222   Set list from THE THE Versus The World Tour
Page 231   Andrew's sketch of Stratford warehouses
Page 237   Early *Dusk* illustration
Page 257   Reading Festival 1993 line-up poster
Page 282   Sketch of figures by Andrew
Page 307   Set list from The Naked Tour
Page 322   Early Cinéola logo design by Cally Calloman
Page 330   *Muscle* poster design by Gary Dalton
Page 346   Save Shoreditch poster by Jonathan Barnbrook
Page 356   Photo of Matt under Radio Cinéola tower by Jacob Sahlqvist
Page 361   Illustration by Andrew used for the cover of the single 'We Can't Stop What's Coming'
Page 372   The Comeback Special Tour early set list planning
Page 379   Barrie Cadogan and Matt Johnson, Royal Albert Hall, photo by Christie Goodwin
Page 398   Insect Man & Friends illustration by Andrew
Page 408   Man & Faces illustration by Andrew
Page 432   Andrew's sketch of London factories
Page 443   Some of Andrew's crow sketches
Page 462   Illustration by Andrew used for the cover of the single 'Cognitive Dissident'
Page 467   Drawings by Stella Johnson and Tess Johnson of THE THE in rehearsal for the Ensouled Tour
Page 479   Crows & Castle sketch by Andrew